Organizations

Structures, Processes, and Outcomes

Tenth Edition

Pamela S. Tolbert

Professor
School of Industrial and Labor Relations
Cornell University

Richard H. Hall

Distinguished Service Professor
University at Albany
State University of New York

PEARSON

Prentice
Hall

Pearson Education International

Editorial Director: Leah Jewell
AVP, Publisher: Nancy Roberts
Editorial Assistant: Nart Varoqua
Editorial Project Manager: Vanessa Gennarelli
Director of Marketing: Brandy Dawson
Senior Marketing Manager: Kelly May
Composition/Full-Service Project
  Management: Satishna Gokuldas,
  TexTech International Pvt Ltd
Production Liaison: Cheryl Keenan

Operations Specialist: Christina Amato
Assistant Marketing Manager:
  Jessica Muraviov
Manager, Cover Visual Research
  and Permissions: Karen Sanatar
Cover Art Director: Jayne Conte
Cover Design: Margaret Kensalaar
Supplements Editor: Mayda Bosco
Printer, Binder, and Cover Printer:
  R. R. Donnelley & Sons

This book was set in 10.5/12 Times.

Credits and acknowledgments borrowed from other sources and reproduced, with permission, in this textbook appear on appropriate page within text.

Pearson Education Ltd., London
Pearson Education Singapore, Pte. Ltd
Pearson Education Canada, Inc.
Pearson Education–Japan
Pearson Education Australia PTY, Limited

Pearson Education North Asia, Ltd., Hong Kong
Pearson Educación de Mexico, S.A. de C.V.
Pearson Education Malaysia, Pte. Ltd.
Pearson Education Upper Saddle River,
  New Jersey

10   9   8   7   6   5   4   3   2   1

ISBN-13: 978-0-13-609225-4
ISBN-10:   0-13-609225-X

For Sherry and for Steve

Brief Contents

Preface   xiii

Part I   **Introduction**
Chapter 1   Thinking About Organizations   1

Part II   **Organizational Structure**
Chapter 2   Organizational Structure: Key Dimensions   19
Chapter 3   Organizational Structure: Explanations   44

Part III   **Organizational Processes**
Chapter 4   Power and Power Outcomes   68
Chapter 5   Leadership   89
Chapter 6   Decision-Making   110
Chapter 7   Communication   121
Chapter 8   Managing Organizational Environments: Conceptions
of the Environment   139
Chapter 9   Managing Organizational Environments: General
Paradigms   161

Part IV   **Outcomes**
Chapter 10   Organizational Performance and Change   186

References   211
Name Index   249
Subject Index   261

Contents

Preface   xiii

Part I   **Introduction**

Chapter 1   Thinking About Organizations   1

Overview   *1*
Why Study Organizations?   *1*
Organizational Impacts   *3*
The Nature of Organizations   *14*
The Plan of the Book   *17*
Summary and Conclusions   *18*
Exercises   *18*

Part II   **Organizational Structure**

Chapter 2   Organizational Structure: Key Dimensions   19

Overview   *19*
Defining Organizational Structure   *20*
Studying Organizational Structure: Early Research
    on the Bureaucratic Form   *21*
Sociological Studies of Formal Structure in Organizations   *25*
Dimensions of Formal Structure   *27*
Relations Between Complexity, Formalization,
    and Centralization   *41*
Summary and Conclusions   *43*
Exercises   *43*

Chapter 3   Organizational Structure: Explanations   44

Overview   *44*
Effects of Size   *46*

Effects of Technology   50
Combined Effects of Size and Technology   53
In Practice: Functional, Product, and Matrix Forms
    of Organization   54
Effects of Internal Culture   57
Environmental Effects on Structure: External
    Culture   58
Creating Formal Structure: Debates over Process   64
Summary and Conclusions   66
Exercises   67

Part III   Organizational Processes

Chapter 4   Power and Power Outcomes   68

Overview   68
The Nature of Power in Organizations   69
Authority and Power   69
Other Types of Power   71
Shifts in Power   77
Power Outcomes: Compliance and Involvement   78
Power Outcomes: Conflict   79
The Components of Conflict Situations   83
The Outcomes of Conflict   85
Summary and Conclusions   86
Exercises   88

Chapter 5   Leadership   89

Overview   89
What Is Leadership?   90
The Outcomes of Leadership for Organizations   98
Leadership in the Voluntary Organization   107
Summary and Conclusions   108
Exercises   109

Chapter 6   Decision-Making   110

Overview   110
Organizations as Systems of Decisions   111
Strategic Decision-Making   115
Strategies of Power and Decision-Making   118
Summary and Conclusions   120
Exercises   120

Chapter 7   Communication   121

Overview   *121*
The Importance of Communication   *122*
Individual Factors   *124*
Organizational Factors   *126*
Vertical Communication   *126*
Horizontal Communication   *130*
Communication Problems   *133*
Communication to and from Outside the Organization   *135*
Possible Solutions   *136*
Summary and Conclusions   *137*
Exercises   *138*

Chapter 8   Managing Organizational Environments:
Conceptions of the Environment   139

Overview   *139*
"Discovering" Organizational Environments   *140*
Defining the Environment   *142*
Perceiving the Environment   *159*
Summary and Conclusions   *160*
Exercises   *160*

Chapter 9   Managing Organizational Environments:
General Paradigms   161

Overview   *161*
The Contingency Paradigm   *162*
The Resource Dependence Paradigm   *163*
The Transaction Cost Paradigm   *171*
The Institutional Paradigm   *176*
The Population Ecology Paradigm   *177*
Combining Paradigms   *183*
Summary and Conclusions   *184*
Exercises   *185*

Part IV   Outcomes

Chapter 10   Organizational Performance and Change   186

Overview   *186*
Problems of Defining Organizational Goals   *187*
Approaches to Organizational Effectiveness   *190*

Evaluating Organizational Performance: Key Issues   *196*
Organizational Change and Transformation   *198*
Organizational Change: Learning and Transformation   *198*
Transformational Change   *204*
Summary and Conclusions   *208*
Exercises   *209*

References   211

Name Index   249

Subject Index   261

Preface

This edition of *Organizations: Structures, Processes, and Outcomes* has undergone yet another major revision. The changes that we've made were guided by three aims: (1) to provide readers with a better sense of the historical development of ideas and concerns that underpin contemporary arguments and debates on the topics that we cover, (2) to update our coverage of research and theorizing on these topics, and (3) to discuss some new lines of research and theory on organizations that we view as especially provocative and promising.

Examples of these changes are provided in Chapters 2 and 3, discussing theory and research on formal structure, an area of organizational studies with a long, venerable tradition. We provide more background on that tradition, tracing its roots to the theoretical concerns of Max Weber with the new form of organization he saw coming to dominate society at the turn of the twentieth century, the pragmatic concerns of the set of analysts prominent in the 1920s and 1930s known as Managerial Theorists, and the empirical concerns of sociologists in the post–World War II years, devising ways to examine the validity of functionalist theory. Moreover, we review some of the more recent explorations of this tradition as manifested in research on high-performance work systems and work that goes under the banner of institutional theory, and consider the links between an institutional theoretic approach and current research on cross-national differences among organizations.

Similarly, in Chapters 8 and 9, addressing research on organizational environments, we discuss factors that led organizational researchers to move their focus from a closed-systems to an open-systems approach and the way in which they wrestled with difficulties inherent in conceptualizing the vast array of factors encompassed in the notion of "the environment." We also examine various strands of research that reflect focalizations on different aspects of the environment as well as broader general paradigms that emerged out of efforts to systematically conceptualize the nature of organizational environments.

The concluding chapter addresses two broad outcomes: (1) assessment of organizational performance and (2) efforts to bring about changes in ongoing organizations. We include in our discussion of organizational performance both a review of the older line of work that was driven by concerns with assessing effectiveness and a critical consideration of economists' standard of "maximizing shareholder value" as a performance criterion. In considering the problem of organizational change, we review two broad streams of research: (1) organizational learning and (2) organizational transformation. In all of our revisions, then, we have sought to give readers a sense of the historical development of sociological studies of organizations along with a systematic overview of contemporary macro-oriented research on organizations, with the goal of facilitating readers' grasp of this very complex and evolving body of research.

As always, we are very grateful to the following reviewers for providing us with helpful comments and suggestions: Issam A. Ghazzawi, University of La Verne; Musa D. Ilu, Central Missouri State University; Kenneth J. Mietus, Western Illinois University; and Patrick Withen, University of Virginia at Wise. And also, as always, we thank our spouses, our own life-long strategic alliances, Steve Carver and Sherry Hall.

Organizations

Chapter 1

Thinking About Organizations

OVERVIEW

This chapter has three aims. The first is to persuade you that having some general understanding of the nature of organizations is critical for members of contemporary society. Organizations dominate the landscape of our world; their activities determine crucial economic, political, and social outcomes that affect all of us, from birth to death. Thus, we argue that it behooves us to give some thought and effort to trying to understand how and why organizations operate the way they do. The second aim is to give you a sense of difficulties inherent in the quest to understand and study organizations. The phenomenon that we call organizations assumes an enormous array of forms, and variations in these forms are related to variations in the outcomes and behaviors that social scientists seek to explain. The third aim relates to the second, that is to give you an overview of the logical structure of the book—how we plan to cover the wide array of theories and research on organizations in order to give you a general sense of this area of study.

WHY STUDY ORGANIZATIONS?

There are two answers to this question. The first has been emphasized so often that it has become clichéd, but is true nonetheless: we have become a society of organizations (Perrow, 1991). Because organizations are such a pervasive feature of social life, it is important to understand the factors that affect their operation. Our lives are shaped by organizations, from birth to death. Although we may be vaguely aware of this fact, we often do not give much thought to just how pervasive organizational influences are. So let's think about this for a moment. Most of us were born in a hospital. The policies, rules, technologies, and other aspects of that organization affected how we came into the world, whether we got appropriate treatment for problems that could affect us throughout our lives, whether we survived. There may have been a brief respite from organizational influences in our early years, though organizations produce most children's toys, books, television shows, and movies, as well as the childcare books that parents rely on for advice. The organizational decisions made about producing these things undoubtedly, though largely imperceptibly, shaped our childhood experiences and early views of the world. Many of us went to preschools where the policies of these organizations affected what we learned, our notions about proper standards of social behavior, even our general level of health. Primary, secondary, and higher education institutions are clearly critical organizations for most of us: the curriculum and teaching protocols adopted by these schools importantly affect the kinds of knowledge and ideas that we acquire, the testing practices they use often determine how we are evaluated and thus the kinds of future educational opportunities we are given, and the certifications they provide affect our work opportunities as well. The ways that work organizations shape our lives are also probably obvious. Their staffing and promotion practices affect the nature of the jobs we hold and the opportunities we are given to hold different jobs; their evaluation and compensation policies affect whether we are recognized and how we are paid for our efforts; scheduling and staffing practices strongly influence the temporal rhythms of our day-to-day lives as well as our residential movements; their rules affect how long we can and want to be employed. Throughout our lives, much of our leisure activities are shaped by products of organizations: the books we read, movies and shows we watch, the games we play, among others. Thus, many, if not most, of the leisure activities available to us are the result of decisions made by these organizations about the products that are to be provided. As we age, many of us will spend the last years of our lives in some sort of care facility; the policies and practices of these organizations will affect how comfortably we are ushered out of the world. Thus, one reason to study organizations is to get some basic understanding of these things that shape our lives in so many fundamental ways.

A second, related reason is practical. Because we live in an organizational society, if we want to change key aspects of our lives and/or society, we almost inevitably must change organizations. We may seek to change organizations because we are unhappy with the outcomes they produce. Organizations have the capacity to do great good or great evil: they are not benign objects. They can spread hate but also save lives and maybe souls. They can wage war but also bring peace. These outcomes can be intentional or unintentional, recognized or not recognized (Arum, 1996; Merton, 1957). Moreover, organizations embody and perpetuate core social values, and if you want to change those values, you must change organizations. If you wish to promote the value of social equality (by reducing the differential economic chances of men and women or of racial groups, for example), you must alter organizational practices—those of businesses, schools, health care organizations, and so forth. Likewise, if you wish to promote values that support only heterosexual relationships, you will need to affect, again, school organizations, the employment practices of work organizations (that may provide benefits to same-sex partners, for example), government organizations such as tax agencies, and so forth. The great social transformations in history have been essentially organization based. The formation and expansion of the Roman Empire, the spread of capitalism and socialism, and the rise of Christian, Jewish, and Islamic states all have been accomplished through organizations. Efforts to address toxic-waste disposal, the use of nuclear energy, unemployment, abortion, and all of the issues facing contemporary society cannot proceed without considering and understanding their organizational contexts. (Having made this point at some length, we also hasten to add that understanding a phenomenon does not necessarily imply the ability to bring about change in it. We understand how gravity works; that doesn't mean that we can easily alter its operation.) But understanding the nature of organizations is an essential first step to trying to alter them.

ORGANIZATIONAL IMPACTS

By discussing a number of levels at which the consequences of organizational activities may be observed, we want to elaborate on the issue of how organizations affect us: for individuals, communities, societies, and international communities.

Organizations and Individuals

Most analyses of the impact of organizations on individuals focus on work organizations. Although some analysts have forecasted an "end of work" (Rifkin, 1995), this has yet to take place, and work organizations still take up a large part of most people's everyday lives. Participation in other kinds of organizations (e.g., political, social, and various voluntary organizations) can provide individuals with many possibilities for growth and development, of course. But for the moment, we will focus on organizations in which people work. Many studies have examined how individuals react to their lives as employees of organizations (Aronowitz, 1973; Hall, 1994; Rosow, 1974; Terkel, 1974; *Work in America,* 1973). These analyses agree that work that is highly routinized, repetitive, and dull is alienating for individuals. (There is no evidence, of course, that work in preorganizational societies was not alienating. Subsistence farming or hunting and gathering is hardly enlightening. Romanticized imageries of preorganizational systems forget that people starved and froze to death, that some were slaves, and so forth. Early industrialization, with its exceedingly low wage rates, child labor, and absence of worker protection, was also alienating, but in a truer Marxian sense than the social–psychological alienation felt by today's worker in a routine job.) Studies of individual reactions to work also reveal that work that provides challenges, potential for advancement, and an opportunity for using creative or expressive capabilities is enjoyable and even enlightening. Thus, variations in organizational arrangements have a strong impact on individuals' sense of engagement and satisfaction with life.

There is also evidence that work organizations affect individuals in other fundamental ways. In a series of studies, Kohn and Schooler (1978, 1982; Kohn et al., 1990) have found consistent tendencies for people who work in more bureaucratized organizations and in occupations with more autonomy to be more intellectually flexible, more open to new experiences, and more self-directed than those working in different contexts. Perhaps even more remarkably, characteristics of their work also have been shown to affect workers' families. Those whose jobs provide them with autonomy and flexibility are more likely to encourage self-direction and self-expression in their children; those whose jobs offer less autonomy and flexibility are more likely to emphasize obedience to rules in their childcare practices. The effects of occupations may vary, to some extent, across organizations. The work of a secretary or an executive can be challenging and have potential for advancement in one organization but not in another. Some jobs allow for idiosyncratic behavior by their occupants, and others do not (Miner, 1987). Here again, organizational characteristics are critical variables as they interact with those of the occupation and the individual.

Thus far, most of the research on the impact of organizations on individuals has been based on studies of full-time, permanent workers. There is, however, a growing trend toward part-time and nonpermanent work. In 1988, for example, one-fourth of all U.S. workers were part-time or nonpermanent workers (Davis-Blake and Uzzi, 1993)—that is, temporary workers, leased workers, or independent contractors. By the late 1990s, some estimates indicated that nearly a third of all workers fell into this category (Barley and Kunda, 2004). The temporary help industry employment level grew from 184,000 in 1970 to 1.5 million in 1993 (Tilly and Tilly, 1998:152). This form of employment typically offers low pay and few benefits. Few studies have examined the impact of these changes in work organizations on the workers themselves. Barley and Kunda's (2004) pathbreaking ethnographic research on technical contractors in the computer industry (programmers, systems technicians, and others) illuminates key aspects of this form of work. Although many of the contractors they studied enjoyed the autonomy, independence, and, often, very high pay that went along with their status as short-term experts brought in to troubleshoot organizational problems, most found their marginality within the organization that employed them psychologically difficult.

> Contractors knew that no matter how appreciated, accepted, and integrated they became, they were still outsiders. Firms repeatedly drove this fact home in countless symbolic ways, from the color of the contractors' badges to the size and location of their office space. For some, the sense of being a second-class citizen was a constant source of anxiety, dissatisfaction, and irritation. Others took it in stride, or even found the distance that it created comforting. But one way or another, all contractors had to learn to live with their liminality. To do so, they carved out roles for

themselves, ranging from "gurus" and "trusted confidants" to "hired guns" and "warm bodies" purchased solely for their "skill sets." These roles allowed contractors to rationalize their status and resolve the practical dilemmas of life on the job. Ultimately, however, their status as outsiders was more than a symbolic issue: all contractors knew that sooner or later they would have to return to the market in search of another job. (Barley and Kunda, 2004:288)

Another growing trend is home-based work, or telecommuting, in which people work from their homes and use electronic communications to link with their employers (Lozano, 1989). Clerical work can be done this way, as can the work of some professionals such as editors and professors. Home workers see themselves as having more freedom than their office-bound counterparts, and such arrangements can allow them to deal more effectively with the integration of work and family life (Hornug, Rosseau, and Glaser, 2008). On the other hand, some work suggests that the lack of regular contact with colleagues and bosses often reduces individuals' sense of identification with the organization and leaves them feeling isolated (Thatcher and Zhu, 2006). That these perceptions may have some validity is suggested by research showing that women who took advantage of flexible work hours and working at home were less apt than those who did not to see wage growth (Glass, 2004). Of course, the individual impact of such arrangements may depend on a variety of other characteristics of the organizations. Organizations vary in their ability to adopt flexible work systems, based on their age and size, their existing labor–management relationships, and their existing work process arrangements (Uzzi and Barsness, 1998). These other characteristics may mediate the way in which flexible work systems are used as well as the way organizations respond to employees who use these systems.

The psychological impacts of organizations on individuals are clearly important, but the most visible and perhaps the most important impacts are those involving individuals' placement and opportunities for advancement within an organization and thus their economic outcomes. Organizational norms and practices define what characteristics of individuals are valued and rewarded (Reskin, 2003). These characteristics may include educational attainment, work experience, length of tenure in an organization, and other characteristics that sociologists refer to as "achieved" (because it is possible for individuals to change them by dint of their efforts and choices). Most economic theories of how organizations affect the economic outcomes of individuals focus on these sorts of characteristics. Organizations may also implicitly or explicitly use demographic characteristics of individuals, such as age, sex, and race, as a basis for selecting, evaluating, and assigning rewards. Sociologists refer to these characteristics as "ascriptive" because they are essentially fixed by birth. Because these characteristics are often assigned different status and social meanings within the larger society, and thus, individuals possessing them are accorded greater or lesser value, they may affect the kinds of rewards and opportunities individuals receive in organizations (Berger, Ridgeway, and Zelditch, 2002; Ridgeway and Correll, 2006). Organizations' use of such characteristics in this way has, in recent decades, been challenged and in most cases ruled as illegal. (It is important to remember, however, that laws forbidding discrimination are indeed a relatively recent phenomenon. For example, "No Irish Need Apply" was frequently seen on signs outside some business firms at the height of Irish immigration to the United States, around the turn of the century. Up through the 1960s, employment advertisements in newspapers were typically divided into two columns: one containing job listings for men and the other for women. In the 1960s, female teachers were routinely assigned salaries that were three-quarters of those received by their male counterparts, because the latter were assumed to be breadwinners whereas the former were not.)

Because organizational policies and practices affect the economic outcomes of individuals, organizations are key components of the system of social stratification; we will discuss this in more detail below. At this point, though, we want to underscore that the impact of these policies and practices is experienced directly by individuals and has consequences for individuals' career choices and outcomes. Figure 1–1 provides a general model that portrays processes that shape individuals' careers (Lawrence and Tolbert, 2007).

FIGURE 1–1   Organizational Influences on Individuals' Career Choices and Outcomes
Source: Barbara S. Lawrence and Pamela S. Tolbert, "Organizational Demography and Individual Careers: Structure, Norms and Outcomes," in *Handbook of Career Studies,* ed. H. Gunz and M. Peiperl (Los Angeles: Sage, 2007), p. 401. Copyright © 2007 by Sage Publications, Inc. Reprinted by permission.

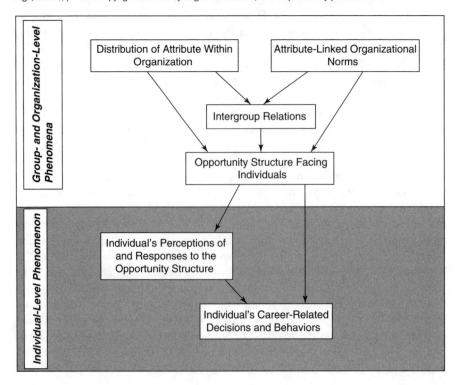

This model suggests that the distribution of a demographic attribute among the members of an organization may affect its salience; in general, research suggests that an increase in the numbers of individuals with a given attribute (e.g., female, Asian) makes members more aware of that attribute (Kanter, 1977). There may also be organizational norms tied to the characteristic. For example, an acquaintance who worked for a major office-equipment firm reported that there was an informal (and probably illegal) company practice of not promoting people who were older than forty-five. Likewise, there may be a long tradition of appointing men to high-level financial offices, so that people *expect* men rather than women to ascend to these offices. In combination, these organizational characteristics shape relations among members with different demographic characteristics—whether they (consciously or unconsciously) communicate easily, feel personally at ease, and generally respect those who have different characteristics. Demographically influenced interaction patterns, in turn, will affect the opportunity structure that individuals face—that is, the statistical likelihood that they will be assigned to certain positions, be given particular rewards and recognition for their work, and have opportunities to acquire new skills and move up within the organization. The objective opportunity structure then affects individuals' perceptions of their opportunities (not everyone will see these chances the same way) and their responses, which in turn affects their career choices. Career choices made by individuals with different demographic characteristics then feed back into the distribution of the characteristics within the organizations and the norms (Reskin and Roos, 1990). These relations may be conditioned by other aspects of organizations. For example, when organizations are growing, there are more promotional opportunities (Rosenbaum, 1979); if such opportunities are made available to those with devalued characteristics as well as others, the representation of people with those less valued characteristics at higher organizational levels may increase. Changes in the distribution of an attribute among organizational members, in turn, may result in changes in organizational norms tied to that attribute.

Organizations and Communities

The practices and decisions of organizations not only affect individuals but also have critical impacts on other collectivities, including towns, cities, and other political communities. The unprecedented role of organizations in contemporary society is based on the fact that organizations are treated as independent entities, just like individual persons. In a perceptive set of essays, Coleman (1974) points out that, just as the individual in modern society is given a set of rights and responsibilities by the state, the state also extends rights and responsibilities to organizations. He refers to organizations as "juristic persons" (since they are created by legal actions) or corporate actors and considers an array of actions that corporate actors are involved in, including buying and selling property, suing and being sued, acquiring debts and savings, and so forth. The granting of such rights to organizations is a fairly recent historical development (Kimberly, 1989), and the possession of these rights, coupled with other features of organizations (e.g., control of relatively large resources, potential immortality), gives organizations an enormous amount of power. Coleman also argues that corporate actors, including the state, are generally more comfortable dealing with other corporate actors than with individual persons and thus tend to provide preferential treatment to organizations in areas as diverse as taxation and rights to privacy. Hence, organizations often wield much greater influence than individual persons, at the communal, societal, and international levels.

The impacts of organizations are easily visible at the community level. A college or a university can be the dominant institution in the town or city in which it is located. One only has to think of Bloomington, Indiana; Ann Arbor, Michigan; or Durham, North Carolina—the homes of large universities—or of Granville, Ohio, a small college town, to see this point. The Mayo Clinic dominates Rochester, Minnesota. The effects of employing organizations on communities can be both positive and negative. One study found that companies vary in the degree to which they encourage their middle managers to participate in community affairs (Christenson et al., 1988). If communities were filled with organizations that encouraged such participation, local life would be enriched. (Interestingly, this same study also found that those middle managers who did get involved in community life were less likely to opt for transfers to other communities.) A dramatic example of the negative effect of an organization on the fate of a community is provided by the case of General Electric Corporation, which once dominated the life of the city of Schenectady, New York. When General Electric (GE) was running its Schenectady operations at full employment, the city prospered. As GE changed its product mix and downsized its Schenectady operations, the city slid downhill. The downsizing of GE has taken retail stores, hotels, restaurants, and a whole series of other small businesses with it.

The impact of a large employer on a community can also be seen clearly in a study reported by Seiler and Summers (1979). They examined the consequences of a large steel manufacturing firm's decision to locate a major new plant in a small town in the Midwestern United States. The steel company Jones and Laughlin engaged in a series of covert actions, such as buying land for their plant through ghost buyers and hiring workers from surrounding counties rather than in the home county. The company also co-opted local community leaders by using key bankers and lawyers as their local representatives. No Jones and Laughlin personnel were active in the community, but their operatives were. The company also directly intervened in plans for a new high school in the community, forcing the building of a less expensive and more practical school, thus reducing their tax liability. Seiler and Summers do not suggest that all the results of the company's actions were bad for the local community. Indeed, some were recognized as positive. The important point is that this organization had a direct and dramatic impact on the local community. The impact of a single powerful organization can thus be great.

Most communities have more than a single dominant organization, but this fact does not dilute the power of organizations in the community. Local power structures reflect interorganizational competition and thus the interests of powerful organizational actors (Galaskiewicz, 1979; Perrucci and Pilisuk, 1970). This is a key reason behind the not infrequent opposition of small towns and cities to the entry of Wal-Mart stores into their community (Bianco, 2006; see also Balser, 2007).

Organizations may affect communities not only through their influence on economic aspects but perhaps even more broadly by decisions and actions that affect the natural environment. Waste disposal practices of organizations in a variety of communities, involving the release of harmful industrial chemicals, such as polychlorinated biphenyls (PCBs), into streams and the air, have crippled commercial fishing, harmed wildlife, and posed a variety of health dangers, ranging from cancer to learning problems in children (Revkin, 1997). Research has shown that larger organizations emit toxins at a significantly higher rate than smaller organizations do (Grant, Jones, and Bergesen, 2002). Organizations dealing with complex technologies that have potentially lethal consequences for wide swaths of human populations are subject to what Perrow (1984) terms "normal accidents." These include organizations that operate nuclear plants, build nuclear weapons systems, engage in recombinant DNA production, ship highly toxic or explosive cargo across distances, and operate chemical plants. His analysis was published before the chemical plant disaster in Bhopal, India, and the Chernobyl nuclear disaster in Russia, in which thousands were killed and the air and soil were contaminated for an indeterminate amount of time, but these cases are consistent with his thesis. He argues that highly complex technical systems that are tightly coupled or integrated have an inherently strong potential for catastrophe and, in consequence, should in most cases, if not all, be abandoned. Most organizational researchers have been reluctant to engage the political implications of Perrow's assessments, although these implications strongly suggest a need for such research to consider more closely the nature of the relationship between organizations and communities.

It is not only individual organizations that have important impacts for communities, but networks of organizations as well. Interorganizational relationships, which will be considered in detail in Chapter 8, can have both positive and negative consequences for a community (Galaskiewicz and Krohn, 1984). For example, Minneapolis, Minnesota, is blessed with an extraordinarily high level of corporate philanthropy (Crittenden, 1978). Much of this is based on the interorganizational linkages among the business firms there; these linkages provide a means for effective coordination of their charity activities. Of course, interorganizational linkages can also provide the means by which organizations effectively shape local policy in ways that specifically favor their own interests, which individually the organizations could not do (Useem, 1979).

Organizations and Societies

If organizations have important outcomes for individuals and communities, it is obvious that they also have important outcomes for the wider society in which they are embedded. Organizations are shaped by societal contexts, as theory and research that we will discuss has emphasized. However, it is clear that they can strongly shape these contexts as well. Among the ways in which organizations affect society is through their impacts on patterns of social stratification and inequality, through their influence on national policy and political decision-making, and through the generation of externalities for which members of society as a whole bear the costs.

Social Stratification.   In the 1980s, there was a dramatic (if, in retrospect, a rather belated) recognition that organizations are a key component in the system of social stratification, and a growing number of organizational researchers began to turn their attention to understanding organizations from this vantage point (Baron, 1984; Baron and Bielby, 1980; Baron and Pfeffer, 1994; Blau, Ferber, and Winkler, 2006; Cohen, Broschak, and Haveman, 1998; England, 1994; Fernandez and Weinberg, 1997; Kalleberg, 1983; Kalleberg and Van Buren, 1996; Reskin, 2003). By selecting people as employees and then assigning them to particular jobs that are associated with greater or lesser rewards and opportunities, organizations play a central role in producing, maintaining, or changing systematic patterns of social inequality. In the preceding paragraphs, we talked about how demographic characteristics may affect the fate of individuals in terms of their personal labor market outcomes. When those individual outcomes are aggregated, they produce systematic, enduring patterns of inequality by gender and by race that indicate unequal life chances of different groups. Given the national credo in the United States of equal opportunity, this is a serious social problem, and this is why organizations have been the ultimate targets of social movements and legislation aimed at addressing this problem. In our earlier discussion, we mainly focused on within-organization factors that contribute to inequality (chances of getting promoted and getting paid well), but differences by race and gender in economic achievements are also produced in part by across-organization factors.

Research has shown that demographic characteristics of individuals affect whether they are likely to be hired by different kinds of organizations; therefore, variations across organizations in terms of compensation and other benefits that they provide may also be related to social inequality. For example, higher-status, larger, research-oriented universities are less likely to hire women as faculty than lower-status, smaller, teaching-oriented institutions. Because the former pay more, the concentration of women in the latter institutions affects the overall patterns of gender differences in earnings (Tolbert, 1986). Differences in the hiring of men and women may reflect differences in research and other aspects of faculty productivity (Johnson and Stafford, 1974), though there is a chicken-and-egg problem here. Considerable research shows that the productivity of scientists is strongly affected by their work context (Allison and Long, 1990; Long, Allison, and McGinnis, 1993; Long and McGinnis, 1981). That is, departments and institutions with more resources encourage scientific productivity through motivation, intellectual stimulation, and good facilities; these attributes of organizations have an independent effect on increasing individuals' productivity. Hence, whether women faculty are less likely to be hired by more elite universities because they are less productive on average than their male counterparts, or whether they are less productive because they are less likely to get the same level of support that average male faculty receive is unclear.

Politics and National Policies. There is little question that large economic organizations wield considerable influence on the formulation of domestic and international policies at the national level (as well as influencing politics at state and local levels). One notable example of this influence is the massive financial support the federal government granted the Chrysler Corporation in the 1980s, when the company teetered on the brink of bankruptcy (Reich and Donahue, 1985). The extent to which the weight given to large organizations' interests in national politics is the result of a concerted effort by corporations to control political decision-making has been heavily debated, though. According to one point of view, corporate elites have opportunities to interact regularly through their shared memberships on their organizations' boards of directors, in social clubs and voluntary organizations and in other organizational venues, which provide them with opportunities to formulate strategies for exercising political influence that are beneficial to them as a group (e.g., Domhoff, 1971; Mills, 1956). In this approach, "inner groups" of business elites are seen as being selected to assist in the governance of other institutions, such as governmental advisory boards, philanthropic organizations, and colleges and universities. Such conscious, concerted action serves to promote the more general interests of the entire capitalist class (Useem, 1979, 1982, 1984).

Few would dispute the assertion that organizations are active participants in the development and implementation of governmental policy, at all levels. One study in the areas of energy and health found that corporate entities in the form of trade associations, professional societies, and public-interest groups were the key actors in these state policy domains (Laumann, Knoke, and Kim, 1985). Organizations can thus be viewed as one source of laws; they are also vital in the selection of judges (Champagne, Neef, and Nagel, 1981). But even without direct lobbying efforts, interests of corporations weigh heavily in political decision-making, and research suggests that this has been true for a large part, if not the entire history of the United States. The embeddedness of large-corporate interests in the U.S. political system is illustrated by one analysis of the State Department's actions for the period 1886–1905, an analysis that persuasively demonstrates the way in which core financial and industrial interests became routinely incorporated into the State Department's decision-making. In consequence, American foreign policy came to reflect these organizational interests (Roy, 1981, 1983a; see also Carstensen and Werking, 1983). However, it is not clear that the influence of large organizations in the political sphere is necessarily the result of the conscious, interlinked efforts of these organizations. It may simply be that the size and wealth of these organizations gives them more power and prominence in political decisions without any necessary collusion among them. Nonetheless, insofar as the interests of these actors are not in line with the interests of most individual members of society, or satisfying those interests imposes costs (not only financial, but personal, such as serving in combat or having a poorer-quality environment) on the average citizen, these political impacts can be highly problematic. This brings us to another way in which organizations have impacts on society—they can create problems with which the rest of society has to cope.

Generation of Externalities. "Externalities" is a term used by economists to refer to the results of an economic transaction that affect others who did not participate in the transaction and whose interests were not taken into account. Externalities can be positive (the nonparticipating party receives benefits from the transaction) or negative (they suffer some damage or have to pay some costs). Organizational decisions often generate externalities of both types, but it is the negative externalities that are often most salient, and these externalities can be very problematic indeed. Organizations can generate externalities through criminal actions (Clinard and Yeager, 1980; Sutherland, 1949). For example, fire insurance companies have been known to facilitate the "torching" of buildings by arsonists. The arsonist owns the building, which is rundown and unsellable. After it burns, the arsonist collects the insurance on the building. The insurance companies may not be directly involved nor benefit themselves, but because they often fail to vigorously investigate or prosecute those involved (either because of the effort involved or because they believe that such investigations might offend or drive away legitimate customers), they often contribute to these property crimes (Needleman and Needleman, 1979). The costs of such arson are borne by other customers in the form of higher insurance premiums. More recent dramatic instances of criminal actions in the stock market (e.g., insider trading on Wall Street) not only have hurt those who invested in specific companies and the unwitting employees of those companies but have had repercussions for the overall performance of the market and therefore consequences for thousands of investors with pension funds and college plans invested in stocks. Even if there is no criminal action involved, organizational actions can be associated with very serious externalities. Levine's (1982) analysis of the case of Love Canal provides an illustration. In this case, toxic wastes were placed in an unused canal, which was later covered with landfill. Homes and a school were built on and near the site. When the homeowners became aware of the situation and its consequences, which included miscarriages, birth defects, and various illnesses, they approached local, state, and federal agencies for help. At each level, agencies worked hard to protect their own interests and in so doing prolonged the harmful outcomes for the residents.

Organizations and the World

Organizations also have impacts that cut across societies. International organizations have been around for a large part of human history, of course. Imperialist organizations that were at the heart of the Roman, Ottoman, and British Empires exemplify this international reach, as does the Catholic Church. Today, many universities have overseas branches. The Red Cross International has sites in hundreds of countries. There are multinational organizations in just about every sphere of life. Much of the contemporary research on organizations, though, focuses on multinational business corporations. There are many explanations for the emergence and rapid spread of the multinational corporation in recent years, all with elements of truth. One explanation emphasizes the role of technology. Mass-production systems and computer information handling have pushed all societies to larger and larger units of production (Heilbroner, 1974) and have made it much easier to communicate and carry on operations across national boundaries. Thus, international expansion is both feasible and necessary.

Another explanation is that local economic independence is impossible for many nations, particularly those with weak political and economic systems. The multinational firm is able to step in to become the dominant economic and political form of organization, superseding the traditional nation-state in weaker parts of the world (Toynbee, 1974). A related explanation is that the multinational corporation is a consequence of corporate choices made to implement product–market strategy: as corporations begin to produce a complex range of products, these are sold in different markets through multiple channels of distribution (Egelhoff, 1982; McMillan, 1973). This explanation—which we will see later is solidly within contemporary organizational theory—suggests that even in a no-growth economic situation, the desire to cut costs or maintain the share of the market would lead to international expansion.

There are important consequences of multinational corporations for individual nation-states. In such organizations, considerations of what is best for a national economy are secondary to considerations of what is best for the corporation as a whole. Although the multinational is frequently welcomed in areas of high unemployment, its presence can create extremely high dependence on the firm. Once the local economy is dependent on such a firm, the firm has a great deal of power. The multinational is also often able to avoid paying taxes at the rate paid by domestic corporations through reporting profits in countries with lower tax rates and other forms of financial shifts. When a multinational moves some of its production operations overseas, of course, domestic employment is adversely affected (Clegg and Dunkerley, 1980). As a consequence, multinationals often have enormous political influence, even in countries in which many multinationals are based, such as the United States. By playing countries off against each other (proposing to move their facilities from one location to another), multinationals can make it difficult for any country to adopt environmental regulations or other rules that multinationals find objectionable. And even when individual countries do succeed in passing such legislation, because the ecosystems of the world are not completely independent (as exemplified by global climate change), the actions of multinationals operating in other countries may still produce negative impacts in those countries.

THE NATURE OF ORGANIZATIONS

So what *are* these things that are shaping the world? We all know intuitively what organizations are, but when pressed to specify the defining elements, it probably doesn't take long for most of us to realize that this is much more difficult to do than one would think at first blush. An organization has no visible corpus, at least outside of the individual members who are part of it. But the individual members are not the organization per se. It is true that for most of us, the representatives of the organization that we deal with determine how we see the organization as a whole. This fact was underscored in a study by Giordano (1974) on the reactions of adolescents who were defined as delinquents to the juvenile courts and social agencies they faced. Her research suggested that if a person felt close to an individual in an organization, his or her interpretation of the total organization was much more positive than if he or she did not. This is why many organizations try to influence the way in which employees respond to customers or clients (Hochschild, 1983). However, the individual members of an organization may leave and be replaced by new ones, but the organization still remains, so clearly there is a difference between the individual members and the organization. An organization may have a building in which its activities take place, but the building itself is not the organization (as vacant office buildings attest—the building remains after the organization is gone). In this respect, organizations are like other abstract social phenomena that have no physical form, including "groups," "markets," and "industries." Because of their lack of tangible, physical representation, it may be useful to conceive of organizations as being much like force fields; we know of them through their effects. This notion is consistent with the definition of organizations offered by Chester Barnard, author of a classic analysis of organizations and who, as the president of New Jersey Bell Telephone Company in the 1930s, had considerable practical organizational experience. He defined an organization simply as being "a system of consciously coordinated personal activities or forces" (1968:72).

Part of the reason that it is so difficult to come up with a good, clear definition of organizations is that there is such a huge amount of variation in the things we deem to be organizations, from two-person, mom-and-pop sandwich shops to huge corporations with establishments in locations spanning the world. Apart from Barnard's minimalist definition, most efforts to define organizations contain some combination of the following four elements: (1) two or more members, (2) a goal or set of goals that guide members' activities, (3) distinctive roles assigned to different members, and (4) an authority system that is accepted as governing decisions. But organizations vary enormously in virtually all of these dimensions, and such variation affects our ability to draw general conclusions about processes and outcomes that characterize organizations as a social phenomenon.

It takes very little thought to recognize the great variance in size among contemporary organizations. There is an interesting statistical paradox that is related to this variance. On the one hand, data indicate that the "typical U.S. employee works in an establishment with 599 full-time workers . . . and

72 part-time workers" (Marsden, Cook, and Knoke, 1996:49). Data from establishments indicate, though, that the "median numbers are 50 full-time and 2 part-time employees" (Dun and Bradstreet, 1995:26). The reason for this apparent discrepancy is that, although there are many very small organizations, most of the people in the United States are employed by a relatively small number of very large organizations (Marsden, Cook, and Knoke, 1996:50). As the preceding statistics suggest, trying to measure the number of members of an organization may be a little problematic. Should we count the number of part-time employees the same way that we count the number of full-time employees? Should we count the number of temporary workers along with those who are permanent or exclude them (or perhaps prorate their number)? Some organizations may be made up of volunteer members whose participation in the organization varies considerably at different points in time; how should they be counted? We will discuss some of these issues in Chapter 3, where we talk about factors that affect the structure of organizations, but the main point we want to make here is that size is an important aspect of the diversity in the phenomenon of organizations.

There is also, obviously, a great deal of variation in organizational goals. (In Chapter 10, we discuss problems of precisely defining organizations' goals, but for now let's consider just the formal goals of organizations, that is, what their officially stated purposes are.) A typology of organizations proposed by Blau and Scott (1962) was premised on the notions that organizations could be characterized in terms of who the primary beneficiaries of their goals were and that organizations driven by different goals would vary in other ways as well. In this context, they distinguished between business organizations, mutual benefit organizations, service organizations, and commonweal organizations. In this scheme, the primary beneficiaries of business organizations are the owners (including stockholders); examples might include restaurants, car dealerships, and producers of computer goods. Clearly, these kinds of organizations vary substantially on other dimensions, but they are alike in their goal of providing revenues for the owners. The primary beneficiaries of mutual benefit associations, on the other hand, are the members themselves; examples of this type of organization include fraternities and sororities, buying cooperatives and labor unions. Again, there is obviously a lot of diversity among organizations in this category, but their key focus on satisfying the needs of the members distinguishes them as a group from business organizations. Service organizations have as their beneficiaries the people who come to the organization for some help or treatment; examples include various treatment-centered nonprofits—hospitals, job counseling and job referral organizations, and social work agencies. These organizations are distinguished both by the lack of profit motive and by concern with helping specific individuals deal with individual problems. Finally, the primary beneficiaries of what Blau and Scott called commonweal organizations are members of the general public; examples are public radio and television stations, libraries, and schools. The boundaries between these different categories are not always sharp (this is a problem for most typologies, unfortunately), but the typology does serve to point up critical aspects of organizational variation associated with different kinds of goals.

Just as organizations vary strikingly in the number of members and in their goals, they also vary strikingly in the type and nature of roles that members are assigned. This aspect of organizations is usually considered under the label "complexity," which we will discuss in detail in Chapters 2 and 3. The kinds of roles that members are assigned are obviously affected by the technology and goals of an organization. These factors affect the distribution of different kinds of occupations that you find in a given organization because organizational roles are often defined by occupations—that is, by the organizational representatives of occupations, professional associations, and educational institutions (Abbott, 1988; Barley and Tolbert, 1991). But even in organizations that have the same technology and set of goals, there is a large variation both in the extent to which roles are clearly defined or not (e.g., whether radiological technicians do many of the same activities that the physicians who supervise them do, or whether these roles are clearly distinguished varies across hospitals; see Barley, 1985) and in the nature of these roles (e.g., what teachers are expected to do in one school may be very different from what they are expected to do in others; see Kidder, 1989).

Finally, although most contemporary organizations operate with a dominant type of authority system, labeled "rational–legal"—discussed in Chapter 4—there is huge variability in how this system operates in practice in different organizations. At one end of the spectrum is the classic example of military organizations, in which the decisions and edicts of higher-level members are expected to be executed without question by lower-level members; at the other end are collectivist organizations (Rothschild-Witt, 1979), in which the authority to make and act on decisions is understood to be equally dispersed among members.

This degree of variation in the phenomenon we want to understand, organizations, makes both thinking about them and studying them a challenging task, to put it mildly. Partly because of this complexity, organizational scholars have taken a number of different tacks to studying the phenomenon. Generally, these are classified as representing three main levels of analysis: (1) individual, (2) group, and (3) organizational. Thus, one tack involves focusing on the properties of a component of organizations, individuals. Research at this level examines variations in personality, motives, needs, and other qualities that define individuals and seeks to link these to organizational characteristics and outcomes (e.g., studies of how individuals' motives are related to the rewards organizations provide). Another tack is to focus on the properties of another organizational component, small groups, or sets of individuals who engage in direct interaction with one another, and to link these to organizational characteristics and outcomes (e.g., studies of the way in which the representation of different "types" of people in a group—defined in various ways, including by areas of expertise, demographic characteristics, organizational tenure—affects the level of conflict and/or creativity of the group). And a third tack involves focusing on properties that characterize the organization as a whole—its size, the kind of technologies that are used in production processes, the length of time it has been in operation, and so on—and relating these to other organizational characteristics and outcomes (e.g., studies examining how the age of an organization affects the chances of continued survival or failure). All of these are valid ways of analyzing and explaining organizational phenomena; which approach is taken depends partly on the intellectual preferences and inclinations of the scholar and partly on the questions that she or he wishes to answer. For example, as far as we can see, it would be completely impossible to use an individual level of analysis to understand and explain patterns of mergers between organizations in different industries.

We were trained as sociologists, and this has led us to be inclined to take an organizational level of analysis in our approach to the subject matter. This orientation is reflected in our treatment of some topics covered in the book (e.g., you will see that when we discuss leadership, which many researchers approach from an individual level of analysis, we tend to emphasize research that has examined the organizational context in which leadership turnover is most likely to occur). We do, however, also discuss other levels of analysis, depending on the topic under consideration. This brings us to the structure or underlying logic of our coverage of research and theory in this book.

THE PLAN OF THE BOOK

We were guided by two main ideas in organizing and presenting work on organizations. One is that, as an organizing device, it would be useful to cover issues and topics that an individual who wants to start an organization would have to think about and cope with in carrying out that project, more or less in the order that he or she would need to deal with these. Thus, we begin in Part I with research and theory on organizational structure and design, because once a person has an idea and some resources to create an organization, that is the first task to be faced. How might the work be divided up and parceled out among different members? This is the core problem that research on formal organizational structure addresses. Next, we turn to the processes that are involved in the day-to-day running of an organization—exercising authority and getting people to do things that need to be done; making decisions; ensuring that everyone gets the information that they need to have in order to function effectively; managing relations with those outside the organization, including customers, suppliers, competitors, and regulators. These are topics that are covered in Part II. Finally, in Part III, we consider two key outcomes that organizations that have been in existence for some time may face: (1) evaluating the performance of the organization and (2) undertaking changes. Thus, the underlying logic of our coverage of the wide array of topics and subjects that have been addressed in various studies and theories of organizations reflects our notion of the processes of development of some prototypical organization.

In addition, we think that having an understanding of the historical context and historical evolution of ideas and thinking on a subject is useful to comprehending the theoretical arguments and conclusions drawn from research by scholars. In this context, we have tried to give you a sense of how research on a given topic developed over time and how current theory and research on a topic is related to and reflective of the history of research and theory on that topic.

SUMMARY AND CONCLUSIONS

In a very real sense, we are living in an "organizational state" (Laumann and Knoke, 1987), in which the major actors in local, national, and international policy events are organizations and networks of organizations. This is why some analysts view organizations as the key to attaining core social values, such as peace, prosperity, and social justice (Etzioni, 1968, 1991, 1993). This may be so, but we would also point out that one of the major contributions that organizational analysis can make is to highlight the limitations to what is feasible for organizations themselves and for the wider social system.

Jackall (1988:3) noted that business is a "social and moral terrain." The same point is true for all kinds of organizations. Moral and ethical issues are confronted whenever decisions are made. In a book prepared under the auspices of the Business Roundtable, an organization made up of the chief executives of many of the largest and most powerful American business firms, Steckmest (1982) (see also Burke, 1986) urges corporate social responsibility. The argument of his book is that corporations need to "develop executives and functions (e.g., government relations and consumer affairs staffs) to effectively monitor and responsibly interact in an increasingly complex sociopolitical environment" (Yeager, 1982:748). Again, the notion of corporations has to be expanded to all organizations, including those that are part of the government itself.

Organizational theory has much to contribute to "clients" of many types, ranging from politicians and journalists, to workers and managers within organizations, to opponents of organizations who operate inside and outside the organizations themselves (Lammers, 1981). The true relevance of organizational theory lies in the following conclusions: *"The more we are able to create worlds that are morally cogent and politically viable, the more we are able as workers and as citizens to manage or resist"* (Brown, 1978:378; italics added).

EXERCISES

1. Write down all of the activities that you do in a day, or in a week. Describe the degree to which each activity is affected by organizations.
2. Think about two organizations with which you are very familiar. They can be places where you worked or are working, athletic teams, fraternities or sororities, clubs, religious organizations, or other organizations that you can describe. What are the outcomes of these organizations? Remember to use the materials in this chapter in your answers.

Chapter 2

Organizational Structure: Key Dimensions

OVERVIEW

Organizations vary considerably in their structure, and this variance has important consequences for both organizational and individual outcomes. We begin by giving you a general sense of what we mean by structure, then offering a more formal definition and describing some of the early work that drew researchers' attention to structure as a key issue in the study of organizations. In this chapter and the next, we discuss research that has concentrated on identifying and explaining key dimensions of structure. In particular, we focus on work on complexity, formalization, and centralization.

Structure is a defining and crucial aspect of any organization. One way to think about structure is as the arrangement of organizational parts, similar in some ways to parts of a building. Buildings have doors through which we enter. Organizations, too, have "ports of entry," such as the admissions office for undergraduates at a university or the hiring department in a business firm. Hallways govern our movements and the forms of activity in a building. Organizations have rules and procedures about how things are to be done, which direct the behavior of their members. Some buildings are small and simple, such as a garage; others are complex and multilayered, with intricate linkages and passageways to other buildings. Similarly, some organizations operate in a single location and have only a few different types of jobs; other organizations operate in many sites, nationally and internationally, and have a wide array of divisions and jobs. In some buildings, the heating and air-conditioning are centrally controlled; in others, each room is essentially autonomous and its temperature is determined by occupants. Likewise, organizations vary in the degree to which people and units are given autonomy in decision-making.

The building analogy isn't perfect. For example, the structure of most buildings rarely changes significantly over time. Although organizational structure has a strong tendency toward inertia, most structures do change (sometimes slowly, sometimes very swiftly) as they are influenced by successive waves of members, interactions among the members, and changes in environmental conditions. However, the analogy provides you with a general sense of how structure affects an organization.

DEFINING ORGANIZATIONAL STRUCTURE

But how do we define structure exactly? There is no single, agreed-upon definition, and indeed, there is wide variation in the ways people have defined this concept. Chester Barnard, in a famous early analysis of organizations, offered the following characterization of structure: "all complex organizations are built up from units of organization, and consist of many units of 'working' or 'basic' organizations, overlaid with units of executive organizations . . ." (1968:113). Robert Merton, whose students helped define organizational sociology as a distinctive subfield, suggested that structure "involves clearly defined patterns of activity in which, ideally, every series of actions is functionally related to the purposes of the organization" (1957:195). Peter Blau, a well-known organizational researcher, defined structure simply as "the distributions, along various lines, of people among social positions that influence the role relations among these people" (1974:12).

One reason that there may be little agreement on a definition of structure is that many scholars have tried to define it broadly enough to encompass both informal and formal aspects of organizations. Informal structure involves norms and social expectations that are not officially prescribed by an organization, but that can be a very powerful force in channeling people's behavior. Formal structure, on the other hand, refers to explicit organizational specifications, such as who is to do what kinds of tasks or jobs, and how these are to be done (including when and where). In offering our own definition of structure, we distinguish between these two aspects. Thus, *formal structure* refers to the official, explicit division of responsibilities, definitions of how work is to be done, and specifications of relationships involving the members of an organization. *Informal structure* refers to the unofficial divisions, definitions, and relations that emerge over time in an organization. As we suggested above, structure (both formal and informal) is important because it shapes people's behavior. Under most circumstances, people enact behaviors that are consistent with structural prescriptions. But you should also recognize that people's behaviors are the source of changes in structure over time. This relationship is sometimes referred to as *structural duality*: "structures shape people's practices, but it is also people's practices that constitute (and reproduce) structure" (Sewell, 1992:4; see also Giddens, 1987). Under what conditions individuals are most apt to deviate from structural pre-scriptions and when such deviations will result in changes in existing structure (i.e., general acceptance of new ways of doing things) are questions with which contemporary organizational theorists are still wrestling (Barley and Tolbert, 1997; Scott, 2007).

Most of the early studies of organizations focused primarily on formal structure, although the importance of informal structure in explaining organiza-tional outcomes has long been recognized (Roethlisberger and Dickson, 1934). Formal structure in particular serves a core function for organizations, minimiz-ing or at least regulating the influence of individual differences on organizational outcomes. Thus, it is intended to ensure reliable, standard organizational outputs and to achieve organizational goals—in other words, to make organizations effective. Formal structure also provides the setting in which leadership is exer-cised, decisions are made, and activities are carried out. Below, we provide a brief history of early research on structure, to help you understand how concep-tions of this aspect of organizations developed over time.

STUDYING ORGANIZATIONAL STRUCTURE: EARLY RESEARCH ON THE BUREAUCRATIC FORM

Up through the nineteenth century, most economic production took place in small organizations and, often, just within family units. In these cases, produc-tion workers typically owned the tools they used in their work, made decisions about what kinds of products to create (presumably based on customers' requests or their own ideas of what would sell), and carried out all the steps in the produc-tion process—including selecting the kinds of materials to be used, deciding on the best techniques for production, and choosing any final, finishing details. This form of production, usually referred to as the craft form, still exists today. Hand-knit sweaters, customized furniture and cabinetry, artisan pottery and glassware, and other such goods are still often created this way. However, by the early twen-tieth century, this form of work organization had largely been supplanted by a very different form, one that allowed production to take place on a much grander scale. Many business firms had grown to proportions rarely witnessed before, and these behemoths had come to wield an unprecedented degree of power and influence in society, both economically and politically.

Max Weber, a German scholar of economic and political history who lived at the turn of the twentieth century, was fascinated by the new form of organiza-tion, which he referred to as *bureaucracy*, and curious about the conditions that had led this type of organization to proliferate and thrive in modern life. To address the latter question, he used the tools of his trade as a historian. He began by constructing an *ideal type* of bureaucracy, a conceptual model that contained the elements he considered to be the defining characteristics of this form. Real organizations, of course, will vary from this ideal type (Hall, 1963) but to different degrees. Weber was interested in identifying the kinds of societies that contained organizations most closely resembling the bureaucratic model. Thus, in order to better understand the conditions that fostered bureaucracy, he compared this model against organizations found in other time periods and in other societies.

Key elements of Weber's ideal type of bureaucracy (Weber, 1946:196–244; 1947:324–341) include such characteristics as

- A clearly defined division of labor, with different tasks and responsibilities assigned to specific individuals and offices or subunits
- A hierarchy of authority in which decisions made by lower-level individuals and offices are subject to review (and possible revision) by those at higher levels
- The use of written rules and documents to govern practice and decisions, promoting consistency across individuals and subunits
- The separation of home and office, such that organizational resources are clearly distinguished from individuals' private, personal resources, and public, official roles are distinguished from private, unofficial ones
- Appointment of members on the basis of their qualifications for particular jobs (versus personalistic ties)

We tend to take these characteristics very much for granted in the organizations we deal with today, but as our brief description of the craft form of organization should suggest, they were *not* common aspects of most organizations before the twentieth century. So what led these organizations to flourish in many societies after this time?

The depth of Weber's knowledge of history and his analytic skills made him one of the most prominent scholars of his era; these qualities are reflected in his analysis of the conditions that gave rise to the dominance of bureaucratic organizations in the contemporary world. He compared the ideal type of bureaucracy against a wide range of organizations, including those that characterized ancient Egyptian, Roman, and Chinese civilizations and those found in more recent Islamic regimes. Based on these comparisons, he identified a number of societal preconditions for the rise of the bureaucratic form, including the development of a monetary-based economy (allowing effective calculation of comparable values for the exchange of goods and services), increasing urbanization and literacy (generating pressures on governments for the efficient provision of expanded state services), and the expansion of governments through colonization and population growth (necessitating both the expansion of existing government services and better methods of controlling officials).

Later, Stinchcombe (1965) elaborated on these preconditions in a classic article and added another important factor influencing the spread of organizations with a bureaucratic form: the existence of other organizations with this form. As more individuals gain experience with this form of organization, either through their own employment or through their daily transactions, the easier it is for newly created organizations to also adopt this form. That is because it is easier to find people with experience that makes them suited for employment in bureaucracies and because it is consistent with the general expectations of how organizations should operate (see our discussion of institutional theory in Chapter 3).

In addition to the conditions listed above, Weber noted that bureaucracy was most compatible with a particular ideology of authority, which he referred to as rational–legal authority. We'll describe this in more detail in Chapter 4, where we discuss power. Although the historical analysis is very provocative, Weber's main impact on subsequent organizational studies came largely through his formulation of the characteristics of the ideal type (Meyer and Brown, 1977). This model drew researchers' attention to specific aspects of organizational structure—in particular, complexity, formalization, and centralization—as we'll discuss below.

But Weber was not the only one to consider structure as key to understanding the nature of contemporary organizations. About the same time that Weber was studying bureaucracy, another set of academics and practitioners was also focused on studying the structure of contemporary organizations. Since Weber's writings were not translated into English until after World War II, however, and most of the latter scholars were from English-speaking countries, their ideas were developed more or less independently of his. Driven largely by practical concerns with effectively managing this new form of organization, this group aptly became known as Managerial Theorists.

Managerial Theory was largely an outgrowth of Scientific Management. Both of these were, as the capitalizations might suggest, a sort of social movement (like the Great Awakening movement of the eighteenth century or the Black Power movement of the 1960s), in the sense that both were spread by adherents who were deeply committed to promoting the cause of rationalized management. (For some insights into what it was like to live with such social movement adherents, you should read *Cheaper by the Dozen*, written by the children of two proponents of Scientific Management, Frank and Lillian Gilbreth.) Scientific Management, developed initially by Fredrick Taylor (1911), first espoused the ideology that managerial practice, generally, and the design of jobs, specifically, should be based on scientific studies that provided systematic evidence of the most efficient ways to accomplish a given task.

Following this basic ideological premise, Managerial Theorists focused on the problem of "scientifically" figuring out the best way to design organizations as a whole—that is, articulating core, universal principles that managers should follow in making decisions about how to group people into departments or subunits, how to create lines of communication and oversight, and so forth (Fayol, 1930; Follet, 1918; Gulick and Urwick, 1937). One key problem they faced in this quest was that of empirically documenting the validity of their proposed principles, that is, scientific methodology. Scientific Management used time and motion studies to determine the efficiency of different job designs. By instructing workers to follow one set of procedures in carrying out their tasks, then instructing them to follow a slightly different set of procedures and timing how long it took them to accomplish their tasks, they could decide which procedures were most efficient. Unfortunately, this sort of experimentation is much less feasible at the organizational level. The analog would involve such things as combining two separate departments (say, product design and production) for some period of time, then separating them into two separate departments for another period of time, then possibly subdividing them into three separate departments, and trying to decide which arrangement was most effective. You can imagine the amount of chaos such experimentation could create in an organization. Hence, in lieu of systematic data collection, Managerial Theorists typically reflected on their own experiences in organizations (many had had administrative experiences in commercial organizations or the military) and used these as the basis for formulating key principles.

Interestingly, many of these principles drew attention to precisely the same aspects of formal structure that Weber had identified as part of the ideal type of bureaucracy—division of labor (the divisionalization principle), hierarchy (the scalar principle), and the use of rules and written documents (the exception principle). The divisionalization principle, for example, indicated that managers should form organizational subunits on the basis of either similar tasks (e.g., everyone doing marketing should be in the same unit) or similar outputs (e.g., everyone involved in producing and selling a particular brand of cereal—from chemists to manufacturing workers to marketing personnel—should be in the same unit). The scalar principle stated that all departments and subunits should be arranged in a clear hierarchy, so that one could easily tell who was to report to whom. And according to the exception principle, managers should make the criteria to be used in routine decisions explicit and then delegate responsibility for making those decisions to subordinates. (Thus, they would deal only with non-routine, "exceptional" decisions.) The validity of the notion of universal principles, however, was challenged by studies conducted in Britain in the mid-1950s by researcher Joan Woodward.

Woodward (1958), as she admits with disarming frankness, stumbled onto a key observation about organizational structure during a research project aimed at empirically examining the validity of some of Managerial Theorists' prescriptions. The researchers collected information on a number of aspects of formal structure from a sample of manufacturing firms in the United Kingdom and on financial measures of firm performance. As Woodward analyzed the data, she became increasingly perplexed: there seemed to be no relationship between the kinds of structural arrangements the firms had and their financial outcomes. However, she noticed that certain kinds of structural characteristics tended to be found in certain types of firms. Thus, she divided the firms into three categories: (1) small-batch or unit-production system, where customized items were produced in small quantities; (2) large-batch or mass-production system, where standardized items were produced in very large quantities; and (3) process or continuous production systems, where nondiscrete items (such as refined oil or chemicals) were produced in large quantities. She found that "typical" organization structure did indeed vary systematically across categories. Moreover, within categories, the type of structure that a firm had was related to financial performance: firms with structures that were more typical of their category performed better overall. Thus, contrary to the assumptions of Managerial Theorists, there was no "one best" structure; rather, what was best depended on the type of organization. But what was it about these categories that made them different? Woodward suggested that it had something to do with the technology but didn't delve into what it was *about* the technology that mattered. We'll return to the question of technological differences in the next chapter, but for now the critical result was that structure varied systematically across different kinds of organizations. Woodward's research laid the foundation for what came to be known as *contingency theory,* a line of research that was predicated on the assumption that the effectiveness of particular structural arrangements depended (was contingent) on the size, technology, and other aspects of an organization. Hence, researchers focused their attention on identifying and explaining such contingencies (Donaldson, 2001). In Chapter 3, we will discuss in more detail key contingencies studied by researchers.

SOCIOLOGICAL STUDIES OF FORMAL STRUCTURE IN ORGANIZATIONS

Sociologists did not turn their attention to studying organizations sui generis, as distinctive social phenomena in their own right, until after World War II. In part, sociological studies of organizations grew out of efforts to empirically examine arguments derived from structural–functionalist theory, a general theoretical approach that was dominant in sociology from the 1930s through the 1960s (see Scott, 2004, and Tolbert and Zucker, 1996, for discussions of the origins of organizations as a subfield in sociology). This approach defined the general task of sociology as explaining structures (in this context, "structure" refers to a widespread pattern of behavior) in terms of their functions, or consequences—that is, understanding how structures affected the survival of a collectivity. Organizations, one type of collectivity, appeared to offer excellent opportunities to conduct comparative analyses guided by functionalist theory. By the time sociologists began studying organizations, Weber's writings on bureaucracy had been translated into English. In addition, Managerial Theorists' arguments about organizations were well established among practitioners; in fact, the latter formed the core of what was taught in management studies in most business schools up through the early 1960s (Massie, 1964). Moreover, Woodward's research pointed to an interesting conundrum about structure. In this context, then, it's not surprising that sociologists focused on the problem of explaining variations in formal structure as a key task for the new subfield of organizational research. Much of this early work focused on three dimensions of structure in particular: complexity, formalization, and centralization (Hage, 1965). As you may notice, these are all aspects that figured prominently in Weber's ideal type of bureaucracy and ones that were the object of Managerial Theorists' key principles. They are not the only dimensions that people studied (others include the size of the administrative component, the average span of supervisory control, and the rates of adoption of new programs), but they received the lion's share of attention by researchers. Before discussing these aspects of formal structure in more detail, there are a few caveats to this research to note.

First, much of the research is comparative in nature; that is, in order to make statements about organizations in general, data were usually collected from more than one organization (Heydebrand, 1973). Some of the research is comparative in the sense that there is an attempt to compare organizations in different settings or societies. Being able to draw broad, generalizable conclusions about what determines formal structure and how it affects organizational outcomes is a noble goal, but there may be problems created by researchers' inadvertently mixing apples and oranges. As Woodward's research suggests, companies that differ in some core aspect could require a different structure to be effective. Thus, if researchers unintentionally compared organizations that varied in some important respects, their findings may reflect "noise" created by this. (The dilemma, of course, is that if a researcher examines only a very limited type of organization— say, hospitals that specialize in treating burns—generalization of the findings to other kinds of organizations is questionable.)

Second, when researchers tried to examine the same aspect of structure, they often used different measures, which makes it hard to know whether differences in the findings are just due to the measures (Pennings, 1973; Price and Mueller, 1986). For example, if you count the number of pages in a personnel manual to measure the degree to which an organization is rule bound, and if you ask members of the organization how much of their work is defined by rules, you may reach different conclusions about the same organization. Research is beginning to show us that there are measures that can be used across diverse sets of organizations (Kalleberg et al., 1996; Leicht, Parcel, and Kaufman, 1992), but as yet we do not have universal measures.

Finally, many studies assume that it is reasonable to characterize organizations as a whole on some dimension (e.g., Organization A is more rule bound than Organization B is), but the validity of this assumption can be debated (Hall, 1962; Heydebrand, 1990; Litwak, 1961; Stinchcombe, 1990). There are often structural differences between work units, departments, and divisions within a given organization. For example, the record-keeping unit of a hospital is likely to have many explicit rules and procedures to ensure consistency, whereas other treatment-oriented units of the same hospital are likely to have relatively few rules. It is possible that when you find differences across two hospitals in the number of rules, it may be because one hospital has a relatively large record-keeping unit and the other has a very small one; they may differ very little in the rules that affect other units.

Perhaps rather remarkably, given these issues, there are a number of common findings and, hence, conclusions to be drawn about the sources of variations in formal structure from this literature. We'll begin by describing the three core dimensions of formal structure in more detail and some of the ways in which they have been measured. Then we'll talk about work by Burns and Stalker (1961), which suggests how these dimensions are apt to covary, and more recent work on "high performance organizations" that also reflects this notion.

DIMENSIONS OF FORMAL STRUCTURE

Complexity

Complexity is one of the first things that you are apt to notice when you join any organization: the range of job titles, different offices, and other divisions are usually readily apparent. Even local voluntary organizations and nonprofits such as the Rotary Club, labor union locals, and garden clubs usually have an array of committees for programs, publicity, membership, community service, education, finance, and other matters, as well as different responsibilities for the main officers. Thus, the vast majority of organizations are divided into many subparts that have different tasks and responsibilities—that is, characterized by complexity. Complexity (or, as it is sometimes termed, differentiation) requires ways to coordinate and control the subparts so that their separate activities mesh, and the more complex an organization is, the more difficult it becomes to achieve such coordination and control. Complexity is not a simple construct. (You could say that it's complex!) It has several dimensions, which do not necessarily covary. To make sense out of the literature, we will discuss the following three dimensions in turn: (1) horizontal complexity, (2) vertical (hierarchical) complexity, and (3) spatial complexity or geographical dispersion.

Horizontal Complexity. Horizontal complexity, the dimension that has received the most attention from researchers, refers to the ways the work tasks performed in an organization are subdivided into different jobs and groups. Such complexity is associated with specialization in the skills and knowledge among the members. For example, if one college has a single office of student counseling, where all the counselors provide a combination of career, academic, and psychological advising, and another college has separate offices for career counseling, academic counseling, and psychological counseling, the latter would be termed more complex than the former.

The fact that complexity entails specialization has led to some key differences in the ways in which researchers have conceptualized, and thus measured, this aspect of formal structure. One approach is exemplified by what is sometimes referred to as "McDonaldization" (after the fast-food restaurant) or "taylorization" (after Fredrick Taylor, the engineer who developed Scientific Management). This approach involves assigning each job a very narrow set of repetitive tasks (Ritzer, 2000) and is usually associated with work tasks that are more routine and predictable. One common way of measuring horizontal complexity, based on this approach, is to count the number of job titles within an organization: the more job titles, the higher the level of complexity (Strang and Baron, 1990). In some organizations, for example, one can find a number of job titles for clerical personnel, such as Typist 1, Typist 2, and Typist 3. Other organizations may have only one generic title, such as Administrative Assistant. This approach to complexity is also reflected in other measures that involve counting the number of divisions, departments, or units within an organization; such measures can be found in the research of Blau and Schoenherr (1971), Hall, Johnson, and Haas (1967), and Pugh et al. (1968). Using measures of this sort, we would find the U.S. Army to be very complex, with its vast array of commands, battalions, brigades, companies, and so on. Organizations low on the complexity scale would be a local church or an automobile dealership, which have only a few main departments. Whether complexity is measured in terms of number of job classifications or number of departments, the underlying assumption is that greater complexity involves a narrower range of tasks and responsibilities, on average, for each subunit.

A second approach taken to conceptualizing and measuring horizontal complexity is often found in studies of more professional or craft-based work settings, such as hospitals or orchestras. Here, complexity is associated with greater knowledge and specialized expertise by jobholders (Hage and Aiken, 1967a). In line with this approach, Hage (1965) defines complexity as the "specialization in an organization . . . measured by the number of occupational specialties and the length of training required by each. The greater the number of occupations and the longer the period of training required, the more complex the organization" (p. 294). In this latter approach, organizations that employ a wide variety of professionals or different kinds of craft workers would be considered as very complex, although the jobs of each worker would normally involve a large number of different tasks over which they had a very high level of control. (For discussions of contemporary craft-organized work, see Barley and Kunda, 2004, and Faulkner, 1985. For a comprehensive discussion of the nature of professionally controlled work, see Leicht and Fennell, 2001.) The more specialized occupational training people have, the more they differ in the knowledge bases that they use in their work from others who might have similar amounts of training but in different occupations. Such specialization often requires extra effort for the individuals to communicate and coordinate their work. A similar conception of complexity is reflected in another well-known study (Lawrence and Lorsch, 1969), comparing workers in different types of jobs (e.g., sales, manufacturing, and research and development). They found that workers in each type of job varied noticeably from those of the others in terms of how they defined the primary goals of the organization, whether they were focused on short-term or long-term problems, and whether they took a more task-oriented or relationship-oriented approach to their work. Their research suggested that these differences created problems among the different groups in coordinating their activities effectively to meet customers' needs.

Consequences of Horizontal Complexity.   Despite the differences in ways of conceptualizing and measuring horizontal complexity, research findings generally suggest certain advantages of increasing complexity as well as common disadvantages. On the positive side, increased complexity (through its attendant increases in specialization) often leads to greater efficiency in carrying out work activities. When people specialize in certain tasks, they are able to hone relevant skills and knowledge and, thus, able to perform those tasks at a higher level of reliability, quality, and speed. In addition, work based on the second approach to conceptualizing horizontal complexity, as involving a greater number of specialists, suggests that organizations with higher levels of complexity are more innovative. Hage and Aiken (1967b), in a study of sixteen welfare organizations, found that new services and techniques designed to increase the quality of the services rendered were more common in more complex organizations. Later studies by Baldridge and Burnham (1975) and Lawrence and Lorsch (1969), conducted in very different types of organizations, also indicated that more complex organizations were likely to have more innovation or, in Hage's (1999) terms, more creative capacities. Work focusing on structural characteristics does not negate the role of individual factors such as creativity but suggests that factors such as complexity also have to be considered in understanding how and why processes such as innovation occur.

On the negative side, as we have suggested, increased complexity often leads to problems of control and coordination across subunits or specialists. For example, if a sales group makes commitments to customers for the delivery of products that a manufacturing group can't meet, the end result will be both very unhappy customers and a lot of unproductive finger-pointing within the organization. Likewise, if a patient is being treated by different medical specialists, the different regimens and prescriptions provided by each specialist may not be compatible. In line with this, Hage and Aiken's (1967b) and Lawrence and Lorsch's (1969) studies suggest that increasing complexity often is associated with higher levels of conflict in an organization, which must be dealt with if the organization is to reap the benefits of complexity. The proper method of handling such conflict is not by suppression—that would probably undermine most of the advantages of employing highly trained personnel—but it must be managed. If they are dealt with properly, conflicts can actually work to the organization's advantage. Research suggests another potential downside to increasing complexity that is interesting. Vaughan (1983, 1999) found that corporate crimes are related to complexity. In this formulation, organizations may become so diversified and complex that top management may not be able to control subunits. The same argument is frequently made in regard to intercollegiate athletics and the illegal recruitment and payment of college athletes.

Vertical Complexity. Vertical, or hierarchical, complexity involves the division of decision-making tasks and supervisory responsibilities. (Just as a small point of note, when people discuss this aspect of formal structure, they often use the alternative term *differentiation* instead of *complexity*.) Although research suggests that even informal social networks are vertically differentiated (Stevenson, 1990), studies of formal structure have often focused on the depth of the hierarchy, or the number of supervisory levels. Meyer (1968a), for example, used the "proliferation of supervisory levels" as a measure; Pugh et al. (1968)

suggested that the vertical dimension can be measured by a "count of the number of job positions between the chief executive and the employees working on the output" (p. 78); and Hall, Johnson, and Haas (1967) used the "number of levels in the deepest single division and the mean number of levels for the organization as a whole" (p. 906) (the total number of levels in all divisions divided by the number of divisions) as their indicators. Although vertical complexity is often discussed along with other aspects of complexity (and it certainly does reflect a kind of division of labor within organizations), it is closely related to a separate dimension, centralization, or the concentration of power in an organization. Because researchers have indeed used the same type of measures just described as indicators of centralization, we will hold off on further discussion of this aspect of structure until we get to centralization.

Spatial Complexity. The final dimension of complexity, spatial (also referred to as *geographical dispersion*), involves the extent to which organizations have different sites in different physical locations. Spatial complexity may encompass horizontal or vertical complexity. Thus, one form of spatial complexity occurs when different kinds of work activities take place in different geographical locations (e.g., a company may have one site where catalytic converters for cars are produced and another site where other automobile parts are produced): this involves horizontal complexity in tandem with spatial complexity. Another form of spatial complexity may occur when different authority groups are in different locations (e.g., a firm may have corporate headquarters located in one city and regional or local offices in other cities): this involves vertical complexity across different locations. Still, a third form of spatial complexity occurs when organizations create separate establishments in different locations that all do the same kinds of tasks. Fast-food restaurant chains offer a prime example of this.

Spatial complexity is relatively simple to measure. One can simply count the number of locations in which an organization has offices or plants. Alternatively, one may count the proportion of an organization's personnel who work away from a headquarters (Hall, Johnson, and Haas, 1967; Raphael, 1967). Although we haven't seen direct data on this, we would expect these different measures to be highly correlated.

Consequences of Spatial Complexity. Like horizontal complexity, increasing spatial complexity has certain advantages as well as disadvantages. One key advantage includes allowing organizations to expand, especially service-based organizations. For example, in order to supply different sets of customers, many grocery stores, banks, dry cleaners, and other organizations have sites in a variety of locations. Simply making a store in a given location larger clearly would not allow the organization to grow to the same extent. Along with expansion, spatial complexity also allows an organization to adapt to local environments. Thus, a fast-food restaurant in one part of the country may add items to its menu that are particularly favored in that location. And finally, spatial complexity allows an organization to take advantage of different labor markets and local resources, which may facilitate its overall functioning; this is a key part of the strategy of many multinational corporations. Also like horizontal complexity, though, spatial complexity often entails problems of coordination and control. Clearly, when different parts of a single product are produced in different locations, it is necessary to coordinate to ensure that the right number and kinds of parts ultimately get to a single location for assembly. Likewise, if headquarters is separate from regional offices, there are potential problems of supervising the regional offices and ensuring that directives issued by the headquarters are not in contradiction to those issued by regional offices and that they are followed. And when corporations create separate establishments that provide the same kind of goods or service, there is always concern that each follows expected procedures in ways that maintain a single corporate identity and reputation.

Covariation in Forms of Complexity.   We have noted that these forms of complexity can vary independently of each other, though they often in fact do covary, partly because each form is likely to increase as organizations get larger. Organizations with low levels of horizontal, vertical, and spatial complexity can easily be identified—small business firms founded by a single entrepreneur, that have a single product or service, and that operate in a single location, abound in cities and towns of all sizes. In direct contrast to this model, think of a multidivisional business firm, like General Mills, whose different divisions create a wide array of products in different places and are overseen by both corporate and regional offices. Similarly, the State University of New York (SUNY), with its multiple campuses in New York and sites in other countries, is an example of a government organization that is complex on all three axes. The Roman Catholic Church provides still another example of an organization characterized by high levels of horizontal, vertical, and spatial complexity. These extreme cases serve as a reminder that organizations can be highly or minimally complex in all facets of complexity.

There are other cases, though, that serve to illustrate that such covariance is not a *necessary* pattern. A liberal arts college, for example, usually has a low degree of vertical differentiation and little geographical dispersion but a high degree of horizontal differentiation. Similarly, many manufacturing plants have a fairly high degree of complexity along the horizontal axis, but may be based in a single location, and, if the production process is very routine, have little vertical differentiation. The offensive unit of a football team is highly specialized but essentially has only two ranks. High vertical differentiation with little horizontal differentiation is exemplified by an army battalion. Thus, different conditions may independently affect the level of complexity that organizations attain on a horizontal, vertical, or spatial dimension.

In general, though, there is a strong tendency for organizations to become more complex on all dimensions as their activities and the environment around them become more complex (Burns and Stalker, 1961; Lawrence and Lorsch, 1967) and as they grow (Blau and Schoenherr, 1971; Heydebrand, 1973; Klatzky, 1970a). Moreover, there is some evidence that increases in horizontal or spatial complexity can directly lead to increases in vertical complexity. The reasons for this increase are suggested by Blau and Schoenherr's (1971) research on government finance and public personnel agencies, which found a significant, positive relationship between the level of horizontal complexity and the level of vertical complexity in an agency. They argued that increased horizontal complexity often engenders problems of communication and coordination between different subunits; in response, organizations add personnel to the managerial hierarchy to deal with these problems. Thus, increases in horizontal complexity lead to increases in what is known as administrative intensity, usually measured as the number of supervisory personnel relative to the number of personnel involved just in production activities. As the number of supervisory personnel increases, so does the number of hierarchical levels, since some supervisory personnel are needed to oversee other supervisors.

The findings of this research thus suggest an interesting paradox in the analysis of organizations. Although large organizations can experience some savings through economies of scale, insofar as increases in size lead to greater horizontal or spatial complexity, growth is likely to be accompanied by cross-pressures to add managerial personnel to reduce the problems associated with control, coordination, and conflict. Therefore, decisions to physically disperse production or to add divisions, made in the interests of greater economy and profits, may be counterbalanced by the added burdens and costs of keeping the organization together. In addition, research on changes in the size of the administrative component of organizations suggests yet another paradox. When an organization is growing, there is a positive relationship between horizontal and spatial complexity, on the one hand, and administrative intensity, on the other; however, the relationship weakens when organizations are in a period of decline (McKinley, 1987). In other words, organizations often do not reduce the size of their administrative component compared to other parts of the organization as much when sales drop or they have other kinds of difficulties.

It's worth pointing out that much of the research on organizational complexity was carried out between 1960 and 1980. However, there is no reason to believe that the conclusions drawn from this research no longer hold—indeed, some recent research has provided confirmation of their continuing validity (Sine, Mitsuhashi, and Kirsch, 2006). In the intervening years, though, some trends that have become increasingly widespread, including downsizing (Baumol, Blinder, and Wolff, 2003; Budros, 1997) and outsourcing (Pfeffer and Baron, 1988), may have affected organizations' propensity to become increasingly complex, at least as we have traditionally thought about and measured complexity. As organizations delegate core functions to outside agencies (e.g., personnel management to temporary service agencies and janitorial work to firms specializing in facilities management), problems of coordination and control are unlikely to disappear but may take a different form, one that entails managing what we've usually thought of as environmental relations. Thus, these trends may necessitate changes in both the way that we think about and measure complexity and the way that we think about the nature of organizations (Scott, 2004). They are also relevant to thinking about the other two dimensions of formal structure that we consider below: formalization and centralization.

Formalization

The concept of formalization taps the extent to which task assignments, procedures for carrying out work, and other prescribed aspects of organizational operations are codified—made relatively permanent in a written record. When people complain about "too much red tape" and bemoan problems of bureaucratic mindsets, formalization is often the aspect that they have in mind. There's no question that a high degree of formalization can have negative consequences for both individuals and organizations—but the absence of formalization certainly produces problems of its own. Formalization involves organizational control over the individual (Clegg and Dunkerley, 1980) and thus has ethical and political implications, in addition to those involving the efficiency and effectiveness of organizations.

You have probably noticed how much different kinds of organizations vary in terms of formalization. If you've ever applied for a driver's license (or any kind of permit) from the Department of Motor Vehicles (DMV), you've undoubtedly experienced one end of the spectrum of formalization. Not only are there a multitude of forms that you must complete to get your license or permit, the instructions on how to complete the forms are often written up in great, booklet-sized detail. Government organizations are often characterized by a high degree of formalization, as are most nongovernmental organizations that have frequent contact with government organizations (though it is by no means only government-related organizations have this property). At the other end of the spectrum are organizations like a roadside vegetable stand, a local poker club or book club, or a newly formed, nontraditional church. Such organizations often have no formal rules at all, only shared understandings of how often meetings will be held or the approximate times and place of the organization's operation.

Most research examining variations in formalization considers written rules and procedures as the basis for assessment and analysis. There are two distinct aspects to this, however: *having* written rules and *following* written rules. In line with this distinction, Hage and Aiken (1967a) commented:

> Formalization represents the use of rules in an organization. Job codification is a measure of how many rules define what the occupants of positions are to do, while rule observation is a measure of whether or not the rules are employed. In other words, the variable of job codification represents the degree to which the job descriptions are specified, and the variable, rule observation, refers to the degree to which job occupants are supervised in conforming to the standards established by job codification. Job codification represents the degree of work standardization while rule observation is a measure of the latitude of behavior that is tolerated from standards. (p. 79)

Thus, some researchers use measures of formalization that rely on members' self-reports of how much their work is regulated by rules, which presumably tap the extent to which rules are actually followed. Others have used more objective measures that, in some sense, "count" how many rules an organization has in place (whether they're followed or not). Hage and Aiken (1967a), for example, used measures based on individuals' perceptions of their work to gauge the level of formalization in different organizations. Another set of researchers, known as the Aston group, after the British university where they held positions (Pugh et al., 1968), used essentially the same conceptualization of formalization but based their measurement on official written records and documents from the British work organizations they studied. For example, if workers were provided with an official handbook describing their tasks and duties, the organization got a high score on formalization. Unfortunately, later research (Dewar, Whetten, and Boje, 1980; Pennings, 1973) has indicated that these different measures are only weakly related. Thus, although there is general agreement in defining the meaning of formalization, measurement problems are not fully resolved.

Organizational Consequences of Formalization.   As noted above, most people are inclined to see formalization as having negative effects. The epithet "bureaucrat" connotes someone who inflexibly adheres to rules and regulations and thus epitomizes this aspect of structure. But formalization is often critical in producing reliable, predictable behavior and outcomes—which is what most of us desire from organizations. Consider the scenario where one person working at the DMV demanded that clients take a written examination, whereas another only asked that they promise that they knew basic road rules—this would be a little problematic. Higher levels of formalization often entail less variable behaviors by organizational members and thus can result in lower variability in outcomes. By the same token, formalization can make it easier to train new members of an organization faster and to transmit expectations about work behaviors more effectively. When newcomers have questions about how to do their work, referring to a written document may be easier than asking a supervisor; formalization can ensure that all members have access to the same, relevant information for their work. Formalization can also enhance equity in the treatment of organizational members. For example, using written examinations and specified standards in making hiring decisions helps minimize the impact of discriminatory preferences (i.e., those that are unrelated to a candidate's ability to do the work). This is a key reason that government organizations are often highly formalized, and some have argued that it is this characteristic that often leads women and minorities to seek employment in such organizations (Spangler, 1986).

On the other hand, formalization can also have negative consequences for organizations. An extreme example of the problems of formalization can be found in Crozier's (1964) analysis of two French organizations. In these organizations, he noted:

> Impersonal rules delimit, in great detail, all the functions of every individual within the organization. They prescribe the behavior to be followed in all possible events. Equally impersonal rules determine who shall be chosen for each job and the career patterns that can be followed. (pp. 187–188)

This extremely high degree of formalization, in addition to several other characteristics of the organizations, created what he termed a "vicious circle," in which managers sought to control workers by creating more and more explicit rules, which in turn actually limited the managers' ability to influence the workers' behavior beyond rule enforcement. The result was an extremely rule-bound, rigid organization that had virtually no flexibility to deal with changes in customers' demands, variations in the availability of supplies, or other such difficulties. Ironically, the rules that were intended to control employees' behavior ultimately provided them with autonomy from managers' direct control.

Thus, one disadvantage of formalization is that it may prevent members from responding to problems in an effective way, especially when the problem is not one that was anticipated by the rule-makers. In much the same way, the presence of many rules may slow work processes in ways that are not productive for an organization. Indeed, when workers wish to protest certain work arrangements or conditions, one way to do this without going on strike is to "work to rule," that is, to strictly follow all of an organization's rules to the letter. This form of protest is related to the way workers used rules, as described in Crozier's analysis. Another related disadvantage of formalization is that it tends to reduce innovation (Hage and Aiken, 1967a); rules may prevent members from experimenting with better ways to accomplish their work.

In sum, formalization can be a double-edged sword and its impact on organizations depends largely on the kinds of conditions an organization faces. We will discuss these conditions in more detail in Chapter 3, but as you might anticipate, one staple finding is that when work processes in an organization are less predictable (or to put it slightly differently, when means-and-ends relations are less well understood), lower levels of formalization are more effective. For example, in a study of hospital emergency rooms, Argote (1982) found that in situations of low uncertainty, programmed coordination (i.e., more rules) contributed to greater effectiveness, whereas in situations of high uncertainty, nonprogrammed modes of coordination were more effective.

Individual Consequences of Formalization. In addition to these organizational-level consequences, high levels of formalization may have effects on individuals as well. Early recognition of this problem is found in Robert Merton's (1957) seminal discussion of the "bureaucratic personality." Merton noted that a trained incapacity can develop when individuals work in highly formalized organizations, where key rewards depend primarily on conscientious adherence to rules. Such a context may foster an overconcern with strict adherence to regulations, inducing "timidity, conservatism, and technicism" (pp. 200–201). The personnel in such a system become increasingly unable to operate on their own initiative and, in fact, seek to reduce the amount of freedom to which they are subject. Thompson (1961) referred to such reactions as "bureaupathic" or "bureautic." To one who values individual freedom, this is a tragedy. It would be presumptuous to say that it is such for the individuals involved, even though the argument could be made that the long-run consequences for them and for the total social system may indeed be tragic from several moral and ethical perspectives.

Professionals and Formalization.   Embracement, or even just passive acceptance, is not the only way that people respond to a high degree of formalization, of course; sometimes they push back. The nature of formalization and conditions under which resistance to formalization occurs are illuminated by the literature on professionals in organizations. There has been a strong interest in this topic because increasing numbers of professionals are working in organizations, and many occupations are attempting to professionalize (Barley and Tolbert, 1991). At one time, almost all analyses of the relationship between professionals and their employing organizations were based on the premise that there are built-in strains between professional and organizational principles and values (Blau and Scott, 1962; Kornhauser, 1963; Miller, 1967). More recent research has challenged that assumption. It is now viewed as quite possible that there can be situations in which professionals are able to carry out their work with minimal interference from the organization, and the organization is able to integrate the work of the professionals for its own benefit. And not all professionals resent and resist organizational control to the same degree (Barley, 2004).

Differences among professionals were pointed up in an early analysis by Hall (1968), examining the relationship between professionalization and bureaucratization. Bureaucratization is a broader concept than formalization, but it contains many of the same implications of control over individuals' behavior. Hall attempted to demonstrate that professionalization, like formalization, is a continuous variable, with some occupations being more professionalized than others. The study included physicians, nurses, accountants, teachers, lawyers, social workers, stockbrokers, librarians, engineers, personnel managers, and advertising account executives. After the occupations were ranked according to their attitudes toward several professional values, the average scores for each occupation were matched with the scores on bureaucratization measures for the organizational units in which these people worked. The results indicated that, in general, bureaucratization is inversely related to professionalization. Examined more closely, these findings reveal some interesting patterns.

A weak relationship was found on the bureaucratic dimension involving the presence of rules. The kinds of rules the organizations developed in these cases apparently did not interfere with the work of the professionals. There was a stronger negative relationship on the procedural-specifications dimension. As more procedures were specified by the organization, the burden on the professionals apparently was stronger. In this case, the professionals were likely to want to utilize procedures that they developed on the job or through their professional training. A major implication of these findings is that formalization and professionalization are actually designed to do the same thing—organize and regularize the behavior of the members of the organization (Child, 1973; Hall, 1962). Formalization is a process in which the organization sets the rules and procedures and the means of ensuring that they are followed. Professionalization, on the other hand, is an occupation-based means of doing the same thing. From the organization's point of view, either technique can be appropriate, as long as the work gets done. One implication of treating formalization and professionalization as alternative means of controlling behavior is that it is very possible to find organizational structures that are compatible with the degree of professionalization of organizational members. As is true of complexity, there are degrees of formalization within the organization.

Formalization, as one way of controlling the behavior of organizational members, is related to the third dimension of structure to which researchers have given much attention—centralization.

Centralization

Centralization has been defined in several ways, but the emphasis is always on the distribution of power within an organization. Hage (1980) defines centralization as "the level and variety of participation in strategic decisions by groups relative to the number of groups in the organization" (p. 65). Alternatively, Van de Ven and Ferry (1980) define centralization as

> [the] locus of decision making authority within an organization. When most decisions are made hierarchically, an organizational unit is considered to be centralized; a decentralized unit generally implies that the major source of decision making has been delegated by line managers to subordinate personnel. (p. 399)

Fundamentally, then, the concept of centralization refers to the degree to which decision-making responsibility and power in an organization are closely held by a few elites, or widely distributed among different organizational members. Although centralization is one of the most interesting aspects of structure for many people (because it is related to power, and most of us find power to be an inherently interesting phenomenon!), it is also one of the most difficult to study. Let's take one example to illustrate some of the problems. At most research universities, the decision of whom to hire for a faculty position lies with individual departments that are adding new members (Blau, 1973). Thus, you might conclude that research universities tend to be decentralized because many different departments separately exercise influence over these decisions. Whether a particular department will be able to hire someone, however, is normally decided by the central administration, which reviews faculty vacancies and determines whether or not there needs to be a redistribution of positions among departments. Departments with declining enrollments and weaker programs are likely to lose positions to departments with high enrollment demands and strong programs. Since the decision to allow departments to search for candidates to hire is often within the purview of one or two top-level administrators, you could conclude that research universities are, in fact, highly centralized. In short, whether it's more appropriate to describe key personnel decisions in research universities as typically centralized or decentralized could be debated.

These issues are reflected in the variety of ways that centralization has been measured and the sometimes fierce debates among researchers over these measures (Child, 1972b; Dewar, Whetten, and Boje, 1980; Donaldson, Child, and

Aldrich, 1975; Greenwood and Hinings, 1976; Mansfield, 1973). One approach to measuring centralization, taken by Blau (1968) in a study of public personnel agencies, used the ratio of managers to nonsupervisory officials. Arguing that higher ratios (relatively more managers) implies less centralization, Blau suggested, "management in a structure with a large proportion of authority positions probably entails more reciprocal adjustments as the result of the greater opportunities for communication between managerial and operating personnel" (p. 458). The assumption that narrower supervisory spans of control imply that supervisors are spending more time consulting with their subordinates (versus simply issuing orders without discussion) is also reflected in studies that used the number of levels of hierarchy as a reverse measure of centralization (Hall, Johnson, and Haas, 1967; Meyer, 1968b; Pugh et al., 1968) because longer hierarchies usually accompany smaller spans of control. As we noted in our discussion of vertical complexity, the length of the hierarchy has often been taken as an index of centralization.

One point that complicates the use of such measures is that although personnel at lower levels in the organization may make many decisions, insofar as the decisions are "programmed" by organizational policies or rules, a high degree of centralization could still remain. In routine situations, rules are often used to govern the actions of the organizational members and there is likely to be little delegation of power through participation. In less routine situations, where there is task uncertainty, activities such as group meetings are likely to be held to try to resolve problems (Van de Ven, Delbecq, and Koenig, 1976). True limits on centralization imply democratic, collective decision-making (Rothschild and Whitt, 1986).

Alternatively, as a general approach, employee surveys have been used to tap individuals' perceptions of the frequency with which they participate in various types of decisions, and how often they were able to make decisions without getting approval from their boss (Hage and Aiken, 1967a). One interesting application of this approach is found in a study by Tannenbaum and his associates (Tannenbaum, 1968). This work is based on surveys of rank-and-file workers concerning how much influence they believe that different hierarchical levels exerted on their work. Aggregated responses were used to construct a "control graph," representing the amount of power that characterizes each hierarchical level. Figure 2–1 is an example of such a graph.

This type of graph can be used to compare organizations in terms of both the slope of the curve across different hierarchical levels and the average height of the curve. The difference between the higher and lower levels provides an indication of the degree of centralization in the organization, and the height of the curve indicates the overall amount of power in the organization. In theory, it would be possible for all levels of the hierarchy to have either a relatively high degree of influence or a very low level of influence.

Although a variety of studies have raised methodological problems with the control-graph approach (Markham, Bonjean, and Corder, 1984), it has been used in many studies. Tannenbaum and his colleagues have used this measure to

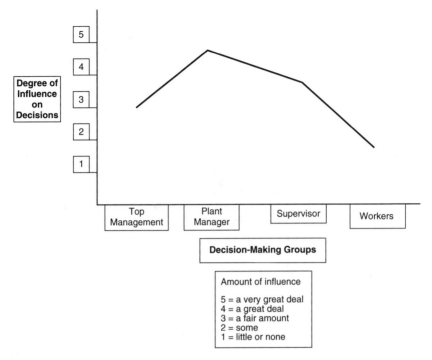

FIGURE 2–1 Example of a Control Graph

conduct interesting cross-national studies of power in organizations (Tannenbaum et al., 1974; Tannenbaum and Rozgonyi, 1986). The original research was carried out in manufacturing plants in Austria, Italy, Israel, the former Yugoslavia, and the United States. Austria and Italy are basically capitalist, like the United States; the Israeli kibbutz is socialist, and the Yugoslav economy was socialist. Organizations in Israel and the United States were most successful, as defined not only by the standards used in these countries but also by such universal factors as efficiency and morale. The kibbutz organizations were highly decentralized; the ones in the United States were relatively more centralized, but the effects of this were mitigated by several factors, including at least some opportunities for upward mobility of workers, and greater worker consultation (though not necessarily greater actual power), and higher rewards.

Although centralization is usually conceived in terms of control of key decisions, it's worth noting that centralized control can also take other, more indirect forms, such as the right to assess work outcomes, to set deadlines and responsibilities, and to allocate resources. Evaluation processes involve determining whether work was done properly, well, or promptly (Dornbusch and Scott, 1975). Evaluation of work outcomes carried out by people at the top of the organization can effectively control people at lower levels, even if the latter appear to be in charge of decisions about how to conduct work activities. This form of centralization is common in organizations of professionals (Freidson, 2001, 2006). Thus, higher-level nonprofessionals may grant professional employees the right to make many decisions involved in the execution of their work; but insofar as the top management has the final right to decide whether the outputs of these activities meet the evaluation criteria they set, much of the control remains vested at the higher level. Similarly, control over work decisions nominally made at lower levels (e.g., by engineering personnel) is often exercised indirectly through such devices as setting internal deadlines and reviews for project development, changing vacation schedules, and allocating extra work assignments (Perlow, 1998).

One final point of note on the issue of centralization, suggested by the Dutch sociologist Cornelius Lammers (1975), involves the distinction between participative management and management by participation. In Lammers's conception, participative management involves taking part in decision-making, whereas both management by participation and self-management involve workers actually taking over organizational management. Participative management is a form of decentralization that may lead to greater efficiency and effectiveness but not to true power-sharing; on the other hand, management by participation and self-management are forms of decentralization that lead to power equalization. True power equalization in organizations is very rare. The very nature of organizations requires some form of hierarchy, once organizations move beyond very small size, simple technologies, and low levels of complexity. As in the wider society, power differences are ubiquitous.

Consequences of Centralization. Two key advantages that higher levels of centralization can provide are greater coordination and faster decision-making. When decisions are made by fewer people, the relations between different decisions are more likely to be recognized, and hence problems of inconsistent and/or conflicting policies are minimized. Moreover, centralization can be an asset when decisions need to be made quickly because when more people are involved in decision-making, the process is slower. On the other hand, these advantages may come at a cost. When decisions are made at higher levels but information relevant to making those decisions is held at lower levels, the decisions may be of poorer quality than would be desired and can be especially ill-suited to addressing local problems or conditions. Efforts to collect information from lower levels may be difficult because communication between top levels and lower levels of an organization is often limited (Stevenson, 1990), and such efforts are apt to undermine the potential for speedy decision-making. Moreover, a long line of psychological studies suggest that, at the individual level, the lack of control over work produces significant negative effects in terms of attitudes toward work and organizational commitment (Hackman and Oldham, 1976; Karasek, 1979).

In general, the degree of centralization in organizations says a great deal about the society in which they are found. A society in which the majority of organizations are highly centralized is one in which workers have little say about their work. A tendency toward high levels of organizational centralization may also provide an index of the capacity of a society for effective political democracy because behaviors learned at work often spill over into other avenues of life (Kohn and Schooler, 1973; Schooler, Mulatu, and Oates, 2004). The degree of centralization of organizations is also an indication of what the organization assumes about its members: high centralization implies that members need tight control, of whatever form; low centralization suggests that members can govern themselves.

RELATIONS BETWEEN COMPLEXITY, FORMALIZATION, AND CENTRALIZATION

Although the three dimensions of formal structure that we've discussed are theoretically and, to some extent, empirically distinct, research does suggest that they tend to covary. As with the different forms of complexity, such covariation is partly due to common factors influencing all of them. For example, as we'll discuss in more detail in Chapter 3, increases in both formalization and complexity tend to occur as organizations get bigger. But research suggests that there are also direct relationships among these dimensions.

In general, research suggests that as organizations become more complex, they tend to become more formalized (Blau and Schoenherr, 1971; Hall, 1963; Pugh et al., 1968) because, as noted earlier, greater horizontal and spatial complexity in particular increase the need for careful coordination in order for the activities of disparate units to fit together; formalization is one key device that organizations can use to accomplish this (Lawrence and Lorsch, 1967). By specifying rules about how production schedules are to be set, who is responsible for providing what kind of information to whom, what the standardized procedures are for various activities, much routine coordination can be effected.

On the other hand, complexity is often negatively related to centralization (Blau, 1973; Pugh et al., 1968), for fairly obvious reasons. Greater complexity makes it harder for a small set of decision-makers to get sufficient information to make decisions within a reasonable timeframe that will be effective for all the parts of the organization. Hence, complexity often leads to greater delegation of decision-making authority, although top-level members can ensure some control over nominally delegated decisions by specifying the criteria to be used. (This is another reason for the relation between complexity and formalization—greater complexity necessitates decentralization, but top-level managers may seek to minimize the exercise of real discretion in those decisions through formalizing how they are to be made.) This may also account for the finding that higher levels of formalization tend to go hand in hand with (what appears to be) lower levels of centralization. Another factor that may account for findings of a negative relation between formalization and centralization is suggested by Blau (1970), who argued that adherence to more formalized, merit-based personnel procedures ensures the employment of highly qualified personnel who can be entrusted with more decision-making responsibility than personnel with fewer qualifications. Formalization in one area of operation may thus be associated with flexibility in another.

On this point, Blau states

> Rigidity in some respects may breed flexibility in others. Not all aspects of bureaucratization are concomitant. The bureaucratic elaboration of formalized personnel procedures and rigid conformity with these personnel standards do not necessarily occur together, and neither aspect of bureaucratization of procedures gives rise to a more rigid authority structure, at least not in employment security agencies. Indeed, both strict conformity with civil service standards and the elaboration of these formalized standards have the opposite effect of fostering decentralization, which permits greater flexibility. (p. 160)

It is important to note that the research of Blau (1970) and Hage and Aiken (1967a, 1967b, 1970) and others who find a negative relation between centralization and formalization deals with relatively professionalized workforces. One of the hallmarks of professionalization is the ability and willingness to make decisions based on professional training and experience. Thus, formalization may be associated with less centralization either because formal rules help maintain control over delegated decisions or because formalization is related to the quality of personnel the organization employs. The organization retains control over the individual in both cases. Selecting highly qualified or indoctrinated individuals assures that the individuals will act according to organizational demands (Blau and Schoenherr, 1971:347–367).

Forms of Organization

The observation of covariation among these dimensions of structure forms the basis for work that posits the existence of distinctive forms of organization. One such early study in this tradition is that of Burns and Stalker (1961). Researching a rather diverse set of organizations, ranging from traditional textile firms to more technologically driven electronics firms, they noted that firms tended to resemble one of two poles. At one end was what they termed the "mechanistic" form, characterized by a high level of "specialisms" (i.e., horizontal complexity), high levels of formalization, and clear top-down control of decisions and activities. At the other end was the "organic" form, which is almost a logical opposite. Thus, instead of being directed by hierarchical authority, organic organizations have a network structure of control; instead of high levels of fixed task specialization, a continual adjustment and redefinition of tasks; instead of formal supervision, a communication context involving information and advice. Burns and Stalker suggested that the form that an organization tended to take was linked to the environment in which it operated: mechanistic forms were more likely to be found in stable environments and organic forms in environments that were characterized by frequent change. However, they noted that the movement of organizations toward one polar form or the other was also importantly shaped by the political struggles between workers and managers over the control of work and the organization.

More recent work on high-performance work systems (HPWS), as a distinctive form of organizing, is related to this distinction between mechanistic and organic forms. Although studies of HPWS reflect some of Burns and Stalker's ideas, their most immediate origin is in democratically oriented arguments concerning the fit between social needs of workers and the technical needs of production organizations (Emery and Trist, 1973). HPWS are characterized in general by broadly defined jobs and work roles, groupings of workers into teams that share tasks and exercise collective responsibility for making work-related decisions, and participation of workers across teams in governance structures to help control and coordinate work in other words, low complexity, low formalization, and low centralization (Appelbaum and Batt, 1994). Such arrangements are posited to provide workers with more interesting and challenging work and thus increased motivation, as well as to enhance contemporary organizations' ability to achieve the kind of flexibility needed to deal with changing environments and increasing competition (MacDuffie, 1995).

SUMMARY AND CONCLUSIONS

This chapter has considered the basic organizational characteristics of complexity, formalization, and centralization. These characteristics have outcomes for individuals who are in organizations and who have contacts with them. They also have outcomes for the organizations themselves and for the wider society of which they are a part.

As we've discussed these aspects of structure, we've often alluded to the topic of Chapter 3—the explanations of structure. Issues such as size, technology, and relationships with the environment have loomed large in analyses of structure. We will examine these issues and pay attention to some of the debates that are generated about underlying assumptions about the nature of decision-making embedded in different explanations for variations in structure.

EXERCISES

1. Construct an ideal type of some phenomenon, such as "democratic government" or "egalitarian marriage." Describe how you might use this in comparative research to understand the conditions that encouraged the development of this phenomenon.

2. Compare the levels of horizontal complexity, formalization, and centralization of your two organizations. Discuss how variations in these dimensions might affect your reactions to being a member.

Chapter 3

Organizational Structure: Explanations

OVERVIEW

In this chapter, we'll examine an array of proposed explanations for variations in the formal structure of organizations (i.e., levels of complexity, formalization, and centralization). We will discuss a key theoretical shift that occurred in these explanations—a shift from what's referred to as a closed-systems approach, which focuses primarily on problems of managing internal relations, to an open-systems approach, which focuses largely on external or environmental influences. We will also consider some of the debates among researchers about underlying assumptions embedded in different explanations of structure, including ones over the extent of managerial freedom (versus constraint) in choosing structural arrangements and ones over the role of calculations of efficiency (versus social conformity) in making such choices.

Let's return to our building analogy to begin thinking about why formal structures are apt to vary. As we noted in Chapter 2, the structure of a building is a major determinant of the movements and activities of the people within it. Thus, the structure, presumably, is designed to fit and facilitate the activities that are planned to take place in it. That's why an office building has a very different structure than a factory and factories where automobiles are made are different from those where computers are made. Buildings are designed to accommodate populations of various sizes—no sane architect would design a huge cathedral for a small religious congregation—and to withstand the environment in which they are located. Buildings in upstate New York are different from those in Arizona. Just as size, the major activity or technology to be used and the environment are important in building design, so is the element of choice—of style, color, and so on. Buildings also reflect the values and ideologies of the persons in control; corporate headquarters and state capitols do not take the form they do just on the basis of technological or functional considerations. Of course, organizations are not built by architects but organizational leaders and other members, who may not be in agreement about how the organization should be arranged nor always realize what the effects of planned arrangements actually will be. Just as one building can be a copy of another, organizational structures can be copies of the structures other organizations. Like buildings, organizations can also reflect the particular fads popular at the time of their construction. And just as buildings can be renovated, organizations can be restructured.

This chapter reviews work that attempts to explain observed variations in organizations' formal structure. Different explanations usually highlight certain types of influences at the expense of others, and each rests on particular assumptions (that may not always be made explicit) about the decision-making processes that result in structural arrangements. Since the formal structure of any organization is undoubtedly the result of the conjoint operation of very complicated processes and influences, each approach is useful in shedding light on factors that are relevant to our understanding.

Most explanations of structure can be placed into one of two basic categories: (1) a closed-systems approach and (2) an open-systems approach. Work categorized as reflecting a closed-systems approach focuses on characteristics or attributes of the organization itself as determinants of its formal structure and typically on characteristics that affect the ease of and the need for coordinating, communicating, and controlling organizational members' activities. Studies in this tradition have given a great deal of attention to two characteristics in particular as having important influences on formal structure: size and technology. Work categorized as reflecting an open-systems approach focuses on how organizations' efforts to manage external relations—with customers, suppliers, competitors, regulatory agencies, and other individuals and groups outside the organization—shape their structure. Many of the earliest studies of organizations could be classified as exemplifying a closed-systems approach. The propensity of scholars to adopt this perspective may have reflected, at least in part, the influence of structural–functionalist theory in the post–World War II years on organizational research. As noted in Chapter 2, the logic of this theoretical framework encouraged researchers to explain structure in terms of its effects on organizations' functioning. The reliance on a closed-systems approach probably also stemmed from pragmatic concerns of some organizational researchers with helping managers and government administrators maximize efficiency in organizational operations. In general, it's easier to change internal arrangements than external factors; hence, for practical purposes, it makes sense to focus on aspects of organizations that are more subject to administrative control.

EFFECTS OF SIZE

Many studies have indicated that organizational size is strongly associated with the three dimensions of structure that we have discussed, and there are logical explanations for this. As organizations grow, the need for greater specialization arises, giving rise to greater complexity. In a small organization, there often are simply not enough people to allow individuals to specialize; each member is likely to be called on to carry out a variety of tasks. As the number of members increases, specialization becomes more feasible. At the same time, increases in personnel are also likely to lead to problems of communication and coordination; specialization helps prevent duplication of effort, which is more apt to occur under these conditions, as well as the possibility that some key tasks will be neglected because of ambiguity about who's responsible for them. As problems of communication and coordination that often accompany organizational growth mount, organizations are likely to respond by greater formalization. And finally, decision-making often becomes more complex as organizations grow, which makes delegation of such responsibilities, and hence decentralization, more desirable.

The preceding arguments about the effects of size on complexity are consistent with findings from a number of studies conducted by Peter Blau and his associates (Blau, 1968, 1970, 1972, 1973; Blau, Heydebrand, and Stauffer, 1966; Blau and Schoenherr, 1971; Klatzky, 1970a; Meyer, 1968a,b, 1971). Their data were collected primarily from studies of government agencies, such as state employment services and municipal finance divisions, with supplementary data from universities and department stores—in other words, from more service-based organizations. In general, this research provides strong evidence that increasing size is related to increasing complexity. Hall, Johnson, and Haas (1967) likewise report positive correlations, albeit more modest ones, between size and several indicators of complexity, as did Rushing (1967). A close relationship between size and complexity was also documented in the studies of the Aston group in England (Child and Mansfield, 1972; Donaldson and Warner, 1974; Hickson, Pugh, and Pheysey, 1969; Hickson et al., 1974; Inkson, Pugh, and Hickson, 1970; Pugh et al., 1963, 1968). This research included manufacturing firms as well as more number of service-based organizations, thus supporting the notion that this relationship was a general one.

Blau (1970) noted that, as a consequence of the association between size and complexity, increases in size do not lead straightforwardly to economies of scale, as might be expected. Economies of scale occur when organizations add more production workers without adding more supervisors; this entails broadening supervisory spans of control. However, because increasing size encourages greater specialization and structural complexity, the addition of more production workers often leads to increases in administrative costs, for more supervisors are needed to oversee and coordinate the activities of specialized subunits, as discussed in Chapter 2. Thus, increases in size are posited to lead to economies of scale in organizations but at a decreasing rate because of the positive effects of size on complexity (Anderson and Warkov, 1961).

In addition, the arguments that higher levels of formalization and lower levels of centralization are found in larger organizations received support from studies by the Aston group (Inkson, Pugh, and Hickson, 1970; Mansfield, 1973; Pugh et al., 1968) as well as those by Blau and his colleagues (Blau, Heydebrand, and Stauffer, 1966; Blau and Schoenherr, 1971; Klatzky, 1970a) and a number of other researchers. Increasing size often creates cross-cutting pressures in organizations, in terms of centralization. Thus, Blau and Schoenherr (1971) conclude that

> the large size of an agency produces conflicting pressures on top management, as it heightens the importance of managerial decisions, which discourages delegating them, and simultaneously expands the volume of managerial responsibilities, which exerts pressure to delegate some of them. (p. 130)

In Chapter 2, where we discussed problems of measuring centralization, we noted that interpreting the nature of the relationship between formalization and centralization is sometimes complicated. This relationship also affects our understanding of how each of these structural characteristics is related to variations in size. In general, research suggests that increasing size is associated with a decline in centralization. However, as noted, the risk of delegation is lessened if organizational personnel have high levels of expertise (though see Kralewski, Pitt, and Shatin, 1985, for an interesting analysis of the effects of size in group medical practices). The relation between the level of professionalization in an organization's workforce and its degree of centralization raises one problem in interpreting research findings that demonstrate an inverse relation between size and centralization: it is impossible to know whether increased size leads to pressures to delegate and thus to hiring individuals with greater expertise or whether the hiring of experts (thereby increasing organizational size) leads to pressures to delegate because experts expect to have more decision-making control. In the latter case, size per se is not really the source of decentralization. Most of the research that has been conducted on this problem is cross-sectional (the organizational characteristics were measured at the same point in time), which makes addressing this question virtually impossible. Both arguments could be true—increases in size may lead to pressures to decentralize, which increases organizations' propensity to hire highly qualified workers, and once individuals with greater skills and qualifications are hired, they may demand greater decision-making autonomy, leading to further decentralization. Exploring the validity of these arguments would require collecting data over time.

Likewise, because increases in formalization often go hand in hand with increases in size, it can be difficult to gauge whether larger organizations are truly less centralized. For example, Mansfield (1973) found that increasing size is related to the increasing use of rules and suggested that size may lead to decentralization of decision-making but not to loss of control for the organization. The relationship between size and centralization is thus complex, with increasing size leading to real delegation in some circumstances and such delegation being tempered by other characteristics in other circumstances.

In addition, other factors may mediate the relationship between size and different aspects of formal structure. For example, a provocative study by Geeraerts

(1984) found that the heads of small organizations who were professional managers were more likely to adopt bureaucratic practices than were heads of small organizations who were owner–managers. Geeraerts explains his finding in terms of both the formal training and career orientation of professional managers. Because movement from one organization to another is more likely to be a part of professional managers' careers, they were more attuned to the need to make visible changes in the organizations they headed; changing formal structure is one way to achieve this.

On the other side of the coin, the relationship between size and formal structure may be important in accounting for the relationship between size and other organizational outcomes found in various studies. The mediating effects of formal structure on the relation between size and organizational outcomes are illustrated by a study of airlines. This research found that smaller airlines were more apt to create competitive challenges in the airline industry than the big carriers (Chen and Hambrick, 1995). Structural characteristics that are often associated with smaller size provide for greater flexibility of organizations and allow them to be more nimble in terms of adapting to environmental changes and entering new markets (Haveman, 1993a). Flexibility can come at a cost, however. Most new organizations are small, and research has consistently shown that new organizations have a low survival rate. Starbuck and Nystrom (1981) note that "nearly all small organizations disappear within a few years" (p. xiv). Interestingly, they provide data that support this conclusion for both governmental agencies and corporations. Apparently, governmental organizations are not as protected as many people think. The corollary of this research, of course, is that large organizations are more likely to survive and are less vulnerable to the often adverse effects of change than small ones. Although the higher survival rates of large organizations may be partly just a matter of resources (larger organizations being likely to have more resources than smaller ones), it may also be related to the lack of reliability associated with less standardization of procedures, lower formalization, and other structural characteristics that are apt to be found in smaller organizations. This, in turn, makes other organizations and individuals have less confidence in a focal organization and less willing to engage in long-term transactions, leading to what has been termed the "liability of newness" for organizations (Stinchcombe, 1965).

Problems of Research on Size and Structure

It is important to recognize that findings from research on the effects of size on various aspects of structure are far from consistent and that the direction of these relationships is subject to dispute. Hall and Tittle's (1966) research, for example, which used a subjective approach to measuring different aspects of organizational structure (i.e., asking individuals about their perceptions), found only a modest relationship between size and the degree of formalization and centralization in organizations. In another study, using an approach similar to that of Blau and the Aston group, Hall and his colleagues they came up with mixed findings in regard to size and structure (Hall, Haas and Johnson, 1967b). Using data from a set of seventy-five organizations of highly varied types, they concluded that although size is important, factors other than size also must be taken into account to understand structure.

Other research has argued that causality may well run in the other direction—decisions about structuring organizations may require certain staffing levels. For example, Argyris (1972) suggests that size may be correlated with, but not generate or cause, differentiation. Similarly, in a reanalysis of the Aston data, Aldrich (1972a,b) posits that size is actually a dependent variable: "the more highly structured firms, with their greater degree of specialization, formalization, and monitoring of role performance, simply need to employ a larger work force than less structured firms" (Aldrich, 1972a:38).

Finally, some researchers have criticized research on size effects for inadequately conceptualizing this construct and failing to fully explicate the theoretical logic of arguments about size. At first glance, organizational size appears to be a simple variable—the number of people in an organization. The size issue is much more complicated than that, however. In a penetrating article, Kimberly (1976) made the case that size can be conceptualized in at least four different ways.

First, size can be considered as the physical capacity of the organization. Hospitals have a fixed number of beds. Hotels have a fixed number of rooms. Airlines have a relatively fixed number of airplanes and seats. Universities have capacities in regard to classroom or dormitory space. Of course, if such capacity isn't fully used, this approach can be misleading. Second, size can be thought of in terms of the personnel available to the organization. This is the most commonly used measure and conceptualization of size, the one used in 80 percent of the studies reviewed by Kimberly. One problem with this approach can be seen with just a little reflection on the nature of organizational boundaries. For example, are the students enrolled in a university part of the organization? Are temporary employees, technically employed by an employment agency, part of the organization in which they are placed? A third way to define size is in terms of organizational inputs or outputs. Inputs can be such factors as the number of clients served and the number of inmates housed in a prison. Sales volume is an important output measure for many businesses. Kimberly correctly suggests that if size is defined this way, research is necessarily limited to making comparisons between organizations of a similar type. The fourth way of thinking about size is in terms of the discretionary resources available to an organization, in the form of wealth or net assets. For a college or a university, the size of its endowment is an important consideration. For a business, it might be capital available for investment. As with the third approach, it would be difficult to include different types of organizations in a study in which size was measured this way. The components of size may be highly intercorrelated in some instances, and indeed they are. But different size measures might, and will, lead to different predictions about the relation between size and various aspects of structure. Thus, Kimberly's argument is that researchers have often failed to think carefully about which measure of size is most meaningful.

These problems also affect research on the relationship between technology and structure, which has proved a very fertile but difficult area of study.

EFFECTS OF TECHNOLOGY

As noted in Chapter 2, research by Woodward (1958, 1965) helped launch the stream of work that became known as contingency theory. Size, as we've just discussed, was identified as one key contingency—a factor that affected both the kinds of structures organizations were likely to adopt and the impact of those structures on organizational performance. Woodward's research suggested another important contingency, the primary production technology used by organizations. Her research indicated that firms dominated by "small-batch" technology (involving the production of relatively small quantities of nonstandardized goods) had a very different structure, in general, than those with "large-batch" technology (involving mass production of standardized goods) and "continuous" technology (involving large-scale production of nondiscrete goods such as chemicals). Likewise, the structure of firms based on large-batch technology differed from that of firms with either of the other two technologies. But the question that Woodward failed to address very clearly was, what was it, exactly, about these different technologies that made certain structural arrangements more or less suitable? Later work tried to address this question, drawing attention to different features of technology that were related to structure.

One such effort is found in a study by James Thompson (1967), who proposed a threefold typology, similar in some ways to that of Woodward, but based explicitly on the notion that the level of interdependence in the activities of different workers is the key to distinguishing among technological types. The nature of the interdependence among workers, he argued, affects the degree to which tight coordination is required and the degree to which such coordination can be scripted or preprogrammed. In this context, one of Thompson's categories is technology that involves *pooled* interdependence, in which each worker carries out a series of actions relatively independent of other workers; the primary interdependence stems from the sharing of common "pools" of resources—cash drawers among bank tellers, telephones among call-center workers, cash registers among supermarket checkers, and so forth. Because technology of this type often occurs in settings where workers broker relations among different sets of individuals (e.g., persons making deposits and those making withdrawals in a bank, individuals seeking technical support and the technical consultants), Thompson referred to this technology as mediating. He termed a second type of interdependence *sequential;* this is used to describe settings where the work of one individual forms the basis of the work of another, and these activities all occur in a predictable order. The classic example of such interdependence is a factory line where, for example, one worker places a bolt in a piece of equipment, the next person tightens it down, the next uses a pneumatic drill to tighten it further, and so on. Thompson referred to this as long-linked technology. And the third type of interdependence, *reciprocal,* involves activities by different workers that are very closely linked but that do not always occur in an orderly fashion, thus requiring mutual adjustments by workers. A surgical team composed of a surgeon, nurses, anesthesiologist, and other medical personnel represents an example of this type of interdependence; scientists and technicians working together on a given project provide another. Thompson referred to this as intensive technology.

It seems reasonable to expect that the level and nature of interdependence associated with different types of technology would be reflected in the formal structure of organizations. Thus, mediating technology, entailing the execution of a fairly wide array of activities by each worker, who is doing essentially the same things as the others, involves low levels of complexity. Although there is only a limited need for coordination, the desire to ensure that workers use the same standards and approaches to dealing with different customers is likely to lead to at least moderate levels of formalization and, by the same token, only moderate levels of centralization (since workers need some autonomy in dealing with variations that may occur in different cases). Long-linked technology, involving relatively high levels of interdependence, would be expected to involve greater levels of complexity and, because the interrelations are predictable, higher levels of both formalization and centralization. And intensive technology, with its hard-to-predict interdependencies, would be expected to be incompatible with high levels of formalization and centralization, though at least a moderate degree of complexity (in terms of differentiated work roles) could be predicted.

The notion of interdependence provides part of an explanation for why different technologies would be associated with different structures, but as may have become clear in the preceding discussion, there's another likely explanatory factor at work: the degree of predictability (or conversely, uncertainty) involved in the execution of work activities. Hence, Perrow (1967) focused on uncertainty in developing an alternative conceptualization of technological differences among organizations. He suggested two distinct aspects of technological uncertainty (Figure 3–1). The first is variability in the inputs (raw materials) that an organization uses in its production activities, indicated by the number of "exceptional cases encountered in the work." The second is the state of knowledge concerning means-and-ends relations in the production process, which determines the nature of the search processes that are set in motion when an exception is encountered (pp. 195–196). Organizations such as hospitals or schools, whose main inputs are human beings, are apt to be characterized by high variability of inputs. Likewise, organizations that involve work on new materials from frontier areas of science

FIGURE 3–1   Perrow's Dimensions of Technological Uncertainty

Variability of Inputs	Knowledge of Means–End Relations	
	Well Understood	*Not Understood*
Low Variation	Low Uncertainty	Moderate Uncertainty
High Variation	Moderate Uncertainty	High Uncertainty

also are apt to have a high level of variability in their inputs. At the other end of the spectrum lie organizations such as steel manufacturers, breweries, or bakeries, where the variations in inputs are typically much more limited (if only by the organizations' arrangements with suppliers). When means-and-ends relations are well understood—when you know that if you do X you will get Y—search processes are usually very limited. When means-and-ends relations are not well understood, search processes often entail some combination of intuition, inspiration, chance, and/or guesswork. The greater the variability in the inputs, and the less-developed knowledge of means-and-ends relations, the more an organization's technology is characterized by uncertainty. Organizations with relatively high levels of technological uncertainty would be expected to have lower levels of formalization and centralization compared with organizations with less technological uncertainty. On the other hand, complexity is likely to be greatest when technological uncertainty is very low; predictability should make it easier to assign different tasks and activities to different units.

Research has used a variety of measures of technology, some reflecting more of Thompson's emphasis on interdependence (e.g., the Aston group's measure of "workflow integration"), others more closely reflecting Perrow's emphasis on uncertainty. Despite the variations in measurement, in general, studies support the idea that higher levels of interdependence and of uncertainty (captured by the notion of *routineness* of technology) are related to high formalization and centralization. For example, Hage and Aiken (1969) divided the sixteen organizations that they studied into those with "routine" and those with "nonroutine" technology. Even though these were all social agencies, they found a marked difference in the degree of routineness and a positive relationship between routinization and formalization. Because these organizations tend to be on the nonroutine end of an overall continuum of routineness, the findings are even more striking. Moreover, the findings are generally consistent with those of the Aston group (Pugh's research team), which proceeded independently and with very different measures. Recall that the Aston group's research, referred to in Chapter 2, was carried out on a sample of English work organizations. Among organizations scoring high on their measure of "workflow integration" (tapping more automated and preprogrammed technologies) were an automobile factory and a food manufacturer. Among those scoring low, with diverse, nonautomated, flexible technologies, were retail stores, an education department, and a building firm (Pugh et al., 1968:103).

Although the organizations in the Aston group's research are more diverse than those in the Hage and Aiken study, they are clustered toward the routine end of the routine–nonroutine continuum. As would be expected from the previous discussion, more routine technology was associated with greater formalization and centralization. Yet another study, by Dornbusch and Scott (1975), examined an electronics assembly line, a physics research team, a university faculty, a major teaching hospital, a football team, schools, a student newspaper, and a Roman Catholic archdiocese. Their evidence, from that diverse set of organizations, is consistent with the technological argument that has been presented.

It's worth noting that the relationship between routinization of work and centralization may partly reflect the level of professionalization of the personnel in the organization (Hall, 1981). More professionalized work is usually less routinized, almost by definition (Abbot, 1988). Lincoln and Zeitz (1980) report that individual professionals desire and often achieve participation in decision-making. They also find that the greater the number of professional employees in an organization, the more likely are nonprofessional employees to exercise decision-making influence. Thus, organizations with less routine technologies are more likely to employ professionals, and these personnel are more likely to explicitly pressure the organization to be less centralized and formalized. This finding is consistent with those of Glisson (1978), who found that procedural specifications (formalization) determine the degree of routinization in service delivery. In this study, a decision made regarding how to structure the organization led to the utilization of a particular service delivery technology (with more professional employees). Although the high correlation between routinization and formalization remains, the reason for the correlation is reversed in this case.

COMBINED EFFECTS OF SIZE AND TECHNOLOGY

Some research suggests that the impact of production technology on organizations' overall structure depends partly on the size of an organization. This possibility was highlighted in research by the Aston group (Hickson, Pugh, and Pheysey, 1969), who broke the general concept of technology into three components: (1) operations technology—the techniques used in the workflow activities of the organization; (2) materials technology—the variability of materials used in the workflow; and (3) knowledge technology—the varying complexities in the knowledge system used in the workflow. In the English organizations they studied, Hickson, Pugh, and Pheysey (1969) focused primarily on operations technology and found that this had a secondary effect in relationship to size. They conclude:

> Structural variables will be associated with operations technology only where they are centered on the workflow. The smaller the organization, the more its structure will be pervaded by such technological effects; the larger the organization, the more these effects will be confined to variables such as job-counts of employees on activities linked with the workflow itself, and will not be detectable in variables of the more remote administrative and hierarchical structure. (pp. 394–395)

The notion that the effects of technology on overall structure depend partly on the size of the organization is also supported in research reported by Miller et al. (1991). They found that the routineness–centralization relationship operates in small organizations but not in large ones.

This finding relates to a major debate that developed in the early 1970s over whether size or technology was a more critical influence on structure (Aldrich, 1972a,b; Blau and Schoenherr, 1971; Pugh et al., 1968). The general conclusion that was drawn once the dust settled on this debate was that both are important influences, which may have interactive effects. This is exemplified by a study of a large state employment security agency that examined task uncertainty, task interdependence (technological variables), and work-unit size as they related to coordination mechanisms (Van de Ven, Delbecq, and Koenig, 1976). As tasks increased in uncertainty, mutual work adjustments through horizontal communications channels and group meetings were used instead of hierarchical and impersonal forms of control. As task interdependence increased, impersonal coordination decreased and more personalized and interactive modes of coordination, in the form of meetings, increased. Increasing size, on the other hand, was related to an increased use of impersonal modes of coordination, such as policies and procedures and predetermined work plans. In a related study, Ouchi (1977) found that both size and homogeneous tasks were related to higher levels of output controls on workers.

In one final example, a study of architectural firms revealed that structural complexity depended upon size when there were uniform tasks, but that size had less of an effect on complexity when tasks were nonuniform (Blau and McKinley, 1979). Thus, size was important under one technological condition but not under the other.

IN PRACTICE: FUNCTIONAL, PRODUCT, AND MATRIX FORMS OF ORGANIZATION

The need to consider the conjoint effects of size and technology in decisions about designing organizations forms a key premise of a prescriptive line of work that draws upon research generated by a contingency approach (Davis and Lawrence, 1977; Galbraith, 1971; Lawrence and Lorsch, 1969). This work defines several distinct structural forms, based on different ways of grouping people into subunits, and suggests how size and technology may be relevant to choosing which form is likely to be most effective. Two of the different forms that are proposed, the functional and product forms, were suggested by the old divisionalization principle from Managerial Theory. A third form, the matrix, was developed in the 1960s in firms in the aerospace industry. These forms are graphically represented in Figures 3–2 to 3–4.

In a functional form, the main divisions are defined by the major areas of skills and knowledge that the organization requires to accomplish its tasks. In Figure 3–2, these are research and development, manufacturing, finance, and marketing. Members of the organization are assigned to one of the main functions, and the heads of these functions have primary oversight of the people within their function. This form of organization has several advantages, including economies of scale and opportunities for people to specialize within a functional group because the groups are often relatively large. The primary disadvantage is that it can be difficult to get people to coordinate across different functional units, partly because their primary identification is with their functional group and because their immediate supervisors are likely to weigh their contributions to the functional unit more

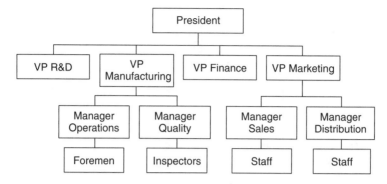

FIGURE 3–2   Functional Form of an Organization

heavily than their ability to work across units in evaluating their performance. It is argued that a functional form is best suited for smaller organizations (organizations that have only one product line fall into this form naturally) and for organizations whose technology and markets are relatively stable and thus do not need to worry about rapid adaptation of products or production processes.

In a product form, the main divisions are formed by separate product groups, each of which has similar sets of functional groups within it, as shown in Figure 3–3. For example, in a company that produced food products, the first line might be cereals, the second line might be cookies and crackers, and the third might be frozen entrées. Each product line would have its own set of people doing research and development on the relevant product, its own manufacturing (operations) staff, and its own marketing group. These units are often relatively small, compared to those in a functional form of organization. Because the main authority is vested in the head of the product line, who is likely to focus on how people have contributed overall to getting the product out and sold in evaluating their performance, coordination across functional units should be comparatively unproblematic within each product line; and this, in turn, should enhance the organization's ability to adapt to specific changes that may affect a given product line. On the other hand, the duplication of functions across product groups means that the organization as a whole cannot capture the benefits of economies of

FIGURE 3–3   Product Form of an Organization

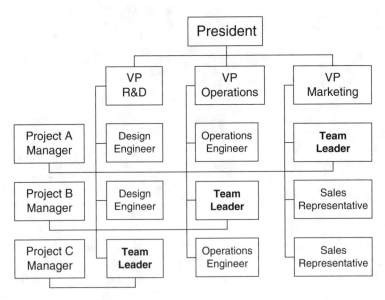

FIGURE 3–4   Matrix Form of an Organization

scale; likewise, because the functional groups within each line are relatively small, it is difficult for members to become specialists—they often need to know a little about all aspects of their functional area. This form of organization is more likely to be found in relatively large organizations (with multiple product lines, of course), especially those with technologies and markets that often change, thus requiring ongoing adaptation within each product line.

The matrix form of organization was developed in an effort to capture the benefits of both functional and product forms. Matrix organizations are divided into functional units, as shown in Figure 3–4, but they also create special product (or project) groups whose members are drawn from the functional units (sometimes on a short-term, sometimes on a longer-term basis). Thus, these organizations have central authority vested in both heads of functional units and managers who oversee the project groups. The distinguishing feature of matrix organizations, then, is a dual-authority structure; this means that some members of the organization report to and are evaluated by two separate supervisors or managers. In Figure 3–4, the team leaders for each product group have this two-boss relationship. They must get other team members to bring their specialized technical knowledge to bear on the project to which they are assigned and to cooperate with other team members who have different knowledge and thus may have very different views of what should be done. The team leaders report to both the head of the product group and the head of the functional unit from which they are drawn. As noted above, this form was originally developed in the aerospace industry in the 1960s, an industry in which organizations faced intense competition to create and develop new products, requiring the application of a very high level of technical knowledge and skill as well as close collaboration among different specialists in order to speed products to the market. It is this kind of context in which matrix forms of organization are expected to be best suited, although the dual-authority structure can require extremely intensive inter- actions and demands, especially on those employees who have two bosses. Partly because of this, it has been suggested that it's most suited to relatively smaller orga- nizations with a limited number (three or four product lines) (Galbraith, 1971).

Information Technology

Before moving on to consider other forces that shape formal structure, there are a few additional points to note about studies of technology and organizations. Research on the effects of technology on organizations dropped off considerably after the 1970s—perhaps because of the shift in researchers' interests from understanding internal influences on organizational operations to understanding more external, environmental influences. This shift seems particularly surprising, however, because it was after this time point that information technologies devel- oped in ways that allowed significant transformations in the way people worked and, hence, in organizational routines and operations (Zammuto et al., 2007). These technologies allow information to be exchanged simultaneously among a large number of individuals working at geographically and temporally dispersed locations; they also provide decision-making tools (simulations, visualization of work processes, etc.) that were largely unknown thirty years ago (Kellogg, Orlikowski, and Yates, 2006; Polzer et al., 2006). Such technological change has potentially enormous implications for the way organizations are structured. Yet we have little systematic knowledge of whether or how this technology has sig- nificantly altered structural patterns or the conditions under which it does or does not lead to structural changes. It remains an intriguing area for further research.

EFFECTS OF INTERNAL CULTURE

Another line of research on determinants of structure that could be classified as belonging to the closed-systems approach is that dealing with internal organiza- tional culture. The importance of internal culture has received varying degrees of attention by organizational scholars and practitioners over time. At one time, internal culture was referred to as "informal structure" and held a prominent spot in Barnard's (1968) important analysis of the functions of the executive. Barnard argued that one of the major functions of top leaders was to "set the tone" for the entire organization, an allusion to the culture of the organization. More contem- porary research suggests that the culture established by executives early in a company's life can indeed leave an enduring legacy, in part through shaping its formal structures (Burton and Beckman, 2007).

Interest in the effects of culture declined after Barnard's work but returned with a vengeance in the 1980s as culture became a buzzword in much of the popular management literature and as organizations sought a culture of "excellence" (Peters and Waterman, 1982). Prompted by its popularity among practitioners, researchers sought to define this concept more precisely. According to Smircich (1985), organizational culture is "a fairly stable set of taken-for-granted assumptions, shared meanings, and values that form a kind of backdrop for action" (p. 58). Similarly, Ott (1989:1) defined culture as "shared values and beliefs, assumptions, perceptions, norms, artifacts, and patterns of behavior." More behavioral aspects of culture include shared jargon, slang, humor, and jokes (Kunda, 2006; Trice and Beyer, 1993).

Organizational culture shapes formal structures by affecting the need for and acceptability of different arrangements for control and supervision. A "clan form" of organization—one in which the culture stresses collective ties and cooperative rather than competitive relations among members—should have less formal division of labor (complexity) and fewer rules and regulations governing behavior than other kinds of organizations (Ouchi, 1980). The culture ensures that members coordinate their behaviors and do what needs to be done to achieve organizational goals, thus making decentralization more feasible. This sort of culture is sometimes consciously fostered in firms through training and socialization procedures for new employees (Kunda, 2006). An alternative means of accomplishing the same end is through the selection of employees with common backgrounds, for example, by recruiting employees from the same professional schools. Professional programs often inculcate students with certain value orientations toward work; thus, having employees who share a common professional socialization/training program can make it easier to create a common organizational culture (Tolbert, 1988). Culture affects not only the extent to which formal structures are needed to accomplish coordination and control but the degree to which certain formal structures are acceptable. Hyde's (1992) analysis of feminist health centers and Zilber's (2002) study of a rape crisis center indicated that formal structures can be seen as symbolizing values and ideologies that the members of the organization accept or reject; thus, the structures themselves may be resisted if they are understood to be contrary to deeply held values.

Although academic studies of culture are still being undertaken, the concept has lost most of the cachet that it once had in the popular management press. This may be because organizational cultures are relatively stable: people come and go, but the culture remains robust. Thus, it is not an easy thing to change, and this makes it less of an attractive management tool.

ENVIRONMENTAL EFFECTS ON STRUCTURE: EXTERNAL CULTURE

Over time, researchers increasingly began to recognize that much of what goes on in organizations is not driven just by concerns about making internal processes more efficient, or even by competition for power among organizational members—rather, much of organizational behavior reflects efforts to cope with pressures that emanate outside organizations' boundaries, in the environment. In later chapters we will discuss in more detail a number of theoretical approaches to thinking about the nature of organizations' environments and how these forces shape organizations. Much of the recent work on environments draws attention to different aspects of organizations than traditional studies of formal structure do—to such outcomes as the formation of interorganizational ties, changes in organizational boundaries, and organizational survival or death. One tradition of research on organizational environments that does seek to explain formal structure developed specifically in reaction to closed-systems explanations. This approach is referred to as institutional theory. We'll describe the general logic of this approach and then link it to research on cross-cultural differences in the formal structure of organizations.

Formal Structures as Institutions: Institutional Theory

There are two basic premises of institutional theory, as expounded in a classic article by John Meyer and Brian Rowan (1977): the first is that specific formal structures can acquire a normative halo—come to be seen as "right and proper" elements of modern, well-run organizations—and the second is that when that happens, organizations are prone to adopt the structures, independent of any specific problems or obvious need for the structures. For example, Six Sigma is a set of formal policies and practices, initially developed at Motorola in the mid-1980s, that are intended to reduce the number of defects in organizational production. Today, these policies and practices are viewed by many people as a sign of organizations' commitment to producing high-quality products, and therefore, even organizations that have had no particular history of problems with high rates of defects (or "scrap") have adopted them. Similarly, in the 1980s and 1990s, Total Quality Management programs were adopted by many organizations independent of size or the kind of technology they used (David and Strang, 2006; Westphal, Gulati, and Shortell, 1997). Institutional theorists argue that organizations adopted such policies because having them, in effect, became a social norm. In line with classic sociological theory (Durkheim, 1964), theorists assume that organizations change their structures to conform to such norms (become "isomorphic" with them) because most decision-makers accept these prescriptions and because even those who are doubtful of their value face social pressures to conform in order to maintain the legitimacy of their organization (DiMaggio and Powell, 1983; Marquis, Glynn, and Davis, 2007). Thus, an institutional approach suggests that the increasing complexity (via the creation of new offices) and formalization (via the adoption of new policies) in modern organizations is at least partly the result of social understandings and expectations held by individuals and other organizations in organizations' environments (Scott, 2007).

An interesting experiment by Zucker (1977) provided some evidence consistent with the idea that organizational structures are subject to institutionalization (becoming taken for granted as "right and proper" elements of organizations).

This experiment made use of what psychologists term *the autokinetic effect:* the tendency for people who are asked to stare at a stationary beam of light in a darkened room to see the light "jump." Subjects in this experiment, who were asked to give estimates of light movement, were assigned to one of three conditions. In the first condition, they were told that they would be working with another student who had been practicing making estimates. In the second condition, they were told to think of themselves as being in an organization and that they would be working with a colleague at this organizational task. In the third condition, they were told to think of themselves being in an organization and that they would be working with a colleague who had more experience and thus would be in charge of working the light switch (suggesting a hierarchical relationship). These three conditions thus represented progressively more bureaucratized settings. In the first part of the experiment, the person sitting in the room with the subject was a confederate, who had been instructed to give a particular estimate for the movement of the light; the confederate gave her estimate first and then the subject did so. This process was repeated twice. In the second part of the experiment, the confederate left, and a new subject was brought in to work with the original subject from the first part of the experiment. Again, they were asked to give their estimates of the light's movement, with the original subject going first.

Zucker found that, in the first part of the experiment, subjects were more likely to make their estimates conform to those of the confederate, and to make them conform sooner, in the second and third conditions—when they had been instructed to think of themselves as being in an organization. This was especially pronounced for subjects in the third condition, which conveyed the idea of hierarchy. She also found that, in the second part of the experiment, original subjects were more likely to stick with the estimates established in the first part of the experiment and that the new subjects were more likely to make their estimates conform to these when they were in the second and third conditions. Zucker argued that these results reflect the fact that we tend to assume that the behavior of people in organizational contexts is purposive and objective, rather than idiosyncratic; this tendency makes it relatively easy to transmit behaviors and practices in organizational settings and also for practices and policies that organizations create to be accepted as "rational." You may have experienced this yourself as a new employee in an organization: given instructions to do your work a certain way, you may have hesitated to do things differently, even if it didn't quite make sense to you, or if you thought you knew a better way, because you assumed (rightly or not, as it may have turned out) that there was a strong rational reason behind the instructions.

How do formal structures become institutionalized or become widely, normatively accepted as components of organizations? There are a number of sources (DiMaggio and Powell, 1983; Meyer and Rowan, 1977). First, there are coercive sources, such as government agencies or other powerful organizations, that can use sanctions to get organizations to adopt specific structural arrangements.

Government regulations, for example, force restaurants to have policies and procedures that (we hope) maintain health standards. The adoption of disciplinary and grievance processes and the formation of internal labor markets have been traced to the development of government mandates for equal employment opportunities (Dobbin et al., 1993; Sutton et al., 1994). Sometimes the mandates don't require specific structures, but as organizations try to show their compliance with the mandates by creating structures (e.g., affirmative action offices), these structures become normatively accepted (Blum, Fields, and Goodman, 1994; Edelman, 1990).

Second, there are mimetic sources: organizations that serve as models for others. Imitation of other organizations is assumed to occur most often when organizations face high levels of uncertainty about how to accomplish their goals (Meyer and Scott, 1983). Rowan (1982) argues, for example, that because of the difficulties in assessing the impact of education processes (given variability in students, uncertainty over the technology of teaching, etc.), schools are particularly likely to follow prescriptions of their institutional environment. As more and more organizations adopt a particular structure, it becomes increasingly institutionalized—understood to be something that legitimate organizations should have (Fligstein, 1985; Goodstein, 1994; Palmer, Jennings, and Zhou, 1993; Tolbert and Zucker, 1983); this fuels adoption by remaining nonadopters. Mimetic processes have been studied most often by organizational scholars (Mizruchi and Fein, 1999). The current vogue of "benchmarking"—watching to see what other organizations are doing, with an eye to imitating things that seem successful—is likely to contribute to institutionalization as an influence on the structure of contemporary organizations.

And third, there are normative sources: groups and organizations who advocate for certain organizational practices and structures and who are considered to be credible, legitimate actors. This includes professional associations, such as the American Medical Association or the American Association of University Professors; trade associations, such as the National Association of Chain Drug Stores or the American Production and Inventory Control Society; and other nonprofit associations, such as the Sierra Club and the Civil Service Reform Association. When such organizations promote a given organizational structure—school health nurses, inventory programs, recycling policies, civil service laws for municipal governments, and so forth—it is apt to become institutionalized and thus adopted by organizations (Terlaak, 2007). For example, Mezias (1990) showed that the spread of financial reporting practices in Fortune 200 business firms reflected the professionalization of accountants and their advocacy of standard practices. In modern businesses, consulting firms often play a key role in the diffusion of structures, serving as normative advocates for new policies and practices (David and Strang, 2006; DiMaggio and Powell, 1983:152).

Thus, in contrast to the older, closed-systems approaches to explaining structure, which treated structure as the result of calculated, direct adaptation to problems of coordination and control, an institutional perspective emphasizes limits on such calculations by decision-makers and pressures for conformity to externally defined norms. Also, in contrast to the older literature, which conceived of structure in broad, abstract terms (levels of formalization, complexity, etc.), an institutional approach emphasizes discrete components that have acquired an institutionalized status (diversity management offices, grievance procedures, stock options for executive compensation, etc.). As noted, responses to institutional pressures are likely to lead organizations to have a higher level of complexity and formalization overall, but research in this tradition typically focuses on explaining the adoption of specific structural elements (Tolbert and Zucker, 1996). Another distinction is that the older literature at least implicitly assumed that components of formal structure were integrated—fit together. An institutional approach explicitly recognizes that organizations can adopt structural elements that are inconsistent (Meyer and Rowan, 1977; Scott et al., 2000). When organizations have constituencies with different and even conflicting norms (e.g., community mental health programs that handle drug abuse treatment), they can develop structures that have conflicting goals and inconsistent structures and practices (D'Aunno, Sutton, and Price, 1991; Zilber, 2002).

Cross-Cultural Variations in Structure

The key insight of institutional theory, that conventional understandings in a society about how organizations "ought" to look affect the kind of structures that organizations have, is relevant to explaining cross-national differences among organizations. Interest in cross-cultural differences among organizations has risen dramatically in recent years, fueled in large part by the growth of multinational enterprises, whose manufacturing, distribution, sales, and administrative operations are often spread around the globe (Morgan, 2004). But it is not only business organizations that are affected by cross-cultural influences. Many international religious organizations have long had multinational operations. One need only think about the well-publicized policy differences between American Roman Catholics and the Vatican to get a glimpse of how national cultural factors may affect the functioning of all types of organizations.

There's ample evidence that national cultures affect in many ways how organizations are structured. For example, clear national differences have been found in levels of formalization and in centralization among organizations in the Nordic countries, the United States, and Canada (Dobbin and Boychuk, 1999). Such cross-national structural variations reflect differences in institutionalized decision-making in different countries (Gooderham, Nordhaug, and Ringdal, 1999). Culture affects the way decision-makers in organizations perceive their environments and thus the "need" for particular structural arrangements (Malan, 1994).

The importance of national cultures for organizations can be seen most clearly, perhaps, in multinational organizations, especially in cases where the norms that affect organizations in the country of origin differ from those of the host country. In an analysis of Japanese companies in the United States, Ouchi and Jaeger (1978) suggested that Japanese and American companies typically exhibited the following distinctive characteristics:

American	Japanese
Short-term employment	Lifetime employment
Individual decision-making	Consensual decision-making
Individual responsibility	Collective responsibility
Rapid evaluation and promotion	Slow evaluation and promotion
Explicit, formalized control	Implicit, informal control
Specialized career path	Nonspecialized career path

They found that Japanese firms with operations in the United States resembled the Japanese model more than the American model, suggesting that the country of origin is of critical importance (see also Ouchi and Johnson, 1978).

There has been some debate, however, over the importance of national culture versus other factors in shaping organizations, that is, whether organizations are mostly "culture free" or largely "culture bound." The culture-free view is that organizational characteristics reflect other differences that characterize organizations in different countries, rather than national cultures per se. These other factors could be size, technology, internal culture, or factors not yet considered. The culture-bound argument is that national cultures are the dominant force in operation. Not surprisingly, perhaps, neither extreme view has decisive empirical support.

In their study of multinational banks in Hong Kong, Birnbaum and Wong (1985) found support for a culture-free determination of structure. Centralization, vertical and horizontal differentiation, and formalization were not related to the cultures in which the multinational banks studied operated. Similarly, Marsh and Mannari (1980) also report that structural relationships found in the West tend to have the same form in Japan, rather than varying with culture. Also in line with these arguments, Conaty, Mahmoudi, and Miller (1983) found that many organizations in prerevolutionary Iran were modeled on Western organizations and showed little signs of the particular culture in which they were located.

On the other hand, those making a case for culture-bound arguments can cite a number of empirical studies. One, a study of manufacturing plants in France, former West Germany, and Great Britain, found that the education, training, recruitment, and promotion processes in each country reflected different "logics" (values), giving rise to particular ways of managing problems of differentiation and integration, and resulting in nationally different organizational shapes (Maurice, Sorge, and Warner, 1980). Distinctive formal structures that are attributed to differences in cultural values have also been documented in studies of organizations in Saudi Arabia and the United States (At-Twarjri and Montansani, 1987), in multinational firms in India (Gupta and Govindarajan, 1991; Rosenweig and Singh, 1991), in business organizations in East Asia (Appold, Siengthai, and Kasarda, 1998), small businesses in China and the

United States (Hall et al., 1993; Nee, 1992), newspapers in Finland (Dalin, 1997), and breweries in Germany and the United States (Carroll et al., 1993).

There are, thus, contrasting findings and interpretations in regard to the importance of cultural differences for organizational structure. Although the relative importance of cultural differences may be debated, it seems most reasonable to assume that organizations are affected by widespread norms and social understandings about appropriate structures and relationships that exist in the countries in which they are located, just as they are affected by size and technology (Guillen and Suarez, 2005; Whitley, 1999). Lincoln, Hanada, and McBride (1986) suggest that national cultural effects are additive in the sense that they are added to the variations in structure introduced by operations technology, size, and market constraints. These authors go on to note that there may be situations in which cultural factors could override technology.

It is also possible that cultural forces affect different aspects of organizations than more material influences. For example, Hamilton and Biggart (1988), in an analysis of South Korean, Japanese, and Taiwanese organizations, argue that both culture-based practices and market factors are important in explaining organizational growth but that authority patterns and legitimation strategies (cultural factors) best explain organizational structure. A comparative analysis by Hall and Xu (1990) of Chinese and Japanese organizations led them to conclude that differences in family and Confucian values in the two countries contribute to crucial differences in structure between the two countries, though they also believe that material and cultural explanations of structure both have validity.

Overall, work that emphasizes the independent effects of distinctive national systems of values and social understandings in shaping organizations is very compatible with the institutional perspective described above (Guler, Guillen, and MacPherson, 2002). Just as an institutional approach, by itself, is not sufficient to explain the formal structure of organizations, purely cultural explanations are also limited. However, these lines of work do draw attention to important, nonmaterial influences on structure that were largely overlooked in most early analyses. Considering them provides a backdrop for discussing some basic debates on assumptions about the nature of organizational decision-making and decision-makers that (at least implicitly) underlie different explanatory approaches. One debate involves the extent to which decision-makers have discretion or are constrained in choices about how to structure their organizations. A related debate involves the question of whether (and when) decision-makers are guided by more external pressures or by independent calculations of costs and benefits in such choices.

CREATING FORMAL STRUCTURE: DEBATES OVER PROCESS

The question of the degree of latitude decision-makers have in choosing particular structural configurations was raised partly as an objection to what was seen as the overly deterministic image of organizations implied by contingency analyses.

Recall that this approach was premised on the notion that the "best" structures depended on the context in which an organization operated—its size, the kind of technology it had, and so forth (Donaldson, 1995, 1996). Critics of empirical work in this tradition pointed out an implicit assumption underpinning much of it: that decision-makers normally responded to these contextual forces by "choosing" the right structure, one that facilitated adaptation and thus maximized the organization's efficiency. This conception of decision-making processes also underpins much of the current work that goes under the banner of "strategy" and more of the economics-oriented analyses in general (Porter, 1998; Williamson, 1983). The idea of strategic choice is not a new one. Chandler (1962) emphasized the importance of strategic choices made by top-level decision-makers for business firms such as Sears, Roebuck, and General Motors as they attempted to take advantage of perceived markets in their environment. When whole sets of organizations are viewed as responding in the same way to similar technological, environmental, or other influences, though, the question can be raised about whether these "choices" are in fact beyond the volition of individual decision-makers and are essentially determined by external conditions. In other words, traditional explanations of formal structure were seen by some theorists as predicated on the assumption that organizational decision-makers must make a given choice in a particular context; otherwise, their organizations will fail.

Child (1972a) challenged this implicit determinism by noting that internal politics often strongly affect the structural forms that organizations assume and that definitions of key environmental features and relevant performance standards are importantly shaped by such political considerations. He also argued that the internal politics are themselves dependent on the existing power arrangements in the organization. There is a fair amount of evidence that chances of organizational failures are much lower among larger, older organizations (Freeman, Carroll, and Hannan, 1983); thus, one could expect that decision-makers in such organizations would indeed have some latitude in making choices about structure and that these choices might well reflect considerations other than efficiency maximization or profitability. In a similar vein, Robert Michels (1949), writing in the early twentieth century, suggested that the leaders of large political organizations often made decisions that were more consistent with their personal interests than with those of the general membership. Likewise, assessing the economic landscape during the Great Depression of the 1930s, Adolph Berle and Gardiner Means (1932) suggested that managers of large, publicly held companies were often inclined to make decisions that advanced their own interests rather than those of the nominal owners, the stockholders (Tolbert and Hiatt, forthcoming). It's not necessary to assume that the heads of organizations are typically guided by their self-interests; the key point is that they may make decisions that reflect concerns other than maximizing efficiency or enhancing the organization's competitive position. The concept of equifinality, which implies that there may be a variety of ways (e.g., structures) to achieve a given end (e.g., organizational survival), is relevant here. Thus, an ongoing debate among organizational researchers centers on the question of whether organizations' formal structure is primarily determined by the need to operate with maximum efficiency in a given environment or whether it is likely to reflect decision-makers' preferences and concerns with other factors than efficiency.

Another, related debate over the decision-making processes that underlie observed structural outcomes revolves around the question of the extent to which decision-makers typically engage in independent calculations of the relative advantages of a particular structure, or just follow the dictates of external groups and organizations. This debate echoes a long-standing concern in sociological analyses about "under-socialized" and "over-socialized" conceptions of action (Wrong, 1961); it also relates to work by economists on "herd" behavior (Banerjee, 1992). While there is little debate over the assertion that organizational decisions are made on the basis of "bounded rationality" (Simon, 1957), there is much less agreement on the *degree* to which rationality is bounded or when it is apt to be more or less bounded. The notion of *bounded rationality* will be considered in detail in Chapter 6, where we discuss organizational decision-making. In brief, it implies that people are inherently incapable of making the sort of full assessments of options that are necessary to make optimal choices. Work based on institutional theory has been criticized for implying that organizational decision-makers are characterized by a very high degree of bounded rationality—or, as it is sometimes put, that they are "cultural dopes" (Wrong, 1961; see also Abbott, 1992; Hirsch and Lounsbury, 1997). On the other hand, some economic approaches to explaining organizations, while explicitly acknowledging problems of bounded rationality, make arguments that imply that decision-makers can and usually do make incredibly complex (and correct) calculations of how much it would cost over the long run to produce goods in-house versus purchasing them in the market; this conception of organizational decision-making is also clearly subject to challenge (Tolbert and Zucker, 1996).

Debates over the decision processes that lead organizations to have a particular structural arrangement are difficult to resolve, in part because we know relatively little about how decisions are "typically" made in organizations, or what kinds of conditions affect tendencies to produce decisions based on efficiency concerns versus other issues, or when decision-makers will be willing to make and follow their own independent judgments versus following the herd. But we think that it is useful for you to be aware of these debates as you consider research on organizational structure (and other aspects of organizations as well), since most research does rest on implicit assumptions that the debates reflect.

SUMMARY AND CONCLUSIONS

We have considered a series of explanations of organizational structure. These have ranged from those emphasizing more material factors, such as size and technology, to those focused on more ideational factors, such as internal and external cultural influences. Which is the correct explanation? It should be obvious by now that neither "all of the above" nor "none of the above" is the appropriate answer. The explanations of structure must be considered in combination.

This has become well recognized among sociologists. There is a growing recognition that market and task contingencies operate along with institutional pressures in influencing organizations (Bugra and Üsdiken, 1997; Gupta, Dirsmith, and Fogarty, 1994; Sutton and Dobbin, 1996). In line with this, Tolbert (1985) combined institutional and more economic explanations to account for variations in the administrative structures of universities. Fligstein (1985) studied the spread of the multidivisional form among large corporations and found support for the strategic choice, member control, and institutional perspectives. Similarly, a study of the development of the thrift industry in California found that market pressures operated in tandem with institutional forces (Haveman and Rao, 1997). Fligstein concludes (and we concur):

> [E]ach school of thought has tended to view its theory as a total causal explanation of organizational phenomena. This suggests that one of the central tasks in organizational theory is to reorient the field in such a way as to view competing theories as contributing to an understanding of organizational phenomena. (p. 377)

The healthy and informed eclecticism that Fligstein calls for has essentially become the norm in organizational analyses. Organizations are structured in a context. Van Houton (1987) analyzed the various approaches to organizational design that were attempted in Sweden in the 1970s and 1980s. He concludes that these cannot be understood out of their historical context. Organizations are thus complex *structures in motion* that are best conceptualized as historically constituted entities (Clegg, 1981:545). There are, then, multiple explanations of structure. When these explanations are taken singly, in opposition to one another, and outside their historical and cultural context, they have little to offer. When combined and in context, they enable us to understand why organizations take the forms that they do.

EXERCISES

1. How well do the contextual explanations of organizational structure fit your two organizations?
2. Explain how well the organizational design explanations do or do not fit your two organizations.

Chapter 4

Power and Power Outcomes

OVERVIEW

One important component of organizational structure is centralization, or the distribution of power. Organizations have been defined as systems of power—an interconnected series of order-givers and order-followers. In this light, organizations can be viewed as tools by which those people with power can use other people to achieve particular goals. But individuals who are not formally designated as order-givers in an organization may also wield power, that is, be able to get others to carry out their wishes. Even individuals who are not official members of the organization may influence others in the organization to do as they wish. Where does power come from in organizations, and what factors influence its distribution as well as changes in this distribution? In this chapter, we focus on these questions. We begin by examining authority as a particular type of power relationship and consider different types and bases of authority. Authority is an important aspect of power in organizations, but authority can be buttressed by or undercut by other kinds of power. Thus, we also look at other types of power that are often found in organizations and the things that affect such power. The exercise of power in organizations has outcomes that are important for the parties involved, and for the organization as a whole. The most common outcome is compliance—power works. But power can also lead to the more dramatic outcome of conflict. We examine the nature and consequences of conflict in organizations. Finally, we consider how organizations exercise power within the larger society.

In many ways, power is a most puzzling phenomenon. On the one hand, power is often stable and self-perpetuating, partly because those in power have the resources to maintain that power (Hardy and Clegg, 1996). On the other hand, as the events in Eastern Europe and the former Soviet Union in 1989 and 1990 demonstrated, long-entrenched systems of power can be overthrown with startling quickness. Different members of an organization, as well as actors outside the organization, can critical influence in decision-making processes and thus affect what organizations actually do, and the relative influence of different actors may vary across time. In Mintzberg's (1983) terms, we can think of power "in and around" organizations. Understanding both the perpetuation of power relations in organizations and how and when shifts in these relations may occur requires consideration of the variety of bases of power in organizations, factors that affect when individuals and groups may be able to use these bases, and different responses to the exercise of power. These are the topics that we focus on in the following discussion.

THE NATURE OF POWER IN ORGANIZATIONS

Power can be rather simply defined. There is general agreement that it has to do with relationships between two or more actors in which the behavior of one is affected by the behavior of the other. Robert Dahl (1957), a political scientist, defines power thus: "A has power over B to the extent that he can get B to do something B would not otherwise do" (pp. 202–203). (For other general discussions of power, see Bierstedt, 1950; Blau, 1964; Kaplan, 1964; Weber, 1947:152–193.) If we remember that the *he* in the definition can also be a *she* and that A and B are not necessarily individuals, this simple definition captures the essence of the power concept. It implies an important point that is often neglected: the power variable is a relational one. A person or a group cannot have power in isolation; rather, the concept describes a relationship between a given individual or collectivity and another specified person or collectivity (Pfeffer, 1982).

Power relationships involve much more than interpersonal power. In organizations, interunit power relationships are an important determinant of organizational outcomes. The units here can be hierarchical levels, such as labor and management, or they can be departments or divisions at the same hierarchical level, such as sales and manufacturing. We will examine interorganizational relationships from the power standpoint at a later phase of the analysis. We have already considered the power of organizations in society. Power is thus a crucial feature of organizations at every level of analysis.

AUTHORITY AND POWER

There are many different bases of power and, hence, different types of power. In this context, a key distinction that is commonly drawn is between authority and other forms of power. Weber (1947), in his classic analysis of bureaucratic organization, emphasized this distinction. Authority is a type of power that is based on the acceptance by others of a given individual's legitimate right to issue orders or directives. Thus, orders are followed because it is believed that they *ought* to be followed; recipients are expected to "suspend judgment" and comply voluntarily. The exercise of this type of power requires a common value system among members of a collectivity, one that defines who has the right to give orders to whom, and under what conditions.

As part of his effort to understand the nature of modern organizations, Weber (1947) developed a widely known typology of authority, one that distinguished among rational–legal, charismatic, and traditional authority. Rational–legal authority characterizes most power relationships in contemporary organizations, as we noted in Chapter 2. It is based on a value system that holds that relations in social groups should be governed by a set of general laws and rules that are created purposively, to deal efficiently and effectively with common problems and questions that people encounter. It is also believed that those laws and rules should be subject to change, if there is a reason to believe that they are not effective or efficient. Consistent with this value system, it is accepted that people with particular knowledge and skills that are relevant to dealing with some set of problems should be assigned to positions or offices that handle those problems. We accept orders that come from those persons and the offices because we assume that they are rational, that is, designed to effectively accomplish some ends (Zucker, 1977). We are not always, and perhaps not even typically, conscious of this assumption, but if pressed to explain our behavior, it is usually reflected in our explanations. For example, at the start of every semester, an instructor hands out a course syllabus to each student. When the students read the assignments, write the papers, and take the examinations, rational–legal authority has operated. They have accepted the professor's right to tell them what to read and what they must do as students in the class, in part because they assume that the professor holds her position because of her relevant knowledge about the topics addressed in the class.

This emphasis on positions takes the person out of the equation—we will put the person back in now. Charismatic authority stems from devotion to a particular power holder and is based on his or her personal characteristics. Members of a collective view these characteristics as being extraordinary, indicating special gifts, talents, and abilities; they accept the person's right to give orders because they believe in the person's superiority. Although this type of authority is not the main form in most modern organizations, it occurs occasionally, and it can help or hinder the regular operations of the organization. If a person with rational–legal authority (gained by virtue of the position that he holds) can extend this through the exercise of charismatic authority, he has more power over subordinates than that prescribed by the organization. This additional power may be harnessed to enhance the performance of the organization. If, on the other hand, charismatic authority is held by persons outside the formal authority system, they may use this to contravene rational–legal authority, and the system itself can be threatened.

The third form, traditional authority, is based on the belief that an established set of social relations is divinely intended. Within this social system, some individuals were destined to hold power, or "born to rule." This was the main basis of political authority in many societies for much of history; Western feudal societies and Eastern dynasties both provide good examples. The Roman Catholic Church serves as at least a partial example of this form of authority in contemporary organizations: the system of pope, cardinals, archbishops, and so on reflects the belief in a divinely ordained set of relations.

Dornbusch and Scott (1975) offer an additional distinction that is useful in thinking about authority in organizations, between endorsed and authorized power. This distinction addresses an old debate over the locus of authority in organizations. On the one hand, Chester Barnard (1968) argued that authority resides in the individual who complies with an order. In this bottom-up view of authority, if one individual does not accept another's right to give an order and fails to comply, the order-giver cannot be said to have authority over that person. On the other hand, Weber's analysis is predicated on the notion that authority resides in a social collectivity and, more specifically, in shared normative beliefs about who has the right to give orders. Weber's top-down approach is based on the assumption that noncompliance with an order given by a person with norma-tively approved authority will result in the application of sanctions by the larger group. By distinguishing between endorsed and authoritative power, Dornbusch and Scott recognized that authority has both bottom-up and top-down aspects. Endorsed power is said to exist when subordinates accept and comply with the orders given by their superiors. Authorized power exists when an individual's orders are supported and enforced by higher-level members of an organization and, ultimately, by the larger society. This distinction is useful in thinking about situations involving different types of organizational conflicts over authority— mutinies, coups d'état, revolutions, and so forth.

OTHER TYPES OF POWER

As noted, although authority is an important type of power in organizations, it is not the only type. Other types of power relationships entail dependency, one party's need or desire for something that another party can provide (Emerson, 1962). When two parties need each other equally, their dependence is mutual— for example, managers need workers to produce goods and services, and workers need managers to provide their pay. But when dependence is *not* balanced, then one actor may have more power over another than vice versa. Or to put it another way, when A wants or needs things that B has more than B wants things from A, this can provide B with power over A.

The things that actors may possess or control that can be sources of power are usually referred to as resources. David Mechanic (1962), analyzing the fac-tors that affected how much power people at lower levels of an organization had, identified three general types of resources in organizations that such members might have access to: persons, information, and "instrumentalities." The last refers to physical or tangible resources, such as machinery, office supplies, and money. If we broaden this list to include nontangible, social factors, such as status and friendship, this constitutes a useful list of basic resources that may provide organizational members with power above and beyond the formal authority they hold.

Access to Resources

Bacharach and Lawler (1980) identify a number of different ways in which actors come to control such power resources. Access to resources can be affected by the official or formal organizational position an individual holds (see also Brass and Burkhardt, 1993; Finkelstein, 1992; Fligstein and Brantley, 1992). Clearly, this is an important source of power for persons who hold high-level positions in organizations and whose jobs involve such tasks as assigning compensation, making decisions about promotions and awards in the organization, and setting working conditions. These are the kinds of key resources that Etzioni (1975) used in formulating a typology of organizations. He referred to these as involving remunerative rewards, normative rewards, and coercion, respectively, and argued that you could classify organizations in terms of which kinds of resources the top-level members primarily relied on to secure compliance by lower-level members. Remunerative rewards involve material, often financial incentives (e.g., salaries and bonuses); normative rewards involve satisfying social or psychological needs (e.g., status, friendship); coercion involves affecting physical conditions (e.g., opportunities to eat, rest breaks).

But lower-level positions can also provide people with access to resources that others need and thus potentially give them power. For example, Crozier's (1964) study of relations in a French cigarette-manufacturing firm found that, although the maintenance personnel were not in high-level positions, they held the most power of any group because of their role in repairing the equipment necessary to the production process. Only the maintenance men were allowed to work on the machines when they broke down, and production workers and their supervisors were essentially helpless unless the maintenance personnel performed their work. Thus, their formal job responsibilities provided them with control of the machines, and this gave them a great deal of power.

> With machine stoppages, a general uncertainty about what will happen next develops in a world totally dominated by the value of security. It is not surprising, therefore, that the behavior of the maintenance man—the man who alone can handle the situation, and who by preventing these unpleasant consequences gives workers the necessary security—has a tremendous importance for production workers, and that they try to please him and he to influence them. (p. 109)

Similarly, think of an administrative assistant or aide whose job involves making appointments for a high-ranking executive in an organization. This job allows him to determine who gets to see the executive, a resource that others are apt to desire highly; thus, although the position may be relatively low level, it provides him with control of an important resource (a person, the executive) that can make others willing to do much to secure his favor.

Bacharach and Lawler (1980) discuss structural position as a determinant of access to resources of power. In this usage, structural position can be thought of in terms of network relations. An actor's position in a network, defined by which other actors are linked to the focal actor, is commonly seen as a key determinant of power (Ansell and Padgett, 1993; Burt, 1992; Gould and Fernandez, 1994; Stevenson and Greenberg, 2000). Links to others are assumed to provide access to two basic resources: information and people; thus, members of a network who have high centrality—are connected to many others, either directly or indirectly—should find it easier to get information and to control people (i.e., affect what others do through their social connections). Some have suggested that *whom* an actor is linked to also needs to be considered in understanding the impact of network position on power (Lin, 1999); links to a few high-status people may have the same, or even more, impact on power as links to many low-status people. This approach is consistent with Allen and Panian's (1982) finding of the role of "family ties" in influencing the choice of top-level executives in organizations.

Finally, personal characteristics have been suggested to have an effect on access to power resources (Bacharach and Lawler, 1980; Etzioni, 1975; French and Raven, 1968; Mechanic, 1962). Such characteristics include social attractiveness, intelligence, and willingness to invest effort in getting such resources. When others find a person attractive, they are likely to value her friendship and esteem (Blau, 1964); as noted, insofar as others find such nontangible, social resources desirable, they can serve as a source of power. Thus, for example, if someone asks a favor of you, you are more likely to comply if you want her to like you than if you are indifferent to her opinion of you. Whether attractive individuals are willing to use this as a source of power may depend on personality characteristics that affect their interest in gaining and using power. Likewise, individuals are apt to vary in their willingness to put in the time to acquire information, to cultivate others' goodwill and favorable recognition, and to make other efforts to acquire resources that can serve as a source of power (Kanter, 1979).

Resources and Strategic Contingencies

Having access to resources that others desire isn't sufficient, by itself, to provide individuals with power. Rather, power rests on how much those resources are highly valued or considered to be important, whether their acquisition is difficult or uncertain, and whether other resources can be substituted for them or not. When resources are viewed as important, when there is high uncertainty surrounding their acquisition, and when they are nonsubstitutable, they represent what's referred to as a "strategic contingency" for the organization. Control of strategic contingencies is fundamental to power in organizations (Hickson et al., 1971; Pfeffer and Salancik, 1974).

The value attached to a resource, or its importance, is affected by whether it's seen as central to the organization's workflow and ability to carry out main production functions. The importance of a resource may also be affected by environmental demands. A study by Hambrick (1981) showed that if executives coped with the dominant requirements imposed by the environment of their industry, they had high power. This finding is consistent with those of other studies that have examined who attains top-level positions in organizations. One study, for example, found that lawyers (coming from legal departments) were disproportionately represented among corporate chief executives. In organizations that face complex legal problems, lawyers move to the top, as they appear to have the information, or knowledge, needed to solve key problems (Priest and Rothman, 1985).

Similarly, another study, a historical analysis of prominent corporations in the United States from 1919 to 1979, reported that people with manufacturing backgrounds dominated corporate presidencies in the early decades of the century. Knowledge of manufacturing processes was key to the success of these organizations. In the middle decades, changes in the kinds of problems facing the corporations led people with backgrounds in sales and marketing to dominate in executive offices. In the more recent decades, personnel from finance tended to occupy presidential positions in the corporations (Fligstein, 1990). The difference in the findings reported here (lawyers versus finance) is undoubtedly due to differences in samples of organizations studied. These findings also indicate an important point: if the environment changes, or the organization develops new markets and concerns, different types of knowledge and other resources can come to be seen as more or less important to the organization's survival and success, and power can shift from one individual or group to another.

It's not only the importance of a resource in an organization that affects whether it provides power to the individual or group that holds it; its scarcity and the relative uncertainty surrounding it affect this as well. The ability to cope with uncertainty has been found to make an important contribution to power differentials (Hickson, Pugh, and Pheysey, 1969). If an organization needs additional financial support (e.g., because it wants to expand), and if its ability to secure funding from banks or other sources is in doubt, the finance department or unit that handles this task will have more power (Salancik and Pfeffer, 1974). In this context, Perrow (1970) used data from twelve industrial firms to examine the question: Which group has the most power? He found that most of the firms were overwhelmingly dominated by their sales departments. This domination is shown in Figure 4–1.

Perrow argued that the power of the sales departments stemmed from the fact that this was the least predictable area of resource flows for most organizations in his study; thus, the departments' ability to cope with uncertainty increased their relative power within the organizations. His findings amplify those of Crozier (1964), described earlier. Part of the reason maintenance workers had such power in cigarette-manufacturing firm, Crozier suggests, was that

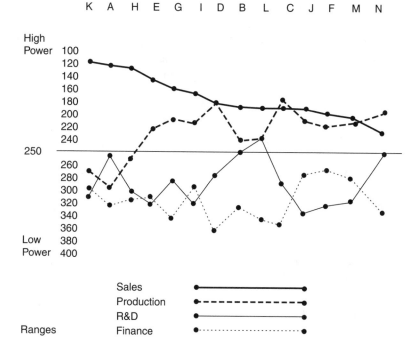

FIGURE 4–1   Overview Power of Departments in Industrial Firms
(Means of Departmental Means)
*Each letter represents a company or separate unit.
Source: Charles Perrow, "Departmental Power and Perspective in Industrial Firms," in *Power in Organizations,*
ed. Mayer N. Zald (Nashville, TN: Vanderbilt University Press, 1970), p. 64. Copyright © 1970. Reprinted by
permission of Charles B. Perrow.

the rest of the organization was highly predictable. The organization was a state-owned monopoly; thus, ensuring sales was not an issue, nor was securing financing. Only the machinery, which was old and apt to break down unexpectedly, was a key source of uncertainty in the organization. Consequently, controlling this uncertainty provided the maintenance men with power.

Finally, whether there are alternative ways of obtaining needed resources, or whether there are other, substitutable resources is important in determining the relevance of a given resource for power. In a hospital, for example, the application of medical knowledge that physicians hold is central to the organization's work processes; this potentially provides physicians with a great deal of power. When there is a shortage of physicians in an area, and the organizations' ability to obtain enough physicians is uncertain, physicians' power increases. However, if there is an oversupply of physicians, there is less uncertainty surrounding organizations' ability to get the needed resource, medical knowledge, and this should decrease physicians' power. Moreover, insofar as other personnel, such as nurses, physicians' assistants, and others, have relevant knowledge and are allowed to use it (which may depend on state regulations), they represent a potential substitute for physicians. This also can lessen physicians' power (Scott et al., 2000). If the production workers in Crozier's study had been allowed to fix their machines when they broke down, the power of the maintenance men would have declined considerably; however, the organization's rules forbade anyone but the maintenance men from doing this task, thus ensuring their nonsubstitutability.

Social Definitions and Strategic Contingencies

It's important to note that the value, uncertainty, and lack of substitutability of resources are not necessarily objectively given; these qualities can be socially constructed, or manipulated (Alvesson and Willmott, 2002). A study by Kanter (1968), for example, documented ways in which leaders of an organization can increase the value of social resources controlled by the organization (status, friendship, etc.) for members and thus secure their compliance. Similarly, Kunda's (2006) research on an engineering firm described the creation of an organizational culture that encouraged employees to set high value on rewards controlled by the management, which enhanced managers' power. It is also possible for groups and individuals to persuade others that the resources they control are unique, and thus not substitutable, or to influence perceptions of the uncertainty of resource flows. To understand changes in power in an organization, then, it is important to pay attention to the way in which various resources are defined and evaluated by members of the organization (Enz, 1988).

Similarly, the use of authority may be affected by the emergence of new social definitions of who *should* be in charge of certain situations and problems. An interesting example of an opportunity for this sort of redefinition is provided by Bucher's (1970) anecdotal account of a confrontation between students and university administration during the 1960s:

> According to the students' statements, the dean asserted that "nobody in the university has the authority to negotiate with the students . . ." "Obviously somebody in the university makes policy decisions," the students said, "and until an official body comes forward, we consider the present situation a refusal to negotiate our demands." (p. 3)

In the situation described above, neither the students nor the university administration could locate an office or an individual who had the authority to negotiate with them. The students' perception that this constituted a refusal to negotiate is only partially accurate. Such a situation simply had not arisen before, and it really was unclear who had the knowledge and skills relevant for assigning authority. In campus situations such as these, student–administration confrontations, issues, and relationships are explored that have not really been part of the preexisting power system. Individuals or groups that are able to define an issue or problem as part of their domain can increase their power.

SHIFTS IN POWER

Because more power is introduced into the system as arrangements are made to handle incidents such as the one described in the preceding section, we see that there is not a fixed amount of power in the system for all time; the amount of power can contract or expand. Thus, Lammers (1967:204), discussing research on increasing workers' participation in organizational decision-making, concludes:

> To sum up, managers and the managed in organizations at the same time come to influence each other more effectively and thereby generate joint power as the outcome of a better command by the organization over its technological, economic, and human resources in the service of certain objectives.

This suggests that the introduction of more cooperative decision-making systems can result in greater power for both managers and workers alike and, thus, overall increases in power.

In addition, power may shift among individuals and groups in organizations over time, as noted above. However, changes in power, either overall or in distribution, do not occur quickly—except perhaps in rare cases, such as a disaster, where dramatic changes in power in an organization may take place in a very short period. There are a number of factors that normally limit such power shifts. First, once an individual or organizational unit gains power, it tries very hard to maintain this power (Michels, 1949). This can account for the observation that an organizational unit's previous power position is the main predictor of its current power (Lachman, 1989). It also explains Boeker's (1989) finding that environmental conditions at the time an organization is formed, along with the background of the founding entrepreneur, determine which departments are regarded as most important in organizations long after the founding period (see also Burton and Beckman, 2007). Likewise, powerful chief executive officers (CEOs) are less apt to be dismissed than their weaker subordinates when their organizations are doing poorly (Boeker, 1992).

Second, because the allocation of organizational resources is affected by the existing power system, it tends to perpetuate the system (Pondy, 1970; Zald, 1970), even in the absence of active efforts by power holders. For example, an analysis of United Fund agencies found that community organizations that were successful in raising funds themselves received greater allocations from the United Fund. These community organizations were less dependent upon the United Fund, and the United Fund feared that they might attempt their own fund-raising efforts (Pfeffer and Long, 1977). Similarly, studies of university budget allocation decisions have found that the more powerful units and departments receive more resources—the rich get richer and the poor get poorer. This pattern is particularly evident in times of financial adversity (Hills and Mahoney, 1978; Pfeffer and Salancik, 1974).

Despite these strong inertial forces, shifts in power systems of organizations *do* occur. External forces often play a key role in such shifts (Zald, 1970). Relationships with similar organizations (e.g., trade associations or baseball leagues), suppliers and customers of the organization's output, regulatory agencies, and others can all affect the amount and distribution of power within the organization. For example, the National Labor Relations Board, after its establishment in the 1930s, facilitated the growth in power of labor unions (Peterson, 1970). At the same time, the increasing complexity of labor laws and regulations led to the development of specialists in labor relations, whose power within the organization was based on managing the organization's relations with unions and legal authorities (Jacoby, 2004). External economic conditions also affect the power system in organizations as markets for labor, raw materials, and outputs shift. The external world thus invades the power structure of these organizations: power, like other organizational phenomena, does not exist in isolation within the organization.

POWER OUTCOMES: COMPLIANCE AND INVOLVEMENT

The most frequent consequence of the exercise of power is compliance. This outcome is so common that it is almost boring. People come to work on time, do what their bosses desire, and produce their goods or deliver their services. Organizational units generally also comply with demands of their superiors. This common occurrence of compliance is frequently overlooked in analyses of power, as the resistance to power—conflict—is more dramatic and exciting. Despite the importance of conflict for organizations, compliance is really their heart.

It was this reasoning that led Etzioni (1975) to make compliance a key component of his typology of organizations, which we mentioned previously. Etzioni argued that lower-level members of organizations could be characterized by the dominant type of involvement they experienced. He also argued that these types of involvement tended to be associated with the dominant types of rewards that top-level members used to induce compliance. The use of coercion should be associated with alienative involvement, remunerative rewards with calculative involvement, and normative (or symbolic) rewards with moral involvement.

Research utilizing Etzioni's approach suggests that when organizations are able to develop moral involvement on the part of their members, their commitment to the organization is higher. For some organizations, such as voluntary organizations, moral involvement is crucial to ensuring members' continued participation and hence the survival of the organization (Kanter, 1968). Consequently, providing opportunities for democratic participation by members is especially important in such organizations because moral involvement is often increased when members are encouraged to participate and actually do participate (Craig and Gross, 1970; Hougland, Shepard, and Wood, 1979; Hougland and Wood, 1980; Wood, 1975). However, this can sometimes create a dilemma for higher-level, full-time staff members of voluntary organizations, since they have more information and skills that are relevant to making core organizational decisions than most members do (Valcour, 2002).

Compliance is clearly not the only response to power, however. The recipient of exercised power has other options, such as withdrawing from the situation or attempting to persuade the power holder to act otherwise (Blau, 1964; Hirschman,

1972). Withdrawal can entail complete departure from an organization, or simply psychological disengagement—making only the barest efforts required to remain in the organization. Persuasion can entail direct discussion with the person who has issued an order, or it may involve "going over the boss's head," which is a risky move but certainly not infrequent. Another example of the latter response would be going to a department chair or college dean to appeal the acts of a professor. The power outcome of greatest interest, however, is conflict.

POWER OUTCOMES: CONFLICT

As will be discussed in Chapter 6, decision-making is a critical organizational process. Power is obviously important in decision-making. Conflict arises whenever individuals or groups perceive differences in their preferences involving decision outcomes, and they use power to try to promote their preferences over others' preferences. There is a strong tendency to view conflicts as necessarily harmful, or "bad" for organizations. Likewise, most people are at least initially inclined to interpret conflict as a problem of individuals, reflecting personality problems, personal rivalries, natural antagonisms, or some combination of these. However, research indicates that conflict can serve positive functions in organizations (Lawrence and Lorsch, 1967). Moreover, the propensity to attribute conflict to individual failings is called into question by the very pervasiveness and constancy of conflict in organizations (Sabel, 1982).

> [C]onflict is *always present* in organizations. Conflict may be personal, interpersonal, or between rival groups and coalitions. It may be built into organizational structures, roles, attitudes, and stereotypes, or arise over a scarcity of resources. It may be explicit or covert. Whatever the reason, or whatever the form it takes, its source rests in some perceived or real divergence of interests. (Morgan, 1986:155; emphasis added)

This pervasiveness suggests that organizational conflict is likely to have systemic rather than individual sources, and in more recent years, researchers have begun to focus on common organizational bases and forms of conflicts. As psychologist R. Nevitt Sanford (1964) states:

> Twenty years ago, it seemed easy to account for organizational conflict by blaming the problem behavior of individuals. But the simple formula, 'trouble is due to trouble-makers,' is unfortunately inadequate in the light of our present knowledge of the social process. (p. 95)

Bases of Conflict

Katz (1964) and others have identified several common bases of organizational conflict. One is "functional conflict induced by various subsystems within the organizations" (p. 105). This form of conflict stems from differentiation, as discussed in Chapter 2, which leads people and units to have different and often opposing interests. The study by Lawrence and Lorsch (1969), described in

Chapter 2, documented the way in which the specialization of organizational departments in different types of tasks led them to have different views of what key organizational problems were, different ideas about what kinds of solutions could best address those problems, even differing orientation toward time—whether to focus on long-term organizational objectives or short-term ones. When this kind of differentiation is coupled with interdependence—the need for different units to coordinate for workflows, decision-making, and so forth—it is likely to result in persistent conflict. This factor is key to explaining one common axis of conflict in many business organizations: between sales and production departments. Members of the sales department typically place very high priority on keeping customers happy and thus are apt to make promises for delivery of goods or for innovations that are difficult for the production department to meet. The production department places more emphasis on minimizing scrap (products that have problems and have to be discarded), and this makes increasing the rate of production and changing production processes to suit new innovations in product design very undesirable. Thus, the two departments have fundamentally different goals as a consequence of the different functions they serve in the organization.

A second basis of conflict suggested by Katz (1964) is the opposite of differentiation; it's overlapping of or similarity in the functions of two units—where two different groups or individuals in an organization have responsibility for handling the same set of tasks. Conflict here can take the form of "hostile rivalry or good-natured competition" (p. 106). For example, members of the human resource (HR) department and the legal department of an organization both have some responsibility for ensuring that the organization conforms to key labor laws; conflict sometimes arises between these areas because of the overlap in responsibility. Such competition can be beneficial, but it can also be destructive. This kind of conflict was reflected in Dalton's (1959) observations of staff–line relations in manufacturing organizations. The staff, trained in engineering and other areas related to production processes, was supposed to provide advice and support to line personnel, to help improve production processes. However, the line managers were concerned that accepting the staff's input would make them seem incompetent or unimaginative, unable to handle the production processes in their charge. The outcome of this competition was a series of conflicts between line and staff that, viewed from outside the organization, were costly to it. This conflict resulted in relatively high levels of turnover among staff personnel, who were frustrated by the line's lack of attention to their recommendations. It also encouraged the staff to moderate proposals for changes, to overlook line practices that didn't conform to technical standards, and generally to be subservient to the line, all of which reduced the effectiveness of the staff. Dalton's study of staff–line relations provides an example of one form of conflict that can take place in organizations that have professional employees.

A third basis of conflict that Katz (1964) made note of is "hierarchical conflict stemming from interest-group struggles over the organizational rewards of status, prestige, and monetary reward" (p. 106). In thinking about this aspect of conflict, it is important to keep in mind that organizations are the means by which societal resources are distributed among social groups (Baron, 1984; Hall, 1994). In allocating people to different positions, and defining the extrinsic rewards attached to these positions, organizations play a key role in reproducing or changing social inequality. Employing organizations affect inequality not only directly, via their hiring, promotion, and compensation practices, but indirectly as well, since parents' employment experiences are a major determinant of the educational attainment of their children. Thus, it is not very surprising that lower-level personnel "try to improve their lot by joining forces as an interest group against the more privileged members of the organization" (Katz, 1964:106).

Although one typically thinks of blue-collar workers and unions in this regard, such conflict can also involve white-collar workers and subgroups in the management hierarchy. In the latter case, workers may use lawsuits and public relations pressures in conflicts that are defined in terms of equity issues, involving the distribution of rewards, or equality issues, involving the allocation of people to different organizational statuses (Kabanoff, 1991). Equity issues have been the focus of various lawsuits and protest actions involving comparable worth, or ensuring that female-dominated jobs that require levels of skills, training, and effort similar to those of male-dominated jobs are similarly compensated. This inequity is a common, much-debated issue for organizational policy (Boraas and Rodgers, 2003; England, 1992). Another organizational policy addressing issues of equality, affirmative action, has also been the source of much recent conflict in contemporary organizations; affirmative action claims are brought by women and minorities when they believe that they have been denied access to positions based on their gender or race (Reskin, 1998).

Since these three key bases of conflict—differentiation, duplication of functions, and hierarchy—are more or less inevitable features of modern organizational life, the potential for conflict is inherent in all organizations. This does not mean, however, that conflict will necessarily take place. In order for conflict to occur, the parties involved must perceive that they are in a position to influence each other in some way (Kochan, Huber, and Cummings, 1975; Schmidt and Kochan, 1972). Otherwise, organizational members may just "work around" problems, without engaging in sustained opposition or efforts to change existing arrangements.

Professional–Organizational Relationships

One of the bases of conflict in organizations, as noted above, is overlapping functions. Often, this entails a problem of ambiguity in authority; it is not absolutely clear who has the "right" to make organizational decisions in a given case. This is a classic problem in organizations whose members are professionals, that is, who belong to occupational groups that society recognizes as having specific knowledge and skills necessary for handling certain tasks or dealing with certain problems (Abbott, 1988). We have talked a little about how organizations with many employees who are professionals often differ from other organizations (Chapters 2 and 3); here, we will discuss in more detail *why* these differences occur.

In organizations with professionals, there are two, potentially competing bases of authority. Freidson (1994) discusses these different types of authority in terms of the difference between the occupational principle and the administrative principle (see also Parsons, 1960). Both principles are consistent with the logic of rational–legal authority, that is, with the belief that individuals who have relevant knowledge and skills for handling problems in particular areas are best able to choose the appropriate means for achieving given ends and therefore have the "right" to give orders in these areas (Satow, 1975). According to the administrative principle, however, authority is tied to the official, hierarchical position a person holds. This principle is based on the assumption that people are allocated to different hierarchical levels because of their organizational knowledge and expertise. Thus, people at higher hierarchical levels are expected to have more knowledge of the operating processes and requirements of an organization and therefore to be better able than people at lower hierarchical levels to make effective decisions. According to the occupational principle, on the other hand, authority derives from occupationally based, specialized knowledge that an individual possesses that is deemed to be relevant and necessary for managing some set of tasks or problems. People with such occupation-specific knowledge are expected to be better able than those lacking such knowledge to make effective decisions.

The administrative and occupational principles, then, point to two very different types of knowledge and skills, both of which may be relevant to rational decision-making in organizations, but which may lead to different conclusions about preferred actions (Freidson, 2001; Tolbert, 2004). Ambiguity about which principle should dominate can lead to enduring and sometimes dramatic conflict within organizations with professional members. For example, one of the most visible instances of changing power relationships between professionals and their employing organizations can be seen in analyses of health maintenance organizations (HMOs). HMOs attempt to control costs, sometimes by limiting referrals to other physicians, limiting the length of hospital stays, and placing other restrictions that infringe on physicians' decision-making. When a physician believes that a patient needs more care than the HMO permits, the likelihood of conflict erupting is evident (Hoff, 1998; Hoff and McCaffrey, 1996).

Such conflict is difficult to manage, but it is not inevitable. Its occurrence depends in part on the degree to which the knowledge base of the professional is apt to lead to decisions that are inconsistent with those of management. For some professions, such as accounting and engineering, there is a very close alignment in professional and organizational points of view (Barley, 2004), and conflict is less apt to be a problem. In other instances, organizations may avoid such conflict by allowing professionals to control themselves, to a large degree, with a fellow professional held accountable for the work of that unit (e.g., a research administrator). This mode allows professionals to work in a situation where there is less direct administrative scrutiny of their day-to-day decision-making but provides the organization with a system of accountability. The reward system in organizations with such arrangements is even altered sometimes to reflect recognition of the importance of using professional criteria in decision-making. Instead of promoting professionals by moving them into higher positions in the administrative system, organizations develop "dual ladders" for their promotion system, whereby professionals can advance either by being promoted into purely managerial positions or by staying in their technical position unit but at increasingly higher salaries, based on recognition of their achievements by the larger profession (Hall, 1968). A more extreme version of this approach, perhaps, is represented by the increasing use of professionals as independent contractors in many contemporary organizations. Some research suggests that working as an independent contractor can provide professionals with a sense of freedom that they do not have traditional employment relations and thus alleviate some of the conflict associated with such arrangements. The degree to which contractors experience such freedom depends, however, on the labor market; when it is tight, and jobs are plentiful, they can easily move across employing organizations if they have problems with one employer (Kunda, Barley, and Evans, 2002).

Not all organizational conflicts involving professionals stem from the question of whether to follow administrative or occupational principles in a given decision-making situation. Conflict can also grow out of the presence of a number of different professional groups in organizations (Barley, 1985). Members of different professions are apt to take differing views on what is good, rational, legal, or effective for the organization. This can happen even in situations of professional dominance, where a clear status hierarchy exists among professional groups, such as physicians, nurses, and nurses' aides (Freidson, 2006). It is even more likely in multidisciplinary partnerships (MDPs), formed from the merger of two or more firms, each composed of the members of one profession, such as the merger of a law firm and an accounting firm (Cooper et al., 1996). Although these are new forms of organizations and little is known about how they actually function, one may surmise that when the perspectives of accountants, lawyers, research scientists, management consultants, and executives are combined, it is extremely unlikely that a common viewpoint will emerge even after serious discussions. Rather, each set of professionals is apt to vie with the others to make their point of view dominant (Hage, 1980).

This discussion has emphasized ways in which conflicts involving professionals and organizations may be resolved. But obviously, in many cases the issues are not resolved, and professional–organizational relations remain an important element of conflict in many organizations.

THE COMPONENTS OF CONFLICT SITUATIONS

We have been looking at the bases of conflict situations and the parties engaged in them. We now examine the conflict situation itself and then turn to the outcomes of conflict. There are four components of the conflict process (Boulding, 1964). The first is the parties involved. Conflict must involve at least two parties—individuals, groups, or organizations. Hypothetically, therefore, there can be nine types of conflict—person–person, person–group, and so on. Boulding suggests that there is a tendency toward symmetry in these relationships, such that person–organizational or group–organizational conflict tends to move toward organizational–organizational conflict. This is based on the power differentials that are likely to exist between these different levels in the organization.

The next component in this framework is the field of conflict, defined as "the whole set of relevant possible states of the social system" (p. 138). What Boulding is referring to here are the alternative outcomes toward which a conflict could move. Thus, the field of conflict includes a continuation of the present state and all the alternative conditions (e.g., both parties gain or both lose power, one gains at the expense of the other). This concept highlights conflict as a process, in that the parties in the situation will seldom have the same position in relation to each other after the conflict is resolved or continued.

The third component is the dynamics of the conflict situation. This refers to the perceptions that the parties have of each other, and the responses that they make to the other on this basis. That is, each party in a conflict will adjust its position to one that it feels is congruent with that of its opponent. If one of the parties becomes more militant, the other will probably do the same. This assumes, of course, that the power available to the two parties is at least moderately comparable. An interesting aspect of the dynamics of conflict is that conflict can "move around" in an organization (Smith, 1989). Parties in a conflict can "take it out on others" as they engage in their conflict.

The field of conflict can thus expand or contract as the dynamics of the conflict situation unfold. The conflict can move around, allies can be sought or bought, and coalitions can be formed. An example of these dynamics can be found in international relations, where national governments intensify their own conflict efforts in anticipation of or reaction to their opponents' moves. This can escalate into all-out war and eventual destruction, or it can stabilize at some point along the way, but the conflict will seldom be limited in its scope to the parties involved. The same phenomenon occurs in business organizations, with the equivalent of all-out war in labor–management conflicts that end in the dissolution of the company involved. The dynamic nature of conflict can also be seen in the fact that there is an increase and decrease in the intensity of a conflict during its course. Although the field of conflict may remain the same, the energies devoted to it vary over time.

The final element in Boulding's model is "the management, control, or resolution of conflict" (p. 142). The terms used suggest that conflict situations are generally not discrete situations with a clear beginning and a clear end. They obviously emerge from preexisting situations and often continue to simmer, even if there is a temporary cessation in overt conflict activities. Boulding notes that organizations attempt to prevent conflict from becoming "pathological" and thus destructive of the parties involved and the larger system. One form of conflict resolution is a unilateral move; according to Boulding, a good deal of conflict is resolved through the relatively simple mechanism of the "peaceableness" of one of the participants. Although it relates primarily to interpersonal conflict, this idea can be utilized in the organizational setting. Peaceableness simply involves one of the parties backing off or withdrawing from the conflict. In most cases, the other party reacts by also backing off, even if it would prefer to continue, and the conflict is at least temporarily resolved. This kind of resolution is seen in labor–management disputes when one of the parties finally decides to concede on some points that were formerly "nonnegotiable."

Relying on some or all parties to make concessions is potentially dangerous, however, because the parties may not exhibit this kind of behavior. For the peaceable party itself, the strategy is hazardous if the opponent is operating pathologically or irrationally to any degree. For that reason, organizations develop mechanisms to resolve or control conflict. One technique is to placate the parties involved by offering them some form of "side payment" as an inducement to stop the conflict. For example, in professional–organizational conflict, the professionals may be given concessions in the form of relaxing some organizational rules they believe to be excessively burdensome.

Conflicts in organizations can also be resolved through the offices of a third party. The third party may be a larger organization that simply orders the conflict behavior to cease under the threat of penalties (as when the government prohibits strikes and lockouts in a labor dispute that threatens the national interest), or it may be a mediator. Since intraorganizational conflict takes place within a larger context, the organization can simply prohibit the conflicting behavior. This does not resolve the issues, but it reduces the intensity of the conflict behavior. Mediation can do the same and can even lead to a complete resolution of the conflict by presenting new methods of solution that may not have occurred to the parties involved or by presenting a solution that would not be acceptable unless it were presented by a third party.

THE OUTCOMES OF CONFLICT

The resolution of a conflict leads to a stage that is known as the aftermath (Pondy, 1967, 1969). This is a useful concept because conflict resolution does not lead to a condition of total settlement. If the basic issues are not resolved, the potential for future, and perhaps more serious, conflicts is part of the aftermath. If the conflict resolution leads to more open communications and cooperation among the participants, that, too, is part of the aftermath (Coser, 1956, 1967). Since an organization does not operate in a vacuum, any successful conflict resolution in which the former combatants are now close allies is not guaranteed to last forever. Changes in the environment and altered conditions in the organization can lead to new conflict situations among the same parties or with others.

Conflict is not inherently good or bad for the participants, the organization, or the wider society. Power and conflict are major shapers of the state of an organization. A given organizational state sets the stage for the continuing power and conflict processes, thus continually reshaping the organization. In this way, conflict plays an important role in the development of variations between organizations. This may contribute to or detract from their survival (Aldrich, 1979).

Any analysis of conflict would be incomplete without noting that conflict can be viewed as a means by which organizational management can manipulate situations to its advantage (Rahim, 1986, 1989). As with any management tool, the morality of using conflict in this manner is in the eye of the beholder and the activities of the managers and the managed.

SUMMARY AND CONCLUSIONS

This chapter has attempted to identify and trace the sources and the outcomes of power in organizations. Common sense suggests that the forms and distribution of power critically affect the operations of any organization and that the lives and behavior of organizational members are vitally affected by their relative power positions. In our analysis, we noted that power involves reciprocal relationships between two or more actors. These relationships can be specified in advance, as lines of authority usually are, or can develop over time, as a result of the acquisition and use of resources by groups and individuals. This point reemphasizes the close connection between organizational structure and processes, since it is the structure that defines the relationship between individuals and subunits initially, and that can determine who has access to certain resources. Studies of power in organizations reiterate the dominant theme of this book—that organizational structure and processes are in constant and reciprocal interaction. Power relationships develop out of and then alter existing structural arrangements.

We discussed authority as a prominent aspect of power in organizations, and the nature of rational–legal authority as a type that characterizes most modern organizations. Authority involves vertical (or hierarchical) relations, but other kinds of power often operate along the lateral or horizontal axis in organizations. Whereas authority rests on social definitions and understandings of who has the legitimate right to give orders and make decisions, other types of power rest on dependencies between actors—the need or desire of one actor for resources that are controlled by another. Such resources can take a variety of forms—people, information (including expertise and knowledge), equipment, and even social or psychological outcomes that people value, such as friendship, status, and sense of belonging. We considered some of the factors that affect people's access to such resources, ranging from the job responsibilities that are associated with a formal position or office, to network connections, to individual characteristics. We noted that the control of resources, in and of itself, is not sufficient to provide individuals or groups with power; rather, power depends on how highly others value the resources or view them as important, whether the resources are scarce or can easily be obtained from other sources, and whether other things can be substituted for a given resource.

If all these conditions are met, an actor controlling resources is likely to be able to get others to do what she or he wishes—but not necessarily in perpetuity. Although there are a number of factors that contribute to the stability of power relations, such as power holders' active efforts to protect their power and systems of resource allocation that typically favor power holders, changes in the environment and/or changes in social definitions of the value of certain resources can lead to shifts in the amount and distribution of power in organizations over time. Thus, a full understanding of power relations requires close attention to the social processes through which resources are defined as valuable and scarce, and authority for various decisions is assigned to particular people and positions.

Compliance is one outcome of the exercise of power, perhaps the least spectacular but probably the most common. The way in which compliance is secured, however, has important consequences for the manner in which individuals attach themselves to organizations and for the more general issue of organizational effectiveness. If inappropriate power forms are used, the organization is likely to be less effective than it might otherwise be. We focused on one particular type of compliance suggested by Etzioni's scheme, moral involvement, and its important role in voluntary organizations.

Conflict is a much more spectacular, and hence often more interesting, outcome of the exercise of power. Although compliance is probably the most common response to power, conflict—the mobilization of resources to resist attempts to exercise power—is far from unusual and thus is reasonably viewed as a normal state of an organization. We discussed many different types of conflicts that commonly occur in organizations, reflecting different bases (differentiation, overlapping functions or responsibilities, and hierarchical relations). One of the most frequently studied types of conflicts in organizations involves relations between professionals and their nonprofessional, hierarchical superiors. This can be seen as a special case of overlapping functions, fundamentally because of the ambiguity in relative authority of managers and professionals. As organizations rely more and more on workers with socially legitimated expertise (sometimes referred to as "knowledge workers"), this is apt to be an increasingly important issue for both researchers and practitioners.

Although there is a tendency to view conflict as "bad," its prevalence in organizations makes this conclusion rather dubious: conflict can yield both positive and negative outcomes for individuals and for organizations. On the one hand, interdepartmental conflict can enhance organizational performance in some situations (Lawrence and Lorsch, 1967). It can also enhance individual performance as attention is focused and more energy is used. As noted in the preceding section, some writers such as Rahim (1986, 1989) see conflict management as a sound management tool.

Unfortunately, there is a darker side to all of this. As Clarke (1989) notes:

> With unabashed commitment to the goals of negotiation, out-of-court settlements of enormous variety, and the powers of information, flexibility, and limited liability . . . risk and conflict management have become enablers of the transformation of many organizational actions from rule-guided competition to a more adventuresome conflict posture. The spirit of deregulation, the calls for improved organizational productivity, and the corporate drive to become "lean and mean," the frantic search for excellence and improved ratings all may be feeding the fires of organizational conflict at the expense of the rules of competition. (p. 154)

Like conflict, conflict management can get out of hand. Conflict becomes a tool by which the powerful can manipulate situations to the detriment of the less powerful, even without their cognizance of being manipulated. To make matters even worse, the civility with which conflict management was accomplished until recently has disappeared. Now, with restructuring and hostile takeovers, honor and dignity have been replaced by a bottom-line mentality that can take the form of vengeance (Morrill, 1991).

Power and its outcomes are central organizational processes. They can contribute to and detract from organizational effectiveness. In the next chapter, we turn to another organizational process—leadership—which also has a relationship to effectiveness, but as we will see, the relationship is much more problematic than is commonly believed.

EXERCISES

1. Describe two resources that provide people with power (not authority) in your two organizations. What allows them to control these resources?
2. Describe three instances of the exercise of power in your organizations, and discuss the outcomes in terms of compliance and conflict.

Chapter 5

Leadership

OVERVIEW

Leadership in organizations is a popular topic. In this chapter, we consider leadership as just one component in understanding organizations. We begin (and conclude) by noting that leadership is not the easy answer for all that is good or bad in organizations. The first step is to define leadership and consider its functions. Next, we review efforts to define what qualities or conditions determine who is apt to be defined as a leader. We then consider some of the outcomes of leadership. The difference between leadership at the top of organizations and leadership at other levels is an important consideration in evaluating the impact of leadership. Studies of top leadership succession or change are analyzed to help determine the importance of leadership. Finally, leadership in voluntary organizations is considered. Here, leadership can play an important role but may require different skills and abilities than leadership in traditional work organizations.

Probably more has been written and spoken about leadership than about any other topic considered in this book. Whether the concern is with a local school district, a business corporation, an athletic team, or the nation, there seems to be a persistent assumption that new leadership can produce dramatic changes in the organization. Anyone who follows sports is aware of the air of expectation surrounding the appointment of a new coach or manager. With extensive inputs from many different parties, blue-ribbon committees select university presidents, and all members of the search committee are acutely conscious of the potential importance of the outcome. The impact on an organization of the appointment of a new chief executive officer at a large corporation is often the subject of lengthy speculation and analysis for several weeks by the business press.

The phenomenal changes in Eastern Europe and South Africa in 1989 and 1990, respectively, were frequently viewed from the perspective of leadership. Interestingly, from the point of view of this analysis, the changes were attributed not only to leadership but also to sweeping historical events. Those sweeping historical events are labeled environmental changes in this analysis. We'll discuss some of the problems of disentangling the effects of leadership and environmental change on organizations later in this chapter.

At election time in labor unions and other political organizations, the assumption is always made that the reelection of the old or the election of new leaders will make an important difference in the continuing operation of the organizations. In short, leadership would seem to be the crucial concept in understanding organizations.

The perspective presented in this chapter is quite different. The research and theory examined indicate that leadership is heavily constrained by many of the factors discussed in previous chapters: organizational structure, power coalitions, and environmental conditions. This is not an "antileadership" position. Rather, it is an examination of leadership in the contexts in which leadership takes place.

WHAT IS LEADERSHIP?

Part of the general fascination with leadership probably is due to the belief that leadership is an easy solution to whatever problems are ailing an organization. Of course, it takes only a little thought to realize that changing the leadership will not necessarily enable an organization to change inappropriate structural arrangements, power distributions that block effective actions, lack of resources, archaic procedures, and other, more basic organizational problems. Despite these common constraints on leaders, leadership is a topic that continues to capture the imagination of people from all walks of life, including academic scholars. As Gary Yukl (2002) notes:

> Leadership is a subject that has long excited interest among people. The term connotes images of powerful, dynamic individuals who command victorious armies, direct corporate empires from atop gleaming skyscrapers, or shape the course of nations. The exploits of brave and clever leaders are the essence of many legends and myths. Much of our description of history is the story of military, political, religious, and social leaders who are credited or blamed for important historical events, even though we do not understand very well how the events were caused or how much influence the leader really had. The widespread fascination with leadership may be because it is such a mysterious process, as well as one that touches everyone's life. (p. 1)

What is leadership? Leadership is a special form of power, one that involves

> the ability, based on the personal qualities of the leader, to elicit the followers' voluntary compliance in a broad range of matters. Leadership is distinguished from the concept of power in that it entails influence, that is, change of preferences, while power implies only that subjects' preferences are held in abeyance." (Etzioni, 1965:690–691)

For our purposes, Etzioni's general definition is a useful one. That followers do in fact alter their preferences to coincide with those of the leader is an important consideration. Leadership entails motivating followers to achieve the outcomes that the leader seeks, and effectively, this requires them to adopt preferences for those outcomes. Katz and Kahn (1978) follow this same line of reasoning when they note: "We consider the essence of organizational leadership to be the influential increment over and above mechanical compliance with the routine directions of the organization" (p. 528). Thus, leadership involves more than simply the normal exercise of authority that is based on a position in the organization or claimed by a member or members of organizations because of the formal requirements of their jobs. It often involves attributions of particular traits and abilities to people by their followers (Meindl, Ehrlich, and Dukerich, 1985).

Functions of Leadership

What do leaders do? Over the years, a variety of efforts to catalog the main tasks and functions of leaders have been made (Borman and Brush, 1993). The list by Yukl, Wall, and Lepsinger (1990), which identifies fourteen separate functions, is one of the most comprehensive. These functions include: planning and organizing, problem solving, clarifying, informing, monitoring, motivating, consulting, recognizing, supporting, managing conflict and team building, networking, delegating, developing and mentoring, and rewarding. Although it may be the case that all leaders must carry out these tasks to some extent, their relative importance for the leadership role is apt to depend on a given leader's hierarchical position in an organization, a point that is sometimes recognized in principle but too often neglected by researchers involved in empirical research on leadership.

As indicated above, leadership is not confined to any particular group or any level within an organization and, at least in theory, does not necessarily involve formal authority. Nonetheless, the vast majority of studies of leadership have focused on persons who have been assigned "a leadership position," that is, who have some authority by virtue of their position. Many of the early leadership studies were concerned, in particular, with first-line supervisors—lower-level military officers, manufacturing foremen, and so forth. This is worth noting because the hierarchical level occupied by a person and, especially, whether a person *has* formal authority or not are apt to be importantly related to the kinds of responsibilities and tasks that are required of him or her as leader.

For example, Selznick (1957) specified four major functions of formal leaders. The first is to define the institutional (organizational) mission and role. This is not a one-time issue but must be viewed as a dynamic process, because the mission must evolve as the world changes. The second task entails the "institutional embodiment of purpose," which involves choosing the means to achieve the ends desired, or ensuring that the structure reflects and is designed to accomplish the mission effectively. The third task is to defend the organization's integrity. Here, values and public relations intermix: leaders must secure support for the organization from both the public and their own members, without allowing either external or internal constituents to fundamentally reshape the organization's mission. Both constituencies must be persuaded of the value of the organization's defined mission. The final leadership task is the ordering of internal conflict. Clearly, these functions are very relevant to leaders at the highest level of an organization.

On the other hand, they are generally much less relevant to the jobs of lower-level managers and supervisors. At this level, the functions of transmitting information, clarifying job expectations, and monitoring individuals' behavior to ensure that it is in compliance with formal structure are likely to be more critical aspects of leadership. Thus, actions that might contribute to effective leadership at one level may be much less appropriate or useful at another level. Leadership at the top level in the organization is likely to have the greatest impact on the organization, at least in the long run, but involves behaviors and actions very different from those taken by leaders in the first-line supervisory position.

As noted, the impact of differences in the organizational level or position a leader occupies has not always been given close attention in research and theories of leadership. This is an important caveat to keep in mind when considering different theories and interpreting findings of various studies that we describe below.

Components of Leadership

Trying to sort through and distill the main findings from the profusion of research on what determines who becomes defined as a leader is a daunting task. We start with the observation that there are three general types of factors that have been the focus of researchers' attention: (1) more or less permanent characteristics of individuals, (2) behaviors and styles that individuals may exhibit (that are, presumably, more subject to conscious alteration by individuals), and (3) characteristics of followers and/or particular situations. Most contemporary theories suggest that leadership is a complex mix of all of these three factors (Yukl, 2002), but for ease of presentation we will begin by considering them separately.

Individual Characteristics. The ideas expressed thus far have implied strongly that individual characteristics are crucial for the leadership role. This notion can easily lead to the conclusion that leadership is an innate quality of individuals, that some people are just "born leaders," while others are not. Indeed, much of the earliest work on leadership was characterized by this notion, and researchers following this tradition spent many years trying to identify the key leadership traits.

However, this effort was largely abandoned by the 1950s because no limited set of common leadership traits could be consistently identified (Gouldner, 1950). A huge set of traits were examined by different researchers, ranging from physical characteristics (e.g., height) to cognitive characteristics (e.g., intelligence) to social psychological characteristics (e.g., extraversion). But studies produced mixed and ambiguous results, and overall, the findings raised serious questions about whether any particular individual characteristics could be found that clearly distinguished leaders from followers.

Within the past decade or so, however, there has been some revival of interest in the link between personality traits and leadership. This revival has been sparked, in part, by focused attention by psychologists on what are referred to as "the big five" personality characteristics:

1. "Surgency" (or extraversion)
2. Conscientiousness
3. Emotional stability
4. Agreeableness or cooperativeness
5. Intellect (Digman, 1990).

Personality theorists argue that these five dimensions capture critical aspects of personality (more or less permanent psychological orientations of individuals) that importantly distinguish among individuals in terms of behavior. On the basis of Stogdill's (1974) review of previous work on personality and leadership, Hogan, Curphy, and Hogan (1994) claim that leaders are distinguished by higher levels of extraversion, conscientiousness, emotional stability, agreeableness, and intellect. They argue that studies of emergent leaders, in particular, suggest the importance of such characteristics in distinguishing leaders from followers. "Emergent leaders" are individuals who are identified as leaders by members of groups in which no one was formally appointed to be leader ("leaderless groups"). It may be that individual characteristics play a more important role in influencing perceptions of leadership when individuals lack formal positions of authority than when they have such authority.

Leader Behavior and Styles.   Researchers' discouragement with trait approaches to leadership led to increased attention to particular kinds of *behaviors* that might characterize leaders. A number of early studies with this focus provided evidence that leadership often involved two very different types of behaviors: one emphasizing the accomplishment of specific tasks and the other emphasizing expressive activities and interpersonal relations. This distinction was confirmed by both laboratory studies (Bales, 1953; Bales and Slater, 1955) and field studies, including two sets of well-known leadership studies conducted at Ohio State University and University of Michigan in the late 1940s. Slightly different terms for these two types of behaviors were used by different researchers. In the Ohio State University research, for example, task-oriented behaviors were referred to as "initiating structure," while the University of Michigan researchers referred to them as "production oriented." Behavior focused on maintaining good interpersonal relations among group members was labeled "consideration" by the Ohio State University group and "employee oriented" by the University of Michigan group.

This distinction provided the basis for a number of theorizing efforts. For example, Etzioni (1965) developed a "dual leadership" approach to organizations, suggesting that, because a task orientation was apt to conflict with an interpersonal orientation, in most cases leadership will rest in the hands of more than one person. He also argued that organizational demands determine which behaviors are most important to effective leadership, with interpersonally oriented behavior more critical in normative organizations, those in which members are motivated primarily by moral or non-tangible rewards, and task-oriented behavior in instrumental organizations, those in which members are motivated largely by financial or other material rewards. On the other hand, others argued that it is possible for leaders to exhibit both types of behavior and that this combined orientation is necessary for truly effective leadership (Blake and Mouton, 1964).

Other lines of work further elaborated on behavioral aspects of leadership by focusing specifically on decision-making behavior, or leadership style. For example, Vroom and Yetton (1973) identified four styles of decision-making:

1. Authoritarian (or autocratic)
2. Consultative
3. Delegative
4. Group-based (or participative)

The first, as it sounds, involves making decisions independently, without seeking input from the group; consultative decision-making entails gathering information and suggestions from group members and then making an independent decision; delegative involves providing relevant information and decision criteria to one or more group members and then allowing them to make decisions; and participative entails involving the group in formulating a problem and possible solutions, as well as in selecting among those options. This typology of decision-making styles is similar to that proposed by House (1971), who also identified four types of leaders based on their decision-making styles. Both approaches assume that a given individual is capable of exercising different styles of leadership, and each suggests particular conditions under which a given style is most effective for leaders.

It is important to reiterate that leadership at the top of an organization is vastly different from leadership at the first-line supervisory level and that different behaviors and decision styles may be more or less appropriate to a given level. For example, the distinction between task-oriented and interpersonally oriented behaviors is most applicable at the first-line supervisory level and is less relevant at top levels because the people at such levels do not engage as much in direct supervisory behavior. By the same token, the use of a delegative or partici- pative style by first-line supervisors is likely to be severely limited by the defi- nitions of their responsibilities. And which kinds of behaviors and styles are more likely to enhance the leadership of individuals who lack formal authority remains to be studied.

Follower/Situational Characteristics.   The recognition that the impor- tance of particular behaviors for being a leader may depend on particular situa- tions that a group or organization is facing led to a number of studies focusing on the conditions that affect leadership. Such work rests on the assumption that in one situation, an individual who exhibits certain behaviors and styles is more likely to be accepted as a leader, whereas in other situations, different individuals, exhibiting different behaviors and styles, are more likely to be accepted as leaders. This focus on situational factors is characteristic of a sociological approach to leadership. Situational approaches draw attention not only to the characteristics of the group and the environment in determining who is defined as a leader, but to the nature of interactions between leader and followers as well. The leader influences the behaviors of followers, of course, but their reactions, in turn, have an impact on the leader's behavior (Hollander and Julian, 1969). Maintaining a leadership role requires the leader to behave in such a way that the expectations of the followers are fulfilled or to modify those expectations in some way.

One situational characteristic that has been suggested as an important determinant of leadership is the degree to which tasks are structured, that is, whether there is consensus within the group about the best way to handle prob- lems and accomplish their work. The importance of this factor has been high- lighted in work by a variety of researchers, including Fiedler (1967), House (1971), Vroom and Yetton (1973), and others. These studies suggest that individ- uals who are more task oriented and use more directive decision-making approaches are more likely to be accepted as leaders when the tasks and prob- lems are highly structured. Interestingly, there is also some indication that this leadership style is also effective under the exact opposite conditions: when tasks and problems are not at all well defined, task oriented, less-participative styles may be more accepted by followers as well (House, 1971).

Other work suggests that intergroup relations—for example, the degree of consensus among members on a given goal and the extent to which conflict is likely—are an important determinant of leadership. When consensus is low and the likelihood of conflict is high, individuals with more-participative decision styles (and presumably, a greater orientation to interpersonal relations) are more likely to be accepted as leaders (Vroom and Yetton, 1973).

One interesting determinant of leadership that has begun to be explored rel- atively recently emphasizes social expectations. Work by sociologists has demon- strated that individuals' perceptions and evaluations of others' behavior are shaped by the expectations those individuals hold initially. These initial expectations, in turn, are based on the others' observable status characteristics—sex, race, age, and so forth. As members of society, we acquire social definitions of those characteristics; for example, we expect men to act in certain ways and to have certain traits, and women to act in different ways and to have different traits. These definitions and expectations, then, shape our perceptions of and reactions to others and can affect whom we see as leaders (Berger et al., 1986). Similar ideas have been expressed by psychologists as implicit theories of leadership (e.g., Lord, DeVader, and Alliger, 1986). The importance of such expectations, or implicit theories, is indicated by many studies of the impact of gender on leadership and, more recently, by some cross-cultural studies of leadership as well.

The limited number of women in high-level leadership positions in organizations strongly suggests that gender affects individuals' ability to assume leadership roles. By the late 1990s, approximately 5 percent of the countries in the world were led by a woman (Adler, 1996), and the number of women at the helms of major corporations in the United States was slightly less—around 3 percent (Ragins, Townsend, and Mattis, 1998). One explanation for such low levels of women's representation in leadership positions is that, according to general social expectations, leaders will be men (Walker et al., 1996). In a classic study by Schein (1973), when individuals were asked to choose adjectives describing "good managers," they chose many of the same words that others had chosen to describe "typical men"; there was very little overlap in the adjectives chosen to describe "typical women" and "good managers." Similar results have been documented in a variety of other studies since this original research (see Carli and Eagly, 1999, for a review). Thus, there is considerable evidence that social expectations make it more likely that men will be assigned leadership roles and make it easier for men to play these roles.

However, as a caveat to this general conclusion, it should be noted that some work suggests that women are more likely to emerge as leaders when group tasks require relatively complex social interaction and sharing of ideas and information (Eagly and Karau, 1991); this finding is consistent with the common expectation that women will demonstrate stronger skills in managing interpersonal relations. Moreover, a study by Filardo (1996) comparing patterns of interaction in mixed-sex groups of African Americans and European Americans found that the propensity of men to assume leadership roles held only for the latter; among African Americans, men and women did not differ in the behaviors that are usually identified with leadership. This finding of subcultural differences within the United States is consistent with international, comparative studies of leadership indicating that *which* characteristics and behaviors are identified with leadership depends on culturally learned values and understandings (e.g., Fu and Yukl, 2000).

As this partial review of leadership research suggests, a very wide range of possible determinants of leadership have been studied. Most current researchers believe that, in practice, individual, behavioral, and situational factors interact to affect definitions of leadership. Figure 5–1, from work by Yukl (1981), provides an idea of the types and range of factors that have been investigated or theorized to affect leadership, as well as leadership outcomes, such as group performance

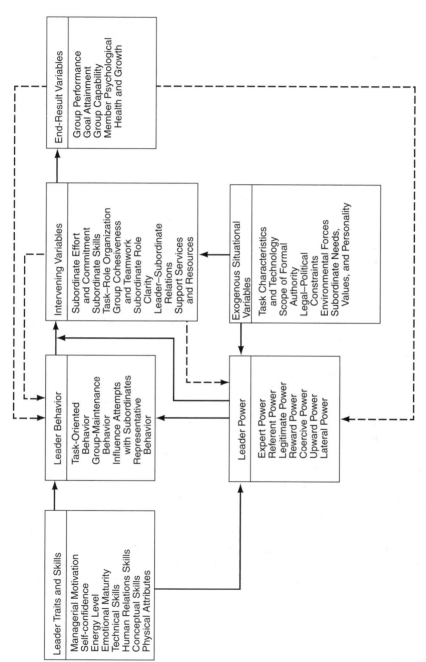

FIGURE 5–1 Leadership Variables

Source: Gary A. Yukl, *Leadership in Organizations* (Upper Saddle River, NJ: Prentice Hall, 1981), p. 270. Copyright © 1981. Electronically reproduced by permission of Pearson Education, Inc., Upper Saddle River, NJ 07458.

and organizational goal attainment (effectiveness in this conceptualization). It is to these latter outcome variables that we now turn.

THE OUTCOMES OF LEADERSHIP FOR ORGANIZATIONS

Many different variables have been examined as outcomes of variations in leadership approaches, but by and large, they reflect two main concerns, as suggested in Yukl's model: (1) group morale and satisfaction and (2) performance/productivity. The focus on these outcomes again reflects the emphasis of much of the research on first-line supervisors. They are much better suited to assessments of leadership in small groups than to leadership of large, complex organizations. However, there is literature that may address issues of top-level leadership outcomes—studies of leadership turnover, or executive succession. Below, we will consider work on group-level outcomes as well as leader turnover.

Satisfaction and Productivity

In general, research suggests that leaders who are more interpersonally oriented and those who use more-participative styles in particular have followers with higher levels of satisfaction and morale. For example, Filley and House (1969), reviewing several studies, found supportive and participative leadership to be commonly related to several indicators of subordinate satisfaction and productivity, including less intragroup stress and more cooperation, lower turnover and grievance rates, and widespread views of the leader as desirable.

The evidence here is confounded, unfortunately, by the possibility that the workers themselves may contribute to their greater satisfaction and productivity by their attitudes and behavior, independent of those of the leader. They may be high-producing, positively oriented employees who do not require close supervision and direction; their abilities and attitudes permit their supervisors to engage in more-participative behaviors, but their attitudes are a cause, not a consequence, of the supervisors' participation. Despite this possibility, most research has taken evidence of a relation between supportive leadership and positive work attitudes among subordinates as indicating the beneficial effects of such leader behaviors.

The impact of leadership approaches on productivity issue is not as clear. Filley and House's (1969) review indicated that the majority of research showed a positive relation between participative leadership and productivity, though others raise questions about this finding. For example, Hamner and Organ (1973), based on their review of a different number of studies, noted:

> Generally speaking, we find that participative leadership is associated with greater satisfaction on the part of subordinates than is nonparticipative leadership, or, at worst, that participation does not lower satisfaction. We cannot summarize so easily the findings with respect to productivity. Some studies find participative groups

to be more productive, some find nonparticipative groups to be more effective, and quite a few studied show no appreciable differences in productivity between autocratically versus democratically managed work groups. (pp. 396–397)

Again, issues of causality can be raised: Does higher productivity among subordinates result in leaders' relaxation of close supervision and direction? Or does participative leadership lead to higher productivity? It is well established in the literature that there is no direct relationship between employee satisfaction and productivity. Thus, in considering leadership outcomes, one obvious question here is, What does the organization want? Another obvious question is, What do the workers want? If satisfied employees are desired, then the supportive approach has clearly been shown to be more effective. But what if the managers want high productivity and the workers want a satisfying work environment? Short-run output gains may well be more easily achieved under an autocratic system, but this may lessen worker satisfaction and lower morale. To complicate matters further, there is evidence that when workers expect to be supervised in an autocratic style, supportive supervision can be counterproductive and threatening to satisfaction. The complexity of leadership choices is also pointed up by Fiedler's studies of the leadership process (Fiedler, 1967, 1972; Fiedler and Chemers, 1982; Fiedler and Garcia, 1987). Fiedler and colleagues found that in stable, structured situations, a stricter, more autocratic form of leadership is more likely to be successful, whereas in a situation of change, external threat, and ambiguity, more lenient, participative forms of leadership work better. Of course, in many organizations conditions will change in one direction or another. Whether shifting from a participative leadership style to a more autocratic one and back again will enhance employee satisfaction and performance or simply alienate employees is debatable.

Most of the studies just cited have relied on data about personnel who are at relatively low echelons in the organization. The general conclusion of this research, that leadership at this level can and often does make a difference in objective performance indicators and the attitudes of the personnel involved, is important. Increased output or rapid acceptance of a new organizational arrangements is not an inconsequential matter for organizations. The extrapolation of the conclusions from these studies to top leadership seems straightforward, but should be made with a good deal of caution because of lack of direct evidence. Whereas the range of behaviors affected by first- or second-line supervisors is rather small, if the jump is made to the range of behaviors affected by those at the top of the organization, the potential for a real impact of leadership can be readily seen. Even in performance and attitudes, the high-level subordinates of top administrators can be affected, and their performance in turn has an impact right down through the organization.

Whether these findings can be generalized to or are relevant to higher levels of an organization is, however, open to question. The nature of the limits on leadership and the leadership process itself can be further understood by evidence from studies of changes in personnel at the *top* of the organization.

Leadership Succession

Leadership or managerial succession takes place when a person in a leadership position is replaced. Replacement can occur for many reasons—transfer, resignation, firing, death, and so on. Succession provides a "test case" for the impact of leadership, since there are seemingly clear before-and-after conditions. Two early case studies of leadership succession provided evidence that leadership could make a huge difference in the functioning of the organization. Later studies, however, raised questions about the direction of causality in the relation of leadership change and organizational performance.

Probably the best-known case study of managerial succession is Gouldner's *Patterns of Industrial Bureaucracy* (1954), an analysis of a gypsum plant and mine that underwent a major and dramatic change in top personnel. The old manager was very casual and indulgent, inclined to overlook company rules and official standards when these were inconvenient. He was well loved by the plant's employees, but productivity often suffered. The parent organization, concerned about the production record of the plant, replaced this manager with a new manager, who was brought in with the specific mandate of increasing production levels. The new manager faced two choices in accomplishing this mandate: either he could try to ingratiate himself with workers by continuing the established pattern of relations—a procedure that probably would not have worked in any event, since he did not have the personal ties of his predecessor—or he could try to change behaviors by enforcing the existing rules of conduct and performance. He chose the latter course, and as a result the organization shifted from an indulgency pattern to one that was "punishment centered." This change led to a severe increase in internal tension and stress among employees and, ultimately, to a strike (described in a later book by Gouldner).

The impact of leadership change in Gouldner's study is in direct contrast to that found in another classic case described by Guest (1962), based on observations in a large automobile factory. Guest compares the studies:

> Both studies [his and Gouldner's] examine the process by which organizational tensions are exacerbated or reduced following the succession of a new leader at the top of the hierarchy. Succession in Gouldner's case resulted in a sharp increase in tension and stress and, by inference, a lowering of overall performance. The succession of a new manager had the opposite results in the present case. Plant Y, as we chose to call it, was one of six identical plants of a large corporation. At one period in time the plant was poorest in virtually all indexes of performance—direct and indirect labor costs, quality of output, absenteeism and turnover, ability to meet schedule changes, labor grievances and in several other measures. Interpersonal relationships were marked by sharp antagonisms within and between all levels.
>
> Three years later, following the succession of a new manager, and with no changes in the formal organizational structure, in the product, in the personnel, or in its basic technology, not only was there a substantial reduction of interpersonal conflict, but Plant Y became the outstanding performer among all of the plants. (p. 48)

The dramatic differences between these two cases might lead one to some sort of "great person" theory of leadership, with Gouldner's successor *not* a great person and Guest's a great one. Guest correctly rejects that simple conclusion and instead attributes the differences to the actions each manager took when confronted with an existing social structure. Although both new managers were expected to improve the situation, the new manager at the gypsum plant believed that, by enforcing rules to the letter, he would get rid of the personnel who were not performing properly—dismissing men, for example, for offenses that had previously been largely ignored. He felt that he was—and probably this was true—under severe pressure to turn the organization around in a short period of time. In Guest's study, the new manager at the automobile plant followed a manager who had tried to improve operations through close and punitive supervision. Consequently, the new manager decided to take a different path by using more informal contacts with his subordinates and bringing them into the decision-making process and by relegating "rule enforcement to a second level of importance." This manager also worked through the existing organizational hierarchy, whereas the new manager at the gypsum plant, after some failures with the established subordinates, brought in some of his own supporting staff, thus setting up a formal hierarchy that was in a sense superimposed on the existing social structure. Thus, Gouldner's new manager and Guest's new manager exhibited very different styles and behaviors.

There were some other important differences in the organizations that may have also affected the consequences of managerial change and, indeed, may have affected the styles the managers "chose." In the gypsum plant, top managers traditionally came from existing members of the organization but the parent company broke with this tradition by sending in an "outsider." In addition, the former manager of the gypsum plant had been active in the small, rural community surrounding the plant and was seen as "one of us." The former manager also had a cadre of subordinates tied to him through personal loyalty, who evinced little inclination to support the successor. The new manager thus had little recourse but to use the more formal bureaucratic mechanisms of control. At the automobile factory, on the other hand, the social setting was radically different. The factory was in a large metropolitan area, and the previous managers had not become involved in the community. The old manager was not particularly well liked within the factory. In addition, the factory had a history of relatively rapid turnover among top managers (the average tenure was three to five years), and it was common for new managers to come from outside the plant. Thus, unlike the gypsum plant personnel, the automobile plant personnel were used to the kind of succession they experienced.

Guest moves beyond his data and draws a conclusion from the comparison of his and Gouldner's cases. He suggests that the success of the automobile plant manager was due in large part to gaining the consent of the governed, or democratization of the leadership process. Gouldner, in a comment on Guest's research, emphasizes differences in the total situations in which the successions occurred. The gypsum plant event occurred during a period of recession, with labor relatively plentiful, but with the pressures for improvement probably more intense.

He suggests that when the total situation is viewed, it is incorrect to conclude that one or another approach to the leadership process is always the correct one, even though in both of these cases the autocratic approach was less successful.

Both studies, however, indicate that top management has the potential for drastic impacts on the operations and performance of the organization. Although not directly contradicting this finding, a later line of studies of succession called into question the direction of causality in this change: Does leadership change directly affect performance? Or is it more a reflection of performance?

Many of the studies focusing on this question use a rather offbeat research site to investigate it—baseball and other sports teams. Baseball managers stand in an unusual organizational position. In relation to the total baseball organization, their role is similar to that of the first-line supervisor; but in relation to the playing team only, their role is similar to that of the top executive. Grusky (1963) was one of the first researchers to use sports teams to examine the relationship between managerial succession and organizational effectiveness. He noted that baseball teams are convenient units for analysis, because of their similarity in "official goals, size, and authority structure" (p. 21). They also offer a ready measure of effectiveness in wins–losses statistics.

His analysis showed that teams with the poorest records had the highest rates of succession. Although this finding may not be surprising, Grusky rejected the commonsense notion built around succession as the dependent variable—that low effectiveness leads to a vote of no-confidence from the owner, then a firing. Instead, he developed a more complicated analysis, arguing that poor team performance leads to managerial role strain, which impairs the manager's performance, and that managerial changes disrupt existing relations among team members and the coaches, thereby further impairing team performance:

> The availability of objective performance standards decreases managerial control and thereby contributes to role strain. The greater the managerial role strain, the higher the rates of succession. Moreover, the higher the rates of succession, the stronger the expectations of replacement when team performance declines. Frequent managerial change can produce important dysfunctional consequences within the team by affecting style of supervision and disturbing the informal network of interpersonal relationships. The resulting low primary-group stability produces low morale and may thereby contribute to team ineffectiveness. Declining clientele support may encourage a greater decline in team morale and performance. The consequent continued drop in profitability induces pressures for further managerial changes. Such changes, in turn, produce additional disruptive effects on the organization, and the vicious circle continues. (p. 30)

This rather complicated explanation was challenged by Gamson and Scotch (1964). Based on a different approach to baseball teams' won–lost records, Gamson and Scotch advanced a "ritual scapegoating no-way casualty theory" (p. 70). This theory essentially suggests that the manager makes no difference:

> In the long run, the policies of the general manager and other front-office personnel are far more important. While judicious trades are helpful (here the field manager

may be consulted but does not have the main responsibility), the production of talent through a well-organized scouting and farm system is the most important long-run determinant. The field manager, who is concerned with day-to-day tactical decisions, has minimal responsibility for such management functions. (p. 70)

Gamson and Scotch note that the players are a critical factor, suggesting that at one point in baseball history, regardless of who was manager, the Yankees would have done as well and the Mets would have (or more accurately, could have) done no worse. When the team is doing poorly, the firing of the field manager is ritual scapegoating.

It is a convenient, anxiety-reducing act which the participants of the ceremony regard as a way of improving performance, even though (as some participants may themselves admit in less stressful moments) real improvements can come only through long-range organizational decisions. (pp. 70–71)

Gamson and Scotch add that there does seem to be at least a short-run improvement in team performance in cases when the manager is changed midseason. They suggest that this improvement might be attributable to the ritual itself.

Grusky (1964), in a reply to the Gamson–Scotch criticism, further analyzes the data regarding midseason changes. Adding the variable of whether the new manager came from inside or outside the organization, he finds that the inside manager is more successful. He takes this finding as partial evidence that his theory of the dysfunctional consequences of disruption in internal relations is more reasonable, since the inside manager is likely to be aware of the interpersonal arrangements and the performance of his predecessor and thus less likely to make the same mistakes again.

Although these analyses were carried out many years ago, when major-league baseball was a kinder and gentler business, without expansion and franchise shifts, free agency, and huge player salaries, the analyses of managerial succession in sports teams remain interesting and timely and provide a unique opportunity for analyzing leadership effects. Further studies of college basketball teams and Major League Baseball teams concluded that managerial succession does not really change things—poor performance in the past leads to poor performance after succession (Allen, Panian, and Lotz, 1979; Eitzen and Yetman, 1972). A study of succession among coaches in the National Football League concluded that succession is cosmetic, a finding that is consistent with the ritual scapegoating approach. The head coach is fired and replaced by a successor, with little opportunity to change policies, procedures, or personnel in the short run (Brown, 1982).

This may seem at first glance to be a lot of words spilled over a relatively minor matter in the larger scheme of things, but the points that these authors are addressing are very relevant for the present analysis. Understanding whether changes in top leadership produce significant changes in the performance of the organization overall, or whether such changes merely reflect performance, is in turn important to understanding the nature and function of leadership.

Studies of leadership turnover in other contexts also suggest that turnover may be as much of a product of organizational conditions and performance as a determinant of performance. Studies of business corporations indicate that political influences often determine leadership turnover. For example, Allen and Panian (1982) studied the effects of the locus of control in business firms on succession. In their study, direct family control of firms was defined as existing when the chief executive officer was a member of the family controlling the organization. Indirect family control characterized firms when the chief executive officer was not a family member, but the family had significant representation on the board of directors. A firm was defined as having managerial control when management dominated the board of directors. On the basis of data regarding 242 large industrial firms in the United States, Allen and Panian conclude:

> To begin with, there was a direct relationship between managerial power and corporate performance, on the one hand, and managerial tenure and longevity, on the other. Chief executives of more profitable firms and those who were members of controlling families usually had longer tenures and were usually older at the time of their succession than the chief executive officers of less profitable firms and those who were not members of controlling families. Similarly, there was an inverse relationship between managerial power and the probability of managerial succession during periods of poor corporate performance. Chief executive officers who were members of controlling families were somewhat less likely to experience succession during unprofitable or only marginally profitable years than chief executives who were not members of controlling families. (pp. 545–546)

What is notable about this piece of research is finding that family ties made top leadership succession less sensitive to performance variation than was the case when a chief executive officer did not have these family ties. Similar results were also documented in a study by Boeker and Karichalil (2002).

Political influences are also indicated in research showing that chief executive officers tend to be succeeded by individuals with the same career specialization, such as finance, sales, or legal (Fligstein and Freeland, 1995). This succession process is based on previous strategies and power coalitions within the organization. This process can involve poor strategy following poor strategy, so that the process is not necessarily beneficial. It is based on the notion of strategic contingencies described in Chapter 4.

Likewise, work on "insider" versus "outsider" succession to leadership positions suggests some of the ways in which organizational politics may moderate the impact of leadership change. As noted earlier, Grusky believes that whether the successor is an insider or an outsider (to the organization) makes a difference, suggesting that, for baseball teams at least, the insider is more successful. In regard to overall change in the organization, however, it appears that the person brought in from the outside will be more able to institute greater changes. The outsider is able to replace subordinates with selected lieutenants of his or her own choice. The constellation of immediate personnel around the outsider can be changed more easily than the insider's could be (Boeker and Karichalil, 2002; Helmich and Brown, 1972). A choice between an insider and an outsider is not always available, of course. Political considerations within an organization, its financial situation, and a dearth of outsiders may force an organization to go with insiders, thus limiting the amount of change possible.

The operation of political processes in leadership behavior can be seen in yet another light. Managers of unstable firms strategically manipulate causal attributions to manage the impression of the degree to which they are in control of the situation, even though they may not have any real control over organizational outcomes. They go so far as to claim responsibility for positive and negative outcomes, indicating their awareness and attempts at controlling the situation. These strategies are designed to maintain their positions (Salancik and Mindl, 1984).

Research also suggests that environmental and organizational conditions determine or moderate the impact of leadership on organizational outcomes. One study examining the length of tenure of academic department heads or chairs found that an important influence was the "paradigm development" of the various disciplines. This refers to the extent to which there is agreement on and use of a common theoretical basis. With higher paradigm development, the tenure of the head was longer. Larger size operated against long tenure. The effects of both size and paradigm development were found to be more pronounced in periods of environmental scarcity (Pfeffer and Moore, 1980). This is in line with the conclusion that the situation in which leadership is embedded needs study. In periods of uncertainty, in regard to both the environment and the nature of the organization itself (low-paradigm-development departments), there is likely to be a greater rate of leadership succession. This, in turn, is likely to have strong effects on leaders' ability to produce significant or enduring changes in the organization.

Other studies have indicated that size affects not only the likelihood of leadership turnover, but its impact as well. A study of the relationship between executive succession and stock-price changes related to the succession found significant positive effects of succession, in the form of stock-price increases, but only for external appointments in small firms. These stock-price increases were found when the departure of the former officeholder was announced along with the appointment of the successor (Reinganum, 1985). In a study of newspaper organizations, size was also found to have a significant effect on the likelihood of organizational failure following the succession of a newspaper's founder (Carroll, 1984b). Since most of these newspaper organizations were small, they were more vulnerable to high failure rates to begin with, and the succession of the publisher would make the situation even more risky.

Another set of constraints on what the top leadership of an organization can do consists of the external environment of the organization. This is dramatically seen in an analysis of 167 major U.S. corporations by Lieberson and O'Connor (1972), who were concerned with the sales, earnings, and profit margins of the corporations over a twenty-year period. Their ingenious research considered the issue of executive succession and its impact on these performance criteria. The authors analyzed the effects of succession over one-, two-, and three-year periods to permit the maximum impact of leadership change to demonstrate itself. They also considered the economic behavior of the industry (e.g., steel versus air transportation), the position of the corporation within the industry, and the state of the economy as a whole. Their findings are startling to those who really believe in leadership: "*All three performance variables are affected by forces beyond a leader's immediate control*" (p. 124; italics added). For sales and net earnings, the general economic conditions, the industry, and the corporation's position within it were more important than leadership. Leadership was important for profit margins but still heavily constrained by the environmental conditions. These findings were replicated (with slight modification) by Weiner (1977) and Salancik and Pfeffer (1977).

Lieberson and O'Connor's findings have created a great deal of controversy, since they fly in the face of much conventional wisdom and in the face of scholars who believe in leadership. Thomas (1988) reexamined the evidence of the sort that Lieberson and O'Connor used and developed an interesting interpretation. Thomas notes that changes in the order in which variables are entered into the regression equation regarding performance can essentially reverse the findings. Rather than reversing Lieberson and O'Connor's findings, which Thomas believes would be implausible, he suggests that the effects of leadership may not be visible at the aggregate level, but such changes can still produce a substantial impact at the *level of the individual firm*. This is because, in the aggregate, the impact of cases of effective leadership cancels out cases of ineffective leadership, and thus there is no obvious impact of leadership change overall.

Another criticism of Lieberson and O'Connor concludes that the impact of organizational size and some contextual effects were not considered sufficiently (Day and Lord, 1988). Like Thomas's analysis, this analysis also argues that leadership ability was not considered, although defining "ability" as a quality that exists independent of the needs of a given firm in a given context, brings us back, unfortunately, to a "great person" perspective.

Lieberson and O'Connor do not claim that leadership is unimportant, nor is that claim made here. Leadership is clearly important in changing organizational directions, developing new activities, considering mergers or acquisitions, and setting long-run policies and objectives. At the same time, from all of the evidence that has been presented, it must be realized that organizational and environmental constraints drastically limit the likelihood of significant change on the basis of leadership alone. The implications of such findings are crucial for organizational analyses. In established organizations, the impact of leadership is heavily constrained, and leadership change may not make much of a difference. For the new organization, leadership is likely to be much more important in determining organizational outcomes. Leadership is also of crucial importance in times of organizational crisis.

A heroic view of leadership can be contrasted with one that sees leadership as helpless to do anything about the events happening to the organization. Neither view of leadership, heroic or helpless, is typically very accurate, or very helpful in thinking about leadership. What is helpful is to realize that, statistically, half of all leaders are below average. Leadership is neither the solution nor the problem. Leadership is an important activity in some situations; in others there is little that a leader can do. Most situations, of course, fall between these extremes.

This discussion of leadership has ignored an important consideration—the motivations of the leaders. More than two generations ago, Berle and Means (1932) argued that corporate executives have become technical managers, separated from the concerns of capitalist owners. Others have argued that corporate leadership represents the modern capitalist class with phenomenal power and wealth in their organizations and in society as a whole (Allen, 1976; Zeitlin, 1974, 1976). From this perspective, organizational decisions are made on the basis of continued acquisition of power and wealth for owners. Spectacular cases of corporate misconduct and managerial greed, such as those at Enron and World Crossing, where corporate leaders intentionally concealed information about organizational performance and received enormous personal compensation and benefits from the corporation even while it was bordering on financial ruin, are consistent with this view (Huffington, 2003). However, whether such cases represent typical patterns of organizational behavior and relations is not clear.

One analysis of corporate presidents found that they are fired on the basis of poor profit performance, regardless of whether they are owners or managers, thus disconfirming the Berle and Means hypothesis about the separation of ownership and management (James and Soref, 1981). We have already noted that such changes in top leadership may be little more than cosmetic. It may not matter if the top leaders are interested in their own power or wealth, if they are really controlled by owners, or if they are simply technocratic managers, because their organizational roles and impacts would not differ. The question of the organization's outcomes for society remains an important one, however, because what is good for the organization may not be good for society. This is true whether the organizations are corporations, school systems, or churches.

LEADERSHIP IN THE VOLUNTARY ORGANIZATION

The discussion thus far has primarily concerned persons who have been formally appointed to positions of authority in work organizations. The situation is somewhat different in the voluntary organization, in which formal leaders are elected to office, or in which members have at least some official input into who is chosen for leadership roles. It has long been noted that in voluntary organizations there is a tendency toward oligarchy, that is, the emergence of a relatively small set of top-level officials who run the organization and who perpetuate themselves in office (Michels, 1949). Tendencies toward oligarchy exist in business organizations as well, of course. But because democratic representation of the members is a key goal or value in many voluntary organizations, its occurrence in these organizations is especially problematic (Osterman, 2006).

Michels identified a number of factors that contribute to the formation of oligarchy (see Tolbert and Hiatt, forthcoming). First, holding office often allows leaders to develop the kinds of skills and knowledge required for leadership—persuasive techniques, an understanding of organizational rules and procedures, and so on. Those who have not held office are apt to lack such inside information and thus are at a disadvantage when they compete for office. Second, existing leaders can reinforce their political power within the organization through patronage and other favors. In addition, over time, leaders become aware that they have a common interest in maintaining their positions and thus help protect each other from challenges by rank-and-file members. Michels believed that because of these processes, the formation of oligarchies in organizations, even those founded on the principle of democratic representation, was inevitable; he referred to this as the "Iron Law of Oligarchy." However, other work suggests conditions that may mitigate such tendencies. A now-classic analysis of the International Typographical Union (Lipset, Trow, and Coleman, 1956) suggests a number of such conditions, including minimizing differences in the compensation and benefits received by leaders and other members and encouraging the high levels of social interaction and a strong sense of community among the membership.

Even when oligarchy is unlikely to be a problem (e.g., in smaller social service organizations, cooperatives, or social clubs), leaders of such organizations face unique challenges because their roles are multiplex—they may be responsible for directing the activities of volunteers, but at the same time they are often viewed as being in the employ of those same volunteers, as well as being expected to provide services to the volunteers, in terms of making their participation enjoyable. Valcour (2002), in an insightful analysis, considers how leaders of such organizations manage these multiplex roles. Her analysis is based on an ethnographic study of a cooperative nursery school, where teachers were responsible for using parent volunteers as classroom aides. In general, her analysis suggests that, to be effective, leaders in such organizations need to get members to adopt and emphasize a conception of role relations in which leader-as-director is most prominent. Strategies for achieving this include using formal training sessions to convey and emphasize desired role relations to volunteers, spending extra time explaining the rationale for behaviors they ask of volunteers, and providing public recognition to volunteers who exhibit the kinds of behaviors (and thus demonstrate appropriate role orientation) that are desired. Overall, her study suggests that the key to leadership rests on detecting the role orientations that volunteers bring with them and carefully reshaping those orientations as needed.

SUMMARY AND CONCLUSIONS

In this chapter, we emphasized the need to consider leadership behavior within the context of a larger framework: the structure of the organization and the environment in which it was set. Leadership is contingent on a combination of factors: individuals' position in the organization, the specific task demands and environmental conditions that are confronted, and the abilities and behaviors of those serving in leadership roles—all of these affect the outcomes of efforts to exercise leadership. Perhaps one useful conclusion from our review of studies of leadership is that it *is* a complex phenomenon. Thus, no single approach or style or set of prescriptions can be counted on to produce desired outcomes. Rather, a nuanced understanding of different approaches and styles, as well as some general idea of the conditions that *may* make one or the other more useful, may be most helpful for practice.

We noted that the impact of leadership may be clearest at the small-group level. Whether leadership normally has an independent effect on the outcomes of large, complex organizations is more problematic. Many factors influence the overall performance of organizations—past performance, changing environmental conditions, and so forth. Studies of leadership succession suggest that these factors may typically be much more important in determining the fate of an organization than the policies and choices of the top leader. However, it may still be asked, Even if these factors are very important, perhaps most important in shaping organizational outcomes, do the top-level leaders' behaviors and decisions have an independent effect? Our intuitive answer to this question is "yes." We believe that the decisions that leaders make often set in motion forces that fundamentally reshape organizations (in unintended as well as intended ways) and determine their fates. But these forces are apt to take time to play out in an organization; hence, the ultimate impact of these decisions is apt to be extremely difficult to evaluate in the short run. This suggests, though, that part of understanding leadership involves understanding decision-making processes in organizations, and it is to that topic that we now turn.

EXERCISES

1. Describe the leadership styles that are present in your two organizations.
2. What has leadership accomplished (or not accomplished) in your two organizations?

Chapter 6

Decision-Making

OVERVIEW

In this chapter, we consider decision-making processes—in many ways, these processes lie at the very heart of understanding organizations. We begin by describing a line of work that has emphasized a view of organizations as systems of decision-making. In this context, we consider research that has identified some of the organizational and environmental factors that shape decision-making. We focus in particular on strategic decisions, those made at the top of organizations, since these decisions usually have the most profound effects on organizations. Decision-making is not easy, nor is predicting the outcomes of decision-making efforts.

The aspect of organizations dealt with in this chapter can be illustrated best with two cases: the tragic launch of the space shuttle *Challenger,* which exploded so dramatically in 1986, killing all on board, and the similar deadly explosion of the second space shuttle, the *Columbia,* seventeen years later. Both launches were the result of complex organizational decision-making processes that were purposively designed to prevent such tragedies, but which were affected by three important biasing factors (Vaughan, 1996, 1999):

1. different units' struggle to obtain scarce resources in a competitive environment;

2. an organizational culture in National Aeronautics and Space Administration (NASA) that contributed to the censoring of information;

3. a regulatory environment that was insufficient for the decision-making task.

No one intended for these tragedies to occur. The launch decisions were not made by stupid or uncaring people. They were made by people like you and me, who were trying to do the best they could. To understand how these decisions were made and why, we first need to understand generally the nature of decision-making in organizations.

ORGANIZATIONS AS SYSTEMS OF DECISIONS

The broadest and most systematic efforts to analyze how decisions get made in organizations are represented in work by Herbert Simon and his students and colleagues. This tradition is sometimes referred to as "the Carnegie School" because much of the work was done at Carnegie-Mellon University, where Simon was a long-time faculty member.

Bounded Rationality and Organizations as Hierarchies of Decisions

Simon's (1957) early efforts to conceptualize decision-making in organizations grew, in part, from his skepticism toward prescriptive models of decision-making processes offered by economists. He argued that such models rested on a conception of "homo economicus" (or economic man) that had little basis in reality.

> Homo economicus is characterized by the following: acting only in his self-interest, possessing full information about the decision problem, knowing all the possible solutions from which he has to choose as well as the consequences of each solution, seeking to maximize utility, having the ability to rank alternatives in order of likelihood of maximizing outcomes. (Zey, 1992:11)

As Simon (1957) pointed out, in contrast to these assumptions, real individuals have a very constrained cognitive capacity—that is, a limited ability to think of the range of possible options in a decision-making situation, to accurately anticipate what the consequences of those options will be, and to know how much they'll actually value one consequence versus another. Thus, rather than being fully rational, as economic models assumed, Simon argued that individuals were characterized by "bounded rationality." This concept implies that individuals typically are able to consider only a limited number of options in making decisions, and often select the first one that meets some minimal criteria, that are "good enough," rather than searching for the very best option. Simon labeled this approach to decision-making "satisficing," in contrast to the economic notion of optimizing. His explication of this view of decision-making contributed to his winning the Nobel Prize in Economics in 1978.

Given bounded rationality, Simon argued, individuals could achieve a greater degree of rationality in decision-making in an organization than they could if they acted on their own. This argument rests on a conception of organizations as a hierarchy of means-and-ends decisions. Individuals at the top of the hierarchy make broad decisions about general courses of action to be taken; these decisions define the ends that individuals at the next level will seek to achieve by making their decisions about more specific actions to be taken, actions that will become the means to achieving higher-level ends. A brief example may make this clearer. Suppose a person decides to make a profit by manufacturing widgets and that two main units need to be created to achieve this objective: manufacturing and marketing. The person recruits two others to be the heads of these two units and charges them with making decisions about how to efficiently manufacture the widgets and market them, respectively. The head of manufacturing decides that there are three tasks that need to be taken care of for efficient manufacturing: (1) obtaining supplies, (2) carrying out production, and (3) inspecting for quality. Thus, she gives three individuals under her command responsibility for making decisions about how to carry out each of these tasks. Each higher-level individual's decisions define the ends that the subordinates will concentrate on in making their decisions, and their decisions will provide the means for accomplishing the objectives of the higher-level members. The process of breaking broad decisions into a series of progressively narrower decisions and assigning these to different individuals or subunits is related to increases in the complexity of organizations, as we discussed in Chapters 2 and 3.

Because of this type of division of labor in decision-making, Simon believed that the decisions made in organizations are likely to reflect a broader and more thoughtful consideration of factors than if a single individual had to think through these alone—that is, to be more rational. Note that this conclusion rests on the assumption that all members of the organization share the general aim of making a profit through the manufacture and marketing of widgets. When one refers to rationality, it's necessary to specify the referent—that is, for whom or what something is rational (Storing, 1962).

Organizational Structure and Decision-Making

Simon followed Chester Barnard's (1968) arguments that when individuals join an organization, they agree to accept the inducements that the organization offers them in exchange for which they will make contributions to the organization. This includes allowing the organization to dictate their behavior within some broad limits, or within their "zone of indifference," and using the criteria and standards set by the organization in making decisions on behalf of the organization. In this context, the aspects of formal structure discussed in Chapter 3 are important because they provide the mechanisms through which organizations shape and control individuals' decision-making (Perrow, 1986). In a series of analyses, Simon and his colleagues (Cohen, March, and Olsen, 1972; Cyert and

March, 1963; March and Simon, 1958) elaborated on the impact of formal structure on decision-making processes in organizations.

They note that the formal division of labor defines the relevant issues that an individual is expected to attend to in making decisions. For example, when the head of manufacturing makes decisions, she focuses on their impact on the production of widgets, rather than on their impact on marketing and distribution. This illustration suggests that as horizontal complexity increases, individuals generally will take a narrower, more specific set of issues into account in decision-making. Such specialization may allow them to be more efficient in making decisions, or more thorough in terms of considering specific factors, but it is likely to lead them to neglect other issues that may bear on the ultimate decision. Hence, there is a need for persons at higher hierarchical levels to review and to coordinate among the decisions made at lower levels.

Likewise, rules and regulations are important because they direct individuals' attention to certain criteria and considerations in making decisions. March and Simon (1958) discuss "performance programs," collections of rules that guide decision-making in particular areas. For example, a performance program for inventory decisions might contain the following rules: When inventory reaches a certain point, more stock should be ordered; to decide how much to order, the rate of sales over the past thirty days should be checked and used as a guide; at least three suppliers should be contacted to get competitive prices; and so forth. Higher levels of formalization thus allow individuals at lower levels of an organization to "make" decisions, leading to a greater degree of decentralization, because the criteria to be used are clear and help ensure standard outcomes. Similarly, the hierarchy of the organization is relevant to decision-making because it defines which decisions are directly related to other decisions.

Politics, Conflict, and Decision-Making

Resting on more realistic notions of individuals' cognitive capabilities than economic models that assume full rationality, this portrayal of organizational decision-making provides an important and useful way of thinking about the connection between individual-level choices and actions, on the one hand, and organizational-level characteristics, on the other (Perrow, 1986). One drawback, though, is that it does not give much attention to the possibility that different members of the organization will have different aims and that an agreement to allow the organization to define the premises of their decisions does not imply that they completely ignore their particular aims and interests. Recognition of this point has led scholars to give more attention to the role of politics and conflict in decision-making.

Consistent with the notion that decision-making in organizations is affected by individuals' bounded rationality, political considerations are assumed to come into play because there is often uncertainty surrounding decision-making processes—uncertainty about which objectives are most important to an

Preferences Regarding Possible Outcomes

		Certainty	Uncertainty
Beliefs About Cause/Effect Relations	Certain	Computation	Compromise
	Uncertain	Judgment	Inspiration

FIGURE 6–1   Decision Processes
Source: James D. Thompson, *Organizations in Action* (New York: McGraw-Hill, 1967), p. 134.

organization and what means should be used to pursue a given objective. These core types of uncertainties were highlighted in the framework for thinking about different types of organizational decisions presented by Thompson (1967). As he noted, "decision issues always involve two major dimensions: (1) beliefs about cause/effect relationships and (2) preferences regarding possible outcomes" (p. 134). "Beliefs about cause/effect" refers to whether there is certainty about the outcome of an action choice. If we decide A, we are sure that B and only B will be the result—this is high certainty about cause and effect. "Preferences regarding possible outcomes" refers to the degree to which there is consensus about what the organization is or should be trying to achieve. (You may note the similarity between Thompson's conception of factors that affect decision-making and Perrow's conception of factors that affect technological uncertainty; we discussed the latter in Chapter 3.)

These basic variables in the decision-making process can operate at the conscious or the unconscious level. As an aid in understanding the process, Thompson suggests that each variable can be (artificially) dichotomized, as indicated in Figure 6–1. In the cell with certainty on both variables, a "computational" strategy can be used. In that case the decision is obvious. For example, in simple inventorying, when the supply of a particular item dwindles to a particular level, a computer reorders it automatically. Obviously, there is not likely to be conflict surrounding these decisions. The other cells present more problems and are thus more crucial for the organization.

When outcome preferences are clear, but cause and effect relationships are uncertain, Thompson suggests that organizational decisions require what he calls a judgmental strategy. This typically involves bringing a group of experts together to share their knowledge and to make recommendations. Where the situation is reversed and there is certainty regarding cause and effect but uncertainty regarding outcome preferences, decision-making requires a compromise strategy. This is exemplified by political arrangements where the members representing different interests and views make decisions by voting. Finally, when there is uncertainty on both dimensions, Thompson argued that an inspirational strategy for decision-making is needed, if indeed any decision is forthcoming. Although Thompson doesn't precisely specify what is involved in an inspirational strategy, it presumably entails a significant effort to forge agreements between parties with different views—that is, skilled and diplomatic leadership (Thompson, 1967:134–135).

STRATEGIC DECISION-MAKING

The higher one goes in an organizational decision-making hierarchy, the greater the uncertainty surrounding both cause and effect relations and preference outcomes. As Cyert and March (1963) and Perrow (1967) point out, high-level goals of an organization are usually so broadly stated—"providing the highest quality education for students," "enhancing community health and well-being," even "maximizing profits"—that it is difficult to get consensus on what they entail, let alone how best to achieve them. Consequently, decisions that would be described as strategic—big, high-risk decisions made at high levels of organizations that significantly affect organizational outcomes—are often fraught with uncertainty and, hence, potential conflict.

Uncertainty and Strategic Decisions

Although we have a tendency to assume that decisions made at high levels of organizations reflect high levels of rationality, or careful consideration of the best means to achieve some given end, evidence suggests that this assumption is very problematic. A good example of this comes from an analysis of General Motors (GM) in the United States. GM was one of the first organizations to adopt a formal structure known as the "M-Form" (for multidivisional); in this form, separate divisions are created for different product lines and divisional heads are given responsibility for running these, much like independent organizations. Classic accounts suggested that this form was chosen for its high level of efficiency (Chandler, 1962). Instead, a more recent analysis suggests that, for most of its history, decisions about structure in GM were driven not so much by efficiency concerns as by efforts to obtain consensus among its managers (Freeland, 1997). This and other detailed accounts of strategic decision-making in organizations (Beamish, 2000; Clarke, 1989; Tickner, 2002) suggest that considerations other than efficiency and effectiveness often influence strategic decisions.

One approach to thinking about how such decisions are made is provided by the "garbage can" model of decision-making (Cohen, March, and Olsen, 1972). This model begins with the points noted by Thompson, that preferences and technology (cause and effect relations) are often unclear. In this context, Cohen and his colleagues argue that decisions are shaped by four more or less independent factors:

1. perceptions of current problems facing the organization;
2. potential "solutions," ideas or actions that individual members of an organization wish to champion (e.g., the adoption of a new computer system, creation of a new office or function);
3. decision-making opportunities, meetings or committees that are assigned to make a recommendation for action;
4. participants, individuals who are present at decision-making opportunities.

The model suggests that, in an organization, decisions result from random combinations of these factors—conceived of as a large garbage can in which the factors are mixed. In other words, decisions are made in the context of particular decision-making opportunities (e.g., meetings) that may have been called to address a particular problem (which is nevertheless subject to redefinition), which are attended by certain individuals (but perhaps not all who were invited, because of scheduling difficulties), and the members may or may not bring current pet projects with them. Needless to say, this approach suggests that decision outcomes are very unpredictable. Other research, though, suggests some structural constraints that "put a lid on the garbage can" (Levitt and Nuss, 1989) and make decision-making somewhat more predictable than the image of garbage-can decision-making suggests.

Constraints on Decision-Making

One constraint on decision-making, and thus on potential conflict surrounding decisions, is the existence of previous decisions that commit organizational resources to certain courses of action (Cyert and March, 1963). Such decisions are often embodied in organizational budgets and are psychologically as well as legally binding. By limiting options, these commitments serve to limit conflict over choices of action.

Although having the benefit of reducing conflict, such commitments can have negative consequences for organizational decision-making. Organizations committed to losing courses of action are apt to continue to make decisions that make matters even worse. These are called *escalation situations*. Escalation situations occur when organizational projects have little salvage value, when decision-makers want to justify their past behavior, when people in a project are bound to each other, and when organizational inertia and internal politics combine to prevent a project from being shut down (Staw and Ross, 1989). A classic example is the process by which a power company on Long Island, New York, persisted in a decision to construct a nuclear power plant in the face of fierce opposition. The power company "stuck to its guns," or escalated, for twenty-three years. The cost of the project went from $75 million in 1966 to $5 billion when the project was abandoned in 1989 (Ross and Staw, 1993).

The concept of social embeddedness (Granovetter, 1985) suggests another factor that often constrains organizational decisions and thus limits conflict. The concept calls attention to the fact that organizations (as well as individuals) have enduring relationships with other actors and are part of ongoing social networks. These relations shape decisions both because they are an important source of information about different choices that may be made and because, in order to maintain the relations, organizations may have to take certain actions.

There are a number of studies that document the ways in which network ties shape the flow of ideas between organizations and thus affect organizational decisions (e.g., Beckman and Haunschild, 2002; Budros, 2002; Guler, Guillen, and MacPherson, 2002; Westphal, Seidel, and Stewart, 2001). For example, a study by Davis (1991) of business firms' adoption of poison pills (legal arrangements that make it difficult for other firms to acquire a given firm without the consent of its board) indicated that such adoptions were strongly affected by whether members of the board of a firm considering adoption were also on boards of other firms that had already adopted this arrangement. Davis (1991) concludes:

> Part of the impact of ties to adopters can be explained with reference to the nature of boards as decision-making groups. When the board is faced with a decision, such as whether to adopt a poison pill, the opinions of those with relevant previous experience naturally will be given more weight. . . . Yet the evidence presented here indicates that the more a firm was tied to others that had adopted a poison pill, the more likely it was to adopt a pill itself (up to a point), a finding that suggests a normative element: The knowledge that several interlock partners had adopted poison pills provides information above and beyond the simple pros and cons of adoption that having one or two directors with prior poison pill experience would give. (pp. 607–608)

As this last point indicates, apart from their informational influence, social ties may affect organizational decisions because they make organizations more responsive to interorganizational norms. A study of the semiconductor industry examined the formation of a research-and-development consortium among highly competitive firms and found that individuals and firms in this consortium developed a "moral community" in which both made contributions to the industry without regard for immediate and specific paybacks (Browning, Beyer, and Shetler, 1995:113). Similarly, research on alliances between firms shows that repeated alliances lead to trust between organizations, which then becomes the basis for additional alliances (Gulati, 1995b).

Although such decisions may or may not be based strictly on economic calculations, they may yield positive economic outcomes. Research on the garment industry in New York City found that embeddedness, in the form of trust between and networks among garment firms, was related to higher survival rates; firms that relied solely on arm's-length economic transactions were more likely to fail (Uzzi, 1996, 1997). On the other hand, a study of the migration of manufacturing plants from New York State between 1969 and 1985 (and there was a lot of migration) found that firms that had links to local communities in the form of material, social, and political ties were less able to make such moves, even when production costs could be considerably reduced. Not surprisingly, the less mobile firms were in more peripheral industries. Firms in core industries were more able to move (Romo and Schwartz, 1995).

Although strategic decisions in organizations may be constrained by the considerations described above, this is not to suggest that decision-makers are purely passive or that these factors necessarily make decision outcomes predictable. As the garbage-can model of decision-making suggests, *who* participates in decision-making processes is a critical factor that affects outcomes; this is not only because different participants see problems differently and bring different "solutions" with them to the table, but because they also have differing amounts of power. Thus, we need to consider how the distribution of power influences decision-making processes.

STRATEGIES OF POWER AND DECISION-MAKING

In Chapter 4, we discussed the nature of power in organizations and some of the factors that influence its distribution in organizations. Authority, typically reflected by the positions individuals hold in an organizational hierarchy, is an important aspect of power. Thus, the opinions and aims of those with more authority often carry more weight in decision-making. But there are potential costs to making decisions under conditions of high uncertainty: decisions that turn out badly may affect decision-makers' credibility and their ability to exercise influence in later decision-making situations. "Well, it seemed like a good idea at the time." That phrase, which we have all used in our lives, also characterizes organizational decisions. The quality of decisions is judged over time. The forty-plus years of Soviet rule in Eastern Europe appeared to be successful decision-making on the part of the Soviets, until the late 1980s. The Ford Motor Company produced both the Mustang and the Edsel. Buying and selling subprime mortgages appeared to be a good investment strategy to many banks before the market collapsed in 2008. What appear to be successful, rational decisions at time 1 are often problematic at time 2. Because of this, those with authority to make strategic decisions, such as chief executive officers and high-level administrators, may resist making the decisions by themselves and leave such decisions to groups or committees (Jackall, 1988). Nonetheless, those in positions of authority have a number of ways to influence decision outcomes in ways that reflect their preferences.

Agenda Setting

One key influence mechanism is through control of the agenda—defining what issues will be discussed and in what order (Bachrach and Baratz, 1962). Defining an agenda shapes not only what issues will be discussed, but what issues will *not* be discussed. Thus, in a meeting held to make decisions about a company's financial situation, workers' compensation levels may be included as an item for discussion, but compensation levels and pension packages for high-ranking managers may be omitted.

Moreover, research suggests that the order in which items and issues are discussed can have strong effects on decision outcomes. This is partly because, given a fixed amount of time for a meeting, items that are placed earlier on the agenda are likely to receive more time and attention; decisions made near the end of the meeting may be made more quickly and participants may have less inclination to debate them. Thus, in setting the agenda, individuals may put the issues that they wish to push through quickly toward the end. In addition, since decisions are made in a sequence, decisions that are made earlier may entail commitments that affect subsequent decisions, resulting in an escalation of commitment to a course of action (Pfeffer, 1981). Suppose in a college faculty meeting there are two issues to be discussed: changing required courses and staffing. If a department can persuade the rest of the college that a particular course should be required, then it is in a position to argue for additional faculty lines (for faculty to teach this course) in the subsequent discussion of staffing.

Controlling Information

Information is part of the communication process within organizations. As will be seen in Chapter 7, the communication process itself is almost guaranteed to withhold, expand, or distort information. And as noted in Chapter 4, control of information can be an important source of power and have clear effects on decision-making outcomes. Although top-level members of an organization usually have access to more information than lower-level members, which can provide them with more influence in decision-making, this is not always the case. As pointed out in Chapter 4, individuals or units that have more contact with organizations, groups, and individuals outside the organization that provide it with critical resources often exercise relatively high levels of power within an organization. By selectively providing information about these resource providers, those individuals or units determine what organizational actions are deemed appropriate and necessary for the continuation of resource support. March and Simon (1958) discuss this aspect of information transmission in terms of the "absorption of uncertainty." Since securing resources from the environment is a major source of uncertainty in most organizations, those who broker information about key aspects of the environment "absorb" the uncertainty—and accrue influence within the organization.

Control of information from *within* the organization may also be becoming increasingly important, as more and more organizations employ sophisticated tools, including complex, electronically accessible databases containing data compiled by organizational members, as sources of information to be used in decision-making. Research suggests that organizational members who limit the amount of information that they make available through such databases, providing an appearance of quality and selectivity, are apt to be more influential (because the data they make available are given more attention) than those who provide a lot of information. This less-is-more strategy is particularly effective when many individuals are entering information in the database. Under these conditions, users of the database pay more attention to sources that appear to offer information more selectively (Hansen and Haas, 2001).

Forming Coalitions

Another way in which decision-making outcomes are influenced is through the selection of individuals to participate in a decision-making group (Padgett, 1980). Selecting organizational members who are likely to form a coalition that will support a particular choice allows top-level managers to ensure that the decision they favor is likely to be recommended. In addition, inclusion of expert outsiders, such as consultants, who may become part of the coalition, can increase the probabilities of this outcome (Bacharach and Lawler, 1980; Pfeffer, 1981).

Most strategic decisions are centered at the top of organizations, since that is where the power lies. At the same time, there are instances in which lower-level subordinates are brought into the process. As we have seen previously in Chapters 2 and 5, participation by subordinates has mixed consequences for the organization and the participants. The same is true of decision-making. Greater participation can actually be dysfunctional if the participants already feel satisfied or even saturated with their role in decision-making (Alutto and Belasco, 1972). Typically, though, bringing them into the decision-making process increases their acceptance of the decision that is made. A useful insight into participation in decision-making is that if a decision is important for the organization, a nonparticipative style is likely to be used; if the decisions are important for the subordinates in regard to their work, a more participative approach will be taken (Heller, 1973). If the organizational decision-makers believe that the subordinates have something to contribute to the decision or its implementation, then participation is more likely.

SUMMARY AND CONCLUSIONS

Decision-making involves both substance and politics and both economic and socially embedded rationality. It also involves limited rationality in all issues. Nonetheless, we plunge ahead. When and if we are participants in decision-making, we do try to do the best we can. To return to our theme, decisions rarely, if ever, provide perfect solutions and they never last over time, but we continue to make them.

Since information is central to decision-making, and since communications allow information to flow, we will now examine this process in organizations.

EXERCISES

1. Describe the decision-making processes in your two organizations. What are the issues? Who participates?
2. Describe the forms of rationality present in decision-making in your two organizations.

Chapter 7

Communication

OVERVIEW

This chapter deals with a topic that has been implicit and explicit throughout the preceding chapters. Power is exercised, leadership is attempted, and decisions are made on the basis of communication. Organizational structure shapes communication. The chapter starts with the obvious fact that individuals are at the core of the communication process. Individuals perceive or misperceive. Organizational factors are then introduced. Both individual and organizational factors contribute to communication problems. The problems are omission, distortion, and overload. Finally, possible solutions to communication problems are presented.

Organizations are information-processing systems. A vivid metaphor portrays the organization as a brain (Morgan, 1986). This imagery captures the idea that organizations receive and filter information, process it in light of what they have already learned, interpret it, change it, and finally act on it. Organizations also have memory lapses. To take the imagery even further, there are mind-altering stimulants and depressants—organizational highs and lows.

The communication process in organizations contains elements that are strongly organizational and strongly individual. At the individual level, consider the simple example of classroom examinations. If there were not individual differences in cognition and interpretation, everyone would give the same answer to an essay question. That obviously does not happen, as every student and faculty member knows. The organizational input into the communication process comes from the structured communication channels and the positions that people occupy. Organizational positions strongly influence the interpretation of communications by individuals. In this chapter, the factors that affect the sending, receiving, perception, and interpretation of communications will be examined.

THE IMPORTANCE OF COMMUNICATION

Organizational structures, with their varying sizes, technological sophistication, and degrees of complexity and formalization, are designed to be or evolve into information-handling systems. The very establishment of an organizational structure is a sign that communications are supposed to follow a particular path. Power, leadership, and decision-making rely upon the communication process, either explicitly or implicitly, since they would be meaningless in the absence of information.

Organizational analysts have ascribed varying degrees of importance to the communication process. Barnard (1968), for example, states: "In an exhaustive theory of organization, communication would occupy a central place, because the structure, extensiveness, and scope of the organization are almost entirely determined by communication techniques" (p. 91). This approach essentially places communication at the heart of the organization. More recently, Stinchcombe (1990) made communication the essence of his analysis. Other theorists, however, pay scant attention to the topic (e.g., Aldrich, 1979; Clegg and Dunkerley, 1980). Instead of declaring that communication is either at the heart or at the periphery of organizational analysis, a more reasonable view is that communication varies in importance according to where one is looking in an organization and what kind of organization is being studied.

Communication is crucial for organizational managers and their work. Managers spend an overwhelming proportion of their time in communications (Kanter, 1977). These communications usually involve face-to-face interactions with subordinates, superiors, peers, and customers. There are also meetings of one kind or another. E-mail and telephone messages have to be answered. In short, the business of the managers is communication. It is estimated that 80 percent of managers' time is spent on interpersonal communications (Klauss and Bass, 1982). The work of clerical personnel is overwhelmingly concerned with information processing. Changing information technology is having a major and unfinished impact on managerial and clerical work and thus on organizations.

These intraorganizational differences are important. Equally important are interorganizational differences. Communication is most important in organizations and organizational segments that must deal with uncertainty, that are complex, and that have a technology that does not permit easy routinization. Both external and internal characteristics affect the centrality of communication. The more an organization is people and idea oriented, the more important communication becomes. Even in a highly mechanized system, of course, communications underlie the development and use of machines. Workers are instructed on usage, orders are delivered, and so on. At the same time, the routineness of such operations leads to a lack of variability in the communication process. Once procedures are set, few additional communications are required. Although communications occur almost continuously in such settings, their organizational importance is more limited unless they lead to severe distortions in the operations.

The communication process is by definition a relational one; one party is the sender and the other the receiver at a particular time. The relational aspect of communication obviously affects the process. The social relations occurring in the communication process involve the sender and the receiver and their reciprocal effects on each other as they are communicating. If a sender is intimidated by a receiver during the process of sending a message, the message itself and the interpretation of it will be affected. Intimidation is just one of a myriad of factors that have the potential to disrupt the simple sender–receiver relationship. Status differences, different perceptual models, sexual attraction, and so on can enter the picture and lead to distortions of what is being sent and received.

These sources of distortion and their consequences will occupy a good deal of attention in the subsequent discussion. Ignorance of the potentiality for distortion has been responsible for the failure of many organizational attempts to improve operations simply by utilizing more communications. Once the importance of communications was recognized, many organizations jumped on a communications bandwagon, believing that if sufficient communications were available to all members of the organization, everyone would know and understand what was going on and most organizational problems would disappear (Katz and Kahn, 1978:430). This communications bandwagon was at the heart of the flurry of interest in organizational "culture" as the cure-all for organizational problems that appeared in the 1980s (Mohan, 1993). Unfortunately, organizational life is not that simple, and mere reliance on more and better communications cannot bring about major, positive changes for an organization.

Before we turn to a more comprehensive examination of communication problems and their consequences in organizations, a simple view of optimal communications will be presented. The view is simple because it is complementary to the earlier discussion of rationality and decision-making.

Communications in organizations should provide accurate information with the appropriate emotional overtones to all members who need the communication content. This assumes that neither too much nor too little information is in the system and that it is clear from the outset who can utilize what is available.

It should be evident that the above scenario is an impossible condition to achieve in a complex organization. Indeed, organizations gather more information than they use but also continue to ask for more (Feldman and March, 1981). This is attributed to decision-makers' need for legitimacy. In addition, the communication process is inherently paradoxical and contradictory (Brunsson, 1989; Manning, 1992). Paradoxes and contradictions permeate organizational life.

In the sections that follow, the factors contributing to the impossibility of perfect communication systems will be examined. These factors range from those that are apparently inherent (through learning) in any social grouping to those that are peculiarly organizational. The focus will be primarily on communication within organizations. Communication with the environments of organizations will be considered later.

INDIVIDUAL FACTORS

Since communication involves something being sent to a receiver, what the receiver does with or to the communicated message is perhaps the most vital part of the whole system. Therefore, the perceptual process becomes a key element in our understanding of communications in organizations.

The perceptual process is subject to many factors that can lead to important differences in the way any two people perceive the same person or message. Even physical objects can be perceived differently. Perceivers may respond to cues they are not aware of, be influenced by emotional factors, use irrelevant cues, weigh evidence in an unbalanced way, or fail to identify all the factors on which their judgments are based. People's personal needs, values, and interests enter the perceptual process. Most communications take place in interaction with others, and how one person perceives the "other" in the interaction process vitally affects how a person will perceive the communication, since other people are more emotion inducing than physical objects are. For example, research has shown that a person's interactions, and thus perceptions, are affected even by the expectations of what the other person will look like (Zalkind and Costello, 1962).

These factors are common to all perceptual situations. For the analysis of perceptions in organizations, they must be taken as basic conditions in the communication process. So it is obvious that perfect perception—that is, perception uniform across all information recipients—is impossible in any social situation. The addition of organizational factors makes the whole situation that much more complex.

Communications in organizations are basically transactions between individuals. Even when written or broadcast forms are used, the communicator is identified as an individual. The impression that the communication receiver has of the communicator is thus crucial in the interpretation of the communication. Impressions in these instances are not created de novo; the receiver utilizes his or her learned response set to the individual and the situation. The individual's motives and values enter the situation. In addition, the setting or surroundings of the act of communication affect the impression. A neat, orderly, and luxuriously furnished office contributes to a reaction different from the one given by an office that looks and smells like a locker room. Since the perceptual process itself requires putting ideas and people into categories, the interaction between communicators is also subject to "instant categorization," that is, you cannot understand other people unless they are placed in some relevant part of your learned perceptual repertoire. This is often done on the basis of a very limited amount of evidence—or even wrong evidence, as when the receiver notes cues that are wrong or irrelevant to the situation in question (Zalkind and Costello, 1962:221).

Organizational position affects how communications are perceived or sent. In almost all organizations, people can be superordinates in one situation and subordinates in another. The assistant superintendent of a school system is superordinate to a set of principals but subordinate to the superintendent and the school board. Communications behavior differs according to one's position in a role set. If the individual is in a role in which he or she is or has been or feels discriminated against, communications are affected. A study found that women who had suffered discrimination in their roles had a lower feeling of autonomy than others in the same role. This in turn was related to distortions in the information that they communicated upward in the organization (Athanassaides, 1974).

All of these factors are further complicated by the well-known phenomenon of stereotyping. This predisposition to judge can occur before any interaction at all has taken place. It can involve the labels "labor," "management," "minority group," and any other group membership. The individuals involved are assumed to have the characteristics of the group of which they are members; in probably the vast majority of cases, however, the characteristics attributed to the group as a whole are distortions of reality. In the sense being used here, stereotyping is the imposition of negative characteristics on the members of the communication system. The reverse situation—attributing socially approved characteristics—can also occur, of course, with an equally strong potential for damage to the communication process.

Other factors that enter the communication process in somewhat the same manner are the use of the "halo effect," or the use of only one or a few indicators to generalize about a total situation: "projection," or a person's assuming that the other members of a communication system have the same characteristics as the person's own; and "perceptual defense," or altering inconsistent information to put it in line with the conceptual framework already developed. All the factors that have been mentioned here are part of the general literature on perception and must be assumed to be present in any communication system. They are not peculiar to organizations.

The characteristics of the perceived person affect what is perceived. Here are four conclusions from research on the perceiver:

1. Knowing oneself makes it easier to see others accurately.
2. One's own characteristics affect the characteristics that one is likely to see in others.
3. The person who is self-accepting is more likely to be able to see favorable aspects of other people.
4. Accuracy in perceiving others is not a single skill (Zalkind and Costello, 1962:227–229).

These findings are linked to the more general considerations, such as tendencies to stereotype or project. It is when the characteristics of the perceived are brought into the discussion that organizational conditions become important. Factors such as age affect how a person is perceived (Zenger and Lawrence, 1989). The person may be labeled a sales manager (accurately or not) by a production worker, and the entire communication system is affected until additional information is permitted into the system. The situation in which the communication takes place also has a profound impact on what is perceived. This is particularly vital in organizations, since in most cases the situation is easily labeled and identified by the physical location.

Organizations are full of all kinds of information, including gossip. There is a great deal of variance in the degree to which people are in social networks and receive information, whether it is gossip or not. Thus, information itself and individuals are part of the paradoxical communication process.

ORGANIZATIONAL FACTORS

It has already been noted that organizations develop their own cultures, with language, rituals, and styles of communications. It is clear that organizations attempt to socialize their personnel so that communication problems are minimized (Pascale, 1985). Despite the presence of a common culture and socialization efforts, however, organizations contain the seeds of communication problems when their vertical and horizontal components are considered.

VERTICAL COMMUNICATION

Patterns of vertical communication have received a lot of attention, primarily because they are so vital in organizational operations. From our discussions of organizational structure, power, and leadership, it should be evident that the vertical element is a crucial organizational fact of life. Since communication is also crucial, the vertical element intersects in a most important way. Vertical communications in organizations involve both downward and upward flows.

Downward Communication

There are five elements of downward communication (Katz and Kahn, 1978:440–443). The first is the simple and common job instruction, in which a subordinate is told what to do through direct orders, training sessions, job descriptions, or other such mechanisms. The intent of job instructions is to ensure reliable and consistent job performance. The more complex and uncertain the task, the more generalized the instructions. As a rule, the more highly trained the subordinates, the less specific the instructions are, because it is assumed that those individuals will bring with them an internalized knowledge of how to do the job, along with other job-related knowledge and attitudes.

The second element is more subtle and less often stressed. It involves the rationale for a task and its relationships to the rest of the organization. It is here that different philosophies of life affect how much this sort of information is communicated. If the philosophy is to keep the organizational members dumb and happy, little such information will be communicated. The organization may feel either that the subordinates are unable to comprehend the information or that they would misuse it by introducing variations into their performance based on their own best judgment of how the task should be accomplished. Even apart from the philosophy-of-life issue, this is a delicate matter. All organizations, even those most interested in the human qualities of their members, have hidden agendas of some sort at some time. If the total rationale for all actions were known to all members, the potential for chaos would be high, since communication overload would quickly occur. The danger of too much communication is matched by the opposite danger—too little communication—which also has strong potential for organizational malfunctioning. If the members are given too little information, and do not and cannot know how their work is related to any larger whole, there is a strong possibility that they will feel alienated from the work and the organization. Obviously, the selection of the best path between these extremes is important in the establishment of communications.

The third element of downward communication is information regarding procedures and practices within the organization. Like the first element (job instruction), it is relatively straightforward and noncontroversial. Here again, whether or not this is linked to the second element is problematic.

Feedback to individuals regarding their performance is the fourth element of the downward communication system. This is almost by definition a sticky issue, particularly when the feedback is negative. If the superior has attempted at all to utilize socioemotional ties to his or her subordinates, the issue becomes even more difficult. It becomes almost impossible when the work roles are so thoroughly set in advance by the organization that the worker has no discretion on the job at all. In these cases, only a totally conscious deviation would result in feedback. In the absence of deviation, there will probably be no feedback other than the paycheck and other routine rewards. Where discretion is part of the picture, the problem of assessment deepens, because feedback is more difficult to accomplish if there are no clear criteria on which to base it. Despite these evident problems, feedback is a consistent part of downward communications.

The final element of downward communication involves attempts to indoctrinate subordinates into accepting and believing in the organization's (or the subunit's) goals. The intent here, of course, is to get the personnel emotionally involved in their work and add this to the motivational system.

Downward communication takes place at all levels, from the top down. At each level it is interpreted by individuals, so that individual factors reenter our picture as information flows and is interpreted downward.

Upward Communication

Contrary to the law of gravity, communication in organizations must also go up, even when nothing is going down. According to Katz and Kahn (1978):

> Communication up the line takes many forms. It can be reduced, however, to what people say (1) about themselves, their performance, and their problems, (2) about

others and their problems, (3) about organizational practices and policies, and (4) about what needs to be done and how it can be done. (p. 446)

The content of these messages can obviously range from the most personal gripe to the most high-minded suggestion for improving the organization or the world; and the messages can have positive or negative consequences for the subordinate, from a promotion or a bonus to dismissal. Whistle-blowers are constantly in fear of dismissal. The most obvious problem in upward communication is again the hierarchy.

People are unlikely to pass information up if it will be harmful to themselves or their peers. Thus, the amount and kind of information that is likely to be passed upward is affected by hierarchy. Anyone who has been in any kind of organization knows that discussions with the boss, department head, president, supervisor, or other superior are, at least initially, filled with something approaching terror, regardless of the source of the superior's power in the organization.

Another facet of upward communication is important: whereas communications downward become more detailed and specific, those going up the hierarchy must become condensed and summarized. Indeed, a major function of those in the middle of a hierarchy is the filtering and editing of information. Only crucial pieces of information are supposed to reach the top. This can be seen in clear relief at the national level, where the president of the United States receives highly condensed accounts of the huge number of issues of national and international concern. Regardless of the party in power, the filtering and editing process is vital in the hierarchy, since the basis on which things are "edited out" can have enormous repercussions by the time the information reaches the top. Here, as well as in downward communication, the perceptual limitations we noted earlier are in operation, so there is a very real potential for distorted communications and, more important, for decisions different from those that would have been made if some other editing process were in force (Halberstam, 1972; Wilensky, 1967).

There is an interesting technological twist here. Computer-based information technology is increasingly important in the organizational communication process. The twist is that top executives, especially older, more senior ones, may leave the handling of computer-based information to their staff and subordinates (March and Sproul, 1990). Only time will tell if this situation will change.

Dysfunctions of Hierarchy and Some Positive Outcomes

There are three specific dysfunctions of hierarchy for the communication process. In the first place, hierarchical divisions inhibit communications. There is a common tendency for people at the same status level to interact more with one another than with those at different levels. At the same time, there is a tendency for those in lower-status positions to look up to and direct friendship overtures toward those in higher-status positions. This increases the flow of socioemotional communications upward, but at the same time it leaves those at the bottom of the hierarchy in the position of receiving little of this type of input. This situation is further complicated by the fact that those in higher-status positions also direct such communications upward rather than reciprocating to their subordinates, thus reducing the amount of satisfaction derived for all parties.

A second dysfunction is that approval is sought from superiors rather than from peers in such situations. Nonperformance criteria enter the communication system, in that respect from peers, which can be earned on the basis of performance, can become secondary to approval-gaining devices that may not be central to the tasks at hand. The plethora of terms ranging from *apple-polishing* to more obscene expressions is indicative of this.

A third dysfunction has to do with the error-correcting function of normal social interaction. Interaction among peers tends to sort out errors and at least provides a common denominator through the interaction process. This is much less likely to happen in upward communication. Subordinates are unlikely to tell a superior that they think an order or an explanation is wrong, fearing for their own positions. Criticism of one's superior is clearly not the most popular form of communication in organizations (Blau and Scott, 1962:121–124).

These problems associated with upward communication in organizations are compounded by the factors affecting individual perception, which we discussed earlier. Since rank in an organization is a structural fact, it carries with it a strong tendency toward stereotyping. The very terms *management, worker, student, general,* and so on are indicative of the value loadings associated with rank. Status differences are necessary and do have their positive side; but the negative connotations attached to many of the stereotypes, and the likelihood that communications will be distorted because of real or assumed differences between statuses, build in difficulties for organizational communications.

In keeping with the earlier discussion in which it was noted that complex organizations contain paradoxes and contradictions, there are also beneficial aspects to hierarchical patterns for the communication process. The studies by Blau and his associates (Blau, 1968; Blau, Heydebrand, and Stauffer, 1966), cited earlier, are a case in point. It will be recalled that in organizations with highly trained or professionalized personnel, a tall or deep hierarchy was associated with effectiveness. The explanation was that the hierarchy provided a continuous source of error detection and correction. The presence of experts in an organization also increases the extent of horizontal communications (Hage, Aiken, and Marrett, 1971). These can take the form of scheduled or unscheduled committee meetings or more spontaneous interactions. Communications are a vital source of coordination when organizations are staffed with a diverse set of personnel offering different forms of expertise (Brewer, 1971). If a tall hierarchy is found in an organization with a low level of differentiation in expertise, it is apparently because of the need for extensive downward communications. There is an additional aspect of hierarchy that is important. Unless one assumes that people always rise to a level just above that of their competence (Peter and Hull, 1969), the superiors may in fact be superior; that is, they may actually have more ability than their subordinates since they have more experience. If this is recognized and legitimated by the subordinates, some of the hierarchical problems are again minimized.

The most obvious contribution of a hierarchy is coordination (Hage, 1980). If one accepts the common model of communications spreading out in more detail as they move down the hierarchy, then the role of the hierarchy becomes clear. It is up to the superior to decide who gets what kind of communication and when. The superior becomes the distribution and filtering center. Given the vast amount of information that is potentially available for the total organization, this role is crucial.

HORIZONTAL COMMUNICATION

Communications in organizations go in more directions than up and down. Horizontal or lateral communication is a regular and important facet of organizational life. The focus of most analyses of communication has been the vertical axis. The horizontal component has received less attention, even though a greater proportion of the communication in an organization appears to be of this type. A study of a textile factory indicates that the lower the level in the hierarchy, the greater the proportion of horizontal communication (Simpson, 1969). This is not surprising, if for no other reason than that in most organizations there are simply more people at each descending level. This fact and the already noted tendency for communication to be affected by hierarchical differences make it natural for people to communicate with those at about the same level in the organization. And those at the same level are more apt to share common characteristics, making horizontal communication even more likely.

Communication within an organizational subunit is quite different from communication between subunits. Within-unit communication is "critical for effective system functioning" (Katz and Kahn, 1978:444). In most cases, it is impossible for an organization to work out in advance every conceivable facet of every task assigned throughout the organization. At some point, there will have to be coordination and discussion among a set of peers as the work proceeds; therefore, this interplay between individuals is vital in the coordination process. Communication within subunits contains much richer content than organizational task coordination materials. Katz and Kahn state:

> The mutual understanding of colleagues is one reason for the power of the peer group. Experimental findings are clear and convincing about the importance of socio-emotional support for people in both organized and unorganized groups. Psychological forces always push people toward communication with peers: people in the same boat share the same problems. *Hence, if there are no problems of task coordination left to a group of peers, the content of their communication can take forms which are irrelevant to or destructive of organizational functioning.* (p. 445; italics in the original)

The implication here is clear. It is beneficial to leave some task-oriented communications to work groups at every level of the organization so that the potentially counterproductive communications do not arise to fill the void. This implication must be modified, however, by a reference back to the general model that is being followed here. Organizational, interpersonal, and individual factors are all part of the way people behave in organizations. If the organizational arrangements are such that horizontal communications are next to impossible, then there is little likelihood of any communication. Work in extremely noisy circumstances or in isolated work locales would preclude much interaction. (These situations, of course, contain their own problems for the individual and the organization.) On the other side of the coin, too much coordination and communications responsibility left to those who, through lack of training or ability, are unable to come to a reasonable joint decision about some matter would also be individually and organizationally disruptive.

Although it is relatively easy, in abstract terms, to describe the optimal mix of vertical and horizontal communications, another element of communications among peers is important. Since the communications among peers tend to be based on common understandings, and since continued communications build up the solidarity of the group, work groups develop collective responses to the world around them. These collective responses are likely to be accompanied by collective perceptions of communications passed to or through the work groups. These collective perceptions can be collective distortions. It is clear that work groups (as well as other interest groups) can perceive communications in a totally different light from what was intended. A relatively simple piece of information, such as a memo about possible reorganization, can be interpreted to mean that an entire workforce will be eliminated.

Interaction among peers is only one form of horizontal communication. Another form, obviously vital, occurs between members of different organizational subunits. There is little research on this subject. The principal reason seems to be that such communications are not supposed to occur. In almost every conceivable form of organization, communications are supposed to go through the hierarchy until they reach the "appropriate" office, at the point where the hierarchies of the two units involved come together. That is, the communications are designed to flow through the office that is above the two departments or units involved, so that the hierarchy is familiar with the intent and content of the communications. In a simple example, problems between production and sales are supposed to be resolved through either the office or the individual in charge of both activities.

In reality, such a procedure occurs in only a minority of such lateral communications. There is a great deal more face-to-face and memo-to-memo communication throughout the ranks of the subunits involved, primarily because the communication system would be totally clogged if all information regarding subunit interaction had to flow all the way up one of the subunits and then all the way back down another. The clogging of the system would result in either painfully slow communications or none at all.

Therefore, the parties involved generally communicate directly with each other. This saves time and can often mean a very reasonable solution worked out at a lower level with good cooperation. However, it may also mean that those further up the hierarchy are unaware of what has happened, and that can be harmful in the long run. A solution to this problem is to record and pass along the information about what has been done, but that may be neglected; even if it is not neglected, it may not be noticed.

Although the emphasis in this discussion has been on coordination between subunits, much of the communication of this sort is actually based on conflict. Professional departments are a good example. When professionals or experts make up divisions of an organization, their areas of expertise are likely to lead them to different conclusions about the same matter (Hage, 1974:101–124). For example, in a petroleum company it is quite conceivable that the geological, engineering, legal, and public relations divisions could all come to different conclusions about the desirability of starting new oil-well drilling in various locations. Each would be correct in its own area of expertise, and the coordination of top officials would obviously be required when a final decision had to be made. During the period of planning or development, however, communications between these divisions would probably be characterized as nonproductive, since the specialists involved would be talking in their own language, one that is unfamiliar to those not in the same profession. From the evidence at hand, each division would also be correct in its assessments of the situation and would view the other divisions as not understanding the "true" meanings of the situation.

This type of communication problem is not limited to professionalized divisions. Communications between subunits inevitably contain elements of conflict. The conflict will be greater if the units involved invest values in their understanding and conceptualizations. Horizontal communications across organizational lines thus contain both the seeds and the flowers of conflict. Such conflict, by definition, will contribute to distortion of communications in one form or another. At the same time, passing each message up the line to eliminate such distortion through coordination at the top has the dangers of diluting the message in attempts to avoid conflict and of taking so much time that the message becomes meaningless. Here again, the endemic complexities of an organization preclude a totally rational operation.

Both horizontal and vertical aspects of organizations create complications for communication. At the same time, there are situations in which these obstacles are overcome. An excellent example is an analysis of aircraft carrier flight decks (Weick and Roberts, 1993). When aircraft are landing, the work pace is furious, the noise overwhelming, and the possibility for tragic error great. Despite these conditions, flight decks operate very effectively. Communication works across ranks and organizational divisions. Weick and Roberts believe that this is based on "heedful interrelating" and a "collective mind" (p. 357). Everyone is extremely focused. Everyone is well trained. Similar situations certainly exist with successful sports teams and in other spheres of life. At the same time, the flight-deck example is striking because it is so different. In the more mundane spheres of organizational life, the vertical and horizontal factors intrude on communication.

Communication Networks

Before we turn to a more systematic examination of the consequences of all these communication problems in organizations, there is a final bit of evidence regarding the manner in which communications evolve. The communication process can be studied in laboratory situations; among organizational characteristics, it is perhaps the most amenable to such experimentation. There has been a long history (Bavelas, 1950; Leavitt, 1951) of attempting to isolate the communication system that is most efficient under a variety of circumstances. These laboratory studies are applicable to both the vertical and the horizontal aspects of communications, since the manner in which the communication tasks are coordinated is the major focus. Three primary communication networks between members of work groups have been studied: (1) the "wheel" pattern, (2) the "circle" pattern, and (3) the "all-channel" system. The wheel pattern requires all persons at the periphery of the wheel to send their communications to the hub. This is an imposed hierarchy, since those at the periphery cannot send messages to each other; it is the task of the hub to do the coordinating. The circle pattern permits each member of the group to talk to those on either side, with no priorities. The all-channel system allows everyone to communicate with everyone else.

Using success in arriving at a correct solution as the criterion of efficiency, repeated investigations have found the wheel pattern to be superior. The other patterns can become equally efficient if they develop a hierarchy, but that takes time, and meanwhile efficiency is reduced. The more complex the task, the more time is required for the communication network to become structured. The importance of these findings for our purposes is that whether the communications are vertical or horizontal, hierarchical patterns emerge. In the vertical situation, the hierarchy is already existing, although the formal hierarchy can be modified through the power considerations of expertise or personal attraction. In the horizontal situation, a hierarchy will emerge. Communication takes place on the basis of organizational structure; it also contributes to the development of structuring.

COMMUNICATION PROBLEMS

It should be clear that communications in organizations are not perfect. The basic consequence of existing communication systems is that messages are transformed or altered as they pass through the system. The fact that they are transformed means that the ultimate recipient of the message receives something different from what was originally sent, thus destroying the intent of the communication process.

Omission

Omission is one of two major forms of transformation, the other being distortion (Guetzkow, 1965). Omission involves the "deletion of aspects of messages"

(p. 551), and it occurs because the recipients may not be able to grasp the entire content of the message and receive or pass on only what they are able to grasp. Communication overload can also lead to the omission of materials, since some messages may not be handled because of the overload. Omission may be intentional, as when certain classes of information are deleted from the information passed through particular segments of the organization. Omission is most evident in upward communications, since more messages are generated by the large number of people and units lower in the hierarchy. As the communications are filtered on the way up, the omissions occur. When omissions are intentional, it is vital to know the criteria for omitting some kinds of information. Omission can occur simply as a removal of details, with the heart of the message still transmitted upward. This is the ideal, of course, but is not usually achieved, since part of the content of the message is usually omitted also.

Distortion

Distortion refers to altered meanings of messages as they pass through the organization. From the earlier discussion of perceptions, it is clear that people are selective, intentionally or unintentionally, about what they receive as messages. Guetzkow (1965) states:

> [B]ecause different persons man different points of initiation and reception of messages, there is much assimilation of meanings to the context within which transmission occurs. Frames of reference at a multitude of nodes differ because of variety in personal and occupational background, as well as because of difference in viewpoint induced by the communicator's position in the organization. (p. 555)

Distortion is as likely to occur in horizontal communications as in vertical, given the differences between organizational units in objectives and values. Selective omission and distortion, or "coding," are not unique properties of organizations. They occur in all communication systems, from the family to the total society. They are crucial for organizations, however, since organizations depend upon accurate communications as a basis for decision-making.

Overload

The communication problem that is perhaps more characteristic of organizations than of other social entities is communication overload. Overload leads to omission and contributes to distortion. It also leads to other coping and adjustment mechanisms on the part of the organization. There are adaptive and maladaptive adjustments to the overload situation. Omission and distortion are maladaptive. They are also normal.

Another device used when overload occurs is queuing. This technique lines up the messages by time of receipt or by some other such criterion. Queuing can have positive or negative consequences. If the wrong priority system is used, less important messages may be acted upon before those that are really crucial reach the recipient. At the same time, queuing does allow recipients to act on messages as they come in without putting them in a state of inaction because of total overload. An example of this is an anecdote from a disaster following a major earthquake. Organizations dealing with the earthquake were besieged with messages. Some organizations allowed victims to plead for help face-to-face, letting them crowd into an office and all talk at once; this quickly brought the organizations involved to a halt. The overload was so great that the communications could not be filtered in any way. Another organization received its messages by telephone, a device providing an arbitrary queuing mechanism based on an operating telephone and the luck of finding an open line. This organization was able to keep functioning, because the messages came in one at a time. In such a queuing situation, of course, there are no real criteria to determine which messages get through and which do not, other than time phasing and luck in getting a telephone line.

A useful modification of queuing is the previously mentioned filtering process, which involves setting priorities for messages. The critical factor here is the nature of the priorities. Many organizations utilize a modified triage system in which the most important messages are permitted to come into the system if it is perceived that the organizations can take relevant actions. Less important messages are then taken in as time permits. This sort of filtering system must be set up in advance. The question always is, What is the principle on which filtering takes place?

All the communication problems discussed derive from the fact that communications in organizations require interpretation. If there is a case of extreme overload, the interpretive process becomes inundated with so much material that it becomes inoperative. Queuing and filtering are techniques designed to sort messages into priorities. Any priority system established in advance means that an interpretation of messages has already been made, with some deemed more important than others. Thus, interpretation occurs regardless of whether priorities are set in advance or simply as messages are received.

Organizations generate and receive a vast amount of material. If we think of an organization as a pyramid, the huge mass at the base is the information entering an organization's communication system. As information moves up and through the organization, it is filtered and condensed. It arrives at the top in the form of an "executive summary." The amount of information, like the pyramid, keeps getting smaller as it rises in the organization. Here the pyramid analogy must be abandoned, since the determination of which information moves up is subject to the types of human and organizationally based interpretations we have been considering.

COMMUNICATION TO AND FROM OUTSIDE THE ORGANIZATION

The focus thus far has been internal organizational communication. The complications and problems that have been identified appear even more severe when we realize that so much of what is really important for an organization comes into it from its environment—competitors, creditors, customers, regulators, taxers, constituents, and so on. In addition, there are the more general environmental messages that are sent to and from an organization, such as changes in prime interest rates, demographic shifts, or petroleum price increases. Communications with the environment greatly compound the communication problems that have already been identified.

POSSIBLE SOLUTIONS

With all the problems, potential and real, in the communication process, it is obvious that a "perfect" communication system is unlikely. But although perfection, like rationality, will not be achieved, organizations do have mechanisms by which they attempt to keep the communication system as clear as they can. There are several devices that are available to reduce the distortions and other complications in the communication process (Downs, 1967). Redundancy, or the duplication of reports for verification, though adding to the flow of messages and paper in an organization, allows more people to see or hear a particular piece of information and respond to it. This is a correction device. There are several ways to create redundancy, including the use of information sources external to the situation—such as reports that are generated outside the organization—thus ensuring that reporting units and individuals coordinate their communications.

A common solution to at least some communication problems is the ubiquitous meeting. Meetings have the potential for yielding common meanings among participants, particularly when the intent of the meetings is to achieve consensus. Although meetings are quite valuable, it is obvious that time spent in meetings is time not spent on other activities. Research indicates that people vary in their perceptions of the usefulness of meetings (Rogelberg et al., 2006), and this may affect whether meetings are effective in helping solve communication problems.

Another way in which communication problems can be reduced is through matrix-like systems. A study of a psychiatric hospital found committees or teams that were composed of personnel from the various occupational specialties in the hospital and from the established departments in the hospital (Blau and Alba, 1982). The teams were designed to deal with various issues and programs of the hospital, and hospital personnel served on multiple teams. In addition, traditional ranks were eliminated. For example, a team could have a nurse as the team leader and psychiatrists as team members. Blau and Alba report that these overlapping circles of weak ties inhibited segmentation and sustained participation because participants were rewarded for participating. Their data indicate that there was extensive interunit communication. There are limitations to this approach, of course. Its applicability in other forms of organizations is uncertain, and the approach requires the commitment of all the participants up through the head of the organization.

Some organizations have turned to "project groups" as a means of solving communication problems. These groups, or *task forces* as they are sometimes called, are typically composed of personnel from a variety of organizational units. Their usual purpose is to develop a new product or service for the organization. They may be isolated from the rest of the organization in the hope that this will enable them to think and work together. One analysis of research and development project groups composed of scientists and engineers found that such groups became increasingly isolated from key information sources within and outside their organizations (Katz, 1982). Over time, their productivity decreased, with the communication process increasingly focused inward. Such project groups or task forces are probably better off with a short span of existence and a sunset clause specifying a termination date.

A major mechanism for achieving consensus about the meaning of communication is putting things in writing, such as contracts. Even though communication in writing is subject to interpretation, lawyers and accountants make much of their living by negotiating consensus in meanings between parties. This is not the answer for all problems, of course, but it is one way to avoid communication chaos.

The nature of, problems in, and suggested solutions for communications all point to the centrality of this process in much of what happens in an organization. But it is evident that the communication system is vitally affected by other structural and process factors. Communications do not exist outside the total organizational framework. They cannot be over- or underemphasized. More and more accurate communications do not lead inevitably to greater effectiveness for the organization. The key to the communication process in organizations is to ensure that the correct people get the correct information (in amount and quality) at the correct time. All of these factors can be anticipated to some degree. If organizations, their members, and their environments were all in a steady state, communication tasks would be easier. Since obviously they are not, the communication process must be viewed as a dynamic one, with new actors, new media, and new definitions constantly entering the scene. As noted at the beginning of this chapter, ambiguities and paradoxes are to be anticipated.

The media of communication in organizations have received little attention in our analysis here. Breakthroughs in the forms of information and word processing, faxing, electronic message sending and receiving, and the Internet continue. Advanced communication technology itself is not the cure for organizational communication problems. The problems are rooted in the nature of organizations, their participants, and their interactions with their environments.

SUMMARY AND CONCLUSIONS

The communication process in organizations in itself is a complicated one because of individual idiosyncrasies, biases, and abilities and is further complicated by organizational characteristics such as hierarchy or specialization. Nonetheless, communications within organizations are central for the other processes of power, leadership, and decision-making. Communications are shaped by organizational structure and continue to reshape structure.

The "perfect" communication system is yet to be devised and probably never will be. Technological changes in various forms have contributed to more rapid processing of information, but the issues and problems considered in this chapter are not erased by advanced technology; in fact, in some instances they are exacerbated.

EXERCISES

1. Describe the extent to which communication omission, distortion, and overload take place in your two organizations. Why does this happen?
2. When communications take place in your two organizations, how are they affected by vertical and horizontal factors?

Chapter 8

Managing Organizational Environments: Conceptions of the Environment

OVERVIEW

Our discussion of organizations has, at various points, underscored the importance of factors that are not directly under an organization's control but that affect what it is likely to do—a vast array of influences included under the rubric of "organizational environments." In this chapter, we consider some of the different approaches to conceptualizing organizational environments, first discussing early efforts to identify broad, key dimensions of environments, then describing a line of work examining interorganizational relations (IORs) as a key aspect of environments, and finally discussing contemporary studies that have focused on a variety of selected aspects of organizations' environments. In the following chapter, we continue this discussion by describing a number of broad theoretical paradigms that focus attention on how particular aspects of organizational environments affect particular outcomes.

One definition of the environment is that offered by Hawley: "all phenomena that are external to and potentially or actually influence the population under study" (1968:330). (Hawley used the term *population* to refer to social collectivities more generally—from societies to ethnic groups—but as used, it would also apply to individual organizations.) This gives you some idea of the scope of the phenomena considered in this chapter. That the environment of an organization strongly affects what it does and its outcomes may seem like such an obvious claim that it's hardly worth spending the ink to print it, but surprisingly, early studies of organizations often gave short shrift to the consideration of environmental influences. As we noted in Chapters 2 and 3, much of this work treated organizations as closed systems, focusing largely, if not exclusively, on relations among different components and features of an organization itself in explaining how and why it had a particular structure, how well it performed, and so forth. We also noted a number of reasons for this focus, such as the pragmatic concerns of some researchers, which led them to concentrate on those aspects more amenable to an organization's control and alteration; environmental factors are often much harder to change. Another possible reason for taking a closed-systems approach, though, is the sheer scope of trying to conceptualize, in some coherent fashion, all of the factors that make up the environment.

"DISCOVERING" ORGANIZATIONAL ENVIRONMENTS

Despite initial predispositions toward a closed-systems approach, a number of studies that ostensibly set out to understand relations among internal components of organizations ended up underscoring the need to consider environmental influences on organizations. One line of research that was particularly important in this respect was that produced by students of sociologist Robert Merton in the years following World War II. We referred to this work earlier (see Chapter 2) when we discussed the influence of structural–functionalist theory on early studies by sociologists of organizations. As we noted, this theoretical framework directed sociologists' attention to the analysis of the functions that existing structures served, in terms of enhancing collectivities' day-to-day interactions and operations and, ultimately, their survival. One of the major architects of this theoretical tradition was a sociologist, Talcott Parsons, and one of the common criticisms of Parsons' work was that its emphasis on the functional consequences (or the benefits) of existing structures made it difficult to explain why structures ever changed (Collins, 1994; Collins and Makowsky, 2005; Turner and Beeghley, 1981).

Robert Merton, a student of Parsons and a prominent theorist in his own right, sought to address this criticism by proposing a theory of structural change that was consistent with the general logic of functionalism. Merton (1949) argued that structures typically develop as solutions to recurring problems faced by a collectivity; thus, existing structures do have manifest or intended consequences. However, structures also often have latent, or unintended, consequences; such latent consequences *can* be beneficial for the collective, but they are often negative—they create new problems. To give an example from a classic functionalist explanation for social stratification offered by Davis and Moore (1945), if a social group has trouble finding individuals who are able and willing to carry out certain tasks that the group wants accomplished, it may assign higher rewards to these tasks in order to induce individuals who have the requisite skills to do them. Getting the tasks done competently would be the intended consequence of this arrangement. An unintended consequence might be envy and conflict among group members, created by perceived inequities in the assignment of rewards. Merton suggested that changes in structures were likely to occur when the positive consequences of existing structures (presumably manifest consequences are always positive) were exceeded by latent, negative consequences. Following the example, if inequality creates too many problems among group members, either the reward system will be changed or the collectivity will implode as its members revolt or leave.

To provide empirical evidence for these sorts of general arguments about structural change, Merton and his students (e.g., Blau, 1955; Gouldner, 1954; Selznick, 1966) began to study organizations, with the notion that an organization could be viewed, in many ways at least, as a society in microcosm. This line of studies has three common characteristics: (1) they are typically case studies—rich, detailed descriptions of day-to-day life in organizations; (2) they focus on the interrelations among different organizational components, particularly on the way in which changes in one component lead to changes in others; and (3) they duly detail both the intended and the unintended consequences of organizational structures. As Perrow (1986:164) noted, work in this tradition provides some of the most interesting and readable academic analyses of organizations that have ever been published.

Perhaps ironically, although the explicit focus of this research was on understanding changes *within* organizations, one of the unintended consequences of this line of work was to draw attention to the importance of environmental forces. For example, Blau's (1964) study of a state employment office examined how changes in the record-keeping system for personnel affected individual behaviors and relations among coworkers, but as he reports, a major force for changing the record-keeping system in the first place came from outside the organization—a very weak labor market at the end of World War II, which made it much more difficult for the organization to achieve its goals of helping job seekers get jobs. Likewise, Gouldner's (1954) study of a gypsum mine and manufacturing company focused on the impact of changes in leadership on the use of rules, supervisory practices, and the general relations between workers and management. However, his account indicated that an important part of the impetus for leadership change came from increasing pressure the company faced from its competitors, raising the need for greater efficiencies in organizational operations. Selznick's (1966) study of the Tennessee Valley Authority focused on how its efforts to ensure the democratic representation of constituents' preferences in its decision-making led to its co-optation by wealthier farmers. As Selznick notes, the initial mandate for democratic representation, though, reflected the influence of widespread, negative social attitudes during this era toward elite-dominated economic organizations. Thus, cumulatively, work in this tradition clearly indicated that neglecting the role of environmental forces in explanations of the behavior of organizations was a key oversight (Hinings and Tolbert, 2008; Tolbert and Zucker, 1996).

DEFINING THE ENVIRONMENT

Core Dimensions

As suggested by our opening remark in this chapter, however, how to think about the vast array of factors denoted by concept, "the environment," is a challenge, one that organizational theorists are still wrestling with today. Some of the earliest efforts to address this problem produced rather abstract catalogs of different dimensions of environments (e.g., Emery and Trist, 1965; Levine and White, 1961; Terreberry, 1968). Because you still see references to these dimensions in more contemporary literature, we follow the synthesis offered by Aldrich (1979; see also Aldrich and Marsden, 1988), to give you a sense of this approach.

One often-mentioned dimension is "environmental capacity," which refers to the level of resources available to an organization. At a general level, this is a joint function of the demand for the goods and services an organization offers and the number of other organizations also offering the same kinds of goods and services. Capacity can be characterized at one extreme as "rich" (lots of resources) and at the other as "lean." Environmental capacity affects organizations' opportunities for growth, the degree of constraint they face in making decisions (March and Simon, 1958), and, ultimately, their chances for survival. This dimension relates to a key focus of one contemporary paradigm known as population ecology, which we'll discuss in the next chapter.

A second dimension is termed "heterogeneity," and this refers to the degree to which the organization faces very different demands by constituents. For example, a hotel that serves a range of clients, from families to business travelers to conventioneers, faces a more heterogeneous environment than one that focuses on serving young, affluent adventure travelers. Dealing with an array of constituents who have different expectations and demands makes decision-making more complicated but may also offer more opportunities for attracting resources and for dealing with fluctuations in support from a given set of constituents (Dowell, 2006).

A third dimension is "stability"; this taps a temporal aspect—the rate at which change occurs in products, clients, funding, or other elements of the environment, changes to which the organization has to respond if it is to survive (Barnett and McKendrick, 2004; Gersick, 1991; Meyer, 1982). High levels of instability require organizations to be able to change quickly without becoming unreliable and/or wracked by internal conflict. Below, we describe in some detail a well-known study by Lawrence and Lorsch (1967) that suggests the ways in which organizations that operate in stable and unstable environments are likely to differ.

A fourth dimension is referred to as "environmental concentration"; this refers to the distribution of resources used by the organization across geographical and/or temporal space. You could think of this as the environmental analog of spatial complexity; the greater the environmental concentration, the less likely is an organization dealing with this environment to be spatially complex. The concentration of resources may also be related to other aspects of the environment, in particular to competition with other organizations (Aharonson, Baum, and Feldman, 2007).

A fifth dimension sometimes discussed in the literature is "domain consensus." This involves the degree to which there is agreement among related organizations and other groups in society about which organizations have the right to provide particular goods and services to whom. For example, when a crime is committed on a university campus, there is sometimes disagreement among different law enforcement agencies (e.g., campus police, municipal police, the Federal Bureau of Investigation) over which agency should direct and control the investigation; this state reflects a lack of domain consensus. A lack of domain consensus often entails increased competition among organizations and may lead them to seek state or even international regulation to reduce this (Abbott, 1988; Halliday and Carruthers, 2007).

The last dimension that we will discuss is one denoted as "environmental turbulence." This is related to environmental instability, but it is instability that is associated with a particular feature of IORs: close interconnections among a set of organizations, or very dense networks, such that change that affects any one of them produces a domino effect among the others. Strong ties between organizations often provide them with access to important information and other resources (McEvily and Marcus, 2005), but as the recent cases of the Enron Corporation and Barings Bank suggest, these can also create problems when one key organization in a network fails.

Interorganizational Relations

In contrast to such an abstract approach to thinking about the nature of organizational environments, an alternative approach taken by some researchers focused on organizations' ties to other organizations, examining both factors that affected the formation of such ties and the exchange of resources through the ties. Implicitly, this approach was premised on the assumption that other organizations represented a key (if not *the* key) aspect of a focal organization's environment (Haunschild and Miner, 1997), and it laid the foundation for some of the general theoretical perspectives that we'll discuss in Chapter 9, especially resource dependence. Early studies of IORs were prompted in part by the rapid growth of government-funded social service agencies in the 1960s, as part of the Great Society and War on Poverty programs begun under President Johnson (Levine, White, and Paul, 1963; Turk, 1975). Such growth, and increased government spending that accompanied it, generated concerns about duplication of efforts by different agencies and interest in bringing about better coordination among agencies in order to reduce inefficiencies and overall costs. Thus, much of the research in this area was focused on factors that affected the development of IORs, with an eye to encouraging such developments (Cook, 1977; Levine and White, 1961; Litwak and Hylton, 1962; Warren, 1967). In line with this, a consistent finding from the research on IORs among social service agencies is that strong ties contribute to improved health and social care at the community level (Alter and Hage, 1993; Goes and Park, 1997; Provan and Milward, 1995). The lack of ties among agencies may partly explain some of the observed social inequality in health care and other social outcomes. For example, a study by Galaskiewicz and Shatin (1981) indicated that poor neighborhoods draw fewer social service organizations and the organizations that are located in these neighborhoods have few interorganizational linkages. Hence, not only do poorer neighborhoods have fewer organizational resources, those resources may not be used as effectively as possible because of the absence of IORs among agencies that provide services.

Forms of Interorganizational Relations.   Three basic forms of IORs have been studied. These are illustrated in Figure 8–1. The dyadic or pairwise relationship is the simplest form of IOR and has probably received the most attention in empirical research. Research focusing on this form typically concentrates on understanding characteristics that make organizations compatible exchange partners.

The notion of an interorganizational set was derived from work on individuals' role sets (Merton, 1957) and was introduced into the literature on organizations by Evan (1966) and Caplow (1964). Analyses focusing on this form typically examine a focal agency (FA in Figure 8–1) and its dyadic relationships with other organizations; key questions addressed by work taking this approach include how do different ties simultaneously affect the functioning of a focal organization and what conditions facilitate or hinder the maintenance of multiple ties.

The third form of IOR is the interorganizational network, which consists "of all organizations linked by a specified type of relation and . . . constructed by finding the ties between all organizations in a population" (Aldrich, 1979:281). Networks are "the total pattern of interrelationships among a cluster of organizations that are meshed together in a social system to attain collective and self-interest

FIGURE 8–1   Forms of Interorganizational Relationships

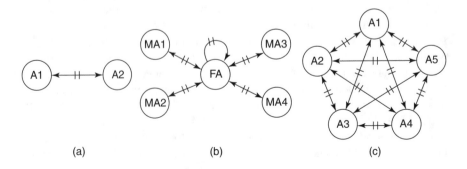

(a)   (b)   (c)

goals or to resolve specific problems in a target population" (Van de Ven and Ferry, 1980:299).

Pairwise or Dyadic Interorganizational Relationships. Most of the early work on IORs dealt with dyadic relations and attempted to identify the conditions under which a given organization might form a tie to another organization and factors that affected the strength of such ties (Klonglan et al., 1976; Levine and White, 1961; Litwak and Hylton, 1962; Molnar, 1978).

A basic precondition for IORs suggested by this literature is awareness. Van de Ven and Ferry (1980) propose two levels of awareness. One level involves basic knowledge of the goals, services, and resources present in other organizations. This awareness provides some insights into potential interdependence or reasons to form ties (Litwak and Hylton, 1962). The second level of awareness involves interpersonal ties among organizational personnel (Boje and Whetten, 1981). These can involve "old school" ties, membership in common professional organizations, membership in common religious or fraternal organizations, simple friendships, or contacts that are based solely on work. Interpersonal ties facilitate the initiation of interorganizational interaction and, ultimately, longer-term relationships (Galaskiewicz and Shatin, 1981). In line with this, a study of hotels in Sydney, Australia, revealed that friendship ties among hotel managers yielded enhanced collaboration and information exchange and mitigated competition (Ingram and Roberts, 2000). Similarly, research has shown that the existence of personal ties between members of auditing firms and their organizational clients contributes to the maintenance of such IORs over time (Seabright, Levinthal, and Fichman, 1992).

A second determinant of IORs that has been suggested is domain consensus. We discussed this previously in terms of work that sought to identify broad dimensions of organizational environments. In the literature on IORs, this concept refers specifically to agreement among organizations about the roles that they can and should play relative to one another, in regard to their programs and services and clients. When organizations have overlapping domains and cannot agree on which organization will be responsible for which set of clients or activities, they are unlikely to form enduring IORs (Aldrich, 1979). Ideological factors, including the compatibility of the goals of the organizations involved, common understanding of the nature of the sources of basic problems, and consensus on accepted treatment approaches, also affect domain consensus (Benson et al., 1973; Boje and Whetten, 1981; Mulford, 1980). For example, research has indicated that reproductive services organizations that are predicated on very different views of client–provider relationships are more likely to have clashes between staff members, making it difficult to sustain a relation (Zilber, 2002).

Yet another influence on the formation of IORs, which has received relatively less attention, is geographical proximity, or the spatial distance between organizations. It is more difficult for both organizations and individuals to establish or maintain relationships across distances. Proximity often enhances knowledge or awareness of other organizations and facilitates interaction among personnel from different organizations. The importance of proximity in shaping IORs may depend on the degree to which organizations are dependent upon a local area for their resources (Galaskiewicz, 1979; Maas, 1979). If organizations with local-ized dependence are successful in commanding local resources, they are more powerful or central in the network of organizations in a community, and this may enhance their ability to form IORs. If, on the other hand, there is high localized dependency with relatively weak access to resources, a given organization may be much less attractive as a partner to other organizations. It can also be noted that the type of unit involved in an IOR interacts with the spatial issue. Modern communication techniques permit the rapid flow of information across space, but clients or staff members are more difficult to transfer.

A final influence on IORs is the size of the actual or potential set or network of organizations (Litwak and Hylton, 1962). This is relevant because it affects the number of organizations available to form ties at any given point in time. Turk (1973) found that the scale of municipal government was positively related to the development of IORs. Increased size may provide general resources that enable organizations to engage in IORs. The number of organizations in a given setting may also affect the strength of IORs that are formed: when organizations form large numbers of IORs, the quality of the relationships weakens (Caragonne, 1978; John, 1977). An analogy with individuals is appropriate here. Many ties reduce the likelihood of each tie being strong, so that there would be a greater proportion of superficial linkages or IORs in a large network than in a smaller network.

Joint Ventures and Strategic Alliances.   Current interest in dyadic IORs is reflected in a spate of studies on joint ventures and strategic alliances among business firms. Such activities represent a relatively strong form of IOR, often involving substantial resource commitment and collaboration between two (and sometimes more) organizations in order to accomplish some common goal (Ahuja, 2000; Beckman, Haunschild, and Phillips, 2004). Participating organiza-tions invest resources and pursue "enduring exchange relationships with one another" (Podolny and Page, 1998:59). One example of such collaboration is provided by the hybrid electric vehicle (HEV) project that was begun in 1993, with funding provided jointly by General Motors, Ford, and Chrysler, along with the support of the Department of Energy. The HEV project involved creating a new, separate research and development unit, whose goal was to produce a market-ready vehicle that could operate on electric power within ten years (http://www.nrel.gov/vehiclesandfuels/hev/about.html); all three firms would share in the benefits of the research outputs of this project.

Interestingly, recent work on joint ventures and strategic alliances among business firms has replicated findings from earlier studies that focused on non-profit social service agencies. It has documented both the importance of interde-pendencies among firms as a basis for forming such IORs (Khanna, Gulati, and Nohria, 1998; Litwak and Hylton, 1962) and the self-perpetuating tendencies of such ties. For example, Gulati (1995b) found that firms that entered into strategic alliances with another firm had a significant probability of entering into another alliance with the same firm at a later time point; this finding echoes the results of earlier research by Aiken and Hage (1968) on joint programs among social service agencies, which showed that establishing one joint program tended to foster other joint programs.

The Interorganizational Set.   As noted, the approach to IORs as an interorganizational set is derived from work on individual-level role sets (Merton, 1957). The key finding of this latter work is that the way a person enacts a given role (e.g., student) is conditioned by other role statuses that she or he occupies (e.g., sorority president, daughter, rock band singer). By the same token, the notion of interorganizational set draws attention to the way in which a given dyadic relation that an organization has with another is likely to be shaped by other IORs the organization has. On the basis of this idea, Evan (1966) offered a number of provocative hypotheses about the way in which the characteristics of the set of organizations to which a focal organization was tied (e.g., the degree of congruence in key values, concentration or dispersion of resources among the organizations in the set, and the total number of interconnected organizations) influenced the focal organization's autonomy and decision-making processes. Many of these arguments are reflected in the theoretic tradition of resource dependence, discussed in Chapter 9.

However, this approach has been given relatively little attention in empirical studies. One key exception is research by Fennell (1980) on hospitals, addressing a problem that initiated much of the IOR studies: factors that affect coordination in the delivery of social services. Her analysis focused on hospital clusters—sets of hospitals within a geographically defined region—and the impact of suppliers to the cluster (doctors in the area) and the set of consumers (potential patients in the area) on differentiation in a cluster. The more each hospital offered distinct services (that didn't overlap with those offered by other hospitals), the more differentiated the cluster was. Her results indicated that cluster differentiation was driven much more by suppliers than consumers: as hospitals within a cluster competed to attract more prestigious physicians, thereby enhancing the organization's prestige, they were led to offer more unique services, regardless of the characteristics of the consumers.

Interorganizational Networks.   In recent years, researchers have given particular attention to interorganizational networks, perhaps partly because of the development of more sophisticated analytic tools for studying networks. (For a good description of the development of network analysis, see Scott and Davis, 2007.) Networks of organizations can be incredibly complex. Figure 8–2 depicts the network of organizations involved in human organ transplantations. The characteristics of the organizations that compose the network are important in determining outcomes—for example, whether patients receive transplants when they need them (Healy, 2004)—but the quality of relationships among the organizations may be equally, if not more, critical.

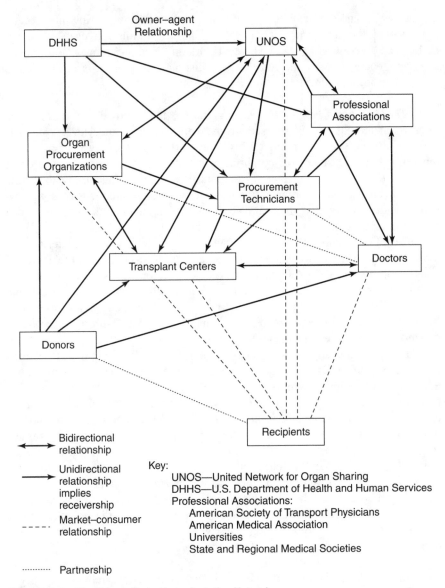

FIGURE 8–2   The Human Organ Transplantation Network

Source: Leslie A. Korb, "The Organ Transplantation Network: A Qualitative Examination of Power, Professionalism, Efficiency, Congruence and Compliance among Stakeholders" (PhD diss., University at Albany, Albany, NY, 2000). Reprinted by permission of Leslie Kolb.

Examination of networks has provided important insights that would be missed in studies of individual organizations. For example, research suggests that when the knowledge base of an industry is both complex and expanding, the locus of innovation is apt to be in networks rather than individual firms (Powell,

Koput, and Smith-Doerr, 1996). Moreover, studies of business organizations have provided ample evidence that network relations strongly influence economic decision-making (Broschak, 2004; Gulati and Gargiulo, 1999; Jensen, 2003; Uzzi, 1997). Network researchers argue that this is because organizational decision-makers are "embedded" in social relations (i.e., are part of networks) that provide them with information about different options and, perhaps more importantly, influence their assessment of the value of different options and thus guide their choices (Burt, 1992; Granovetter, 1985). Hence, in contrast to traditional economic approaches, which treat decision-makers as essentially atomistic (unaffected by the constraints of social norms), network research is predicated on the assumption that social relationships, and the norms associated with these relationships, are key to understanding economic behavior, including organizational actions. In line with this approach, studies have shown that, independent of other factors, network ties influence firms' decisions to enter new markets (Jensen, 2003), to engage in mergers with other firms (Kogut and Walker, 2001), and to charge different rates to different sets of customers (Uzzi and Lancaster, 2004)—decisions that, ultimately, shape firms' chances of survival (Uzzi, 1996).

Interlocking Directorates.   So how do organizational networks work? How do they influence what organizations do? Much of the existing research on this topic has concentrated on ties between organizations created by connections among top-level members of organizations and, in particular, on ties between individuals who are on the boards of directors of different organizations. These ties are referred to as "interlocks," and organizations that are connected by shared board memberships are characterized as having "interlocking directorates." Interlocks can take different forms. Direct interlocks occur when a member of one organization joins the board of directors of another organization. Indirect interlocks occur when members of two organizations sit on the board of a third organization (Burt, Christman, and Kilburn, 1980), thus providing a link between the first two organizations.

A common assumption in this literature is that individuals from different organizations who regularly attend board meetings for a given organization share information about policies and practices at such meetings (and perhaps outside the meetings as well), based on their own experiences and observations. In the most benign view, such interactions provide organizations with similar information about common problems and contribute to the development of shared responses to such problems (Haunschild and Beckman, 1998). Less benignly, interlocks are viewed as providing a foundation for collusion, co-optation, monitoring, and social cohesion among organizations (Mizruchi, 1996). This more negative view goes back at least to 1913, when U.S. Supreme Court Justice Louis Brandeis warned that such interlocks contain many evils, such as the suppression of competition (Pennings, 1980b).

This jaundiced view of the potential power associated with interlocking directorates is reflected in one line of research that draws on Marxist theory in portraying interlocks as a mechanism through which a capitalist class can act in concert to protect its economic interests. C. Wright Mills (1956), a prominent sociologist, expounded on this approach, echoing President Eisenhower's suggestion that a "military–industrial complex" had come to dominate in the United States' political and economic life, formed through regular interactions among the leaders of large business corporations, the military, and government organizations. Interlocking directorates, presumably, provided a key vehicle for such interactions. The extent to which a self-conscious capitalist class existed and whether the members acted coherently to advance class interests were ongoing points of debate among researchers studying interlocking directorates throughout the 1970s and 1980s (Domhoff, 1971, 1983; Galaskiewicz et al., 1985; Mintz and Schwartz, 1981; Palmer, Friedland, and Singh, 1986; Useem, 1979, 1982, 1984). Based on Canadian evidence, Ornstein (1984) concluded that corporate imperatives and class solidarity factors operate in interlocks. Using data from a U.S. Senate committee, Kerbo and Della Fave (1983) found evidence of an "intercorporate complex" of major corporations, with banks in a central coordinating position. They also found evidence for an inner group of the "corporate class." An analysis of the 1980 congressional elections found that corporate contributions to political action committees (PACs) for these elections were based on class-wide rational actions (Clawson and Neustadt, 1989).

Many network studies have documented the key role played by financial institutions as sources of interlocks in the United States (Keister, 1998; Mizruchi, 1989, 1992). By World War I, commercial banks, investment banks, and insurance companies were the most likely organizations to have their members on the boards of other types of organizations (Pennings, 1980a,b). This situation was, however, a shift from the one that prevailed in the previous century, when railroads, along with the telegraph and coal industries, were at the core of interlocks (Roy, 1983a,b; see also Mizruchi and Bunting, 1981). More recent work suggests, though, that neither banks nor any particular sector dominated interlocks by the late twentieth century. Beginning in the late 1980s and through the 1990s, corporations began to rely more on markets than commercial banks as sources of financing, and banking representatives were found less and less often on corporate boards of directors (Davis and Mizruchi, 1999; Mizruchi, 2004).

Current work on interlocks has focused less on these as a reflection of self-conscious class action and more as a means by which organizations can attempt to manage uncertainty in their environments. Interlocks can provide access to resources. Although banks may have become a less prominent part of interlocking directorates overall, research suggests that organizations experiencing financial problems such as declining solvency and declining rates of profit are apt to seek out directors from financial institutions (Mizruchi and Stearns, 1988). Interlocks also provide organizations with access to information, including ideas about how to deal with common problems. In the 1980s, when many corporations were facing the threat of takeovers by corporate raiders, interlocking directorates became a key source for the spread of poison pills (Davis, 1991), a strategic arrangement that substantially raised the cost to individuals or organizations of taking over a targeted firm through stock purchase. Interlocks also result from organizations' efforts to increase their prestige by putting individuals from high-status organizations on their boards. Research carried out in the Minneapolis–St. Paul metropolitan area (Galaskiewicz, 1997; Galaskiewicz et al., 1985) found that socially elite individuals who were associated with large corporations were disproportionately represented on boards of directors. According to Galaskiewicz et al. (1985; Galaskiewicz, Bielefeld, and Dowell, 2006), both "clout and grace" contributed to the densest interlocks, as economic power and higher social standing made companies and people attractive to one another.

The Galaskiewicz studies dealt with interlocks and corporate philanthropy and documented some interesting linkages at levels below the boards of directors. This research showed that "corporate contributions officers," who hold staff positions well below the top executive level, often have cohesion with one another since they have similar-to-identical role relationships, and ties at this level importantly contributed to the "contagion" in philanthropy that was identified in the Minneapolis–St. Paul area (Galaskiewicz and Burt, 1991). Less research has focused on organizational ties created by individuals at lower levels of the organization (though see Levinthal and Fichman, 1988), despite the fact that such ties may have important influences on organizational decision-making as well as ties at higher levels.

Although research has demonstrated the importance of boards for organizations as diverse as the Young Men's Christian Association (YMCA) (Zald, 1970) and the United Way (Provan, Beyer, and Kruytbosch, 1980), as well as large corporations, some analysts believe that the actual power of boards of directors is often much more limited than their position in the organizational hierarchy would indicate. Although, technically, boards of directors have the right to remove top administrative officers (James and Soref, 1981), frequently the executive officers have greater knowledge of the problems facing organizations than members of the board and can thus control the situation (Berle and Means, 1932). Some studies have shown that at least in some cases the board of directors has little effect on the behavior of managers (Fligstein and Brantley, 1992). Researchers are still seeking to identify conditions under which outside board members (excluding those employed by the organization) will have relatively more or less power vis-à-vis top corporate officers (Belliveau, O'Reilly, and Wade, 1996; Boeker, 1992; Davis, 2005; Ocasio, 1994; O'Connor et al., 2006; Zajac and Westphal, 1996), an issue that has become increasingly salient in the wake of the array of spectacular cases of corporate official misconduct in the last decade (Tolbert and Hiatt, forthcoming).

Selected Aspects

Yet another tack taken by researchers to understanding environmental influences on organizations has been to concentrate on analyzing the effects of selected aspects of environments. To give you a sense of this approach, we discuss four streams of research that have addressed one of the following aspects of the environment: (1) rates of technological change, (2) the passage of laws and regulations, (3) pressures from political actors, and (4) shifts in the demographic composition of clients and/or the workforce.

Technological Conditions.   We discussed work on the impact of technology on the formal structure of organizations in Chapter 3. Much of that work was premised on the assumption that an organization was characterized by a given technology, which might vary in terms of how difficult for individuals to apply it (how much knowledge and skill they must have) or to what extent it required coordination of the activities of different individuals. However, little attention was given to the issue of how often the technology itself was apt to change. When we talk about technological conditions as part of the environment, we are talking about the latter aspect: how much the equipment, knowledge and skills needed in the production process, and the products themselves change over time.

New ideas come into circulation and become part of the environment as soon as they cease being the private property of any one individual or organization. Since sciences have norms of distributing knowledge, scientific developments become part of the public domain as a matter of course. A development that can be patented is a different matter, but if it is thought to be significant, other organizations will seek to buy it, copy it, or further extend the previous development. Thus, technological change is determined by conditions that are external to the organization, conditions that can lead to "creative destruction"—forcing organizations to keep up with the changes or die (Schumpeter, 1934). In consequence, organizations face pressures to respond to technological developments in the environment that are crucial to their continued success (McEvily, Eisenhardt, and Prescott, 2004; Zucker, Darby, and Brewer, 1998).

A classic study by Lawrence and Lorsch (1967) focused on this aspect of organizations' environment. Their research examined firms in three industries that varied in terms of the level of change in customers' demands for new kinds of products (a dimension they denoted as "the market"), the frequency with which new production equipment required to create the products was developed (called the techno-economic dimension), and the certainty of means-and-ends knowledge that characterized production (the science dimension). One industry contained firms involved in the production of plastic goods; this industry was characterized by a high level of technological uncertainty. According to interviews with firm managers, firms in the industry faced the continual need to develop new and revised products, which typically had very short life cycles. Perhaps most importantly, the state of knowledge involved in producing new products was extremely uncertain. Lawrence and Lorsch (1967) quote one manager on this issue:

> We very often know the performance characteristics required by a customer or for a new application, but as far as research is concerned, you might as well be asking for the perfect plastic. We have to be concerned with technical feasibility right from the start, and then you don't know as you are involved in a lengthy testing and development process. (p. 25)

In all of the firms in this industry (they studied six), special organizational divisions devoted to research and development were established to keep the organization technologically current.

To more fully understand the impact of such technological conditions on organizations, Lawrence and Lorsch also studied organizations in two other industries: two firms in the standardized container industry (beer bottle manufacturers) and two firms in the packaged foods industry. The first industry was by far the most stable of the three: in the 1960s, beer bottles were almost all brown and held 12 ounces, and no significant changes in the products had occurred in years. The main problems facing organizations in this industry were ensuring "prompt delivery and consistent product quality while minimizing operating costs" (Lawrence and Lorsch, 1967:86). As one of the managers interviewed put it:

> As far as this business is concerned, there is no innovation. If you really want to grow in this business, you have got to have strategically located plants . . . well-placed throughout the country to give instant service. (Lawrence and Lorsch, 1967:89)

The technological conditions facing organizations in the packaged foods industry were intermediate to those faced by firms in the standardized container industry, on the one hand, and those in the plastics industry, on the other. There was some pressure to be innovative (to come up with "new and improved" products), but core changes in the products and production processes were much less frequent and more predictable than in the plastics industry. Again, quoting a manager from this industry:

> This is a profitable business, which is an intensely competitive market, but not a very price-sensitive one. The top competition takes the form of a very intensive merchandising effort around new product innovations. (Lawrence and Lorsch, 1967:89)

Lawrence and Lorsch's main conclusions were compatible with the basic logic of contingency theory: the kind of structure that was most effective (i.e., associated with strong financial performance) varied by the kinds of technological conditions with which the organizations had to deal. Key departments within the firms in the plastics industry tended to be highly differentiated in terms of formalization, members' definition of organizational goals, views of appropriate interpersonal relations, and time orientations. High levels of differentiation, Lawrence and Lorsch suggest, were beneficial to firms in managing the complex and changing environment. Increasing differentiation, though, created problems of conflict and coordination among the departments, and this required more elaborate arrangements to ensure coordination and deal with conflict (e.g., creation of specific positions and offices just to manage these problems)—to achieve integration, in their terms. Thus, the most effective firms in the plastics industry were both highly differentiated *and* highly integrated. This did not hold for the firms in the container or packaged foods industries. Successful firms in the former industry were much less differentiated, whereas firms in the latter industry were somewhere between those in the container and plastics industry; and this characteristic was much less strongly related to firm effectiveness.

Thus, whether an organization's environment is characterized by frequent or infrequent changes in core technology strongly shapes its formal structure, by influencing the relative importance of adaptation versus reliability as critical determinants of survival. Moreover, the structure of "high technology" firms, those in which the key technologies are rapidly evolving, often reflects the occupational standards and practices (another aspect of the environment) that subgroups in the organization accept—research scientists, engineers, and other professional groups (Barley and Tolbert, 1991; Burton and Beckman, 2007; Zucker, Darby, and Torero, 2002).

Legal Conditions.   Another environmental dimension that has received an increasing amount of attention from organizational researchers in recent years involves the laws that govern organizations. As Coleman (1974) pointed out, organizations are, fundamentally, legal creations—laws define the right of organizations to exist as well as the kinds of actions they can undertake and the rules that they must follow. Laws even define how organizations can "die," via dissolution or merger. Both the existence and the integral role of growing staffs of legal experts in many organizations and the trend toward lawyers serving as chief executive officers are indicative of the critical nature of legal conditions for organizations (Priest and Rothman, 1985). Given the importance of laws and regulations, researchers gave surprisingly little attention to the ways in which the legal environment shapes the structure or the outcomes of organizations for a long time. It is only within the last two decades that researchers have begun to explore these issues.

As Edelman and Suchman (1997) point out, the legal environment affects organizations in at least three major ways. One effect they refer to as "facilitative," which means laws provide procedures to be followed in forming organizations, in creating contracts and engaging in transactions both with individuals and with other organizations, in merging with other organizations, and so forth. In short, the legal environment can facilitate decision-making in organizations by providing guidelines so that terms and arrangements don't always have to be negotiated or created de novo. A second effect is termed "regulatory," which refers to the active monitoring and sanctioning of organizations when they fail to comply with laws, such as requirements related to worker health and safety, nondiscrimination in employment, environmental pollution. A third effect, which is a little more esoteric, is referred to as "constitutive." This refers to the law's ability to create social categories or definitions that, once accepted, almost invisibly shape organizational decision-makers' understandings of what issues should be taken into account in designing and operating organizations. For example, the idea that it is unfair to treat individuals differently because of gender was, not so long ago, completely foreign to many employers (and employees) in the United States. The Civil Rights Act of 1964 created gender discrimination as a new form of discrimination, and this categorization has had a major impact on organizations.

Edelman and Suchman (1997:484) note that "this aspect [the constitutive] of the legal environment provides the fundamental definitional building blocks that undergird the other two [facilitative and regulative]." Work on the latter aspect of the law is closely tied to an institutional theoretic approach to analyzing organizations, which we described in Chapter 3.

Much of the current work on legal environments has focused on the way in which organizations respond to changes in employment law by modifying their formal structures. For example, Baron, Dobbin, and Jennings (1986) examined the way in which government regulations of employment practices, put in place during World War II to minimize disruptions in industrial production, led to the development of many now-commonplace organizational arrangements, including the use of job analyses to determine the appropriate wage for a job, the use of tests for selecting and promoting employees, and the creation of personnel directors to oversee compliance with government rules. Analyses by Edelman (1990, 1992) suggest that there is a mutual relationship between organizations and the development of law: laws may be passed that identify problems that organizations must address (e.g., preventing discrimination), but the way in which organizations typically respond to the law (e.g., creating distinct units or personnel that are assigned responsibility for preventing discrimination) is often used in judicial interpretations of whether organizations have complied with the law (see also Edelman, Fuller, and Mara-Drita, 2001). More recent work has explored the extent to which formal structures, created by organizations in response to the legal environment, have a real impact on what organizations do or whether they serve primarily symbolic functions and produce few material changes in organizations (Dobbin and Kelly, 2007; Edelman and Suchman, 1997; Kalev, Dobbin, and Kelly, 2006).

Political Conditions.   Political conditions represent another broad dimension of the environment studied by organizational researchers—one that is partly, but not perfectly, related to the legal dimension. Work focusing on political conditions has examined both the level of stability of political groups and relationships in a country and the impact of mobilization of groups that seek to change existing arrangements in society (social movements).

Only a few studies have systematically examined the impact of general instability or broad changes in a political system on organizations within the system. Two studies of rates of founding and failure of newspapers in countries during periods of significant changes in national regimes provide examples of such research (Carroll and Delacroix, 1982; Delacroix and Carroll, 1983). Using historical data from two countries, Argentina and Ireland, this research found that increasing political turbulence fueled the founding of newspapers, probably because conflicting actors sought to influence public opinion through publications. They also found, though, that newspapers founded during turbulent conditions had higher rates of mortality than newspapers born under stable conditions, perhaps because they were established *too* quickly, without enough capital or planning. Another study of the collapse of the former East Germany suggests that the changed political system had ramifications for almost all organizations, even cultural organizations, such as symphony orchestras (Allmendinger and Hackman, 1996). Interestingly, the onset of socialism in East Germany had less impact on orchestras than its collapse. Under a socialist system, the level of homogeneity among different orchestras in the country increased but little else changed. However, the demise of the system and the spread of capitalism set in motion increased competition and differentiation among the orchestras, which were especially problematic for lower-status, smaller orchestras.

Another line of research concerned with the impact of political conditions on organizations has focused on the mobilization of groups seeking to change society (although not necessarily completely revamping the political system, as the work we described above). A growing literature has begun to document the interplay between social movement activity, organizational change, and broad social changes (Davis and Zald, 2005; King and Soule, 2007; McCarthy and Zald, 1973; Tilly, 1978).

Bringing about enduring changes in society almost inevitably involves bringing about changes in organizations, since organizational policies and practices typically embody and perpetuate core values that underpin societal arrangements. Take, for example, the Civil Rights movement of the 1960s, a general movement that was spearheaded by a variety of specific social movement organizations that shared the common aims of reducing racial discrimination and thereby decreasing economic and political inequality. Because organizations are key mechanisms through which discrimination and inequality are produced and perpetuated—through the hiring, compensation, and promotion practices of employing organizations; through the admissions and curricular policies of schools; through lending and service policies of financial organizations; and so forth—achieving the general aims of the movement entailed changing the policies and practices of many organizations. Thus, successful outcomes of almost all contemporary social movements, from the environmental movement (Bartley, 2007) to the pro-choice and antiabortion movements (Staggenborg, 1986) to gay-rights and family-values movements (Ash and Badgett, 2006), have implications for organizations. Movements affect organizations either through changing the policies and practices of existing organizations (Lounsbury, 2001) or by fostering the creation of new forms of organizations and/or the demise of existing ones (Schneiberg, King, and King, 2008).

There are a number of strategies social movements may use to bring about changes they desire; while all may reshape organizations' environments, they do so in rather different ways. One of the most common strategies involves changing laws that regulate organizational activities—that is, changing organizations' legal environments (Wade, Swaminathan, and Saxon, 1998). (This is why we noted that political conditions and legal conditions that organizations face are often related.) But social movements pursue other strategies that also affect organizations' environments. They may attempt to persuade individuals to consciously accept and follow particular social norms (Haveman, Rao, and Paruchuri, 2007). For example, the organic foods movement has sought to portray the purchase of produce or meat raised by organic standards as a moral choice, one that contributes to the protection of the environment (Lee, 2007; Weber, Heinze, and DeSoucey, forthcoming). Likewise, the Temperance Movement, at the turn of the nineteenth century, encouraged people to refrain from drinking alcohol on normative grounds. Even in the absence of regulatory laws, if people follow the social norms espoused by the movement, the availability of resources for organizations that provide related services or products is affected.

A related but slightly different strategy involves changing individuals' taken-for-granted beliefs and cognitions. This strategy usually entails some kind of education campaign, such as Drug Abuse Resistance Education (DARE) programs or sex education programs offered in public schools. These programs are often championed by social movement organizations with the aim of instilling beliefs about the logic and utility of particular behaviors and practices (Stimson, 2007). Insofar as they are successful, they also alter the environments of organizations that provide services or products that are involved, such as contraceptive providers and manufacturers, breweries, and alcohol retailers. Thus, different strategies are related to changing the regulative, normative, and cognitive dimensions of organizations' environments (Scott, 2008). Whether changing one or the other dimensions (or some combination) is more effective in bringing about change in organizations has not been assessed by researchers.

Demographic Conditions. Demography—the distribution of social characteristics such as age, race, and gender among members of a population—is another important aspect of organizational environments. As suggested in Chapter 1, the distribution of such characteristics among work-age individuals and among potential consumers of organizational products and the presence of social norms related to the characteristics affect both the demographic composition of organizations (work on this is sometimes referred to as organizational demography) and arrangements involving relationships with external constituents. The impact of this aspect of the environment is often most visible among organizations located in areas where the demography of the local population is changing rapidly. In such cases, it's not uncommon to find that businesses, schools, and police departments have a very different demographic composition than the people they serve, and this can create problems for the organizations. Transitions to adapt the organizations to address changes in their constituencies are often fraught with difficulties (Fernandez, 2001).

At a national level, the demographic composition of the workforce may shift over time as a result of a variety of economic and political forces. Such shifts are apt to lead to changes in social norms that are related to workforce participation by different groups and to changes in organizational practices (Lawrence and Tolbert, 2007). For example, the Great Depression of the 1930s resulted in a small birth cohort between 1930 and the mid-1940s (Easterlin, 1987); when members of these cohorts entered the labor markets in the expansionary post–World War II period, their small numbers contributed to a relatively tight labor market, fueling rapid advancement and high wages. This made it feasible for families to live reasonably well on the earnings of one wage earner, reinforcing traditional gender norms of male-earner, female-homemaker (Kessler-Harris, 2003). With single-earner families as the modal family type, it was relatively unproblematic for organizations to expect blue-collar workers to put in overtime and for white-collar workers to be willing to relocate as the organizations needed. The affluence and family structure of this period contributed to a relatively large birth cohort, born between the mid-1940s and 1960; the size of this cohort increased competition for stable, well-paying jobs when its members entered the workforce. This, in combination with the rise of the Women's Movement, led to a major increase in women's labor force participation rates and to dual-earner families as the dominant type (Blau, Ferber, and Winkler, 2006). In consequence, many organizations are still struggling to create policies and practices that are "family friendly," to fit with the changing needs and demands of the workforce (Reskin and Bielby, 2005).

The demographic composition of organizations, then, is often driven by larger demographic changes in society. Whatever their source, variations in organizational demography have been linked to a wide variety of organizationally important issues, such as levels of conflict, innovation and adaptability, turnover, and interorganizational linkages (DiTomaso, Post, and Parks-Yancy, 2007; Lawrence, 1988; Pfeffer, 1983; Wharton and Baron, 1987; Williams and O'Reilly, 1998).

Work on organizational demography has focused on the impact of the proportional representation of groups on intergroup relations. This work draws on two different literatures: one focusing on conflictual race relations in communities (e.g., Blalock, 1967), which emphasized intergroup competitive processes that could be set in motion as a minority group began to increase in size; and the other focusing on social psychological processes that foster prejudice (e.g., Kanter, 1977), which emphasized perceptions of and attitudes toward dissimilar others. These two traditions lead to different expectations about the effect of group proportions on group relations. The first literature, on community race relations, suggests that as a minority group grows, the dominant group is apt to feel threatened and to increasingly discriminate against minority group members. The second literature, on the social psychology of prejudice, suggests that as a minority group grows, the dominant group has more opportunities for contact with minority members, reducing the power of preexisting stereotypes and decreasing prejudice (at least under certain conditions).

Studies within organizations have found support for both arguments. For example, in a study of academic departments, Tolbert et al. (1995) found that increases in the representation of female faculty led to increasing rates of turnover among the women; the authors attributed this to increasing conflict between male and female faculty in the department as gender ratios became more equal. On the other hand, a study of officers in the Israeli army by Pazy and Oron (2001) found that female officers were evaluated more negatively than male officers when the proportion of women in the unit was lower. Conflicting effects of increasing group heterogeneity have also been found by other work using dissimilarity indexes to measure group heterogeneity. Dissimilarity indexes yield higher values (indicating more heterogeneity) as groups approach equality in proportionate representation. Work using such measures has often found that increasing heterogeneity is associated with greater intergroup conflict, reduced intergroup communication, and lower group performance (Williams and O'Reilly, 1998); at the same time, it is also associated with groups' greater use of information and higher levels of creativity and innovation (Reagans and McEvily, 2003). This suggests that there is need for more research specifying scope conditions: *When* will increases in the size of a smaller, subordinate group lead to improved or more conflictual group relations?

PERCEIVING THE ENVIRONMENT

Our discussion thus far reflects an assumption, common in much of the existing research, that the environment is simply something "out there" beyond the organization, which anyone in the organization can readily spot and identify. It would be handy if that were the case, but it is not. The environment comes into the organization as information and, like all information, is subject to the communications and decision-making problems that have been identified.

People have different positions in organizations. Some people are identified as "gate keepers" or "boundary spanners," who are designated to admit certain information that is relevant to the organization. Their perceptions are influenced by their positions within the organization. Of course, it is difficult to determine where the organization stops and the environment begins. Different positions are at an organization's boundaries, depending on what the activity at the moment is. At times it can be the switchboard operator; at other times it is the president or the chief executive officer (Starbuck, 1976).

An organization selects those aspects of the environment with which it is going to deal (Starbuck, 1976:1078–1780). The selection process is affected by the selection processes of other organizations with which it is in contact. At the same time, of course, interorganizational linkages are affected by environmental pressures. In this manner, organizations go about constructing or inventing their environments. The scope of the domain or environment claimed or selected by organizations has an impact on its operations. Narrow domain claims are associated with stability, broad and inconsistent claims with loss of functions. Broad claims coupled with technological capacity and newness lead to domain expansion (Meyer, 1975). Domain claims seldom contract.

Organizational theory has stressed the importance of perceived uncertainty in the environment (Duncan, 1972). It is equally important to stress that much of the environment that is perceived is actually quite certain, rather than uncertain. Colleges and universities, for example, face a certain demographic profile of the number and distribution of potential students. Business firms face a certain environment of governmental regulations. The environment thus contains elements of certainty and uncertainty. Even when an environment is certain, of course, there is no guarantee that it will be perceived as such (Milliken, 1990).

Just as the perceptions of individuals are shaped by their experiences, so are the perceptions of organizations. Organizations may actually be more realistic than individuals because of their constant comparisons with and sharing personnel among comparable organizations (Starbuck, 1976:1080–1081), but it has not yet been clearly demonstrated that this is the case. It must be remembered that the perceivers of the environment are themselves individuals, all with idiosyncrasies in perception.

SUMMARY AND CONCLUSIONS

This chapter has identified a number of different approaches to conceptualizing "organizational environments" and different ideas about how environments may shape organizations. We began by considering efforts to define the environment in terms of broad, analytical dimensions, then turned to work that focused more concretely on links between organizations as the key to understanding the nature of the environment, and finally discussed a number of lines of work, each of which draws attention to a different, specific aspect of the environment, from technological change to population demography. Today, less attention is being given to developing broad, abstract dimensions, although, as we noted, people still use such concepts as "turbulence" and "domain consensus" in trying to describe environmental conditions. There is still much work being conducted on IORs (especially on networks and interlocking directorates) and on the different aspects of the environment that we discussed in the latter part of the chapter.

In addition, there have also been several major theoretical "paradigms" of the environment that have been developed in the last half century, each of which draws attention to certain aspects of the environment and to certain selected types of organizational outcomes. These paradigms are the focus of the next chapter.

EXERCISES

1. What are the most critical elements of the environments of your two organizations?
2. Describe some of the most important interorganizational linkages between your two organizations and their environments.

Chapter 9

Managing Organizational Environments: General Paradigms

OVERVIEW

This chapter describes several major contemporary organizational paradigms, lines of theory, and research that are based on a particular view of organizational environments and their impact on organizations. Our discussion here focuses on resource dependence, transaction costs, and population ecology; we also refer back to two paradigms discussed in Chapters 2 and 3: contingency theory and institutional theory. We consider similarities and points of convergence in work conducted under the banner of different paradigms as well as differences among these. To provide broader insights into organizational phenomena, we conclude by considering the way in which different paradigms may be used in combination.

As organizational scholars continued to wrestle with the question of how to conceptualize organizational environments, they developed a number of paradigms (alternatively referred to as "perspectives," "models," "theories," or just "approaches"). Merriam-Webster (2002) defines paradigm as a "theoretical framework of a scientific school or discipline within which theories, laws, and generalizations and the experiments performed in support of them are formulated." We propose a rather more casual definition of this term: a paradigm is a way of looking at some phenomenon, which emphasizes or draws attention to certain aspects of it—and thus away from other aspects—as key to understanding the phenomenon. This definition is consistent with the way the term was used by Thomas Kuhn (1970) in a famous analysis of the development of physical sciences. As Kuhn noted, paradigms are not right or wrong, but they are predicated on the notion that certain questions are "more important" and certain approaches to answering those questions are "more useful." At least as originally formulated, different organizational paradigms tended to focus on different kinds of outcomes to be explained (ranging from the creation of formal structure, to the formation of interorganizational relations, to the failure of existing organizations, and to the foundings of new ones) as well as on different aspects of organizational environments in explaining those outcomes (Pfeffer, 1993). As various scholars developed different paradigms over time, they tended to draw on one another's arguments, so the boundaries have become more blurred than they were originally. In this chapter, we will try to give you a sense of the original formulations, to make the differences between these paradigms as clear as possible, but will also note points of intersection as well.

Before beginning our discussion of the different paradigms, we should make clear that we are not proposing a scheme for classifying these approaches in terms of underlying assumptions or causal arguments. For this sort of analysis, you may want to see Burrell and Morgan (1979) and Astley and Van de Ven (1983) as well as Donaldson's (1995) provocative assessment of contemporary organizational studies.

Here, we simply describe key assumptions and arguments of each paradigm to help you understand the logic and findings of research generated by these.

THE CONTINGENCY PARADIGM

Much of the research on sources of variation in organizations' formal structure that we discussed in Chapters 2 and 3 can be categorized as representing what is usually referred to as contingency theory. Although the "theory" guiding this research was often more implicit than explicit (Schoonhoven, 1981), Donaldson (1995, 1996) suggests that the basic tenets essentially reflect the logic of structural–functionalist arguments from sociology, as described in Chapter 2. Thus, organizations' structure is viewed as being created to serve certain functions, particularly the coordination and control of members' activities. The effectiveness of different structural arrangements in carrying out these functions depends on (is contingent upon) conditions that an organization faces—its size, the kinds of technology that people use in their work, and so forth. Most of the early research within this tradition focused on internal characteristics as key contingencies, as we noted; that is, it reflected closed-systems approach to thinking about organizations.

However, some of the research also considered environmental conditions, particularly change in technology and customer demands for new products. A key example of this research is a study by Lawrence and Lorsch (1967), which we described in some detail in Chapter 8. To briefly recap, this study compared the structures of organizations in three industries: plastics (rapid change in the production technologies firms used and in the products they made), packaged foods (not as much change in production technologies but fairly frequent changes in products), and containers (little change in either technologies or products). They noted that differences in environmental conditions were closely related to the formal structure of successful firms: firms operating in environments characterized by frequent technological and product change generally were more structurally complex (differentiated) and had more elaborate structures to bring about integration among the differentiated units. Likewise, an earlier analysis by Burns and Stalker (1961) suggested very similar conclusions about the relation between the level of environmental change and formal structure. Thus, Scott (1981) summarizes the logic of contingency theory: "The best way to organize depends on the nature of the environment to which the organization must relate" (p. 114).

One issue that critics have raised about this approach (e.g., Child, 1972a) involves assumptions about the role of organizational decision-makers' choice in bringing about the fit between formal structure and environmental contingencies (or for that matter, internal contingencies, such as size). There are two ways in which fit could be obtained, but work in this tradition rarely, if ever, spells out the mechanisms that are assumed to be at work. One mechanism involves strategic choice by decision-makers. Thus, decision-makers facing the same conditions simply draw the same conclusions about how to adapt their organizations and adopt the same structural arrangements. This argument would be consistent with much of the current literature that goes under the banner of strategy (e.g., Eisenhardt, 2002; Porter, 1980). Another mechanism through which fit between organizations' structures and environmental conditions could be produced is selection—the demise of organizations whose structures were not consistent with the requirements of the environment and other conditions. This mechanism is emphasized by population ecologists, as we'll discuss below.

THE RESOURCE DEPENDENCE PARADIGM

As noted in Chapter 8, work on interorganizational relations provided an important foundation for the development of another major paradigm, known as resource dependence theory. Evan's (1966) work on interorganizational sets, which we described in the previous chapter, articulated some of the key arguments of resource dependence, as did an early analysis by Thompson and McEwen (1958) discussing the process of goal setting in organizations. In general, the resource dependence theory closely reflects the influence of the decision-making analyses of Herbert Simon and other members of the Carnegie School, described in Chapter 6. However, the development of the basic logic of this paradigm (and the assignment of the label, "resource dependence," to it) is identified primarily with two main theorists: Jeffrey Pfeffer and Gerald Salancik (1978).

Key arguments of the resource dependence paradigm reflect two main assumptions about forces that drive organizational activities. The first is that organizations seek to ensure access to a stable flow of resources. That no organization is totally self-sustaining, a point underscored by Pfeffer and Salancik (1978:2), appears to be axiomatic. Even organizations that seem completely self-contained, such as isolated monasteries or agricultural communes, require some critical resources from outside their boundaries—new members, metal tools, even prosaic goods like salt and other materials necessary for the group's survival and functioning. In order to ensure orderly operations, then, organizations must have access to those resources, either from individuals outside a focal organization or, more often, from other organizations. This means that all organizations must deal with resource dependencies.

A second key assumption that is underscored particularly in the forerunning work by Thompson and McEwen (1958) and Evan (1966) is that organizational decision-makers seek to maximize their autonomy. If an organization is to pursue its interests effectively (however those interests are defined), decision-makers need freedom to operate, to take whatever actions necessary for attaining specified ends. But dependencies on other individuals and groups for resources pose a threat to this autonomy because resource providers may withhold or threaten to withhold their exchanges if they are unhappy with organizational decisions. These sorts of considerations make power a key issue for decision-makers. Resource dependence, then, draws attention to power motives in explaining organizations' actions. Following Emerson (1962), power is treated as a property of an exchange relationship, rather than a general characteristic of an actor (including organizational actors). As noted in Chapter 4, we can talk about A's power vis-à-vis B but not about the absolute power of A (i.e., without reference to a given partner). Given these assumptions, a resource dependence paradigm focuses attention on power in dyadic exchange relations involving key resources and on different strategies that organizations may use to manage power relations.

Note that concerns with ensuring stable resource flows and with ensuring decision-making autonomy may sometimes lead to conflicting choices. For example, establishing long-term contracts with a given supplier might guarantee a stable flow of resources, but this would limit the organization's ability to find and establish relationships with other suppliers who might provide a better deal. The choice of strategies, therefore, presumably reflects consideration of possible trade-offs between these two concerns.

Strategies for managing resource dependencies can be classified into two broad categories. One category involves actions that an organization can take independently, without securing the cooperation of a given exchange partner or set of partners. Thompson (1967:19) described a number of such actions an organization could take to, in his words, "seal off their core technologies from environmental influences." We refer to these as autonomous strategies, and they include buffering, smoothing, forecasting, and rationing. The other broad category of strategies involves establishing ties to other organizations that provide resources to a focal organization; thus, we refer to these as interorganizational strategies. These ties vary in the level of resource commitments an organization must make and in the length of time that the commitment entails; they include contracts, co-optation, coalitions (or strategic alliances), and mergers.

Autonomous Strategies

Buffering refers to arrangements that allow an organization to absorb the effects of changes in resource flows, without necessarily trying to shape the flows directly (Thompson, 1967:20). On the input side, this involves stockpiling resources—obtaining resources when they are plentiful and relatively cheap and storing them for future use. So, for example, biodiesel fuel producers may purchase corn or soy products when there is a large supply of these and then store them for conversion into fuel at a later time point. Another, more subtle illustration of this scenario is when organizations provide managerial training for more employees than the number of open managerial positions or the numbers that are likely to be open in the near future; that way, the organization has a ready supply of management candidates available when positions do become open. On the output side, a buffering strategy takes the form of warehousing—storing goods that have been produced for exchange at a later time. Carpet manufacturers, for example, make different types of carpeting and store them so that they can be shipped when ordered by customers. The practice in some universities of hiring their own Ph.D. students who did not find a job in a given year as temporary lecturers could also be viewed as a form of this strategy. The effectiveness of buffering strategies depends largely on the degree to which the resources involved are subject to becoming obsolete or unusable over time. If demands for a resource change quickly—products go out of style or technology changes so that different types of resources are needed—organizations may end up holding resources that they can't use.

Smoothing strategies (sometimes called leveling) entail practices that are designed to reduce variability in resource flows directly, rather than simply adapting to such variations, as in buffering (Thompson, 1967:21). These strategies often are aimed at variations in flows on the input side. An administratively oriented form of this involves scheduling. Thus, for example, medical clinics normally reserve some time slots and assign nonemergency patients to these; another example is the assignment of days and times to students for online enrollment. Both of these arrangements have the same goal: an orderly flow of resources (people, in these cases) through the organizational system. Smoothing can also take a market-oriented form, usually involving inducements to encourage transactions at particular times. Commuter railroads commonly offer off-peak rates (lower prices for travel in the middle of the business day, or on weekends); airlines offer lower fares during periods when fewer people are apt to travel; stores offer mid-January sales, when consumers are less likely to be in a buying mood. You could also think of organizations' offers of early-retirement packages to their employees in this light; this can be a way to encourage the regular flow of personnel through the organization. The effectiveness of this strategy depends to a large degree on whether the demand for the resources is elastic (using economists' terminology)—whether consumers and suppliers can and are willing to wait to transact with the organization. To give an obvious (if slightly dark) illustration of inelastic demand: patients who need pacemakers will not wait for a sale.

A third type of autonomous strategy that organizations may use is *forecasting* (Thompson, 1967:21). Like buffering, forecasting does not involve efforts to alter the flow of resources but does involve active monitoring of changes in flows and adaptation by the organization in response to expected changes. One prosaic example of this is the practice in many grocery stores of stocking more canned pumpkin in the late fall and early winter than in the spring or summer; they forecast that increased demand for this resource will occur around the holidays and lessened demand in summer months. Similarly, some hotels in resort areas open up in the late spring and summer (or late fall and winter, in skiing areas) and shut down in the opposite seasons, again based on expectations of changes in the flow of customers. This strategy can be effective when changes in flows are predictable and orderly; when changes are random (e.g., based on fads), forecasting is clearly not of much use to organizations—although, despite norms of rationality (Thompson's favorite caveat), they may still try to use it.

And a final type of autonomous strategy is *rationing* (Thompson, 1967:23). This entails coping with uncertainty over the demand for a good or service produced by the organization by limiting its provision; the goal here is to minimize excess production of resources. One example of this strategy is provided by book publishers: when printing a book by an unknown author, publishers often make first runs fairly small. If the book is successful, more copies can be produced, but a smaller number of initial printings helps reduce "remainders" on the shelves at bookstores. Another example is provided by free legal services clinics, where the number of staff members is usually low; when there are more clients than counselors available, the clients simply have to wait. This strategy is effective primarily when the organization is the sole producer or in a position of monopoly or near-monopoly control. Since this often holds for public service agencies, it is not uncommon for such organizations to use this strategy. This condition holds less often for business organizations; by limiting production, businesses may run the risk of losing transactions to others who produce the same or substitutable goods and services. (In publishing, organizations enter into contracts with authors for copyright, which effectively gives these organizations a sort of monopoly power, at least for some specified period of time.)

Interorganizational Strategies

Buffering, smoothing, forecasting, and rationing may help minimize dependence on other organizations and thus maintain autonomy in decision-making, but they are not always adequate to ensure stable resource flows to an organization. Consequently, organizations frequently pursue interorganizational strategies to deal with this issue. The use of such strategies is the major focus of contemporary research conducted under the banner of resource dependence (see Pfeffer and Salancik, 1978, for a summary of much of this research), which has investigated a number of different types, including bargaining, co-optation, strategic alliances, and mergers. As we'll discuss in another section of this chapter, where we describe the transaction cost paradigm, the first and last of these strategies—bargaining and mergers—have also been of central concern.

Bargaining refers to the establishment of formal but relatively short-term exchange agreements with another organization (Thompson and McEwen, 1958). There are abundant examples of this strategy: a company enters into an agreement with a union to pay a specified wage for labor for a specified period of time; one firm agrees to buy a given quantity of some good from another firm; an organization rents space from another organization for a defined leasing period, and so on. Such exchange relationships are not necessarily limited to monetary transactions. For example, in one case that we're familiar with, a nonprofit agency that provides workforce training for the unemployed entered into an agreement with a local bank, permitting the latter to use its computer facilities for training bank employees, in exchange for allowing some of the nonprofit's clients to receive the training. This strategy goes beyond a pure market relationship, that is, one where the exchanges are immediate and involve no ongoing relation, but not much. It does secure a flow of resources to an organization but only for a limited period of time; on the other hand, it also entails little or no threat to its decision-making autonomy, since once the exchange agreement is up, a focal organization may simply choose not to renew it.

The second form of interorganizational strategy, *co-optation,* involves bringing representatives of another organization that provides (or can provide) important resources into the decision-making structure of a focal organization. Often, this involves appointments to the board of directors of an organization, as exemplified in the case of Chrysler automobile company, which, in the early 1980s, took the unprecedented step of appointing the president of the United Auto Workers union, Douglas Fraser, to its board. Similarly, examination of the board of trustees of most business schools will also illustrate this strategy: most, if not all, have individuals from large corporations or important local employers represented on their board.

As we noted, when we discussed work on interlocking directorates in Chapter 8, interlocks sometimes have been viewed as co-optative devices, a way of securing commitments from key resource-providing organizations. Thus, co-optation was commonly offered as an explanation for why banks and other financial institutions were so often selected to be on other organizations' boards throughout most of the twentieth century (Mizruchi, 2004). Creating ties to other organizations this way can help an organization ensure a flow of resources in a number of ways (Perrow, 1961; Pfeffer, 1972; Pfeffer and Salancik, 1978). First, it provides a channel of communication that can be important in facilitating resource exchanges. For example, a board member who is employed by a bank that is considering changes in its loan policies may convey this information to members of a focal organization during a board meeting; that may affect the focal organization's ability to prepare for these changes to make sure it can obtain needed loans. Second, when a member of one organization is appointed to the board of another, she or he may feel an obligation to help direct resources to the latter. Thus, representatives of large corporations who sit on university boards of trustees are apt to help direct the donations of their corporation to the university. And finally, having representatives of other, powerful organizations on an organization's board can help provide it with legitimacy, and this can increase support not only from the organization represented on the board but from others as well. Hence, a new organization formed to lobby for regulations involving environmental issues might put a member of the Audubon Society or Sierra Club on its board to help legitimate itself with possible donors; such legitimacy is likely to affect individuals' and organizations' willingness to provide donations and support to the new organization (Meyer and Rowan, 1977; Zucker, 1986).

However, this strategy also poses a much greater threat to a focal organization's decision-making autonomy than bargaining, since resource providers are in a direct position to shape decision outcomes. A prime example of this is provided by Selznick's (1966) now-classic study of the Tennessee Valley Authority (TVA). The Tennessee Valley Authority Act was passed by the U.S. Congress in 1933 with the aim of helping southern farmers who had been especially hard-hit by the Great Depression, by providing electric power to the region, manufacturing cheap fertilizers, and providing other forms of support for agricultural production. One of the mandates of the Act was that the organization created to operate these projects be democratic by having local organizations and citizens participate in its decision-making processes. Doing this could be viewed as a co-optative process, whereby the organization gained political support from local constituents. As Selznick's account underscores, however, co-optation is a two-way process. He documents how the TVA ended up largely representing the interests of the wealthier farmers in the area (who were active members of the local organizations from which the TVA recruited participants), rather than the truly economically disadvantaged ones, whom it was presumably intended to help the most. The inherent threats to autonomy associated with this strategy suggest that it is more likely to be used by organizations that are relatively weaker— where the need to ensure resource flows outweighs the potential costs of loss of autonomy. This is consistent with findings from research by Davis (1996), showing that less than 5 percent of large corporations had representatives of firms that served as key buyers or suppliers to the corporation on their boards; large corporations presumably have sufficient resource flows to make the potential costs of co-optation efforts not worth paying.

A third strategy, which is broadly referred to as *coalition* (Thompson and McEwen, 1958), involves the commitment of resources by two or more organizations to some relatively long-term joint activities. Our use of the term *coalition,* then, encompasses arrangements that go under an array of labels: joint ventures, alliances (or strategic alliances), and joint programs (Child, 2005). One example of the use of this strategy is provided by the hybrid electric vehicle (HEV) project that was begun in 1993 with financial support from General Motors (GM), Ford, Daimler-Chrysler (then Chrysler), and the Department of Energy's National Renewable Energy Laboratory (NREL). The project's purpose was to conduct research leading to the production of a market-ready hybrid vehicle in a decade (http://www.nrel.gov/vehiclesandfuels/hev/about.html). Although the ultimate goal is still being pursued, the contributing firms all were able to make use of the research findings from the project. Another example of a coalitional strategy is provided by the Inter-University Consortium for Political and Social Research (ICPSR), which is a data archive (a place where researchers can find data sets to use in research) that is headquartered at the University of Michigan. This organization is supported by a large number of academic organizations, whose faculty and students are given the rights to use the data and resources of the organization. Still another example is represented by Butachimie, an organization that manufactures a chemical used by two competing chemical companies, DuPont and Rhône-Poulenc Rorer. Although competitors, the companies cooperated in forming Butachimie to serve as a supplier for both companies (Child, 2005).

These kinds of arrangements help participating organizations secure resources that they may need in the present, or that they anticipate needing in the future, while sharing the costs and potential risks associated with getting those resources. However, such arrangements often also require a substantial amount of initial and ongoing investment of resources to the coalition project. Because the contributing organizations lose unilateral control over those resources once they've been committed (because decisions about their use are made by some joint governance arrangement), there is some loss of autonomy for participating organizations (Coleman, 1974). For example, the HEV project was put under the authority of the NREL, a separate organization that ran the research. The automakers who contributed to the project could try to influence NREL's decisions (and almost certainly did so), but none of them had complete individual control of how their investments were spent by the project. Likewise, at ICPSR, no one university sets policy on what data sets are acquired or what the rules for use are. The potential costs of allowing other organizations to have some say over resources that a focal organization has contributed may be a key reason that one of the strongest predictors of two organizations forming an alliance is a past alliance (Aiken and Hage, 1968; Gulati, 1995a; Gulati and Gargiulo, 1999); this allows organizations to develop trust and knowledge of the other that aides in facilitates joint decision-making.

A final form of interorganizational strategy involves *mergers,* the joining of two organizations so that they become, legally, a single one. There are different types of mergers, each of which deals with different aspects of resource dependence. A symbiotic merger involves organizations that carry out different but related activities, that is, ones that are exchange partners (actual or potential). This kind of merger is also referred to as vertical integration, because it involves combining organizations at different "levels" of a supply chain. Thus, for example, when Will Durant purchased a bankrupt automobile manufacturing business in 1904, Buick Motors, and then created franchise businesses that were responsible for sales and distributions of Buick automobiles, he engaged in "forward integration"; when he bought companies that provided parts used in the manufacturing of the automobiles, he was involved in "backwards integration" (Chandler, 1962).

Symbiotic mergers ensure control over a set of resources that a focal organization requires (Pfeffer and Salancik, 1978:114). A competitive merger, on the other hand, involves organizations that carry out the same kinds of activities, that is, competitors, as the term suggests. This is sometimes called horizontal integration, and one example is provided by the merger in 2003 of two unions: Hotel Employees and Restaurant Employees (HERE) and UNITE (which to represented laundry workers and other service industries). This merger, resulting in UNITE HERE!, allowed the unions to avoid expending resources on competitive unionizing drives and to pool resources for organizing, lobbying, and mobilizing workers. This type of merger not only allows more effective use of resources through economies of scale, but also limits options available to exchange partners, and this facilitates resource flows as well (Pfeffer and Salancik, 1978).

There is another type of merger, diversification, that involves one or more organizations that are unrelated—neither potential exchange partners nor competitors. Such mergers may result in conglomerates, extremely large organizations composed of businesses in many different industries. One example is Beatrice Foods, which started out as a small dairy products company in the 1890s but by the 1970s owned such diverse companies as Avis (car rentals), Playtex (women's undergarments), Good and Plenty (candy), and Riley Tannery (leather goods). The logic behind such mergers is that the organizations in the conglomerate face different markets that are likely to rise and fall independently. Thus, the combined organization diversifies its risks: when one part of the organization faces conditions that lower its revenues, it can be subsidized by other parts that are (it is hoped) facing more promising conditions. This strategy, then, is intended to address problems of resource flows (although its efficacy was called into general question in the 1980s; see Davis, Diekmann, and Tinsley, 1994).

Mergers can provide a very strong means of ensuring ongoing flows of resources, especially symbiotic mergers. However, firms that use this strategy for this purpose also must commit a large amount of resources to the acquisition, and there are potential problems in terms of the decision-making autonomy, for the acquiring firm as well as the one acquired (Casciaro and Piskorski, 2005). This is because efforts to integrate two sets of decision-makers into a single governance structure are difficult despite careful planning and can produce unexpected conflicts and negotiations (Graebner and Eisenhardt, 2004). Pfeffer and Salancik's research examining industry-level data on rates of mergers (1978; see also Pfeffer, 1972) suggests that symbiotic mergers are likely to be undertaken primarily when exchanges are very frequent, that is, when there is a high level of resource dependence between firms. Competitive mergers, on the other hand, are more likely to occur in industries with an intermediate level of concentration (i.e., not those dominated by a few large firms, nor those characterized by a large number of small, competing firms). The explanation offered for this finding is that in concentrated industries, competitor firms are often so large that the costs of acquisition outweigh the benefits (and antitrust regulations could prevent such mergers), whereas in industries with very low levels of concentration, a merger with a competitor produces very small gains, because the number of competitors is so great. Thus, the greatest gains to merging horizontally occur at intermediate levels of concentration in an industry.

Internal Power Relations

Of the various paradigms that we'll discuss in this chapter, resource dependence is the only one that explicitly considers how environmental relations may affect relations among different units and groups within an organization. Drawing on the image of organizations suggested by the Carnegie School as coalitions of groups that simultaneously have common and competing interests (Cyert and March, 1963), Pfeffer and Salancik have examined how an organization's dependence on external resources shapes decisions about the internal distribution of resources to different groups. They argue that groups or subunits that broker important resource dependencies for an organization will be more powerful coalitional members (Perrow, 1970) and thus are likely to receive a larger share of the organization's resources. In line with this, their research on a university showed that departments that brought in higher levels of external research funds and contracts and that external agencies ranked higher in levels of prestige (an important resource for academic organizations) were assigned more valued and scarce organizational resources, such as support for graduate students (Pfeffer and Salancik, 1974). Moreover, the relative power of a department affected the proportion of the university's general budget that it received, independent of the number of students taught in department course or the number of faculty members in the department. In general, these findings are consistent with the notion that subunits and groups that are involved in the acquisition of key resources by an organization will exert more influence on decision-making within an organization. This is also consistent with later work by Fligstein (1990) and others linking changes in the representation of various functional groups in top-level management to changes in corporations' environments that made different types of resources more valued by corporations.

THE TRANSACTION COST PARADIGM

A third paradigm, transaction cost, is similar in many ways to that of resource dependence. One point of similarity is that both focus on the problem of organizational decision-making in response to environmental conditions. This common focus probably reflects the fact that the major architect of transaction costs analysis, Oliver Williamson, received graduate training at Carnegie Mellon University, as did Jeffrey Pfeffer, one of the theorists most closely identified with resource dependence. As we've noted, this institution was home base for Herbert Simon, James March, and others deeply engaged in studying decision-making processes in organizations. Also like resource dependence, transaction cost analysis seeks to explain the conditions that affect which strategies decision-makers use to manage exchange relationships. The latter, though, draws on work by an economist, John Coase (1937), to frame a key question underlying this paradigm, namely: Why do organizations draw their boundaries where they do? (To be more precise, Coase asked why there are organizations at all; this is a more extreme version of the boundary question and more clearly reflects the underlying faith of economists in the normal efficiency of markets for the creation and distribution of resources.) That is, a transaction cost paradigm focuses on explaining why organizations externalize some transactions—rely on the market to manage exchange relationships—and internalize others—rely on hierarchical control to manage exchanges (David and Han, 2004).

Reflecting its roots in economics, a transaction cost analysis starts with the notion that, theoretically, production units can obtain any resource they need in the market. Consider the case of producing some simple object, such as a coffee cup. In theory, one unit (which we'll call A Company) could dig up the clay used for forming parts of the cup, another unit (B Company) could purchase clay to create the bowl of the cup, another unit (C Company) could also purchase clay to create the handles of the cup, while another unit (D Company) could purchase the bowls and handles and attach these together to form the cup, still another (E Company) could purchase the cups and apply a glaze, and so on. The question is: Under what conditions are these units likely to be combined, to become a single organization (e.g., the ABCDE Company, producing whole finished cups from clay), rather than continuing to operate as discrete exchange partners? This, Williamson (1981, 1983) argues, depends on transaction costs.

Transaction costs are those that are associated with the transfer of goods or services "across a technologically separable interface" (Williamson, 1981:552). The notion of a "technologically separable interface" implies that there are some activities that are inherently bundled, because of either temporality or necessary physical proximity or both. To have one person assigned responsibility for putting a button in place and another to push the needle through the button hole to sew it on makes little sense. But within those sorts of limits, it is possible to have a very high degree of specialization, as the cup-producing example above suggests. Whenever individuals or units specialize in one part of the production process and then pass the product along to another unit specializing in another part of the process, there are transaction costs—for example, from a buyer's standpoint, there are costs associated with being sure that a particular good or resource is available when it's needed, at a reasonable price, and at a level of quality that's required (all this is apt to entail time and financial costs involved in specifying, enforcing, and renegotiating contracts and/or monitoring sellers).

These costs are affected by, in Williamson's words, "human nature as we know it" (1981:553). In particular, there are two posited characteristics of human nature that are relevant here: (1) bounded rationality, which limits people's ability to anticipate future events and states and thus to design exchange agreements that cover all contingencies; and (2) propensities toward opportunism, that is, inclinations to take advantage of exchange partners when possible, by misrepresentation, extortion, and so forth. If people were not opportunistic, bounded rationality would be much less problematic; when circumstances affecting the exchange changed unexpectedly, new agreements could be readily constructed if everyone could be counted on to act in good faith. Without bounded rationality, opportunistic behavior presumably would be recognized and anticipated and thus pose no threat to workable contracts or agreements. But opportunism in combination with bounded rationality can make market-based exchanges, very problematic.

Williamson argues that the extent to which these characteristics of individuals create problems for market exchanges depends on three characteristics of the transaction: (1) uncertainty, which involves the reliability with which some needed good or service is available when needed; (2) frequency, the degree to which a given producer regularly needs access to a good or service from an exchange partner in order to carry out its activities; and (3) asset specificity, the degree to which a good or service is specialized to a particular set of exchange partners. (Note that these conditions are very similar to those that define "strategic contingencies," discussed in Chapter 4.) Asset specificity is viewed as an especially critical dimension of transactions, one that is related to the number of alternative exchange partners available. If asset specificity is very high, a seller may have a product that can only be used by one buyer; likewise, from a buyer's standpoint, high asset specificity may mean that there is only one seller of a product that a buyer needs. On the other hand, with low asset specificity, there are apt to be many sellers and buyers available to transact with. Asset specificity can take a variety of forms. One is site specificity, which occurs when exchange partners are in such close proximity that it affects the costs associated with a particular exchange relation compared to other possible ones (e.g., a steel mill located right next door to a mining company). Physical specificity describes situations where parts or equipment needed to produce a product or the product itself is specialized for a particular exchange (e.g., a company produces catalytic converters that are used by only one car manufacturer). And human asset specificity is said to exist when individuals have particular knowledge or skills that are valuable only for a particular exchange relationship (e.g., an administrator who is well versed in an idiosyncratic bookkeeping system of a company). (Economists usually refer to the latter skills and knowledge as "firm-specific"; see Becker, 1964.)

Frequent need for a good or service and uncertainty over its provision can increase transaction costs, insofar as exchange partners have to be located and exchanges negotiated and renegotiated over and over again. These problems are lessened, though, when there is no asset specificity—when there are many potential exchange partners available. The greatest problem for market exchange is created by asset specificity, because this implies a "small numbers problem"—a lack of alternatives when a given exchange relationship turns out to be unsatisfactory. If an unanticipated problem is encountered with an exchange agreement (because bounded rationality limited the ability to specify how such problems will be handled), time and effort must be spent negotiating a new contract; the option of simply finding a new exchange partner is foreclosed. Moreover, under these circumstances, it's more likely that at least one of the exchange partners will act opportunistically and seek to exploit the other, because they know the other has no alternative.

As the costs of market exchange rise, the attractiveness of bringing transaction partners together under the umbrella of a single organization increases. The hierarchical authority that characterizes organizations allows for resolution "by fiat" of conflicts surrounding transactions, thus eliminating time-consuming and potentially expensive negotiations. Moreover, as part of a single organization, information about production costs and other characteristics of goods and services is generally accessible to all parties, reducing the ability to engage in opportunistic behavior. However, there are costs associated with transactions that occur within the boundaries of organizations as well; these are referred to as "governance costs." They include costs associated with administration and coordination—hiring people to supervise production, to handle personnel issues, and to keep records, expanding physical facilities, maintain excessing capacity perhaps (having more employees and space than needed when business slows), and so forth. When goods and services are purchased on the market, other organizations bear these costs. Thus, transaction cost theorists argue that only when transaction costs (those of market-based exchanges) exceed governance costs (those of organizationally based exchange) will organizations internalize exchanges; otherwise, they will rely on the market to manage exchange relations. This is sometimes described as "make or buy" decisions; internalization involves "make" decisions, whereas externalization involves "buy" decisions. David and Han (2004), reviewing a large number of empirical studies derived from a transaction cost paradigm, find that there is generally a fairly high level of support for its predictions of make-or-buy decisions.

Comparing Transaction Costs with Resource Dependence

You may notice that "buy" decisions map on to the strategy that resource dependence theorists discuss as bargaining, whereas "make" decisions map on to the strategy of merger (symbiotic mergers, in particular). Thus, the two paradigms draw attention to some similar kinds of strategies that organizations may use to manage environmental relations. In both cases, the choice of strategies is assumed to be primarily conditioned by dependencies. The notion of dependence is inherent in the concept of asset specificity and its implication of limited numbers of alternative exchange partners. In line with this, resource dependence theorists recognize that "concentration of control" of needed resources in the hands of a few exchange partners or a single one is a key element of dependence (Pfeffer and Salancik, 1978:52). Moreover, both paradigms emphasize conscious, calculated choices by organizational decision-makers in explaining organizational structure. Although work in each tradition explicitly recognizes that decision-makers are characterized by bounded rationality, the emphasis is more on the rationality than the bounds. For example, although Williamson discusses the way in which bounded rationality limits people's ability to formulate complete contracts, the notion that decisions to make or buy are based on comparison of governance costs with market-based transaction costs is predicated on the assumption that decision-makers are able to forecast and make complex calculations of the impact of various factors on exchanges (Tolbert and Zucker, 1996).

The primary differences between these paradigms stem from assumptions or emphases that characterize the academic disciplines of the primary theorists, namely, economics and sociology. In line with economics, transaction costs analysis assumes that decision-makers are concerned with maximizing profit (of which minimizing costs is an important part). Resource dependence analyses, on the other hand, assume that organizational decision-makers are also concerned with maximizing their organization's power and autonomy; this loosening of the emphasis on profit maximization is more consistent with a sociological approach. Perhaps partly because of its focus on more purely cost concerns as a driver of behavior, a transaction costs paradigm seems in some ways to be more elegant. However, this focus may limit its utility in explaining various types of organizational behavior. Thus, it is not easily extended to consideration of how organizations seek to manage relations with competitors; its use in addressing questions about conditions that are likely to increase the occurrence of competitive mergers, coalitional behavior, or co-optation is unclear. Williamson (1991) does consider a third type of strategy, in addition to market-based and organizationally based exchange relationships, that involves what he refers to as a hybrid form. This is an arrangement where an exchange relationship between partners who are more or less independent is brokered by a third party; as examples, he offers the case of a public utility, whose relationship with customers is overseen by a regulatory agency, and franchises, who operate fairly independently of one another but are governed by a parent company. But the idea that one organization might actually cultivate the dependence of another organization, and be able to do so because of the relative power imbalance between the organizations, does not rest easily within a transaction cost framework. This is precisely what GM did with its suppliers, though, and it was able to do so because it was the biggest game in town. As Pfeffer and Salancik (1978:54) note, GM used to insist that its suppliers (who were nominally independent—certainly not part of the formal structure of GM) allow the company to audit the suppliers' financial records; suppliers were willing to do this because GM had large contracts to award. Auditing further increased GM's power because it then had information about what suppliers' actual costs were and could determine what charges were within a "reasonable" profit margin. By explicitly drawing attention to the use of power in exchange relations, resource dependence provides some additional insights into organization and environment relations that might be missed with a transaction cost paradigm alone.

THE INSTITUTIONAL PARADIGM

The underlying assumptions about the nature of organizational decision-making contained in both resource dependence and transaction costs paradigms, as described above, contrast sharply with those suggested by two other major paradigms: institutional theory and population ecology. We described the basic logic of institutional theory in Chapter 3 in some detail, so as with contingency theory, we'll just offer a short recap and a little elaboration here.

Whereas resource dependence and transaction cost underscore interorganizational exchange relations as key to understanding how environments affect organizations, institutional theory emphasizes the effects of widespread social definitions of how organizations "ought" to look and "ought" to operate; these sorts of normative forces are referred to as the institutional environment. As we noted previously, theorists have suggested a number of sources that help create the institutional environment: government and other powerful resource-controlling organizations that set requirements; professional associations and organizations that have special claims to expert authority and that promote particular practices and arrangements; and networks of organizations whose members observe and often imitate one another (DiMaggio and Powell, 1983; Meyer and Rowan, 1977). Scott (2008) refers to these, respectively, as the regulative, normative, and cognitive dimensions of the institutional environment. In general, institutional theorists predict that as elements of formal structure (e.g., affirmative action offices, chief financial officers, total quality management programs) become institutionalized—defined as right and proper components of well-run organizations by these sources—organizations that don't have these elements will be increasingly likely to adopt them, regardless of whether they have particular problems or issues that might make such structures useful to the organization's functioning (Tolbert and Zucker, 1983).

A key problem with much of the empirical work based on institutional theory is that it gives almost no attention to measuring whether some element of structure *is* institutionalized—widely, normatively accepted or not—independent of the number of organizations that has adopted the structure. (This is also a problem for population ecology's approach to measuring legitimation—a concept that's virtually identical to that of institutionalization—as we'll discuss below.) This lack of separate measures of institutionalization makes it difficult to compare the utility of an institutional explanation with those that emphasize highly calculated, rational choices by organizational decision-makers; the latter approach could conclude that all decision-makers simply reached the same conclusion about the need to adopt a given structure by independent avenues (Tolbert and Zucker, 1996).

This issue is tied to an assumption underlying this paradigm, that organizational decision-makers are very vulnerable to pressures for conformity and prone to follow the herd, particularly as uncertainty surrounding decisions increases. This assumption has served as the source of some criticism for this paradigm (Hall, 1992; Hirsch and Lounsbury, 1997; Oliver, 1991). Critics suggest that it is based on an "oversocialized" conception of individuals (Wrong, 1961) and that there is no place in it for agency, or independent, purposive action (DiMaggio, 1988). There is certainly some validity to these criticisms. As we noted at the outset of this chapter, one of the things that paradigms do is to focus attention of some selected aspects of phenomena that are to be explained and ignore other aspects. Hence, the resource dependence and transaction costs paradigms emphasize agency and choice and ignore more conformity-driven, less independently calculated aspects of decision-making. Both characterizations of organizational decision-making probably represent accurate depictions, although perhaps at different points in time and under different circumstances.

In line with institutional theory's arguments, though, there are a number of studies that indicate that, once a certain number of organizations or individuals have adopted some practice, the strongest predictor of adoption by others is the number of previous adopters (Banerjee, 1992; Bikchandani, Hirshleifer, and Welch, 1992; Fligstein, 1985; Palmer, Jennings, and Zhou, 1993; Tolbert and Zucker, 1983). The popular press also provides some insights into how institutionalization processes shape organizational decision-makers' choices. For example, a *New York Times* article reported that business firms are establishing formal intelligence departments to keep tabs on competitors from home and abroad. One source is quoted as saying that "understanding your competitors' positions and how they might evolve is the essence of the strategic game" (Prokesch, 1985).

THE POPULATION ECOLOGY PARADIGM

Like institutional theory, the line of work known as population ecology also underscores the "boundedness" of decision processes in organizations, although this issue is relevant to this tradition primarily because of a key underlying assumption, namely, most organizations do not change fundamentally over time (they are "inert"). One of the distinguishing features of population ecology is that it was not developed to explain changes in individual organizations (such as the creation of formal structure or the formation of relations with other organizations); rather it was formulated with the aim of accounting for large-scale shifts that characterize groups of organizations, or organizational populations (Aldrich, 1979, 1999; Aldrich and Pfeffer, 1976; Bidwell and Kasarda, 1985; Carroll, 1985; Carroll and Swaminathan, 2000; Hannan and Freeman, 1977b, 1989; Haveman, 1992, 1993a; McKelvey, 1982). As an example of this kind of change, consider the case of the hotel industry in the United States. For many years, up through the early 1950s at least, this industry was dominated by stand-alone, independent organizations—from the small mom-and-pop motor courts that dotted U.S. highways to the grand Plaza Hotel in New York City and the classic Hotel Del Coronado in San Diego. Today, the industry is dominated by big chains—Howard Johnsons, Hiltons, Sheratons, Marriotts, etc.—that have largely replaced the small individually owned motor courts and that have acquired most, if not all, of the original urban classic hotels. Population ecologists would describe this as the replacement of one form of organization (in this case, independently owned, single establishments) by another (corporately owned, multisite chains). Similar population shifts can be seen in higher education, where the once-dominant form of organization, liberal arts colleges, has largely been eclipsed by the rise of larger research universities at one end and community colleges at the other (Kraatz and Zajac, 1996). Yet another example is provided by gas stations, where what used to be common, the full-service gas station with a mechanic on the premises, has been replaced by self-service stations with no mechanic—albeit often with a small food mart. Population ecology seeks to explain how such large-scale shifts come about. This focus on the forest rather than the trees (i.e., population change rather than individual organizational change) provided a new and very generative approach to examining organizations.

Given the focus on populations, the first natural question that you might raise is: How do you define an organizational population? This question turns out to be surprisingly difficult to answer simply. Although population ecology draws heavily on biological imagery and evolutionary theory, organizations differ in a number of key ways from biological phenomenon, which can make the analogies problematic (Carroll and Hannan, 2000). In a seminal article, Hannan and Freeman (1977b:937) identify a *population* as a set of organizations that share a common organizational form and an *organizational form* as a "blueprint for organizational action, for transforming inputs into outputs." They elaborate:

> The blueprint can usually be inferred, albeit in somewhat different ways, by examining any of the following: (1) the formal structure of the organization in the narrow sense—tables of organization, written rules of operation, etc.; (2) the patterns of activity within the organization—what actually gets done by whom; or (3) the normative order—the ways of organizing that are defined as right and proper by both members and relevant sectors of the environment.

In empirical practice, much of the research in this tradition has relied largely on the latter approach, using commonly accepted distinctions among organizations, much like those given in the examples above (i.e., individually owned motor courts, liberal arts colleges, full-service gas stations). More recent formal definitions have underscored this; a form is defined as a "recognizable pattern that takes on rule-like standing" (Carroll and Hannan, 2000:67).

So how do the kinds of population changes described above occur? As we noted, population ecology is premised on the assumption that most organizations do not change fundamentally over time. That is, organizations are assumed to be characterized by a high degree of inertia, and adaptation to environmental changes is expected to be a rare phenomenon. They may change on the margins (e.g., adding new positions, altering bookkeeping systems) but not in "core" aspects such as their main technology, customer base, goals. For example, special-language newspapers have rarely (if ever) morphed into general, mass-audience newspapers (Carroll and Delacroix, 1982) or large convention-oriented hotels do not normally turn into specialized boutique hotels (Ingram and Inman, 1996).

Hannan and Freeman (1984) list a number of factors that are important sources of inertia. One source is sunk costs in equipment, personnel, and location. For example, switching to a new operating system in a computer-manufacturing company requires a very large investment not only in hardware but in training and/or recruiting new people who are knowledgeable of the system. Even going from an all-women's college to one that is coeducational requires changes in facilities (dorms, bathrooms, locker rooms, etc.) and personnel that are more costly than you might expect and that often limit such changes (Perratta, 2007). A second contributor to inertia is limited information about changes that are occurring in the environment, which make it hard for decision-makers to recognize the need for change and to decide what kind of change will be effective. Thus, in the 1970s, U.S. automakers were completely surprised by the impact of the oil embargo on customer preferences and severely underestimated the length of time the embargo would have its effects; consequently they continued to produce large, gas-guzzling autos (Katz, 1985). Even if decision-makers are able to recognize the need for change, there may be such high political costs associated with a change that they are unwilling to pay those costs; this is a third source of inertia. Major changes in organizations necessarily involve major reallocation of resources among groups and divisions, and such reallocation efforts can become a key source of significant infighting among members (Bacharach, Bamberger, and Sonnenstuhl, 1996). Given the uncertainties surrounding the outcomes of change processes, anticipation of such politics can provide strong incentives not to undertake the changes (Lawler, Thye, and Yoon, 2008). Legal and fiscal barriers to entry or exit from an industry constitute a fourth major source of inertia. Thus, a group medical practice cannot simply become a hospital because the requirement for this transformation-purchasing additional equipment, meeting the standards for accreditation, to locate increased staffing, and so forth–barriers to entry. Likewise, public universities cannot simply declare themselves independent of state governments and become private universities (Tolbert, 1985).

Moreover, population ecologists argue that when older organizations overcome these sorts of inertial pressures and actually undertake significant major changes, their chances of failing increase because they become subject to the "liability of newness." This concept refers to a commonly observed positive relationship between organizational age and chances of surviving; newly founded organizations have a much higher death rate than older organizations (Aldrich and Marsden, 1988). There are several reasons for this relationship. One is that in relatively new organizations, routines and procedures are less well worked out and understood by organizational members. In consequence, they often function with less reliability than older organizations, and customers will not continue to transact with an organization that is undependable (Aldrich, 2005). A second, related factor is that newer organizations often lack legitimacy; they don't have an established record of performance, so when errors or problems occur, customers or other exchange partners are less likely to give them the benefit of the doubt, to see these as a one-time issue (Zimmerman and Zeitz, 2002).

Hence, instead of adaptation by individual organizations, population ecologists argue that the major motor of population change is evolution, resulting from the deaths of organizations with a given form and the births of new organizations with a different form. You may recall from basic biology that there are four main processes involved in evolution: variation, competition, selection, and retention (Aldrich, 1999). Thus, population change starts with variation, the emergence of one or more organizations with a form that is different from those of existing organizations. Ecologists have typically not been particularly concerned with explaining *why* variations occur or the conditions that give rise to such variations (though see Burton and Beckman, 2007). They assume that an entrepreneur or set of entrepreneurs, in a search for competitive advantage, are apt to try new forms of organization, and that this happens with some frequency. Such variations are necessary for the second process, competition, to occur. From a theoretical standpoint, population ecologists are interested in competition between different forms of organization rather than competition among organizations with the same form (Hannan and Freeman, 1977b), although this is not always evident in empirical analyses. It is assumed that organizations with different forms but occupying the same niche (i.e., requiring the same set of resources—labor, customers, materials, etc.) will ultimately begin to compete for resources. When that happens, the growth of one population will occur at the expense of the other; organizations in the latter set will have increasing rates of failure as more and more organizations with a different form are founded and expand. Thus, the outcome of competition is selection, the death of organizations whose forms are less well fit to environmental conditions. And the counterpart of selection for the surviving form of organization is retention. In biology, of course, retention occurs because individual members have certain "successful" genes that they pass along to their offspring. Presumably, for organizations, this process entails the observation by entrepreneurs of the success of a given form of organization and the subsequent adoption of that form when they found new organizations.

While population ecologists' original theorizing focused on the dynamics of competition *between* two or more populations of organizations, many of the empirical studies in this tradition and later theorizing focused primarily on competition *within* a population of organizations. Thus, researchers gave attention to the way in which the number of organizations in a given population (referred to as organizational density) affected the survival and founding rates of organizations within that same population. A common finding from an array of studies conducted of organizations within different industries and at different points in historical time was that there was a curvilinear relationship between the number of organizations in a population and both survival and founding rates. These relations are described in terms of "density dependence" and are portrayed in Figures 9–1 and 9–2.

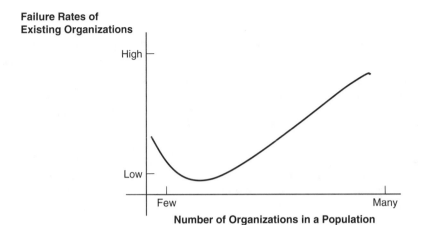

FIGURE 9–1   Density Dependence and Failure Rates Within an Organizational Population

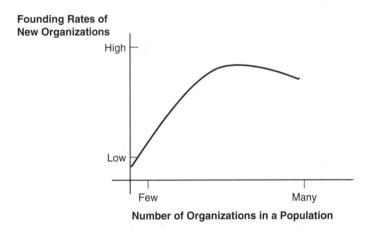

FIGURE 9–2   Density Dependence and Founding Rates Within an Organizational Population

The initial downward slope of the line in Figure 9–1, portraying the relation between density dependence and organizational failure, indicates that as the number of organizations in a population increases, the likelihood of any given organization failing decreases, at least up to a point. However, the upturn in the slope means that after that point, increases in the number of organizations lead to *increases* in the likelihood of organizational failures. The curve shown in Figure 9–2, the relation between density dependence and foundings of new organizations, implies the reverse: Increases in the number of organizations of a given type lead to more foundings of that type, again up to a point; once a threshold number is reached, the rate of foundings begins to decline with further increases.

Carroll and Hannan (2000) have labeled this line of research as the demography of corporations, since it examines patterns and processes of organizational births and deaths, much as human demography investigates general patterns of increases and declines in human populations. These common curvilinear relations between density and organizational death and founding rates are explained in terms of two key processes: legitimation and competition. When new types of organizations are created, because people are unfamiliar with them, they are likely to be concerned about whether the organizations will be reliable and a little reluctant to transact with them—the sort of problems we discussed earlier in terms of the notion of "liability of newness." Another way to put this is that they lack legitimacy. As more organizations of that type get founded and become more commonplace, they gain legitimacy. Thus, increases in density are associated with greater legitimacy, leading to lower rates of failure, and to further foundings of that type of organization. As more and more organizations are created, however, competition between organizations for resources begins to intensify so that at some level of density, the forces of competition outweigh those of legitimacy, and rates of failure begin to rise. Presumably, entrepreneurs observe this and become less willing to invest their time and effort in creating new organizations of that same type, resulting in declining rates of founding.

Both the older and newer versions of population ecology have led to some novel and provocative insights into the nature of organizations and generated a vast array of studies on the conditions that increase organizations' chances of being founded, and of failing. It should be noted, however, that the empirical evidence in support of some key arguments in this tradition is quite mixed, particularly evidence for the key claims that organizations are characterized by a very high degree of inertia and rarely engage in substantial change and that when they do, they are very apt to die. While there is some evidence that is consistent with this claim (e.g., Amburgey, Kelly, and Barnett, 1993; Barnett and McKendrick, 2004), there is also a fair amount of evidence that organizations do indeed change and that this is likely to enhance their survival chances. For example, in a series of studies of organizations involved in the savings and loan business, a business that was hit by a major environmental shift in the early 1980s in the form of deregulation, Haveman (1992, 1993b) found that many organizations substantially changed their core customer base and markets and that making such changes contributed to the organizations' survival. Likewise, a review of research by Miner and Haunschild (1995) also provided evidence of adaptational changes that occurred across several populations of organizations. Other research by Haveman (1993a) indicated that smaller organizations often found it more difficult to undertake such significant adaptive changes, which is consistent with the suggestion that population ecology arguments of strong inertial forces may be more applicable to younger and smaller organizations than to larger organizations with more resources (Aldrich and Pfeffer, 1976).

Other criticisms of this approach include that of Van de Ven (1979), who suggests that the notion of "fit" between the environment and organizations is unclear. According to Van de Ven, population ecologists appear to use fit as

> either an unquestioned axiom or inductive generalization in a causal model that asserts that organizational environment determines structure because effective or surviving organizations adopt structures that fit their environmental niches relatively better than those that do not survive. To avoid a tautology, the proposition implicitly reduces to the hypothesis that organizational survival or effectiveness moderates the relationship between environment and structure. (p. 323)

This is interesting, because effectiveness is scarcely mentioned by population ecology theorists. Van de Ven goes on to criticize the population ecology model for drawing too heavily on analogies with biological systems, a criticism that is echoed by Young (1988, 1989), who argues that the approach may be suited for only a narrow range of organizational phenomena. To illustrate this issue, compare the notion of the death of a biological organism with that of an organization. Death in the former case is usually quite clear, but this is more difficult to judge for organizations. When a restaurant changes owners without ceasing operations (although perhaps undergoing a substantial change in menu, hours of operation, and so forth), it can be debated whether the first organization died and a new one came into existence, or whether the same organization survived over time. Likewise, when an organization is acquired by another organization through a merger, whether to count that as a death is also open to question.

All paradigms have their limitations, however, as we noted repeatedly; by definition, each offers ways of explaining some organizational phenomena, while ignoring other phenomena. Thus, some of the most promising avenues of research often involve combining ideas and insights from different paradigms. Below, we describe just a few examples of such research to give you a sense of how different paradigms can be used in combination.

COMBINING PARADIGMS

A number of studies have suggested the utility of combining resource dependence and institutional paradigms. Oliver (1991), for example, suggested that organizations' responses to institutional pressure were strongly shaped by patterns of dependence. Thus, when organizations have more diversified dependencies, they may be better able to resist pressures by some constituents to follow institutional prescriptions, by pointing to the competing demands of other constituents. The more concentrated dependencies, presumably, the more an institutional perspective may be relevant to explaining the adoption of new structures. Goodstein (1994) combined institutional and resource dependence paradigms in an examination of the extent to which organizations get involved with work-family issues; similar evidence comes from studies by Blum, Fields, and Goodman (1994), in an analysis of the proportion of women in management, and by Gooderham, Nord-haug, and Ringdal (1999), in an analysis of the adoption of human resource practices in a set of European firms. Taking a slightly different tack, Tolbert and Zucker's (1983) analysis of the spread of civil service procedures among city governments suggested that resource dependencies are likely to affect the adoption of structures before the structures become institutionalized. However, once institutionalization processes begin, dependencies have less and less of an effect on decisions to adopt the structures. Instead, the number of other organizations having previously adopted it becomes the most powerful predictor of adoption. Thus, these studies suggest that the impact of institutionalization on organizations' adoption of formal structures may be mediated by dependency patterns, and the converse may hold as well: the impact of dependencies on the adoption of structures may lessen as structures become progressively more institutionalized.

Other studies have demonstrated points of convergence between institutional and population ecology paradigms. A study by Haveman, Rao, and Paruchuri (2007) indicated that as certain structural arrangements in banks became more institutionalized (accepted as consistent with core values of modern, bureaucratic organization), banks that had these structures were more likely to survive. Likewise, a study by Sine, Haveman, and Tolbert (2005) of organizations in the new, independent power sector combines insights from both population ecology and institutional paradigms. This study indicated that organizations with technologies that were more innovative (less consistent with institutionalized technologies) were more likely to be founded and to survive when resources were more abundant (because of favorable tax policies), when court rulings provided more stability for the industry, and before industry associations began to promote (i.e., institutionalize) particular technologies.

And a growing body of work on resource partitioning combines insights from resource dependence and population ecology to explain the emergence and survival of small, specialized firms in niches dominated by a few large firms (e.g., Baum and Haveman, 1997; Dowell, 2006; Ingram and Inman, 1996).

SUMMARY AND CONCLUSIONS

The claim that forces outside of organizations, the environment, fundamentally affect the form that organizations take, their ability to achieve their goals, and their chances of survival is hardly earthshaking. Yet grasping the processes through which these outcomes are produced is a difficult and complex task. Because of this complexity, different theorists have often resorted to focusing on a selected set of environmental factors and a selected set of organizational outcomes in developing an understanding of organizational–environment relations. At this point in time, there appears to be a strong sentiment among organizational theorists that the time has come to cease being paradigm warriors, advocating one approach as "the best," and to seek fuller explanations through combining perspectives. As this is done, we should increasingly be able to move toward the elusive goal of specifying which theoretical explanations work in which settings and thus have truly meaningful explanations of organizations.

EXERCISES

1. Which theoretical paradigms do you find most appealing? Why?
2. For each paradigm, discuss a situation you've experienced (or read about) in organizations that it would help explain. What aspects of the situation were not accounted for by a given paradigm?

Chapter 10

Organizational Performance and Change

OVERVIEW

Formal organizations are, presumably, created for some purpose; hence, at the end of the day, one key outcome involves the evaluation of an organization's performance in terms of its achievement of this purpose. Moreover, if the performance is deemed inadequate, another outcome is change, "righting" the organization to achieve its purpose. Although on the surface these issues seem straightforward, a long line of theoretical and empirical studies provide testimony to how complicated they really are. In this chapter, we review this literature to help you understand why both assessment of organizations' performance and efforts to bring about intended, significant changes in organizations are so difficult.

Many if not most definitions of formal organizations include the concept of "goal" or "purpose" as a key element. For example, Blau and Scott (1962:5) assert:

> In contrast to the social organization that emerges whenever men are living together, there are organizations that have been deliberately established for a certain purpose. If the accomplishment of an objective requires collective effort, men set up an organization designed to coordinate the activities of many persons and to furnish incentives for others to join them for this purpose.

The idea of a shared goal as a defining feature of organizations is consistent with commonsense notions of organizations as being deliberately created to accomplish some task collectively that individuals, acting alone, cannot. Barnard's classic epitome of an organization as five people trying to move a large rock also reflects this notion. In line with this, it seems reasonable to step back, at various points in an organization's life, to assess how well it's performing with respect to its goals. This idea underlies the definition of organizational effectiveness as the degree to which "an organization realizes its goals" (Etzioni, 1964:8). It did not take long, however, for organizational theorists and researchers to recognize the problems inherent in conceptualizing effectiveness this way and in trying to use this approach in assessing organizational performance (Simon, 1964). Below, we discuss some of the problems of specifying exactly what the goals of an organization are, and some of the ways this is dealt with in different proposals for assessing organizational performance.

PROBLEMS OF DEFINING ORGANIZATIONAL GOALS

Let's begin by thinking about how we might determine what the goals of an organization are. One tack we could take would be to examine the mission statement or some other document that offers a formal statement of the organization's key objectives. The plural term, "objectives," should signal one potential problem here: most organizations have multiple and, not infrequently, conflicting aims. ExxonMobil's Financial and Operating Review section of their 2006 annual report (pp. 4–5) provides one example of this. The company's focal business operations involve the production and sale of gas and oil, and you might assume that its goal is to maximize profits in this business. However, its list of key objectives includes the following (http://exxonmobil.com/corporate/files/corporate/xom_2006_SAR.pdf):

- Promoting safety, health, and the environment
- Demonstrating sound corporate governance and high ethical standards
- Capturing quality investment opportunities
- Maintaining one of the strongest financial positions of any company

These goals are not necessarily inconsistent, but it is not hard to imagine circumstances under which the aim of ensuring individuals' health and the maintenance of the natural environment in this industry might be at odds with that of maintaining a strong financial position. Thus, in gauging the extent to which the organization has realized its goals, one problem is: Which goal should be used?

Along with the multiplicity of goals that characterize most organizations, this list also serves to highlight another common problem in defining goals, the difference between what Perrow (1961:855) refers to as "official" and "operative" goals. He defines official goals as "the general purposes of the organization as put forth in the charter, annual reports, public statements by key executives and other authoritative pronouncements." Official goals are usually stated in very abstract, broad, and hard-to-measure terms, such as those shown above from ExxonMobil. Operative goals, on the other hand, "designate the ends sought through the actual operating policies of the organization; they tell us what the organization actually is trying to do, regardless of what the official goals say are the aims." Examining the operative goals entails examining the allocation of organizational resources: to what kinds of activities is the organization devoting relatively more of its money, time, and personnel? Operative goals *may* be linked directly to official goals, but the fact that they are defined by the relative alloca-tion of organizational resources means that they probably reflect choices among competing values embodied in the latter. Thus, they could contribute to one offi-cial goal, while subverting another. An illustration of this is provided by an early study of two state employment agency units by Blau (1955), who found that although the agencies had the same official goals, they were clearly differentiated in terms of what they really were attempting to accomplish. One unit was highly competitive, with members striving to outproduce each other in the numbers of individuals placed, regardless of whether the placements resulted in a good "fit" for individuals and thus job retention. In the other unit, cooperation among the members and quality of placement for job seekers was stressed.

To make matters even more complicated, operative goals may develop that are unrelated to official goals. Perrow (1961) goes on to note:

> Unofficial operative goals, on the other hand, are tied more directly to group inter-ests, and while they may support, be irrelevant to, or subvert official goals, they bear no necessary connection with them. An interest in a major supplier may dictate the policies of a corporate executive. The prestige that attaches to utilizing elaborate high speed computers may dictate the reorganization of inventory and accounting departments. Racial prejudice may influence the selection procedures of an employ-ment agency. The personal ambition of a hospital administrator may lead to commu-nity alliances and activities which bind the organization without enhancing its goal achievement. On the other hand, while the use of interns and residents as "cheap labor" may subvert the official goals of medical education, it may substantially fur-ther the official goal of providing a high quality of patient care. (p. 856)

Thus, another issue in defining the goals of an organization is whether to take the official or operative goals as the "real" ones.

Even if we were able to construct a reasonable rationale for making the choice between using official or operative goals and for assigning primacy to one or two as *the* critical goals, we would encounter yet another definitional problem—specifying the temporal boundary of the goals. Attaining a particular goal in the short run, such as maximizing stock price, could be disastrous for a company in the long run if it achieved this by failing to invest sufficient resources in technology or basic staffing. Not making such investments might raise profits and lead investors and analysts to increase the stock value in the short run but create serious functional problems at a later date. This is a key limitation of the classic economic definition of business organizations' goals, which is simply to "maximize shareholder value" (Davis, 2005). A rather ironic illustration of the importance of considering time in the context of defining goals and assessing goal achievement is provided by the once-popular management book *In Search of Excellence* (Peters and Waterman, 1982). In the early 1980s, the authors identified a number of companies as high achievers and sought to define the common properties of the companies that contributed to this position. Within five years of the book's publication, however, a substantial number of the companies were in very serious financial trouble. Thus, it may be difficult to decide what the appropriate time frame for assessing goal attainment should be.

Apart from examining documents that specify official goals, or examining the allocation of resources to ascertain the operative goals, another tack to take in determining what the goals of an organization are might simply be to ask current members. You could even ask them to specify what *the* single most important goal is. This approach, however, would likely lead to the identification of another, rather different problem with the concept of organizational goal, one summed up by Cyert and March (1963:26), who assert, "People (i.e., individuals) have goals; collectives of people do not." This distinction partly reflects concern over the potential confounding of individuals' motivation for cooperating in an organizational context with the outcomes of that cooperative effort. To go back to Barnard's favorite example of five people trying to move a stone, each person may have a different reason for wanting the stone moved (e.g., to make it easier to travel some route, to provide a dam in a stream, to test a theory of how to move stones with minimal effort). Thus, if you asked them what the goal of the enterprise is, each might well provide you with a different answer.

One way that Cyert and March (1963) propose to deal with this issue is to conceive of the goals of an organization as the intersection of the goals of key participants, or what they call "the dominant coalition" (pp. 30–31). The goal in Barnard's example (the intersection of the five individuals' personal goals) would be moving the rock to some particular spot. Given this objective, other individuals may be recruited to participate in the enterprise in exchange for "side payments," or inducements that the key participants provide; in exchange for these, individuals agree to contribute their activities to achieve the goals as defined. (You may remember this model of organizations being discussed in Chapter 6 on decision-making.) This doesn't quite get us out of the thicket of trying to define goals by asking members, however, since members are still apt to have different perceptions of what "the organization's goals" are, and these will probably be closely allied to what their main duties are in the organization (Barnard, 1968:231). Thus, the members of the research and development group at Exxon-Mobil might be expected to perceive the development of new technology as the key goal of the organization, members of the legal department might see maintaining safety and health (thus avoiding crippling lawsuits) as the key goal, and so forth.

Temporal boundaries are also a problem with this approach, since subjectively defined organizational goals may also shift over time. This can be the result of a number of forces, including environmental changes that lead to new emphases within the organization as well as changes in members of the dominant coalition (i.e., turnover in top executives) who set new priorities for the organization. Michels's (1949) classic study of the development of oligarchy in political parties and labor unions is illustrative of this. As an oligarchical elite becomes entrenched, the goals that the elites once shared with the rank and file tend to be displaced by other goals among elites—such as perpetuating themselves in office (Tolbert and Hiatt, forthcoming).

There are other sources of shifts in goals, of course. Organizations may begin to emphasize goals that are easily quantifiable, at the expense of those that are not so easily quantified. Universities look at the number of faculty publications rather than at the more-difficult-to-measure goal of classroom teaching; business firms look at output per worker rather than at "diligence, cooperation, punctuality, loyalty, and responsibility" (Gross, 1968:542). If organizations do begin to emphasize that which is easily quantifiable, then there is a shift of goals in that direction. Goal shifts are also possible when there is slack in the organization and it is secure. A study of the National Council of Churches found that staff interactions guided by a new professional ideology and strong purposive commitments contributed to major and radical goal shifts within the organization (Jenkins, 1977). This study also suggests that threats to the organization's domain would probably lead to a more conservative stance. Finally, an additional source of goal shifts lies outside the organization and involves indirect pressures from the general environment. Economic conditions lead to expansion or contraction of operations; technological developments must be accommodated; core social values and legal requirements shift. Organizational goals are adjusted to these environmental conditions.

A classic study of changing goals is provided by Sills's (1957) analysis of the March of Dimes Foundation, which had been created to raise funds for the treatment of individuals who suffered the crippling effects of polio and for research on this disease. A technological development, the discovery of an effective vaccine, essentially eliminated the need for the continued existence of the organization. You could say that its effectiveness created the conditions for the organization's demise. Since the organization had grown very large at this point, with a regular, salaried staff that ran it, as well as legions of volunteer workers, closing down the organization was not viewed as a desirable option. Hence it shifted its goals, to raising funds for research on and ultimately elimination of all kinds of birth defects; this is not a goal that is likely to be achieved any time soon.

APPROACHES TO ORGANIZATIONAL EFFECTIVENESS

The preceding discussion of the nature of organizational goals has convinced you, we hope, that the seemingly straightforward approach to assessing organizational performance in terms of goal achievement is fraught with problems (Campbell, 1977). Nonetheless, the desire of investors, government agencies, charitable foundations, and others to be able to evaluate the performance of organizations spurred efforts to develop other ways of assessing effectiveness, leading to a variety of proposed approaches, or models (Georgiou, 1973; Pennings and Goodman, 1977;

Seashore and Yuchtman, 1967; Steers, 1977; Yuchtman and Seashore, 1967). We describe some of these below.

System-Resource Approach

One approach advocated by Seashore and Yuchtman (1967), labeled as the system-resource model, defines an effective organization in terms of its "ability to exploit its environment in the acquisition of scarce and value resources to sustain its functioning" (p. 393). Implicitly, this approach assumes that the key goal of an organization is to survive; this is, in the authors' terminology, the ultimate criterion of effectiveness, which can only be assessed over a long period of time. However, they suggest that there are also penultimate criteria, whose level of attainment at given points in time will affect the ability of the organization to achieve the ultimate goal. In their conception, penultimate criteria have a number of defining characteristics:

> [T]hey are relatively few in number; they are "output" or "results" criteria referring to things sought for their own value; they have trade-off value in relation to one another; they are in turn wholly caused by partially independent sets of lesser performance variables; their sum in some weighted mixture over time wholly determines the ultimate criterion. (p. 379)

These penultimate criteria, in turn, are determined by a large number of short-term performance measures; Seashore and Yuchtman refer to these as "subsidiary variables." Thus, the conception of effectiveness reflects the idea that the long-run performance of an organization depends on how well it performs overall on a variety of dimensions, even though performance on any single dimension at any given point in time may be unrelated (or even inversely related) to its performance on another.

They applied these ideas in a study of seventy-five insurance companies, from whom they collected all kinds of financial and other information (over two hundred variables!) for an eleven-year time period, 1952–1962. They reduced the number of variables to seventy-six based on redundancy, missing or poor-quality information, and so forth, and conducted a factor analysis to determine which variables "hung together" as indicators of performance. This resulted in a set of ten factors, such as business volume (e.g., number of policies written), new member productivity (relative number of policy sales by new sales staff compared to those of older staff), and manpower growth. Some of these factors, such as business volume, were very stable over time, whereas others, such as new member productivity, varied considerably across time—that is, the level of new member productivity at one point in time was not related to the level of the same factor at a later point. Moreover, the strength of the relations among the different factors was not very consistent. They conclude:

> These sales organizations are maximizing their ability to get resources when they optimize, as an interdependent set, the ten performance factors isolated. This

optimizing process involves balancing off some exploitative strategies against others; for example, increased market penetration against temporarily higher production costs; short-run gains against deferred gains; exploiting the manager for current sales as against exploiting him for staff growth and development. The optimum pattern of performance for each of the organizations may be unique to the extent that their histories and environments differ, and they may fall into a limited number of types of alternative general strategies that are equally effective as long as each type maintains its own internal balancing principle. (p. 394)

From the standpoint of thinking about how to assess the effectiveness of an organization, the primary implications of this approach are that the conclusions one draws will depend on what measures are chosen and at what point in time the data are collected on these measures (since not all measures of performance at a given point in time are positively related), and the autocorrelations of a given measure over time may not be very high, or even negative. Thus, it offers important caveats, though not necessarily clear directions for how to assess effectiveness.

Participant-Satisfaction Approach

Barnard (1968) set the tone for participant-satisfaction models in his discussion of efficiency, which he defined in terms of the ability of the organization to attract contributions from members that were needed for the organization to continue to exist. (Note that Barnard used the term *efficiency* in a way that is a little confusing, given contemporary definitions of efficiency as the ratio of inputs to outputs—that is, maximizing outputs with minimal inputs.) Thus, organizational success was not viewed as the achievement of goals but rather as survival of the organization through securing contributions by providing sufficient rewards or incentives. Georgiou (1973), building on the work of Barnard, argues:

[T]he emergence of organizations, their structure of roles, division of labor, and distribution of power, as well as their maintenance, change, and dissolution can best be understood as outcomes of the complex exchanges between individuals pursuing a diversity of goals. Although the primary focus of interest lies in the behavior within organizations, and the impact of the environment on this, the reciprocal influence of the organization on the environment is also accommodated. Since not all of the incentives derived from the processes of organizational exchange are consumed within the interpersonal relations of the members, organizational contributors gain resources with which they can influence the environment. (p. 308)

The implication of Georgiou's argument for effectiveness is that incentives within organizations must be adequate for maintaining the contributions of organizational members and must also contain a surplus for developing power capabilities for dealing with the environment. A basic problem with this argument is that it does not disclose how the incentives are brought into the organization in the first place. If a major incentive is money, the money must be secured. To be sure, money is brought into the organization through exchanges with the environment, but it appears that the system-resource approach or a goal model dealing with profit is necessary before considering individual inducements.

Cummings (1977) approaches effectiveness from a related perspective. He states:

> One possibly fruitful way to conceive of an organization and the processes that define it is as an instrument or an arena within which participants can engage in behavior they perceive as instrumental to their goals. From this perspective, an effective organization is one in which the greatest percentage of participants perceive themselves as free to use the organization and its subsystem as instruments for their own ends. It is also argued that the greater the degree of perceived organizational instrumentality by each participant, the more effective the organization. Thus, this definition of an effective organization is entirely psychological in perspective. It attempts to incorporate both the number of persons who see the organization as a key instrument in fulfilling their needs and, for each person, the degree to which the organization is so perceived. (pp. 59–60)

According to this approach, factors such as profitability, efficiency, and productivity are necessary conditions for organizational survival and are not ends in themselves. The organization must acquire enough resources to permit it to be instrumental for its members. A loosely related approach argues that more effective organizations are those in which the members agree with the goals of the organization and thus work more consistently to achieve them (Steers, 1977).

Approaching organizational effectiveness from the perspective of individuals and their instrumental gains or their goals has three major problems. The first problem, which is particularly the case for Steers's approach, is that individuals have varying forms of linkages to the organizations of which they are a part. People's involvement in organizations can be alienative, calculative, or moral (Etzioni, 1961, 1975). These different forms of involvement preclude the possibility of individual and goal congruence in many types of organizations. A second, and more basic, problem in these psychological formulations is that their focus on instrumentality for individuals neglects the activities or operations of the organization as a whole or by subunits. Although the instrumentality approach is capable of being generalized across organizations, it misses the fact that organizational outputs do something in society. The outputs may be consumed and enjoyed by some, but they also could be environmentally harmful in general. The outputs may affect people in other organizations as much as people within a focal organization. The psychological approach also downplays the reality of conflicts among goals and decisions that must be made in the face of environmental pressures. The problem is basically one of overlooking a major part of organizational reality. For example, some research indicates that there is a positive relationship between workers' commitment to the organization and some effectiveness indicators such as adaptability, turnover, and tardiness. No such relationship was found with the effectiveness indicators of operating costs and absenteeism, however (Angle and Perry, 1981). Reducing effectiveness considerations to the individual level misses the point that there can be conflicts between desirable outcomes, such as lowered operating costs and lowered turnover.

A third problem with this individualistic approach is that it misses the fact that individuals outside the organization are affected by what organizations do.

A study of the juvenile justice system found that the "clients" of a juvenile justice system network had clearly different views of the effectiveness of organizations such as the police, courts, and probation departments from those of the members of those agencies (Giordano, 1976, 1977). That is hardly surprising, of course, since the clients in this case were juveniles who had been in trouble with the law. Nonetheless, a client perspective on effectiveness would seem to be a critical component of any comprehensive effectiveness analysis.

Stakeholder Approach

Inherent in many of these models and in the debates surrounding them is the idea that it is folly to try to conceptualize organizations as simply effective or ineffective (Campbell, 1977). Some (e.g., Pennings and Goodman, 1977; Perrow, 1977) began to suggest that the concept of effectiveness requires a referent: you need to specify for *which set of interests* an organization can be said to be effective. This view underlies what has come to be called a stakeholder approach (or sometimes, multiple constituency approach) to assessing effectiveness (Cameron and Whetten, 1981; Connolly, Conlon, and Deutsch, 1980; Tsui, 1990). This approach recognizes that different sets of people who contribute to and are important for the organization are apt to have differing objectives they seek to satisfy through the organization and that these differences should be explicitly recognized (Donaldson and Preston, 1995). Although work in this tradition shares the recognition that there are different (and probably conflicting) organizational goals associated with different (and also possibly conflicting) groups, it differs in terms of the relative weight that is assigned to the preferences of different groups in coming up with an overall assessment of the organization. Zammuto (1984) identified four distinct stakeholder approaches on this basis, what he terms *relativistic, power, social justice,* and *evolutionary*.

A *relativist approach* entails identifying key constituencies, collecting information from each set of constituents about the effectiveness of the organization based on their own criteria, and then presenting the results to whatever audience seeks it (e.g., Connolly, Conlon, and Deutsch, 1980). According to Zammuto (1984), in this approach

> an overall judgment of organizational effectiveness is viewed as being neither possible nor desirable because the approach does not make any assumptions concerning the relative primacy of one constituency's judgments over those of any other constituency. Instead the relativist evaluator takes the position that overall judgments should be made by someone else, preferably the consumer of the evaluative information. (p. 607)

While the agnosticism of this approach to the question, "effective for whom?" has some appeal, it's worth noting that it provides little or no guidance for possible organizational change, unless of course all constituencies converge in a common assessment—intuitively, an unlikely outcome (Meyer and Zucker, 1989). It also ignores the likelihood that the constituency that commissions such collection of data is very likely to be one controlling critical resources.

A *power approach,* on the other hand, explicitly uses assessment criteria based on the goals of the group that is most critical to the organization, or what has been referred to as the "dominant coalition." One way to do this, presumably, is to let the organizational members negotiate the criteria to be used in assessing an organization's performance; the outcome of such negotiation can be assumed to reflect the preferences of the most powerful internal constituents of the organization (Pennings and Goodman, 1977). Pennings and Goodman recognize that there are requirements set by both internal and external stakeholders that must be met if an organization is to survive, but just meeting these constraints does not imply that an organization has a high degree of effectiveness. Rather, effectiveness is indicated by the degree to which an organization meets or exceeds the objectives defined by the dominant coalition. If an organization is a publicly traded firm, many economists would argue that effectiveness is indicated very simply in the stock price of the firm (Jensen, 2002); this is the logic behind the notion that "maximizing shareholder value" should be the goal of all publicly held businesses. Of course, this ignores the fact that shareholders are not an undifferentiated group with a single objective. Employee shareholders, small investors, and large investors may have very different time frames for their investments and thus different values at any given point. In this context, a power approach is consistent with making "maximize shareholder value" equate to "maximize the current goals of a few large investors." A logical problem with this approach is that achieving these goals may result in the demise of the organization, insofar as keeping current stock value high results in inability of the organization to function in the long run, as it did at Enron (McLean and Elkind, 2004). Interestingly, partly in response to the power of external shareholders, many corporations have in recent years launched stock repurchase plans, allowing business firms to buy back stock. Although this practice runs counter to the logic of "market discipline," it may have acquired increased legitimacy as a result of some of the failures of market discipline, as exemplified by Enron (Zajac and Westphal, 2004).

The exact opposite of a power approach is what is referred to as the *social justice approach,* as advocated by Keeley (1978, 1984). Building on the work of the social philosopher John Rawls, Keeley suggests that a guiding principle for organizational evaluation should be "maximization of the least advantaged participants in a social system" (1978:285). Keeley proposes that this approach could be operationalized by minimizing the regret that participants experience in their interactions with the organization. Keeley's (1984) later work shifts to the idea of minimizing organizational harm but retains the same flavor. He recognizes the difficulties associated with the actual application of the approach but claims that the approach contains an optimization principle that goal models do not contain. He argues that it is possible to specify the manner in which group regret or harm can be minimized across organizations, though it is not possible to specify how goal attainment can be optimized across organizations, given the diversity of goals. Although this seems hopelessly idealistic at first blush, Keeley argues for its essential pragmatism in the long run:

> It may seem perverse to focus on regretful organizational participants rather than on those, possibly more in number, who enjoy the outcomes of cooperative activity. But the point is that generally aversive system consequences ought not, and, in the long run, probably will not, be tolerated by some participants so that positive consequences can be produced for others. Systems that minimize the aversive consequences of interaction are, therefore, claimed to be more just as well as more stable in the long run. (p. 290)

Finally, an *evolutionary approach,* as described by Zammuto (1982), takes into account the possibility that the relative power and the importance of different constituencies will change over time and that constituencies' preferences may change as well. Thus, this approach downplays the utility (and even underscores the potential harm) of attempting to evaluate the effectiveness of organizations at a single point in time. This is certainly consistent with the cautionary example offered by *In Search of Excellence,* which we discussed in the preceding paragraphs. It suggests that organizations that can adapt to best meet the demands of an organization's most important constituents as these change over time should be considered to be most effective.

While a stakeholder approach in general seems to be more sensible than a simple goal-based approach, one implication of this review is that a stakeholder approach in fact requires analysts to prioritize stakeholders on the basis of some underlying values or goals that they ascribe to the organization—whether this be satisfaction of the needs of powerful members, realization of social justice values, or long-term survival of the organization. Recognizing that such choices need to be made explicit is a useful contribution of a stakeholder approach.

Although the ambiguities and problems in assessing organizational effectiveness have led some to argue that effectiveness as an overall concept has little or no utility (e.g., Hannan and Freeman, 1977a), we think that it would be a serious mistake simply to ignore issues and findings that have been developed in regard to organizational effectiveness. As we noted, the perceived need to evaluate organizations as part of deciding whether to transact with them—whether by investors, government agencies, private charities, or others—remains as strong today as it ever was. If organizational researchers throw up their hands in the face of problems involved in assessment, this is not going to mitigate this pressure. Instead, we advocate the importance of recognizing issues that have been raised in our review of previous efforts to help guide efforts to conduct performance assessment, and to interpret (with due caution) the outcomes of these efforts. In this light, let us summarize issues that any effectiveness study should take into consideration, both in terms of design and in terms of drawing conclusions.

EVALUATING ORGANIZATIONAL PERFORMANCE: KEY ISSUES

1. Organizations face multiple and conflicting environmental constraints. These constraints may be imposed on an organization; they may be bargained for; they may be discovered; or they may be self-imposed (Seashore, 1977). Imposed constraints are beyond organizational control. They involve our familiar environmental dimensions such as legal requirements and economic pressures. To be sure, organizations lobby for legal and regulative advantage, but taxes and regulations are essentially imposed on organizations. This imposition is not just from government. A computer or software manufacturer, such as Microsoft, that develops new systems is imposing this environment on users, if those users must adopt the new system to stay "state of the art." Bargained constraints involve contractual agreements and competitive pressures in markets. Discovered constraints are environmental constraints that appear unexpectedly, as when a coal company finds that its vein of ore has run out. Self-imposed constraints involve the definitions of the environment that organizations utilize. For example, a study of newspaper coverage of an oil spill documented the fact that newspapers differed markedly in the amount of space given to the spill (Molotch and Lester, 1975). Organizational policy thus defines the importance of environmental elements.

Regardless of the source of the constraints, the fact that they frequently conflict must be stressed, since efforts to deal with one constraint may operate against the meeting of another. Indeed, organizational units facing multiple contingencies are more prone to face design misfit and lower performance than those in simpler situations (Gresov, 1989). As a general rule, the larger and more complex the organization, the greater the range and variety of constraints it will face. Organizations have to consider their environments, recognize and order the constraints that are confronted, and attempt to predict the consequences of their actions—all within the limitations on decision-making and rationality we have considered.

2. Organizations have multiple and conflicting goals. This point has been beaten to death, but one more pass is necessary here. A case from the University at Albany is instructive. It involved a threatened budget cut, which is an annual event that sometimes results in real cuts and sometimes does not. In the case being described, the threatened cuts were severe. Each vice president had to make up a list of "target" positions in his or her area. We know that decisions that are made in such situations are the result of power coalitions. At the same time, goals do not just disappear. Issues such as the emphasis on research, needs for the continued recruitment and retention of high-quality students and faculty to achieve the goal of being a high-quality university, and reiterations of the importance of having a safe and attractive campus were voiced and were much more than rhetoric. When the cuts were made, they were based on goals and power coalitions. Both contained contradictions that were played out in actions.

3. Organizations have multiple and conflicting internal and external stakeholders, a point that is partly related to the preceding one. By stakeholders we mean those people affected by an organization (Marcus and Goodman, 1991; Tsui, 1990). They may be employees, members, customers, clients, or the public at large. Stakeholders can also be other organizations such as suppliers and customers. Individual and organizational stakeholders obviously can have different and contradictory interests (Harrison and Freeman, 1999; Somaya, Williamson, and Zhang, 2007). Although it may be necessary to draw conclusions about organizations' performance, prioritizing the objectives of one set of stakeholders is very likely to create problems and pressures from other stakeholders in response.

4. The outcomes of any assessment effort will almost certainly depend on the time frame that it used. There are intraorganizational variations in the time frames that may affect efforts to understand the performance of the organization as a whole (Lawrence and Lorsch, 1967). The degree and mix of environmental constraints also vary over time. Constraints that were critical at one point may disappear as threats. New problems arise. Time also plays a role in the history of an organization, since new organizations are more vulnerable. How to incorporate the temporal dimension in assessing effectiveness is essentially one of judgment. Decisions must be made with regard to the time frame of reference for analyzing goal attainment, the nature and phasing of environmental constraints, and the historical situation of the organization. Failing to recognize this can lead the analyst and the practitioner to real problems. For the analyst it is only a poor study; for the practitioner it is organizational decline or death.

ORGANIZATIONAL CHANGE AND TRANSFORMATION

There is another key outcome for organizations, one that is often a corollary of efforts to assess performance: change. With the exception of population ecology, most organizational research is predicated on the assumption that change is a pervasive aspect of organizations. Child and Kieser (1981), for example, assert:

> Organizations are constantly changing. Movements in external conditions such as competition, innovation, public demand, and governmental policy require that new strategies, methods of working, and outputs be devised for an organization merely to continue at its present level of operations. Internal factors also promote change in that managers and other members of an organization may seek not just its maintenance but also its growth, in order to secure improved benefits and satisfactions for themselves. (p. 28)

But how do such changes take place? Many changes may occur, if not completely haphazardly, in a piecemeal fashion that doesn't reflect consideration of long-term direction but simply immediate solutions to immediate problems as they are perceived. At some point, though, members of an organization may stop to take a longer-term view of how it is functioning (either voluntarily or because circumstances—e.g., imminent failure—dictate this) and decide that some significant alterations in operations are needed. There are a number of different lines of work that address the challenges of bringing about change in organizations, ranging from problems of organizational learning to those of large-scale organizational transformation. Below, we review some of the main ideas from these literatures.

ORGANIZATIONAL CHANGE: LEARNING AND TRANSFORMATION

Closely aligned with work on organizational decision-making, research and theory on organizational learning has examined how organizations get, interpret, and act on information that leads to changes that are designed to improve their functioning. Glynn, Lant, and Milliken (1994) distinguish two different strands of research and theory on this topic. One, referred to as adaptive learning, is very directly tied to work from the Carnegie School on processes of decision-making (Cyert and March, 1963; March and Simon, 1958; Simon, 1957). This work focuses on linking the cognitive processes of individuals to structural properties of organizations (Argote and Greve, 2007). The other, referred to as the knowledge development approach, comes out of research on small groups in social psychology and focuses primarily on factors that affect communication and patterns of interaction among members of a group.

An Adaptive Learning Approach

The adaptive learning approach is predicated on the view of organizations as a series of programs, or sets of rules, for making decisions that lead to the accomplishment of various tasks. Routine use of these programs economizes on individuals' decision-making efforts and contributes to the efficiency and reliability of organizations' outcomes. However, when programs fail to yield outcomes that are at or above some standard that has been set (e.g., the organization's revenues drop below the past quarter's or those of the past year), a search for new programs, or a nonroutine revision of the existing programs, is set in motion. March and Simon (1958:174–175) suggest that the beginning of a round of learning in organizations entails the "devising and evaluation of new performance programs that have not previously been a part of the organization's repertory and cannot be introduced by a simple application of programmed switching rules." (Their view of programs includes the notion that organizations may have established rules for changing programs; when the programs yield unsatisfactory results and the established rules for changing the programs also fail to yield satisfactory results, search processes—and learning—begin.) This approach assumes that organizational search is usually relatively limited, in part because choices for new programs are shaped by existing programs because these create cognitive frameworks and categories for analyzing problems (Cohen and Levinthal, 1990). Thus, learning (and hence change) in organizations is viewed as occurring incrementally and as being reflected in the systematic alteration of standard sets of decision rules, or programs. This latter point is important because "organizational learning" connotes more than the acquisition of knowledge by individuals; for individuals' knowledge to become part of the knowledge of an organization, it must be embedded in rules and common procedures that enable it to persist (Carley, 1992; Levitt and March, 1988).

An illustration of research in this tradition is provided by a study of accidents among U.S. commercial airlines by Haunschild and Sullivan (2002). The question the authors address is whether organizations are more likely to learn from accidents that have complex, more ambiguous causes (what they call heterogeneous accidents) or clearer, easier-to-diagnose causes (homogeneous accidents). Heterogeneous accidents often involve a series of events (e.g., a warning light coming on indicating engine problems, a pilot's failure to notice and/or notify anyone of this, a lack of required maintenance checks by the crew), thus requiring a deeper analysis of a broad range of possible underlying sources of problems. They note that this complex analysis is likely to generate debate among people charged with evaluating the causes, entailing more a carefully developed articulation of suspected problems and possible solutions. In this light, heterogeneous accidents might be expected to produce greater organizational learning. On the other hand, they also make the case that homogeneous accidents, especially when they occur repeatedly, may make a particular problem more salient and increase the perceived need to address it. Hence, the opposite prediction, that learning will increase as the number of homogeneous accidents increases, could be seen as plausible. Using reduction in the rates of accidents over time (between 1983 and 1997) as an indicator of organizational learning, Haunschild and Sullivan found that, in general, heterogeneous accidents were more likely to lead to organizational learning. However, the impact of this depended partly on whether the organization was a generalist (indicated by having a variety of types of airplanes in its fleet) or a specialist (having only a single type of airplane). They argue that the complexity of generalist organizations makes processing of information more difficult, and this makes learning from heterogeneity more difficult as well. In line with this, they found that heterogeneous accidents led to greater learning among specialist airlines, but not among generalists. However, unlike specialists, generalists also seemed to learn from others' experiences as well as from their own. This may be because generalists are often larger and are apt to have the resources to engage in more intensive monitoring of what is happening in the industry in general. Thus, this research focuses on the link between structural conditions (organizational complexity) and processes involved in organizational learning (drawing causal inferences), which is characteristic of an adaptive learning approach. Because the authors use archival data, they could not directly examine the creation or modification of programs that presumably underpin the reduction of accidents. (For a more close-grained analysis of such processes, see the interesting observational study of product development teams in two firms conducted by Miner, Bassoff, and Moorman, 2001.)

There is a separate line of studies of innovation in organizations (e.g., Damanpour and Evan, 1984; Hage, 1980, 1999; Moch, 1976; Moch and Morse, 1977; Pennings, 1987; Zaltman, Duncan, and Holbek, 1973) that could also be viewed from an adaptive learning approach, although the connections are not always drawn between these studies and the latter approach. Part of the reason for this is that many studies of innovation do not explicitly focus on the interaction between the cognitive properties of individuals and structural properties of organizations, as an adaptive learning approach does. Instead, much of the work on innovation has been concerned with identifying characteristics of innovations that make them more "adoptable" and characteristics of organizations that make them more "adopting." An innovation is defined as a significant departure from existing practices or technologies (Kimberly and Evanisko, 1981). (The parallels between this concept and that of March and Simon's notion of changing performance programs, as we described above, are worth noting. To repeat, March and Simon defined change as involving "new performance programs that have not previously been a part of the organization's repertory and cannot be introduced by a simple application of programmed switching rules.") Zaltman, Duncan, and Holbek (1973) proposed a long list of factors that make innovations more likely to be adopted, including lower cost, compatibility with the existing organizational systems, the ability to be modified later, a lack of complexity. On the other side, Hage and Aiken (1970) proposed a list of organizational characteristics that were posited to increase the propensity to adopt innovations. These included greater decentralization, less formalization, greater emphasis on quality (versus volume) in production, and higher levels of training among organizational members. There was, over a period, some debate in this literature over the relative importance of the characteristics of the innovation, organizational characteristics, and characteristics of decision-makers in determining the propensity of organizations to adopt innovation (e.g., Hage and Dewar, 1973 versus Baldridge and Burnham, 1975), which ultimately concluded that all factors interacted as influences (Damanpour, 1991).

In general, work from the adaptive learning tradition, in combination with some of the older studies of innovation, suggests a number of factors that often impede organizational learning. One is that individuals' cognitive preferences for stability and the use of routine programs often lead to a lack of recognition of "failures" in the programs (Milliken and Lant, 1991). This is consistent with the findings of a study by Manns and March (1978) of university departments, that under conditions of financial constraint, more powerful departments were less likely to innovate, in terms of offering a wider variety of courses, changing the number of credits assigned to courses, and so forth, than weaker ones. One way to interpret this finding is that increased power and resources enable members to indulge their cognitive preferences for stability. Another impediment to learning is organizational structure, particularly structure that contributes to the perpetuation of existing programs. This notion is consistent with the findings of Hage and Aiken, that greater formalization leads to less innovation. In other words, encoding performance programs in writing makes them less likely to be targeted by "problemistic search" (Cyert and March, 1963) and thus less likely to be modified. Interestingly, another barrier to learning, suggested by March (1991), is incremental learning itself. Incremental learning, in March's terms, involves "exploitation" of an organization's existing knowledge base—members become used to making small alterations in organizational practices and procedures and viewing this as the right way to go about changing the organization. This typically limits what he calls "exploration," the search for very different knowledge and ideas that might call the organization's existing knowledge base into question. Thus, when the conditions facing organizations change dramatically, those organizations that have acquired the greatest competence in operating in previous conditions are apt to find it most difficult to adapt and are most vulnerable to failure.

A Knowledge Development Approach

Although adaptive learning and knowledge development approaches overlap, a distinguishing feature of work that we would characterize as part of the latter tradition is the attention given to relational influences and social processes that affect knowledge transfer—the understanding, sharing, and accepting (or not) of information and ideas that lead to different ways of doing things in organizations. Researchers have examined a variety of group characteristics that may affect such transfer processes. For example, Edmondson (1999) studied the impact of culture, in particular, a culture that fosters a sense of psychological safety, "confidence that the team will not embarrass, reject, or punish someone for speaking up." Using data collected from a number of independent teams in a manufacturing company, she concluded that psychological safety led to enhanced team performance, as measured by self-reports from members of each team and her own observations of each team's performance. On the basis of her research, she attributes this relationship to the greater efforts of team members in psychologically safe groups to engage in learning behaviors such as discussions about how to improve the team's operations and collection of data relevant to the team from a wide variety of sources. Another example is provided by a study by Darr and Kurtzberg (2000), who considered the impact of similarity among franchises (including location, customer base, and strategy) on franchisees' propensity to adopt ideas and practices from each other. They found that firms were most attentive to others that were pursuing similar business strategies and were more likely to learn from them, indicated by the relationship between a given firm's changing production costs and those of other firms.

One last example that we'll offer comes from an experimental study examining the impact of shared social identity on the transfer of knowledge (Kane, Argote, and Levine, 2005). Following a line of studies that have suggested personnel changes as an important mechanism for transferring ideas and information across groups and organizations (e.g., Boeker, 1997), participants in the experiment were divided into sets of two teams, each containing three members, and each team was given the task of assembling origami sailboats. To manipulate a sense of shared social identity, some pairs of teams were given a common superordinate team name along with name tags of the same color and were intermixed around a table while the general task was explained to them. The pairs of teams without a shared identity were not given a common name, each team had different colored name tags, and the teams were seated on opposite sides of the table while the task was explained. The teams were then separated into two rooms, where one team was provided with a set of instructions for constructing the sailboats very efficiently, while the other team was provided with instructions that were less efficient. After the teams had worked for awhile, one member of each team was rotated into the other team. The researchers were interested in seeing whether having a superordinate team identity would affect the ability of the rotated member to influence the methods the team used in constructing the sailboats. They hypothesized that when the rotated member had been trained using the more efficient method (had superior knowledge), the team would be more likely to change their method than when the rotated member had been trained with the less efficient method (had inferior knowledge), but this would only occur when the two teams had a superordinate identity. The results of the study supported their hypotheses. When teams shared a superordinate identity, they adopted the superior method 67 percent of the time in the first trial, and 75 percent of the time in the second. (Surprisingly, teams with a superordinate identity adopted an *inferior* method brought by the rotating member 8 percent of the time!) In contrast, when the teams did not share a superordinate identity, they only adopted the superior method brought by the rotating member 25 percent of the time. Thus, this study provides strong evidence of the influence of social relationships on groups' willingness to accept ideas and information and thus to learn.

Percentage of Teams Adopting Methods of Rotated Team Member

Trial	Rotating Member Has Superior Knowledge	Rotating Member Has Inferior Knowledge
Superordinate Identity Condition		
1	67	8
2	75	0
No Superordinate Identity Condition		
1	25	0
2	25	0

Adapted from Aimee A. Kane, Linda Argote, and John M. Levine, "Knowledge Transfer between Groups via Personnel Rotation: Effects of Social Identity and Knowledge Quality," *Organizational Behavior and Human Decision Processes* 96 (2005): 62.

In general, work in this tradition, like that of adaptive learning, also indicates that there are many barriers to organizational learning (Argote, 1999), although, as noted, the barriers underscored by the knowledge development literature involve relational influences rather than the sorts of cognitive tendencies and limitations emphasized by work in the adaptive learning tradition.

In combination, the two traditions suggest that there are substantial barriers to incremental organizational learning and, hence, to organizational change. To make matters worse, there are occasions when even incremental learning and incremental organizational change are not sufficient, when organizational survival requires major transformational changes. This brings us to the debates and research on organizational transformation.

TRANSFORMATIONAL CHANGE

Although bringing about incremental change in organizations may not be easy, particularly change that truly improves organizational functioning, both research and everyday observations of organizations attest that this sort of change does occur with some frequency. On the other hand, there is much more debate about both the frequency of occurrence and the general efficacy of transformational change. The concept of transformational change connotes a significant alteration in some core property of organizations, such as official goals and mission, basic technology, or other aspects that are central to their identity. By identity, we mean features that members and nonmembers use to "distinguish the organization from others with which it might be compared" (Albert and Whetten, 1985:265; see also Dutton, Dukerich, and Harquail, 1994). As we noted in our discussion of population ecology in Chapter 9, two key premises underlying this theoretical framework are that fundamental change in organizations is extremely rare (excluding death as a type of change, of course) and that efforts to bring about transformational change are almost always fatal. A huge practical management literature on how to change organizations certainly provides strong testimony to arguments of powerful inertial forces in organizations and the difficulties inherent in bringing about significant organizational change. This was also acknowledged by an early analyst of organizational change, Herbert Kaufman (1971), who noted:

> In short, I am not saying that organizational change is invariably good or bad, progressive or conservative, beneficial or injurious. It may run either way in any given instance. But it is always confronted by strong forces holding it in check and sharply circumscribing the capacity of organizations to react to new conditions—sometimes with grave results. (p. 8)

Kaufman went on to describe the factors within organizations that contribute to resistance to change. These include the "collective benefits of stability" or familiarity with existing patterns, "calculated opposition to change" by groups within the organization that may have altruistic or selfish motivations, and a simple "inability to change" (p. 3). The last point refers to the fact that organizations develop "mental blinders" that preclude change capability. This happens as personnel are selected and trained to do what was done in the past in the manner in which it was done in the past.

However, whether the likelihood of transformational change in organizations is quite as miniscule as suggested and whether such change is likely to do mortal harm, especially, are subject to contention.

Case Studies of Organizational Transformation

There is a venerable tradition in sociology of case studies that have examined instances of transformational change. We've discussed some of these, such as

Sills's (1957) study of the March of Dimes Foundation, the organization that redefined its key mission to be the eradication of birth defects after its original mission, eradication of polio, was accomplished through the discovery of a vaccine. As described in Chapter 9, the case of the Tennessee Valley Authority (TVA)—the organization that was founded to provide services for the desperately impoverished farmers of the Deep South during the Great Depression, but that ended up serving primarily the wealthier farmers in the region as a result of co-optation—is another example (Selznick, 1966). This is a case where the operative goals, as we discussed in a preceding section, were substantially changed, though the official goals remained the same. Clark (1972) compared three cases of private colleges, Reed, Antioch, and Swarthmore, each of which underwent major transformations in its curricular emphases and academic orientations. Still another case of transformational change is provided by a study by Zald (1970) of the Young Men's Christian Association (YMCA) (see also Zald and Denton, 1963). Zald's analysis provides very useful insights into factors that affect organizational transformation, so we'll describe this in a little more detail.

Founded in London in the mid-1800s, the YMCA was originally created to recruit young men who had migrated from the country to urban areas in pursuit of new industrial jobs to evangelical Christianity. In exchange for cheap meals and information on "wholesome" boarding houses and jobs, the migrants were expected to attend missionary church services and ultimately to become members of evangelical churches associated with the YMCA. In the United States, new immigrants to the country were often the targets of the organization's outreach efforts. However, as the flood of immigrants in the late 1800s turned into a small stream by the early 1900s and as secularization became a prominent trend, the emphasis of the organization on religious conversion shifted to developing the "whole man" by providing an array of physical, social, and intellectual activities. In addition to changing the primarily goal, the organization also changed its primary client group as well, from exclusively young Protestant men to include women and members of other religious denominations as well.

Zald's analysis focuses on the characteristics of the organization that enabled it to undertake this transformation successfully. One is the broad formulation of the organization's initial goal, which was to contribute to members' development of strong moral character. As he points out, this goal permits enormous potential diversification, since a wide range of activities can be viewed as being perfectly consistent with that objective; it also does not limit the set of target clients served by the organizations' activities. In addition, the organization's primary means of financing, through the dues paid by members, encouraged it to pay close attention to changing environmental conditions—that is, to the wants and interests of potential members. As he suggests, dependence on a single constituent, such as a particular church or charity, would almost certainly have muted the impact of changes in societal preferences and attitudes on organizational decision-makers' choices of services to provide. Adaptation to the environment was also facilitated by the federated structure of the organization, in which local associations were provided with considerable autonomy, allowing them to make changes that were consistent with local conditions. More recent research suggesting the importance of "interconnected organizational forms," such as franchises and strategic alliances (e.g., Baum and Ingram, 1998; Powell, Koput, and Smith-Doerr, 1996), in helping spread ideas and information (Argote et al., 2000) supports the idea that this structure may also have facilitated organizational learning among different parts of the organization.

All of these studies provide fascinating insights into processes that promote and accompany organizational transformations. As a set, they suggest that transformations are apt to occur when major environmental changes take place that limit organizations' ability to continue to get resources without changing (e.g., technological advances in the March of Dimes Foundation, changes in demographics and dominant cultural values in the YMCA). Clark's (1972) study of the three colleges, in particular, underscores the key role played by organizational leaders in selecting and promoting a specific response to changing environmental conditions. This is consistent with the popular management literature on the importance of transformational leaders (Bass, 1985; Burns, 1978; Judge and Piccolo, 2004). It's worth noting, however, that Lipset's (1960) study of the way in which the efforts by socialist party leaders, swept into office by Canadian elections in the 1930s, to transform provincial governance were effectively sabotaged by lower-management civil servants sounds a cautionary note for this literature. Zald's study suggests the importance of diversified resource dependencies, rather than more concentrated dependence, in enabling organizations to undertake transformational efforts. However, there is one important point to note here: because they are all studies of organizations that undertook and survived the transformation process, we are limited in drawing conclusions from these cases about the kinds of organizations that are likely to undertake transformations (since we have no comparative information on organizations that faced similar conditions and did *not* seek to transform themselves), or the conditions that allow transformations to be successful (since we lack information on organizations that tried to transform themselves and failed). However, a number of more recent studies coming out of the tradition of population ecology, based on comparative data from organizations undergoing transformational change, provide more systematic insights.

Comparative Studies of Organizational Transformation

As we discussed, population ecologists' arguments for selection as the key mechanism in producing observed shifts in organizational populations rest on the assumption that organizations rarely undergo significant change and that when they do, it's likely to be fatal to their survival (Hannan and Freeman, 1984). The latter assumption, in particular, has been put to test by a number of studies in this tradition, with less than overwhelming support for it.

For example, Kelly and Amburgey (1991) studied the impact of going from a specialist airline (carrying only one type of product—mail, passengers, cargo, and so on) to a generalist airline (carrying mixed types of products) and vice versa, using data from the airline industry between 1962 and 1985. This industry was affected by a significant environmental jolt (Meyer, 1982) in 1978, in the form of deregulation. A rapid increase in the foundings of new airlines in the wake of this change increased competition among airlines enormously and led many of the airlines to make key shifts in their strategy, reflected in changes from specialists to generalists and the reverse. This is notably inconsistent with the argument that organizations tend toward inertia; moreover, Kelly and Amburgey's findings indicate that neither a shift toward specialism nor one in the opposite direction, toward generalism, had any significant impact on the airlines' chances of survival. Likewise, Kraatz and Zajac (1996) found that the adoption of business and other professional programs by liberal arts colleges—a shift that sharply contradicted their identity as generalist educational institutions—had no significant negative effect on their survival chances. Research by Haveman (1992) on savings and loan organizations (thrifts), members of an industry that was also significantly shaken up by the wave of deregulations that swept the United States in the 1980s as well as by rapid computerization during this decade, also challenges the notion that transformational changes generally raise rates of organizational failure. As deregulation and other economic changes made the two key traditional activities of thrifts, maintaining savings account for small investors and providing fixed-rate residential mortgages, less and less profitable, many attempted to move into new domains, such as nonresidential (commercial) mortgages, various types of investment activities, and other consumer loans (e.g., credit cards, automobile loans). Haveman examined the impact of these kinds of domain shifts on thrifts' financial performance and their survival chances. She found evidence of substantial change in these organizations over time: the average level of firm assets invested in residential mortgages dropped from nearly 80 percent in 1977 to just about half in 1986. Moreover, the more thrifts diversified into other financial domains, generally, the better their financial performance, at least in the short term. Not all domain changes had a positive effect in terms of enhancing survival; most had no effect on this, although a few actually increased the likelihood of survival. Again, as with the Kelly and Amburgey study, these results run counter to arguments that selection is almost inevitably the primary motor of population change. Other studies, however, have provided some evidence that core changes in organizations have negative consequences (e.g., Amburgey, Kelly, and Barnett, 1993).

As Baum (1996) cautions, much remains to be understood about the conditions under which organizational transformations will yield successful outcomes or the opposite. Older and larger organizations, for example, may have the resources and the reputation to invest in making significant changes and to ride out the difficulties in operations that are apt to occur with change, whereas smaller, younger organizations may lack these. This is in contrast to the usual image of the latter sorts of organizations as being more flexible and more adaptive; perhaps this holds for smaller changes, but not transformational ones. Some evidence along these lines is provided by another study of the thrift industry by Haveman (1993a). In this study, she examined how size affected the organization's propensity to shift domains. Her results suggested that for some types of domain changes, both very large and very small organizations were at a disadvantage. Her proposed explanation is that small organizations lack the resources to undertake significant change, whereas the largest organizations tend to be the most bureaucratized; thus, it takes much more effort to bring about significant alterations in practices. For some types of domain changes, though, it appeared that the larger the organization, the more likely it was to make the change. It may be that entry into some markets, or some kinds of transformation, simply requires such concentrated efforts and large expenditures of resources that only very large organizations can undertake them. In other cases, the level of resources required may be high, but not so high as to make it out of reach of more medium-sized organizations, who are less held back by high levels of formalization, complexity, and other correlates of size.

SUMMARY AND CONCLUSIONS

In this chapter, we have considered two basic outcomes for organizations: evaluation of performance and change. We assume that generally the latter outcome reflects the former, although performance evaluations may not be conducted as fully as the literature that we discussed on effectiveness and performance suggests they should be. The absence of regular, full-blown assessments of effectiveness in many organizations is understandable, in light of our discussion of the complexities involved in this task. However, as we argued, awareness of such complexities may be useful and shouldn't necessarily lead to abandoning these efforts in despair. As some of the literature on adaptive learning suggests, organizations may undertake changes with little sense of what the nature of the problem to be solved is, which of course stymies efforts to produce outcomes that have real benefits (Cohen, March, and Olsen, 1972). And there is an underlying theme in much of the practical management literature, at least, that organizational change is inherently desirable. We suspect that acting on this assumption is very conducive to garbage-can-model processes. Moreover, as a sterling example of contemporary organizational malfunctioning and mismanagement, the case of the Enron Corporation should highlight the dangers of undertaking change without careful reflection of where this might lead. This corporation embodied, in many ways, current prescriptions for changing organizations: strong, charismatic leaders who imbued members with a sense of complete commitment to the organization, the creation of a strong culture through careful selection of members to fit with the organization's values and through rituals that embodied these values, alignment of the reward system with that culture and the organization's objectives, and so on. These features did in fact result in the transformation of a relatively small organization operating routinely in the business of selling gas and oil properties into a mammoth investment corporation and, to the dismay of many stockholders and employees, into a fraudulent operation on a scale not witnessed within the last century or more (McLean and Elkind, 2004). Periodic evaluations of organizational performance may be fraught with ambiguities and difficult choices, but they do have the advantage of encouraging reflection on what the organization is doing.

This brings us to the point of departure for this book. Organizations are powerful members of our society; their actions and outcomes affect not just those directly involved in day-to-day operations—employees, stockholders, suppliers, customers and clients—but whole societies and international communities. They are very complex actors indeed, and many puzzles about how and why they operate the way that they do and under what conditions they change or refuse to change remain. By surveying research and theory, we have tried to provide you with insights into their functioning that we hope will prove useful to you both as a member of organizations and as a member of society who will participate in shaping the rules and environments that govern these powerful actors.

EXERCISES

1. Discuss the goals, environments, and stakeholders of your two organizations. To what degree are contradictions or conflicts present?
2. Pick a change that occurred within your organizations that you witnessed, or heard about. What were the factors that led to the change, and what was the process through which change occurred (how did the search take place, what solutions were considered, why was a given solution chosen)? Were the changes successful, would you say?

References

Abbott, Andrew. 1988. *The System of Professions*. Chicago: University of Chicago Press.

———. 1992. "An Old Institutionalist Reads the New Institutionalism." *Contemporary Sociology*, 21, 754–56.

Adler, Nancy J. 1996. "Global Women Political Leaders: An Invisible History, an Increasingly Important Future." *Leadership Quarterly*, 7, 133–61.

Aharonson, Barak S., Joel A. C. Baum, and Maryann P. Feldman. 2007. "Desperately Seeking Spillovers? Increasing Returns, Industrial Organization and the Location of New Entrants in Geographic and Technological Space." *Industrial and Corporate Change*, 16, no. 1, 89–130.

Ahuja, Gautam. 2000. "Collaboration Networks, Structural Holes, and Innovation: A Longitudinal Study." *Administrative Science Quarterly*, 45, 425–55.

Aiken, Michael, and Jerald Hage. 1968. "Organizational Interdependence and Interorganizational Structure." *American Sociological Review*, 33, 912–30.

Albert, Stuart, and David A. Whetten. 1985. "Organizational Identity," in *Research in Organizational Behavior*, Vol. 14, 264–95. Greenwich, CT: JAI Press.

Aldrich, Howard E. 1972a. "Technology and Organizational Structure: A Reexamination of the Findings of the Aston Group." *Administrative Science Quarterly*, 17, 26–43.

———. 1972b. "Reply to Hilton: Seduced and Abandoned." *Administrative Science Quarterly*, 17, 55–57.

———. 1979. *Organizations and Environments*. Upper Saddle River, NJ: Prentice Hall.

———. 1999. *Organizations Evolving*. Thousand Oaks, CA: Sage.

——— 2005. "Entrepreneurship," in *The Handbook of Economic Sociology*, eds. N. J. Smelser and R.Swedberg, 451–77. Princeton, NJ: Princeton University Press.

Aldrich, Howard E., and Peter V. Marsden. 1988. "Environments and Organizations," in *Handbook of Sociology*, ed. Neil J. Smelser, 361–92. Newbury Park, CA: Sage.

Aldrich, Howard E., and Jeffrey Pfeffer. 1976. "Environments of Organizations," in *Annual Review of Sociology*, Vol. 2, 78–106. Palo Alto, CA: Annual Reviews.

Allen, Michael Patrick. 1976. "Management Control in the Large Corporation: Comment on Zeitlin." *American Journal of Sociology*, 81, 885–94.

Allen, Michael Patrick, and Sharon K. Panian. 1982. "Power, Performance, and Succession in the Large Corporation." *Administrative Science Quarterly*, 27, 538–47.

Allen, Michael Patrick, Sharon K. Panian, and Roy E. Lotz. 1979. "Managerial Succession and Organizational Performance: A Recalcitrant Problem Revisited." *Administrative Science Quarterly*, 24, 167–80.

Allison, Paul D., and J. Scott Long. 1990. "Departmental Effects on Scientific Productivity." *American Sociological Review*, 55, 469–78.

Allmendinger, Jutta, and J. Richard Hackman. 1996. "Organizations in Changing Environments: The Case of East German Symphony Orchestras." *Administrative Science Quarterly,* 41, 337–69.

Alter, Catherine, and Jerald Hage. 1993. *Organizations Working Together.* Newbury Park, CA: Sage.

Alutto, Joseph, and James A. Belasco. 1972. "A Typology for Participation in Organizational Decision Making." *Administrative Science Quarterly,* 17, 117–25.

Alvesson, Mats, and Hugh Willmott. 2002. "Identity Regulation as Organizational Control: Producing the Appropriate Individual." *Journal of Management Studies,* 39, 619–44.

Amburgey, Terry, Dawn Kelly, and William P. Barnett. 1993. "Resetting the Clock: The Dynamics of Organizational Change and Failure." *Administrative Science Quarterly,* 38, 51–73.

Anderson, Theodore R., and Seymour Warkov. 1961. "Organizational Size and Functional Complexity: A Study of Administration I Hospitals." *American Sociological Review,* 26, 23–28.

Angle, Harold L., and James L. Perry. 1981. "An Empirical Assessment of Organizational Commitment and Organizational Effectiveness." *Administrative Science Quarterly,* 26, 1–14.

Ansell, C. K., and John F. Padgett. 1993. "Robust Action and the Rise of the Medici, 1400–1434." *American Journal of Sociology,* 98, 1259–1319.

Appelbaum, Eileen, and Rosemary Batt. 1994. *The New American Workplace: Transforming Work Systems in the United States.* Ithaca, NY: ILR Press of Cornell.

Appold, Stephen J., Sununta Siengthai, and John D. Kasarda. 1998. "The Employment of Women Managers and Professionals in an Emerging Economy: Gender Inequality as Organizational Practice." *Administrative Science Quarterly,* 43, 538–65.

Argote, Linda. 1982. "Input Uncertainty and Organizational Coordination in Hospital Emergency Units." *Administrative Science Quarterly,* 27, 420–34.

———. 1999. *Organizational Learning: Creating, Retaining and Transferring Knowledge.* Norwell, MA: Kluwer Academic Publishers.

Argote, Linda, and Henrich R. Greve. 2007. "A Behavioral Theory of the Firm: 40 Years and Counting." *Organizational Science,* 18, 357–69.

Argote, Linda, Paul Ingram, John M. Levine, and Richard L. Moreland. 2000. "Knowledge Transfer in Organizations: Learning from the Experience of Others." *Organizational Behavior and Human Decision Processes,* 82, 1–8.

Argyris, Chris. 1972. *The Applicability of Organizational Sociology.* London: Cambridge University Press.

Aronowitz, Stanley. 1973. *False Promises.* New York: McGraw-Hill.

Arum, Richard. 1996. "Do Private Schools Force Public Schools to Compete?" *American Sociological Review,* 61, 29–46.

Ash, Michael, and M. V. L. Badgett. 2006. "Separate and Unequal: The Effect of Unequal Access to Employment-Based Health Insurance on Same-Sex and Unmarried Different-Sex Couples." *Contemporary Economic Policy,* 24, 582–99.

Astley, W. Graham, and Andrew H. Van de Ven. 1983. "Central Perspectives and Debates in Organization Theory." *Administrative Science Quarterly,* 28, 245–73.

Athanassaides, John C. 1974. "On Investigation of Some Communication Patterns of Female Subordinates in Hierarchical Organizations." *Human Relations,* 27, 195–209.

At-Twarjri, Mohammad I., and John R. Montansani. 1987. "The Impact of Context and Choice on the Boundary Spanning Process: An Empirical Extension." *Human Relations,* 40, 783–98.

Bacharach, Samuel B., Peter Bamberger, and Walter Sonnenstuhl. 1996. "The Organizational Transformation Process: The Micropolitics of Dissonance Reduction and the Alignment of Logics of Action." *Administrative Science Quarterly,* 41, 477–506.

Bacharach, Samuel B., and Edward J. Lawler. 1980. *Power and Politics in Organizations.* San Francisco: Jossey-Bass.

Bachrach, Peter, and Morton S. Baratz. 1962. "The Two Faces of Power." *American Political Science Review,* 56, 947–52.

Baldridge, J. Victor, and Robert A. Burnham. 1975. "Organizational Innovation: Individual, Organizational, and Environmental Impacts." *Administrative Science Quarterly,* 20, 165–76.

Bales, Robert F. 1953. "The Equilibrium Problem in Small Groups," in *Working Paper in Theory of Action,* eds. Talcott Parsons, Robert F. Bales, and Edward Shils, 111–61. New York: Free Press.

Bales, Robert F., and Philip E. Slater. 1955. "Role Differentiation in Small Decision Making Groups," in *Family Socialization and Interaction Processes,* eds. Talcott Parsons and Robert Bales, 259–306. New York: Free Press.

Balser, Deborah B. 2007. "The Bully of Bentonville." *Administrative Science Quarterly,* 52, 161–64.

Banerjee, Abhijit. 1992. "A Simple Model of Herd Behavior." *Quarterly Journal of Economics,* 107, 797–817.

Barley, Stephen R. 1985. "Technology as an Occasion for Structuring: Evidence from Observations of CT Scanners and the Social-Order of Radiology Departments." *Administrative Science Quarterly,* 31, 78–108.

———. 2004. "What Sociologists Know (and Mostly Don't Know) About Technical Work," in *Handbook of Work and Organizations,* eds. Stephen Ackroyd, Rose Batt, Paul Thompson, and Pamela Tolbert, 376–403. Oxford: Oxford University Press.

Barley, Stephen R., and Gideon Kunda. 2004. *Gurus, Hired Guns and Warm Bodies: Itinerant Experts in a Knowledge Economy.* Princeton, NJ: Princeton University Press.

Barley, Stephen R., and Pamela S. Tolbert. 1991. "At the Intersection of Organizations and Occupations," in *Research in the Sociology of Organizations,* eds. P. S. Tolbert and S. R. Barley, 1–19. Greenwich, CT: JAI Press.

———. 1997. "Institutionalization and Structuration: Studying the Links Between Action and Institution." *Organization Studies,* 18, 93–118.

Barnard, Chester I. 1968. *The Functions of the Executive: 30th Anniversary Edition.* Cambridge, MA: Harvard University Press.

Barnett, William P., and David G. McKendrick. 2004. "Why Are Some Organizations More Competitive than Others? Evidence from a Changing Global Market." *Administrative Science Quarterly,* 49, 535–71.

Baron, James N. 1984. "Organizational Perspectives on Stratification," in *Annual Review of Sociology,* ed. Ralph Turner, 37–69. Palo Alto, CA: Annual Reviews.

Baron, James N., and William T. Bielby. 1980. "Bringing the Firms Back In: Stratification, Segmentation and the Organization of Work." *American Sociological Review,* 45, 737–65.

Baron, James N., Frank R. Dobbin, and P. Devereux Jennings. 1986. "War and Peace: The Evolution of Modern Personnel Administration in U.S. Industry." *American Journal of Sociology,* 92, 350–83.

Baron, James N., and Jeffrey Pfeffer. 1994. "Social Psychology of Organizations and Inequality." *Social Psychology Quarterly,* 67, 190–209.

Bartley, Timothy. 2007. "Institutional Emergence in an Era of Globalization: The Rise of Transnational Private Regulation of Labor and Environment Conditions." *American Journal of Sociology,* 113, 297–351.

Bass, Bernard M. 1985. *Leadership and Performance Beyond Expectations.* New York: Free Press.

Baum, Joel A. C. 1996. "Organizational Ecology," in *Handbook of Organizational Studies,* eds. S. R. Clegg, C. Hard, and W. R. Nord, 77–114. London: Sage.

Baum, Joel A. C., and Heather Haveman. 1997. "Love Thy Neighbor? Differentiation and Agglomeration in the Manhattan Hotel Industry, 1998–1990." *Administrative Science Quarterly,* 42, 304–38.

Baum, Joel A. C., and Paul Ingram. 1998. "Survival Enhancing Learning in the Manhattan, 1898–1980." *Management Science,* 44, 996–1016.

Baumol, William J., Alan S. Blinder, and Edward N. Wolff. 2003. *Downsizing in America: Reality, Causes and Consequences.* New York: Russell Sage Foundation.

Bavelas, Alex. 1950. "Communication Patterns in Task Oriented Groups." *Journal of the Acoustic Society of America,* 22, 725–30.

Beamish, Thomas D. 2000. "Accumulating Trouble: Complex Organization, a Culture of Silence and a Secret Spill." *Social Problems,* 47, 473–98.

Becker, Gary S. 1964. *Human Capital: A Theoretical and Empirical Analysis.* New York: Columbia University.

Beckman, Christine M., and Pamela R. Haunschild. 2002. "Network Learning: The Effects of Partners' Heterogeneity of Experience on Corporate Acquisitions." *Administrative Science Quarterly,* 47, 92–124.

Beckman, Christine M., Pamela R. Haunschild, and Damon J. Phillips. 2004. "Friends or Strangers? Firm-Specific Uncertainty, Market Uncertainty and Network Partner Selection." *Organization Science,* 15, no. 3, 259–75.

Belliveau, Maura A., Charles A. O'Reilly, and James B. Wade. 1996. "Social Capital at the Top: Effects of Social Similarity and Status on CEO Compensation." *Academy of Management Journal,* 39, no. 12, 1568–93.

Benson, J. Kenneth, Joseph T. Kunce, Charles A. Thompson, and David L. Allen. 1973. *Coordinating Human Services.* Columbia, MO: Regional Rehabilitation Institute, University of Missouri.

Berger, Joseph, Cecilia Ridgeway, and Morris Zelditch. 2002. "Construction of Status and Referential Structures." *Sociological Theory,* 20, 157–79.

Berger, Joseph, Murray Webster, Celia L. Ridgeway, and S. J. Rosenholtz. 1986. "Status Cues, Expectations, and Behaviors," in *Advances in Group Processes,* Vol. 3, ed. E. J. Lawler, 1–22. Greenwich, CT: JAI Press.

Berle, Adolph A., and Gardiner C. Means. 1932. *The Modern Corporation and Private Property.* New York: Macmillan.

Bianco, Anthony. 2006. *The Bully of Bentonville: How the High Cost of Wal-Mart's Everyday Low Prices Is Hurting America.* New York: Random House.

Bidwell, Charles E., and John D. Kasarda. 1985. *The Organization and Its Ecosystem: A Theory of Structuring in Organizations.* Greenwich, CT: JAI Press.

Bierstedt, Robert. 1950. "An Analysis of Social Power." *American Sociological Review,* 15, 730–38.

Bikchandani, Sushil, David Hirshleifer, and Ivo Welch. 1992. "A Theory of Fads, Fashion, Custom and Cultural Change as Informational Cascades." *Journal of Political Economy,* 100, 992–1026.

Birnbaum, Phillip H., and Gilbert Y. Y. Wong. 1985. "Organizational Structure of Multinational Banks from a Culture-Free Perspective." *Administrative Science Quarterly,* 30, 262–77.

Blake, R. R., and J. S. Mouton. 1964. *The Managerial Grid.* Houston, TX: Gulf Publishing.

Blalock, Hubert M. 1967. *Toward a Theory of Minority-Group Relations.* New York: Wiley.

Blau, Francine D., Marianne A. Ferber, and Anne E. Winkler. 2006. *The Economics of Women, Men and Work.* Upper Saddler River, NJ: Prentice Hall.

Blau, Judith R., and Richard D. Alba. 1982. "Empowering Nets of Participation." *Administrative Science Quarterly,* 27, 363–79.

Blau, Judith R., and William McKinley. 1979. "Ideas, Complexity, and Innovation." *Administrative Science Quarterly,* 24, 200–19.

Blau, Peter M. 1955. *The Dynamics of Bureaucracy.* Chicago: University of Chicago Press.

———. 1964. *Exchange and Power in Social Life.* New York: John Wiley.

———. 1968. "The Hierarchy of Authority in Organizations." *American Journal of Sociology,* 73, 453–67.

———. 1970. "Decentralization in Bureaucracies," in *Power in Organizations,* ed. Mayer N. Zald, 221–61. Nashville: Vanderbilt University Press.

———. 1972. "Interdependence and Hierarchy in Organizations." *Social Science Research,* 1, 1–24.

———. 1973. *The Organization of Academic Work.* New York: John Wiley.

———. 1974. *On the Nature of Organizations.* New York: John Wiley.

Blau, Peter M., and Richard A. Schoenherr. 1971. *The Structure of Organizations.* New York: Basic Books.

Blau, Peter M., Wolf Heydebrand, and Robert E. Stauffer. 1966. "The Structure of Small Bureaucracies." *American Sociological Review,* 31, 179–91.

Blau, Peter M., and W. Richard Scott. 1962. *Formal Organizations.* San Francisco: Chandler.

Blum, Terry C., David Fields, and Jodi Goodman. 1994. "Organizational-Level Determinants of Women in Management." *Academy of Management Journal,* 37, 241–68.

Boeker, Warren. 1992. "Power and Managerial Dismissal: Scapegoating at the Top." *Administrative Science Quarterly,* 37, 400–21.

———. 1997. "Executive Migration and Strategic Change: The Effect of Top Manager Movement on Product Market Entry." *Administrative Science Quarterly,* 42, 213–36.

Boeker, Warren, and Richard Karichalil. 2002. "Entrepreneurial Transitions: Factors Influencing Founder Departure." *Academy of Management Journal,* 45, 818–26.

Boje, David M., and David A. Whetten. 1981. "Effects of Organizational Strategies and Contextual Constraints on Centrality and Attributions of Influence in Interorganizational Networks." *Administrative Science Quarterly,* 26, 378–95.

Boraas, Stephanie, and William M. Rodgers. 2003. "How Does Gender Play a Role in the Earnings Gap? An Update." *Monthly Labor Review,* 126, no. 3, 9–15.

Borman, W. C., and D. H. Brush. 1993. "More Progress Toward a Taxonomy of Managerial Performance Requirements." *Human Performance,* 6, 1–21.

Boulding, Kenneth E. 1964. "A Pure Theory of Conflict Applied to Organizations," in *Power and Conflict in Organizations,* eds. Robert L. Kahn and Elise Boulding, 75–78. New York: Basic Books.

Brass, Daniel J., and Marlene E. Burkhardt. 1993. "Potential Power and Power Use: An Investigation of Structure and Behavior." *Academy of Management Journal,* 36, 441–70.

Brewer, John. 1971. "Flow of Communication, Expert Qualifications, and Organizational Authority Structure." *American Sociological Review,* 36, 475–84.

Broschak, Joseph P. 2004. "Managers' Mobility and Market Interface: The Effects of Managers' Career Mobility on the Dissolution of Market Ties." *Administrative Science Quarterly,* 49, 608–40.

Brown, M. Craig. 1982. "Administrative Succession and Organizational Performance: The Succession Effect." *Administrative Science Quarterly,* 27, 1–16.

Brown, Richard Harvey. 1978. "Bureaucracy as Praxis: Toward a Political Phenomenology of Formal Organizations." *Administrative Science Quarterly,* 23, 365–82.

Browning, Larry D., Janice M. Beyer, and Judy C. Shetler. 1995. "Building Cooperation in a Competitive Industry: SEMATECH and the Semiconductor Industry." *Academy of Management Journal,* 38, 113–51.

Brunsson, Nils. 1989. *The Organization of Hypocrisy: Talk, Decisions, and Actions in Organizations.* New York: John Wiley.

Bucher, Rue. 1970. "Social Process and Power in a Medical School," in *Power in Organizations,* ed. Mayer N. Zald, 3–48. Nashville, TN: Vanderbilt University Press.

Budros, Art. 1997. "The New Capitalism and Organizational Rationality: The Adoption of Downsizing Programs, 1979–1994." *Social Forces,* 76, no. 1, 229–50.

———. 2002. "The Mean and Lean Firm and Downsizing: Causes of Voluntary and Involuntary Downsizing Strategies." *Sociological Forum,* 17, 307–42.

Bugra, Ayse, and Behlül Üsdiken. 1997. "Introduction: State, Market and Organizational Form," in *State, Market and Organizational Form,* eds. Ayse Bugùra and Behlül Üsdiken, 1–14. Berlin: Walter de Gruyter.

Burke, John P. 1986. *Bureaucratic Responsibility.* Baltimore: Johns Hopkins University Press.

Burns, James M. 1978. *Leadership.* New York: Harper and Row.

Burns, Tom, and G. M. Stalker. 1961. *The Management of Innovation.* London: Tavistock Publications.

Burrell, Gibson, and Gareth Morgan. 1979. *Sociological Paradigms and Organizational Analysis.* London: Heinemann Press.

Burt, Ronald S. 1992. *Structural Holes: The Social Structure of Competition.* Cambridge, MA: Harvard University Press.

Burt, Ronald S., Kenneth P. Christman, and Harold C. Kilburn Jr. 1980. "Testing a Structural Theory of Corporate Cooptation: Interorganizational Directorate Ties as a Strategy for Avoiding Market Constraints on Projects." *American Sociological Review,* 45, 821–41.

Burton, M. Diane, and Christine M. Beckman. 2007. "Leaving a Legacy: Position Imprints and Successor Turnover in Young Firms." *American Sociological Review,* 72, 239–66.

Cameron, Kim, and David A. Whetten. 1981. "Perceptions of Organizational Effectiveness over Organizational Life Cycles." *Administrative Science Quarterly,* 26, 524–44.

Campbell, John P. 1977. "On the Nature of Organizational Effectiveness," in *New Perspectives on Organizational Effectiveness,* eds. Paul S. Goodman and Johannes M. Pennings, 13–55. San Francisco: Jossey-Bass.

Caplow, Theodore. 1964. *Principles of Organization.* New York: Harcourt Brace Jovanovich.

Caragonne, P. 1978. "Service Integration: Where Do We Stand?" Paper prepared at the 39th National Conference on Public Administration, April, Phoenix, Arizona.

Carley, Kathleen. 1992. "Organizational Learning and Personnel Turnover." *Organization Science,* 3, 20–46.

Carli, Linda, and Alice H. Eagly. 1999. "Gender Effects on Social Influence and Emergent Leadership," in *Handbook of Gender and Work,* ed. G. N. Powell, 203–22. Thousand Oaks, CA: Sage.

Carroll, Glenn R. 1984b. "Dynamics of Publisher Succession in Newspaper Organizations." *Administrative Science Quarterly,* 29, 93–113.

———. 1985. "Concentration and Specialization: Dynamics of Niche Width in Populations of Organizations." *American Journal of Sociology,* 90, 1262–83.

Carroll, Glenn R., and Jacques Delacroix. 1982. "Organizational Mortality in the Newspaper Industries of Argentina and Ireland: An Ecological Approach." *Administrative Science Quarterly,* 27, 169–98.

Carroll, Glenn R., and Michael T. Hannan. 2000. *The Demography of Corporations and Industries.* Princeton, NJ: Princeton University Press.

Carroll, Glenn R., Peter Preisendoerfer, Anand Swaminathan, and Gabriele Wiedenmayer. 1993. "Brewery and Branerei: The Organizational Ecology of Brewing." *Organizational Studies,* 14, 155–88.

Carroll, Glenn R., and Anand Swaminathan. 2000. "Why the Micro-Brewery Movement? Organizational Dynamics of Resource Partitioning in the U.S. Brewing Industry." *American Journal of Sociology,* 106, 715–62.

Carstensen, Fred V., and Richard Hume Werking. 1983. "The Process of Bureaucratization in the U.S. State Department and the Vesting of Economic Interests: Toward Clearer Thinking and Better History." *Administrative Science Quarterly,* 28, 56–60.

Casciaro, Tiziana, and Mikotaj J. Piskorski. 2005. "Power Imbalance, Mutual Dependence and Constraint Absorption: A Closer Look at Resource Dependence Theory." *Administrative Science Quarterly,* 50, 157–99.

Champagne, Anthony, Marian Neef, and Stuart Nagel. 1981. "Laws, Organizations, and the Judiciary," in *Handbook of Organizational Design,* Vol. 1, eds. Paul C. Nystrom and William H. Starbuck, 187–209. New York: Oxford University Press.

Chandler, A. D., Jr. 1962. *Strategy and Structure.* Cambridge, MA: MIT Press.

Chen, Ming-Jer, and Donald Hambrick. 1995. "Speed, Stealth, and Selective Attack: How Small Firms Differ from Large Firms in Competitive Behavior." *Academy of Management Journal,* 38, 453–82.

Child, John. 1972a. "Organizational Structure, Environment, and Performance: The Role of Strategic Choice." *Sociology*, 6, 1–22.

———. 1972b. "Organizational Structures and Strategies of Control: A Replication of the Aston Study." *Administrative Science Quarterly*, 71, 163–77.

———. 1973. "Strategies of Control and Organizational Behavior." *Administrative Science Quarterly*, 18, 1–17.

———. 2005. *Organization: Contemporary Principles and Practice*. Malden, MA: Blackwell Publishing.

Child, John, and Alfred Kieser. 1981. "Development of Organization over Time," in *Handbook of Organizational Design*, Vol. 1, eds. Paul C. Nystrom and William H. Starbuck, 169–98. New York: Oxford University Press.

Child, John, and Roger Mansfield. 1972. "Technology, Size and Organizational Structure." *Sociology*, 6, 369–93.

Christenson, James A., James G. Hougland Jr., Thomas W. Ilvento, and Jon M. Shepard. 1988. "The 'Organization Man' and the Community: The Impact of Organizational Norms and Personal Values on Community Participation and Transfers." *Social Forces*, 66, 808–26.

Clark, Burton. 1972. "The Organizational Saga in Higher Education." *Administrative Science Quarterly*, 17, 178–84.

Clarke, Lee B. 1989. *Acceptable Risk? Making Decisions in a Toxic Environment*. Berkeley: University of California Press.

Clawson, Dan, and Alan Neustadt. 1989. "Interlocks, PACs and Corporate Conservatism." *American Journal of Sociology*, 94, 749–73.

Clegg, Stewart. 1981. "Organization and Control." *Administrative Science Quarterly*, 26, 545–62.

Clegg, Stewart, and David Dunkerley. 1980. *Organization, Class, and Control*. London: Routledge and Kegan Paul.

Clinard, Marshall B., and Peter Yeager. 1980. *Corporate Crime*. New York: Free Press.

Coase, R. H. 1937. "The Nature of the Firm." *Economica*, 4, 386–405.

Cohen, Lisa E., Jospeh P. Broschak, and Heather A. Haveman. 1998. "And Then There Were More? The Effects of Organization Composition on Hiring and Promotion." *American Sociological Review*, 63, 711–27.

Cohen, Michael D., James G. March, and Johan P. Olsen. 1972. "A Garbage Can Model of Organizational Choice." *Administrative Science Quarterly*, 17, 1–25.

Cohen, Wesley M., and Daniel A. Levinthal. 1990. "Absorptive Capacity: A New Perspective on Learning and Innovation." *Administrative Science Quarterly*, 35, 128–52.

Coleman, James S. 1974. *Power and the Structure of Society*. New York: W. W. Norton.

Collins, Randall. 1994. *Four Sociological Traditions*. London: Oxford University Press.

Collins, Randall, and Michael Makowsky. 2005. *The Discovery of Society*. Boston: McGraw-Hill.

Conaty, Joseph, Hoda Mahmoudi, and George A. Miller. 1983. "Social Structure and Bureaucracy: A Comparison of Organizations in the United States and Prerevolutionary Iran." *Organization Studies*, 4, 105–28.

Connolly, Terry, Edward J. Conlon, and Stuart J. Deutsch. 1980. "Organizational Effectiveness: A Multiple-Constituency Approach." *Academy of Management Review*, 5, 211–17.

Cook, Karen S. 1977. "Exchange and Power in Networks of Interorganizational Relations." *Sociological Quarterly,* 18, 62–82.

Cooper, David J., Bob Hinings, Royston Greenwood, and J. L. Brown. 1996. "Sedimentation and Transformation in Organizational Change: The Case of Canadian Law Firms." *Organization Studies,* 17, 623–47.

Coser, Lewis. 1956. *The Functions of Social Conflict.* New York: Free Press.

———. 1967. *Continuities in the Study of Social Conflict.* New York: Free Press.

Craig, John G., and Edward Gross. 1970. "The Forum Theory of Organizational Democracy: Structural Guarantee as Time Related Variables." *American Sociological Review,* 35, 19–33.

Crittenden, Ann. 1978. "Philanthropy, the Business of the Not-So-Idle Rich." *New York Times,* July 23, sec. F.

Crozier, Michael. 1964. *The Bureaucratic Phenomenon.* Chicago: University of Chicago Press.

Cummings, Larry L. 1977. "The Emergence of the Instrumental Organization," in *New Perspectives on Organizational Effectiveness,* eds. Paul S. Goodman and Johannes M. Pennings, 56–62. San Francisco: Jossey-Bass.

Cyert, Richard M., and James G. March. 1963. *A Behavioral Theory of the Firm.* Upper Saddle River, NJ: Prentice Hall.

Dahl, Robert. 1957. "The Concept of Power." *Behavioral Science,* 2, 201–15.

Dalin, M. Tina. 1997. "Isomorphism in Context: The Power and Prescription of Institutional Norms." *Academy of Management Journal,* 40, 46–81.

Dalton, Melville. 1959. *Men Who Manage.* New York: John Wiley.

Damanpour, Fariborz. 1991. "Organizational Innovation: A Meta-Analysis of Effects of Determinants and Moderators." *Academy of Management Journal,* 34, 555–90.

Damanpour, Fariborz, and William M. Evan. 1984. "Organizational Innovation and Performance: The Problems of 'Organizational Lag.' " *Administrative Science Quarterly,* 29, 392–409.

Darr, Eric, and Terri Kurtzberg. 2000. "An Investigation of Partner Similarity Dimensions on Knowledge Transfer." *Organizational Behavior and Human Decision Processes,* 82, 28–44.

D'Aunno, Thomas D., Robert I. Sutton, and Richard H. Price. 1991. "Isomorphism and External Support in Conflicting Institutional Environments: A Study of Drug Abuse Treatment Units." *Academy of Management Journal,* 34, 636–61.

David, Robert J., and Shin-Kap Han. 2004. "A Systematic Assessment of the Empirical Support for Transaction Cost Economics." *Strategic Management Journal,* 25, 39–58.

David, Robert J., and David Strang. 2006. "When Fashion Is Fleeting: Transitory Collective Beliefs and the Dynamics of TQM Consulting." *Academy of Management Journal,* 49, no. 2, 215–33.

Davis, Gerald F. 1991. "Agents Without Principles? The Spread of the Poison Pill Through the Intercorporate Network." *Administrative Science Quarterly,* 36, 583–613.

———. 1996. "The Significance of Board Interlocks for Corporate Governance." *Corporate Governance,* 4, 154–59.

———. 2005. "New Directions in Corporate Governance." *Annual Review of Sociology,* 31, no. 1, 143–62.

Davis, Gerald F., Kristina A. Diekmann, and Catherine H. Tinsley. 1994. "The Decline and Fall of the Conglomerate Firm in the 1980s: The Deinstitutionalization of an Organizational Form." *American Sociological Review,* 59, 547–70.

Davis, Gerald F., and Mark Mizruchi. 1999. "The Money Center Cannot Hold: Commercial Banks in the U.S. System of Corporate Governance." *Administrative Science Quarterly,* 44, 215–39.

Davis, Gerald F., and Mayer N. Zald. 2005. "Social Change, Social Theory and the Convergence of Movements and Organizations," in *Social Movements and Organization Theory,* eds. G. F. Davis, D. McAdam, W. R. Scott, and M. N. Zald, 335–50. New York: Cambridge University Press.

Davis, Kingsley, and Wilbert Moore. 1945. "Some Principles of Stratification." *American Sociological Review,* 10, 242–49.

Davis, Stanley M., and Paul R. Lawrence. 1977. *Matrix.* Reading, MA: Addison-Wesley.

Davis-Blake, Allison, and Brian Uzzi. 1993. "Determinants of Employment Externalization: A Study of Temporary Workers and Independent Contractors." *Administrative Science Quarterly,* 38, 195–223.

Day, D. V., and R. G. Lord. 1988. "Executive Leadership and Organizational Performance: Suggestions for a New Theory and Methodology." *Journal of Management,* 14, 453–64.

Delacroix, Jacques, and Glenn R. Carroll. 1983. "Organizational Foundings: An Ecological Study of the Newspaper Industries of Argentina and Ireland." *Administrative Science Quarterly,* 28, 274–91.

Dewar, Robert D., David A. Whetten, and David Boje. 1980. "An Examination of the Reliability and Validity of the Aiken and Hage Scales of Utilization, Formalization, and Task Routineness." *Administrative Science Quarterly,* 25, 120–28.

Digman, J. M. 1990. "Personality Structure: Emergence of the Five-Factor Model." *Annual Review of Psychology,* 41, 417–40.

DiMaggio, Paul J. 1988. "Interest and Agency in Institutional Theory," in *Institutional Patterns and Organizations: Culture and Environment,* ed. Lynne G. Zucker, 3–22. Cambridge, MA: Ballinger.

DiMaggio, Paul J., and Walter W. Powell. 1983. "The Iron Cage Revisited: Institutional Isomorphism and Collective Rationality in Organizational Fields." *American Sociological Review,* 48, 147–60.

DiTomaso, Nancy, Corinne Post, and Rochelle Parks-Yancy. 2007. "Workforce Diversity and Inequality: Power, Status and Numbers." *Annual Review of Sociology,* 33, 473–501.

Dobbin, Frank, and Terry Boychuk. 1999. "National Employment Systems and Job Autonomy: Why Job Autonomy Is High in the Nordic Countries and Low in the United States, Canada, and Australia." *Organization Studies,* 20, 257–91.

Dobbin, Frank, and Erin L. Kelly. 2007. "How to Stop Harassment: Professional Construction of Legal Compliance in Organizations." *American Journal of Sociology,* 112, no. 4, 1203–43.

Dobbin, Frank, John R. Sutton, John M. Meyer, and W. Richard Scott. 1993. "Equal Opportunity Law and the Construction of Internal Labor Markets." *American Journal of Sociology,* 99, 396–427.

Domhoff, G. William. 1971. *Higher Circles: The Governing Class in America.* New York: Viking.

———. 1983. *Who Rules America Now? A View for the 80s.* Englewood Cliffs, NJ: Prentice Hall.

Donaldson, Lex. 1995. *American Anti-Management Theories of Organization: A Critique of Paradigm Proliferation.* Cambridge: Cambridge University Press.

————. 1996. "The Normal Science of Structural Contingence Theory," in *Handbook of Organization Studies,* eds. Stewart R. Clegg, Cynthia Hardy, and Walter R. Nord, 57–76. Thousand Oaks, CA: Sage.

————. 2001. *The Contingency Theory of Organizations.* Thousand Oaks, CA: Sage.

Donaldson, Lex, John Child, and Howard Aldrich. 1975. "The Aston Findings on Centralization: Further Discussion." *Administrative Science Quarterly,* 20, 453–60.

Donaldson, Lex, and Malcolm Warner. 1974. "Bureaucratic and Electoral Control in Occupational Interest Associations." *Sociology,* 8, 47–59.

Donaldson, Thomas, and Lee E. Preston. 1995. "The Stakeholder Theory of the Corporation: Concepts, Evidence and Implications." *Academy of Management Review,* 20, 65–91.

Dornbusch, Sanford M., and W. Richard Scott. 1975. *Evaluation and the Exercise of Authority.* New York: Basic Books.

Dowell, Glenn. 2006. "Product Line Strategies of New Entrants in an Established Industry: Evidence from the U.S. Bicycle Industry." *Strategic Management Journal,* 27, no. 10, 959–79.

Downs, Anthony. 1967. *Inside Bureaucracy.* Boston: Little, Brown.

Dun and Bradstreet. 1995. *Census of American Business.* New York: Dun & Bradstreet.

Duncan, Robert B. 1972. "Characteristics of Organizational Environments and Perceived Environmental Uncertainty." *Administrative Science Quarterly,* 17, 313–27.

Durkheim, Emile. 1964. *Rules of the Sociological Method.* New York: Free Press of Glencoe.

Dutton, Jane E., Janet M. Dukerich, and Cecilia V. Harquail. 1994. "Organizational Images and Member Identification." *Administrative Science Quarterly,* 39, 239–63.

Eagly, Alice H., and Steven J. Karau. 1991. "Gender and the Emergence of Leaders: A Meta-Analysis." *Journal of Personality and Social Psychology,* 60, 685–710.

Easterlin, Richard A. 1987. *Birth and Fortune: The Impact of Numbers on Personal Welfare.* Chicago: University of Chicago Press.

Edelman, Lauren B. 1990. "Legal Environments and Organizational Governance: The Expansion of Due Process of the American Workplace." *American Journal of Sociology,* 95, 1401–40.

————. 1992. "Legal Ambiguity and Symbolic Structures: Organizational Mediation of Civil Rights Law." *American Journal of Sociology,* 97, 1531–76.

Edelman, Lauren B., Sally Riggs Fuller, and Iona Mara-Drita. 2001. "Diversity Rhetoric and the Managerialization of Law." *American Journal of Sociology,* 106, no. 6, 1589–1641.

Edelman, Lauren B., and Mark C. Suchman. 1997. "Legal Environments of Organizations." *Annual Review of Sociology,* 23, 479–515.

Edmondson, Amy C. 1999. "Psychological Safety and Learning Behavior in Work Teams." *Administrative Science Quarterly,* 44, 350–83.

Egelhoff, William G. 1982. "Strategy and Structure in Multinational Corporations: An Information Processing Approach." *Administrative Science Quarterly,* 27, 435–58.

Eisenhardt, Kathleen M. 2002. "Has Strategy Changed?" *MIT Sloan Management Review,* 43, 88–90.

Eitzen, D. Stanley, and Norman R. Yetman. 1972. "Managerial Change, Longevity and Organizational Effectiveness." *Administrative Science Quarterly,* 17, 110–18.

Emerson, Richard M. 1962. "Power-Dependence Relations." *American Sociological Review,* 27, 31–40.

Emery, Fredrick E., and Eric L. Trist. 1965. "The Causal Texture of Organizational Environments." *Human Relations,* 18, 21–32.

———. 1973. *Towards a Social Ecology: An Appreciation of the Future in the Present.* New York: Plenum Press.

England, Paula. 1992. *Comparable Worth: Theories and Evidence.* New York: Aldine de Gruyter.

———. 1994. "Neoclassical Economists' Theories of Discrimination," in *Equal Employment Opportunity,* ed. P. Bursein, 59–69. New York: Aldine De Gruyter.

Enz, Cathy A. 1988. "The Role of Value Congruence in Intraorganizational Power." *Administrative Science Quarterly,* 33, 284–304.

Etzioni, Amitai. 1961. *A Comparative Analysis of Complex Organizations.* New York: Free Press.

———. 1964. *Modern Organizations.* Upper Saddle River, NJ: Prentice Hall.

———. 1965. "Dual Leadership in Complex Organizations." *American Sociological Review,* 30, 688–98.

———. 1968. *The Active Society: A Theory of Societal and Political Processes.* New York: Free Press.

———. 1975. *A Comparative Analysis of Complex Organizations,* rev. ed. New York: Free Press.

———. 1991. *A Responsive Society: Collected Essays on Guiding Deliberate Social Change.* San Francisco: Jossey-Bass.

———. 1993. *The Spirit of Community Rights, Responsibilities and the Communitarian.* New York: Crown Publishers.

Evan, William. 1966. "The Organization Set: Toward a Theory of Interorganizational Relations," in *Approaches to Organizational Design,* ed. James Thompson, 173–88. Pittsburgh, PA: University of Pittsburgh Press.

Faulkner, Robert R. 1985. *Hollywood Studio Musicians: Their Work and Careers in the Recording Industry.* Lanham, MD: University Press of America.

Fayol, Henri. 1930. *Industrial and General Administration,* trans. J. A. Coubrough. London: Sir I. Pitman & Sons.

Feldman, Martha S., and James G. March. 1981. "Information in Organizations as Signal and Symbol." *Administrative Science Quarterly,* 26, 171–86.

Fennell, Mary C. 1980. "The Effects of Environmental Characteristics on the Structure of Hospital Clusters." *Administrative Science Quarterly,* 29, 489–510.

Fernandez, Roberto M. 2001. "Skill-Biased Technological Change and Wage Inequality: Evidence from a Plant Retooling." *American Journal of Sociology,* 107, 273–320.

Fernandez, Roberto, and Nancy Weinberg. 1997. "Sifting and Sorting: Personal Contacts and Hiring in a Retail Bank." *American Sociological Review,* 62, 883–902.

Fiedler, Fred E. 1967. *A Theory of Leadership Effectiveness.* New York: McGraw-Hill.

———. 1972. "The Effects of Leadership Training and Experience: A Contingency Model Explanation." *Administrative Science Quarterly,* 17, 453–70.

Fiedler, Fred E., and M. M. Chemers. 1982. *Improving Leader Effectiveness: The Leader Match Concept,* 2nd ed. New York: Wiley.

Fiedler, Fred E., and J. E. Garcia. 1987. *New Approaches to Leadership: Cognitive Resources and Organizational Performance.* New York: Wiley.

Filardo, E. K. 1996. "Gender Patterns in African American and White Adolescents' Social Interactions in Same-Race, Mixed-Gender Groups." *Journal of Personality and Social Psychology*, 71, 71–82.

Filley, Alan C., and Robert J. House. 1969. *Managerial Processes and Organizational Behavior*. Glenview, IL: Scott, Foresman.

Finkelstein, Sydney. 1992. "Power in Top Management Teams: Dimension, Measurement and Validation." *Academy of Management Journal*, 35, 505–38.

Fligstein, Neil. 1985. "The Spread of the Multidivisional Form Among Large Firms." *American Sociological Review*, 50, 377–91.

———. 1990. *The Transformation of Corporate Control*. Cambridge, MA: Harvard University Press.

Fligstein, Neil, and Peter Brantley. 1992. "Bank Control, Owner Control, or Organizational Dynamics: Who Controls the Large Modern Corporation." *American Journal of Sociology*, 98, 280–307.

Fligstein, Neil, and Robert Freeland. 1995. "Theoretical and Comparative Perspectives on Corporate Organization," in *Annual Review of Sociology*, eds. John Hagan and Karen S. Cook, 21–43. Palo Alto, CA: Annual Reviews.

Follet, Mary P. 1918. *The New State, Group Organization the Solution of Popular Government*. New York: Longmans, Green and Co.

Freeland, Robert F. 1997. "The Myth of the M-Form? Governance, Consent, and Organizational Change." *American Journal of Sociology*, 102, 483–526.

Freeman, John H., Glenn Carroll, and Michael Hannan. 1983. "The Liability of Newness: Age-Dependence in Organizational Death Rates." *American Sociological Review*, 48, 692–710.

Freidson, Eliot. 1970. *Professional Dominance*. Chicago: Aldine de Gruyter.

———. 1994. *Professionalism Reborn: Theory, Prophecy and Policy*. Chicago: University of Chicago Press.

———. 2001. *Professionalism: The Third Logic*. Chicago: University of Chicago Press.

———. 2006. *Professional Dominance: The Social Structure of Medical Care*. New Brunswick, NJ: Aldine Transaction.

French, John R. P., and Bertram Raven. 1968. "The Bases of Social Power," in *Group Dynamics*, 3rd ed., eds. Dorwin Cartwright and Alvin Zander, 259–69. New York: Harper and Row.

Fu, P. P., and Gary Yukl. 2000. "Perceived Effectiveness of Influence Tactics in the United States and China." *Leadership Quarterly*, 11, 251–66.

Galaskiewicz, Joseph. 1979. "The Structure of Community Organizational Networks." *Social Forces*, 57, 1346–64.

———. 1997. "An Urban Grants Economy Revisited: Corporate Charitable Contributions in the Twin Cities, 1979–81, 1987–89." *Administrative Science Quarterly*, 42, 445–71.

Galaskiewicz, Joseph, Wolfgang Bielefeld, and Myron Dowell. 2006. "Networks and Organizational Growth: A Study of Community Based Nonprofits." *Administrative Science Quarterly*, 51, 337–80.

Galaskiewicz, Joseph, and Ronald S. Burt. 1991. "Interorganizational Contagion in Corporate Philanthropy." *Administrative Science Quarterly*, 36, 88–105.

Galaskiewicz, Joseph, and Karl R. Krohn. 1984. "Positions, Roles, and Dependencies in a Community Interorganizational System." *Sociological Quarterly*, 25, 527–50.

Galaskiewicz, Joseph, and Deborah Shatin. 1981. "Leadership and Networking Among Neighborhood Human Service Organizations." *Administrative Science Quarterly,* 26, 434–48.

Galaskiewicz, Joseph, Stanley Wasserman, Barbara Rauschenbach, Wolfgang Bielefeld, and Patti Mullaney. 1985. "The Influence of Corporate Power, Social Status, and Market Position on Corporate Interlocks in a Regional Network." *Social Forces,* 64, 403–31.

Galbraith, Jay R. 1971. "Matrix Organization Designs." *Business Horizons,* 14, no. 1, 29–40.

Gamson, William, and Norman Scotch. 1964. "Scapegoating in Baseball." *American Journal of Sociology,* 70, 69–72.

Geeraerts, Guy. 1984. "The Effects of Ownership on the Organization Structure in Small Firms." *Administrative Science Quarterly,* 29, 232–37.

Georgiou, Petro. 1973. "The Goal Paradigm and Notes Toward a Counter Paradigm." *Administrative Science Quarterly,* 18, 291–310.

Gersick, Connie J. G. 1991. "Revolutionary Change Theories: A Multilevel Explanation of the Punctuated Equilibrium Paradigm." *Academy of Management Review,* 16, 10–36.

Giddens, Anthony. 1987. *Social Theory and Modern Sociology.* Stanford, CA: Stanford University Press.

Giordano, Peggy C. 1974. "The Juvenile Justice System: The Client Perspective." PhD diss., University of Minnesota.

———. 1976. "The Sense of Injustice: An Analysis of Juveniles' Reaction to the Justice System." *Criminology,* 14, 93–112.

———. 1977. "The Client's Perspective in Agency Evaluation." *Social Work,* 22, 34–39.

Glass, Jennifer. 2004. "Blessing or Curse? Work-Family Policies and Mothers' Wage Growth over Time." *Work and Occupations,* 31, 367–94.

Glisson, Charles A. 1978. "Dependence of Technological Routinizations on Structural Variables in Human Service Organizations." *Administrative Science Quarterly,* 23, 383–95.

Glynn, MaryAnn, Theresa K. Lant, and Frances J. Milliken. 1994. "Mapping Learning Processes in Organizations: A Multi-Level Framework Linking Learning and Organizing." *Advances in Managerial Cognition and Organizational Information Processing,* 5, 43–83.

Goes, James B., and Seung Ho Park. 1997. "Interorganizational Linkages and Innovation: The Case of Hospital Services." *Academy of Management Journal,* 40, 673–96.

Gooderham, Paul N., Odd Nordhaug, and Kristen Ringdal. 1999. "Institutional and Rational Determinants of Organizational Practices: Human Resource Management in European Firms." *Administrative Science Quarterly,* 44, 507–31.

Goodstein, Jerry D. 1994. "Institutional Pressures and Strategic Responsiveness: Employer Involvement in Work-Family Issues." *Academy of Management Journal,* 37, 350–82.

Gould, Roger V., and Roberto M. Fernandez. 1994. "A Dilemma of State Power: Brokerage and Influence in the National Health Policy Domain." *American Journal of Sociology,* 99, 1455–91.

Gouldner, Alvin, ed. 1950. *Studies in Leadership.* New York: Harper and Row.

———. 1954. *Patterns of Industrial Bureaucracy.* New York: Free Press.

Graebner, Melissa A., and Kathleen M. Eisenhardt. 2004. "The Seller's Side of the Story: Acquisition as Courtship and Governance as Syndicate in Entrepreneurial Firms." *Administrative Science Quarterly,* 49, no. 3, 366–403.

Granovetter, Mark. 1985. "Economic Action and Social Structure: The Problem of Embeddedness." *American Journal of Sociology,* 91, 481–510.

Grant, Donald Sherman, II, Andrew W. Jones, and Albert J. Bergesen. 2002. "Organizational Size and Pollution: The Case of the U.S. Chemical Industry." *American Sociological Review,* 67, 389–407.

Greenwood, Royston, and C. R. Hinings. 1976. "Centralization Revisited." *Administrative Science Quarterly,* 21, 151–55.

Gresov, Christopher. 1989. "Exploring Fit and Misfit with Multiple Contingencies." *Administrative Science Quarterly,* 34, 431–53.

Gross, Edward. 1968. "Universities as Organizations: A Research Approach." *American Sociological Review,* 33, 518–43.

Grusky, Oscar. 1963. "Managerial Succession and Organizational Effectiveness." *American Journal of Sociology,* 69, 21–31.

———. 1964. "Reply." *American Journal of Sociology,* 70, 72–76.

Guest, Robert. 1962. "Managerial Succession in Complex Organizations." *American Journal of Sociology,* 68, 47–54.

Guetzkow, Harold. 1965. "Communications in Organizations," in *Handbook of Organizations,* ed. James G. March, 534–73. Chicago: Rand McNally.

Guillen, Mauro F., and Sandra L. Suarez. 2005. "Explaining the Global Digital Divide: Economic, Political and Sociological Drivers of Dross-National Internet Use." *Social Forces,* 84, no. 2, 681–708.

Gulati, Ranjay. 1995a. "Does Familiarity Breed Trust? The Implications of Repeated Ties for Contractual Choices in Alliances." *Academy of Management Journal,* 38, 85–112.

———. 1995b. "Social Structure and Alliance Formation Patterns: A Longitudinal Analysis." *Administrative Science Quarterly,* 40, 619–52.

Gulati, Ranjay, and Martin Gargiulo. 1999. "Where Do Interorganizational Networks Come From?" *American Journal of Sociology,* 104, 1439–93.

Guler, Isen, Mauro F. Guillen, and J. M. MacPherson. 2002. "Global Competition, Institutions and the Diffusion of Organizational Practices: The International Spread of ISO 9000 Quality Certificates." *Administrative Science Quarterly,* 47, no. 2, 207–32.

Gulick, Luther, and L. Urwick, eds. 1937. *Papers on the Science of Administration.* New York: Institute of Public Administration, Columbia University.

Gupta, Anil, and Vijay Govindarajan. 1991. "Knowledge Flows and the Structure of Control Within Multinational Corporations." *Academy of Management Review,* 16, 768–92.

Gupta, Parveen P., Mark W. Dirsmith, and Timothy J. Fogarty. 1994. "Coordination and Control in a Government Agency: Contingency and Institutional Theory Perspectives on GAO Audits." *Administrative Science Quarterly,* 39, 264–84.

Hackman, J. Richard, and Greg R. Oldham. 1976. "Motivation Through the Design of Work: Test of a Theory." *Organizational Behavior and Human Performance,* 16, 250–79.

Hage, Jerald. 1965. "An Axiomatic Theory of Organizations." *Administrative Science Quarterly,* 10, 289–320.

————. 1974. *Communications and Organizational Control*. New York: Wiley.

————. 1980. *Theories of Organizations*. New York: Wiley.

————. 1999. "Organizational Innovation and Organizational Change," in *Annual Review of Sociology*, Vol. 25, 597–622. Palo Alto, CA: Annual Reviews.

Hage, Jerald, and Michael Aiken. 1967a. "Relationship of Centralization to Other Structural Properties." *Administrative Science Quarterly*, 12, 72–91.

————. 1967b. "Program Change and Organizational Properties." *American Journal of Sociology*, 72, 503–19.

————. 1969. "Routine Technology, Social Structure, and Organizational Goals." *Administrative Science Quarterly*, 14, 366–77.

————. 1970. *Social Change in Complex Organizations*. New York: Random House.

Hage, Jerald, Michael Aiken, and Cora Bagley Marrett. 1971. "Organizational Structure and Communications." *American Sociological Review*, 36, 860–71.

Hage, Jerald, and Robert Dewar. 1973. "Elite Values versus Organizational Structure in Predicting Innovation." *Administrative Science Quarterly*, 18, 279–90.

Halberstam, David. 1972. *The Best and the Brightest*. New York: Random House.

Hall, Richard H. 1962. "Intraorganizational Structural Variation: Application of the Bureaucratic Model." *Administrative Science Quarterly*, 7, 295–308.

————. 1963. "The Concept of Bureaucracy." *American Journal of Sociology*, 69, 32–40.

————. 1968. "Professionalization and Bureaucratization." *American Sociological Review*, 33, 92–104.

————. 1981. "Technological Policies and Their Consequences," in *Handbook of Organizational Design*, Vol. 2, eds. Paul C. Nystrom and William H. Starbuck, 320–35. New York: Oxford University Press.

————. 1992. "Taking Things a Bit too Far: Some Problems with Emergent Institutional Theory," in *Issues, Theory, and Research in Industrial/Organizational Psychology*, ed. Kathryn Kelley, 73–87. New York: Elsevier Science Publishers.

————. 1994. *Sociology of Work: Perspectives, Analyses, and Issues*. Thousand Oaks, CA: Pine Forge Press.

Hall, Richard H., Shanhe Jiang, Karyn A. Loscocco, and John K. Allen. 1993. "Ownership Patterns and Centralization: A China and U.S. Comparison." *Sociological Forum*, 8, 595–608.

Hall, Richard H., Norman J. Johnson, and J. Eugene Haas. 1967. "Organizational Size, Complexity, and Formalization." *American Sociological Review*, 32, 903–12.

Hall, Richard H., and Charles R. Tittle. 1966. "Bureaucracy and Its Correlates." *American Journal of Sociology*, 72, 267–72.

Hall, Richard H., and Weiman Xu. 1990. "Run Silent, Run Deep: A Note on the Ever Pervasive Influence of Cultural Differences on Organizations in the Far East." *Organization Studies*, 11, 569–76.

Halliday, Terence C., and Bruce G. Carruthers. 2007. "The Recursivity of Law: Global Norm Making and National Lawmaking in the Globalization of Corporate Insolvency Regimes." *American Journal of Sociology*, 112, no. 4, 1135–1201.

Hambrick, Donald C. 1981. "Environment, Strategy and Power Within Top Management Teams." *Administrative Science Quarterly*, 26, 253–76.

Hamilton, Gary L., and Nicole Woolsey Biggart. 1988. "Market, Culture, and Authority: A Comparative Analysis of Management and Organization in the Far East." *American Journal of Sociology*, 94, S52–S94.

Hamner, W. Clay, and Dennis Organ. 1973. *Organizational Behavior: An Applied Psychological Approach.* Dallas, TX: Business Publications.

Hannan, Michael T., and John H. Freeman. 1977a. "Obstacles to Comparative Studies," in *New Perspective on Organizational Effectiveness,* eds. Paul S. Goodman and Johannes Pennings, 106–31. San Francisco: Jossey-Bass.

―――. 1977b. "The Population Ecology of Organizations." *American Journal of Sociology,* 82, 929–64.

―――. 1984. "Structural Inertia and Organizational Change." *American Sociological Review,* 49, 149–64.

―――. 1989. *Organizational Ecology.* Cambridge, MA: Harvard University Press.

Hansen, Morten T., and Martine R. Haas. 2001. "Competing for Attention in Knowledge Markets: Electronic Document Dissemination in a Management Consulting Company." *Administrative Science Quarterly,* 46, 1–28.

Hardy, Cynthia, and Stewart R. Clegg. 1996. "Some Dare Call It Power," in *Handbook of Organization Studies,* eds. Stewart R. Clegg, Cynthia Hardy, and Walter R. Nord, 622–41. Thousand Oaks, CA: Sage.

Harrison, Jeffrey S., and R. Edward Freeman. 1999. "Stakeholders, Social Responsibility, and Performance: Empirical Evidence and Theoretical Perspectives." *Academy of Management Journal,* 42, 479–85.

Haunschild, Pamela R., and Christine M. Beckman. 1998. "When Do Interlocks Matter? Alternate Sources of Information and Interlock Influence." *Administrative Science Quarterly,* 43, 815–44.

Haunschild, Pamela R., and Anne S. Miner. 1997. "Modes of IOR Imitation: The Effect of Outcome Salience and Uncertainty." *Administrative Science Quarterly,* 42, 477–500.

Haunschild, Pamela R., and Bilian N. Sullivan. 2002. "Learning from Complexity: Effects of Prior Accidents and Incidents on Airlines' Learning." *Administrative Science Quarterly,* 47, 609–44.

Haveman, Heather A. 1992. "Between a Rock and a Hard Place: Organizational Change and Performance under Conditions of Fundamental Environmental Transformation." *Administrative Science Quarterly,* 37, 48–75.

―――. 1993a. "Organizational Size and Change: Diversification in the Savings and Loan Industry after Deregulation." *Administrative Science Quarterly,* 38, 20–50.

―――. 1993b. "Follow the Leader: Mimetic Isomorphism and Entry into New Markets." *Administrative Science Quarterly,* 38, 593–627.

Haveman, Heather A., and Hayagreeva Rao. 1997. "Structuring a Theory of Moral Sentiments: Institutional and Organizational Coevolution in the Early Thrift Industry." *American Journal of Sociology,* 102, 1606–51.

Haveman, Heather A., Hayagreeva Rao, and Srikanth Paruchuri. 2007. "The Winds of Change: The Progressive Movement and the Bureaucratization of Thrift." *American Sociological Review,* 72, 117–42.

Hawley, Amos H. 1968. "Human Ecology," in *International Encyclopedia of the Social Sciences,* ed. D. L. Sills, 328–37. New York: Macmillan.

Healy, Kieran. 2004. "Altruism as an Organizational Problem: The Case of Organ Procurement." *American Sociological Review,* 69, no. 3, 387–405.

Heilbroner, Robert. 1974. "Nobody Talks About Busting General Motors in 500 Companies." *Forbes,* 113, 61.

Heller, Frank A. 1973. "Leadership Decision Making and Contingency Theory." *Industrial Relations,* 12, 183–99.

Helmich, Donald, and Warren B. Brown. 1972. "Succession Type and Organizational Change in the Corporate Enterprise." *Administrative Science Quarterly,* 17, 371–81.

Heydebrand, Wolf V. 1973. *Comparative Organizations: The Results of Empirical Research.* Upper Saddle River, NJ: Prentice Hall.

————. 1990. "The Technocratic Organization of Academic Work," in *Structures of Power and Constraint: Papers in Honor of Peter M. Blau,* eds. Craig Calhoun, Marshall W. Meyer, and W. Richard Scott, 271–320. New York: Cambridge University Press.

Hickson, David J., C. R. Hinings, C. A. Lee, R. E. Schneck, and J. M. Pennings. 1971. "A 'Strategic Contingencies' Theory of Interorganizational Power." *Administrative Science Quarterly,* 16, 216–29.

Hickson, David J., C. R. Hinings, C. J. McMillan, and J. P. Schwitter. 1974. "The Culture Free Context of Organizational Structure: A Tri-National Comparison." *Sociology,* 8, 59–80.

Hickson, David J., Derek S. Pugh, and Diana C. Pheysey. 1969. "Operational Technology and Organizational Structure: An Empirical Reappraisal." *Administrative Science Quarterly,* 14, 378–97.

Hills, Frederick S., and Thomas A. Mahoney. 1978. "University Budgets and Organizational Decision Making." *Administrative Science Quarterly,* 23, 454–65.

Hinings, C. R., and Pamela S. Tolbert. 2008. "Organizational Institutionalism and Sociology: A Reflection," in *Sage Handbook of Organizational Institutionalism,* eds. R. Greenwood, C. Oliver, R. Suddaby, and K. Sahlin, 473–91. New York: Sage.

Hirsch, Paul M., and Michael Lounsbury. 1997. "Putting the Organization Back into Organization Theory: Action, Change and the 'New' Institutionalism." *Journal of Management Inquiry,* 6, no. 1, 79–88.

Hirschman, Albert O. 1972. *Exit, Voice, and Loyalty.* Cambridge, MA: Harvard University Press.

Hochschild, Arlie Russell. 1983. *The Managed Heart: Commercialization of Human Feeling.* Berkeley and Los Angeles: University of California Press.

Hoff, Timothy. 1998. "Same Profession, Different People: Stratification, Structure, and Physicians' Employment Choices." *Sociological Forum,* 13, 133–56.

Hoff, Timothy, and David McCaffrey. 1996. "Resisting, Adapting, and Negotiating: How Physicians Cope with Organizational and Economic Change." *Work and Occupations,* 23, 165–89.

Hogan, Robert, Gordon J. Curphy, and Joyce Hogan. 1994. "What We Know About Leadership." *American Psychologist,* 49, 493–504.

Hollander, Edwin P., and James W. Julian. 1969. "Contemporary Trends in the Analysis of Leadership Processes." *Psychological Bulletin,* 71, 387–97.

Hornug, Severin, Denise M. Rosseau, and Jurgen Glaser. 2008. "Creating Flexible Work Arrangements Through Idiosyncratic Deals." *Journal of Applied Psychology,* 93, 655–64.

Hougland, James G., Jon M. Shepard, and James R. Wood. 1979. "Discrepancies in Perceived Organizational Control: Their Decrease and Importance in Local Churches." *Sociological Quarterly,* 20, 63–76.

Hougland, James G., and James R. Wood. 1980. "Control in Organizations and Commitment of Members." *Social Forces,* 59, 85–105.

House, Robert J. 1971. "A Path-Goal Theory of Leader Effectiveness." *Administrative Science Quarterly,* 16, 321–38.

Huffington, Arianna. 2003. *Pigs at the Trough: How Corporate Greed and Political Corruption Are Undermining America.* New York: Crown.

Hyde, Cheryl. 1992. "The Ideational System of Social Movement Agencies: An Examination of Feminist Health Centers," in *Human Services as Complex Organizations,* ed. Yeheskel Hasenfeld, 113–26. Thousand Oaks, CA: Sage.

Ingram, Paul, and Crist Inman. 1996. "Institutions, Intergroup Competition and the Evolution of Hotel Populations Around Niagara Falls." *Administrative Science Quarterly,* 41, no. 4, 629–58.

Ingram, Paul, and Peter W. Roberts. 2000. "Friendships Among Competitors in the Sydney Hotel Industry." *American Journal of Sociology,* 106, 387–423.

Inkson, J., Derek S. Pugh, and David J. Hickson. 1970. "Organizational Context and Structure: An Abbreviated Replication." *Administrative Science Quarterly,* 15, 318–29.

Jackall, Robert. 1988. *Moral Mazes: The World of Corporate Managers.* New York: Oxford University Press.

Jacoby, Sanford. 2004. *Employing Bureaucracy: Managers, Unions and the Transformation of Work in the 20th Century.* Mahwah, NJ: Lawrence Erlbaum.

James, David R., and Michael Soref. 1981. "Profit Constraints on Managerial Autonomy: Managerial Theory and the Unmaking of the Corporate President." *American Sociological Review,* 46, 1–18.

Jenkins, J. Craig. 1977. "Radical Transformation of Organizational Goals." *Administrative Science Quarterly,* 22, 568–86.

Jensen, Michael C. 2002. "Value Maximization, Stakeholder Theory, and the Corporate Objective Function." *Business Ethics Quarterly,* 12, 235–56.

Jensen, Michael. 2003. "The Role of Network Resources in Market Entry: Commercial Banks' Entry into Investment Banking, 1991–1997." *Administrative Science Quarterly,* 48, 466–97.

John, D. 1977. *Managing the Human Service System: What Have We Learned from Services Integration?* Project SHARE Monograph Series. Rockville, MD: National Institute of Mental Health.

Johnson, George, and Frank Stafford. 1974. "The Earnings and Promotion of Female Faculty." *American Economic Review,* 67, 214–17.

Judge, Timothy A., and Ronald F. Piccolo. 2004. "Transformational and Transactional Leadership: A Meta-Analytic Test of Their Relative Validity." *Journal of Applied Psychology,* 89, 755–68.

Kabanoff, Boris. 1991. "Equity, Equality, Power, and Conflict." *Academy of Management Review,* 16, 416–41.

Kalev, Alexandra, Frank Dobbin, and Erin Kelly. 2006. "Best Practices or Best Guesses? Assessing the Efficacy of Corporate Affirmative Action and Diversity Policies." *American Sociological Review,* 71, no. 4, 589–617.

Kalleberg, Arne. 1983. "Work and Stratification: Structural Perspectives." *Work and Occupations,* 10, 251–59.

Kalleberg, Arne L., David Knoke, Peter V. Marsden, and Joe L. Spaeth. 1996. "Organizational Properties and Practices," in *Organizations in America: Analyzing Their Structures and Human Resource Practices,* eds. Arne L. Kalleberg, David Knoke, Peter V. Marsden, and Joe L. Spaeth, 2–21. Thousand Oaks, CA: Sage.

Kalleberg, Arne L., and Mark E. Van Buren. 1996. "Is Bigger Better? Explaining the Relationship Between Organizational Size and Job Rewards." *American Sociological Review,* 61, 47–76.

Kane, Aimee A., Linda Argote, and John M. Levine. 2005. "Knowledge Transfer Between Groups via Personnel Rotation: Effects of Social Identity and Knowledge Quality." *Organizational Behavior and Human Decision Processes,* 96, 56–71.

Kanter, Rosabeth Moss. 1968. "Commitment and Social Organization: A Study of Commitment Mechanisms in Utopian Communities." *American Sociological Review,* 33, 499–517.

———. 1977. *Men and Women of the Corporation.* New York: Basic Books.

———. 1979. "Power Failure in Management Circuits." *Harvard Business Review,* 57, 65–75.

Kaplan, Abraham. 1964. "Power in Perspective," in *Power and Conflict in Organizations,* eds. Robert L. Kahn and Elise Boulding, 11–32. New York: Basic Books.

Karasek, Robert A. 1979. "Job Demands, Job Decision Latitude and Mental Strain: Implications for Job Design." *Administrative Science Quarterly,* 24, 285–307.

Katz, Daniel. 1964. "Approaches to Managing Conflict," in *Power and Conflict in Organizations,* eds. Robert L. Kahn and Elise Boulding, 105–14. New York: Basic Books.

Katz, Daniel, and Robert L. Kahn. 1978. *The Sociology Psychology of Organizations,* rev. ed. New York: Wiley.

Katz, Harry C. 1985. *Shifting Gears: Changing Labor Relations in the U.S. Automobile Industry.* Cambridge, MA: MIT Press.

Katz, Ralph. 1982. "The Effects of Group Longevity on Project Communication and Performance." *Administrative Science Quarterly,* 27, 81–104.

Kaufman, Herbert. 1971. *The Limits of Organizational Change.* Tuscaloosa: University of Alabama Press.

Keeley, Michael. 1978. "A Social Justice Approach to Organizational Evaluation." *Administrative Science Quarterly,* 23, 272–92.

———. 1984. "Impartiality and Participant-Interest Theories of Organizational Effectiveness." *Administrative Science Quarterly,* 29, 1–12.

Keister, Lisa A. 1998. "Engineering Growth: Business Group Structure and Firm Performance in China's Transition Economy." *American Journal of Sociology,* 104, 404–40.

Kellogg, Katherine C., Wanda J. Orlikowski, and JoAnne Yates. 2006. "Life in the Trading Zone: Structuring Coordination Across Boundaries in Postbureaucratic Organizations." *Organization Science,* 17, no. 1, 22–44.

Kelly, Dawn, and Terry L. Amburgey. 1991. "Organizational Inertia and Momentum: A Dynamic Model of Strategic Change." *Academy of Management Journal,* 34, 591–612.

Kerbo, Harold R., and L. Richard Della Fave. 1983. "Corporate Linkage and Control of the Corporate Economy: New Evidence and a Reinterpretation." *Sociological Quarterly,* 24, 201–18.

Kessler-Harris, Alice. 2003. *Out to Work: A History of Wage-Earning Women in the United States.* New York: Oxford University Press.

Khanna, Tarun, Ranjay Gulati, and Nitin Nohria. 1998. "The Dynamics of Learning Alliances: Competition, Cooperation and Relative Scope." *Strategic Management Journal,* 19, 193–210.

Kidder, Tracy. 1989. *Among Schoolchildren*. Boston: Houghton-Miflin.

Kimberly, John R. 1976. "Organizational Size and Structuralist Perspective: Review, Critique and Proposal." *Administrative Science Quarterly, 21*, 571–97.

———. 1989. "Organizational, Institutional, and Societal Evolution: Medieval Craft Guilds and the Genesis of Formal Organizations." *Administrative Science Quarterly, 34*, 540–65.

Kimberly, John R., and Martin J. Evanisko. 1981. "Organizational Innovation: The Influence of Individual, Organizational and Contextual Factors on Hospital Adoption of Technological and Administrative Innovations." *Academy of Management Journal, 24*, 689–713.

King, Brayden G., and Sarah A. Soule. 2007. "Social Movements as Extra-Institutional Entrepreneurs: The Effects of Protests on Stock Price Returns." *Administrative Science Quarterly, 52*, no. 3, 413–42.

Klatzky, Sheila. 1970a. "The Relationship of Organizational Size to Complexity and Coordination." *Administrative Science Quarterly, 15*, 428–38.

Klauss, Rudi, and Bernard M. Bass. 1982. *Interpersonal Communication in Organizations*. New York: Academic Press.

Klonglan, Gerald E., Richard D. Warren, Judy M. Winkelpleck, and Steven K. Paulson. 1976. "Interorganizational Measurement in the Social Services Sector: Differences by Hierarchical Level." *Administrative Science Quarterly, 21*, 675–87.

Kochan, Thomas A., George P. Huber, and Larry C. Cummings. 1975. "Determinants of Interorganizational Conflict in Collective Bargaining in the Public Sector." *Administrative Science Quarterly, 20*, 10–23.

Kogut, Bruce, and Gordon Walker. 2001. "The Small World of Germany and the Durability of National Networks." *American Sociological Review, 66*, 317–35.

Kohn, Melvin L., Atsushi Naoi, Carrie Schoenbach, Carmi Schooler, and Kazimierz M. Slomczynski. 1990. "Position in the Class Structure and Psychological Functioning in the United States, Japan and Poland." *American Journal of Sociology, 95*, 964–1008.

Kohn, Melvin L., and Carmi Schooler. 1973. "Occupational Experience and Psychological Functioning: Assessment of Reciprocal Effects." *American Sociological Review, 38*, no. 1, 98–117.

———. 1978. "The Reciprocal Effects of Substantive Complexity of Work and Intellectual Flexibility: A Longitudinal Assessment." *American Journal of Sociology, 84*, 1–23.

———. 1982. "Job Conditions and Personality: A Longitudinal Assessment of the Reciprocal Effects." *American Journal of Sociology, 87*, 1257–86.

Kornhauser, William. 1963. *Scientists in Industry*. Berkeley and Los Angeles: University of California Press.

Kraatz, Matthew S., and Edward J. Zajac. 1996. "Exploring the Limits of the New Institutionalism: The Causes and Consequences of Illegitimate Organizational Change." *American Sociological Review, 61*, 812–36.

Kralewski, John E., Laura Pitt, and Deborah Shatin. 1985. "Structural Characteristics of Medical Practice Groups." *Administrative Science Quarterly, 30*, 34–45.

Kuhn, Thomas S. 1970. *The Structure of Scientific Revolutions*. Chicago: University of Chicago Press.

Kunda, Gideon. 2006. *Engineering Culture: Control and Commitment in a High-Tech Corporation*. Philadelphia, PA: Temple University Press.

Kunda, Gideon, Stephen R. Barley, and James Evans. 2002. "Why Do Contractors Contract? The Experience of Highly Skilled Technical Professionals in a Contingent Labor Market." *Industrial and Labor Relations Review,* 55, 234–62.

Lachman, Ron. 1989. "Power from What? A Reexamination of Its Relationship with Structural Conditions." *Administrative Science Quarterly,* 34, 231–51.

Lammers, Cornelius J. 1967. "Power and Participation in Decision Making." *American Journal of Sociology,* 73, 201–16.

———. 1975. "Self-Management and Participation: Two Concepts of Democratization in Organizations." *Organization and Administrative Sciences,* 5, 35–53.

———. 1981. "Contributions of Organizational Sociology: Part II: Contributions to Organizational Theory and Practice—A Liberal View." *Organization Studies,* 2, 361–76.

Laumann, Edward O., and David Knoke. 1987. *The Organizational State: Social Choice in National Policy Domains.* Madison: University of Wisconsin Press.

Laumann, Edward O., David Knoke, and Yong-Hak Kim. 1985. "An Organizational Approach to State Policy Formation: A Comparative Study of Energy and Health Domains." *American Sociological Review,* 50, 1–19.

Lawler, Edward J., Shane Thye, and Yeongkoo Yoon. 2008. "Social Exchange and Micro Social Order." *American Sociological Review,* 73, 519–42.

Lawrence, Barbara S. 1988. "New Wrinkles in the Theory of Age: Demography, Norms and Performance Ratings." *Academy of Management Journal,* 31, 309–37.

Lawrence, Barbara S., and Pamela S. Tolbert. 2007. "Organizational Demography and Individual Careers: Structures, Norms and Outcomes," in *Handbook of Career Studies,* eds. H. Gunz and M. Peiperl, 399–421. Thousand Oaks, CA: Sage.

Lawrence, Paul R., and Jay W. Lorsch. 1967. *Organization and Environment.* Cambridge, MA: Harvard University Press.

———. 1969. *Developing Organizations: Diagnosis and Action.* Reading, MA: Addison-Wesley.

Leavitt, Harold J. 1951. "The Effects of Certain Communications Patterns on Group Performance." *Journal of Abnormal and Social Psychology,* 46, 38–50.

Lee, Brandon H. 2007. "Cultivating the Niche: A Study of the Origins and Consequences of Standards-Based Certification Organizations in the U.S. Organic Food Industry." Unpublished PhD diss., Cornell University, Ithaca, NY.

Leicht, Kevin T., and Mary Fennell. 2001. *Professional Work: A Sociological Approach.* Malden, MA: Blackwell Publishers.

Leicht, Kevin T., Toby L. Parcel, and Robert L. Kaufman. 1992. "Measuring the Same Concept Across Diverse Organizations." *Social Science Research,* 21, 149–74.

Levine, Adeline Gordon. 1982. *Love Canal: Science, Politics, and People.* Lexington, MA: D. C. Heath.

Levine, Sol, and Paul E. White. 1961. "Exchange as a Conceptual Framework for the Study of Interorganizational Relationships." *Administrative Science Quarterly,* 5, 583–610.

Levine, Sol, Paul E. White, and Benjamin D. Paul. 1963. "Community Interorganizational Problems in Providing Medical Care and Social Services." *American Journal of Public Health,* 52, no. 8, 1183–95.

Levinthal, Daniel A., and Mark Fichman. 1988. "Dynamics of Interorganizational Attachment: Auditor-Client Relationships." *Administrative Science Quarterly,* 33, 345–69.

Levitt, Barbara, and James G. March. 1988. "Organizational Learning." *Annual Review of Sociology,* 14, 319–40.

Levitt, Barbara, and Clifford Nuss. 1989. "The Lid on the Garbage Can: Institutional Constraints on Decision Making in the Technical Core of College-Text Publishers." *Administrative Science Quarterly,* 34, 190–207.

Lieberson, Stanley, and James F. O'Connor. 1972. "Leadership and Organizational Performance: A Study of Large Corporations." *American Sociological Review,* 37, 117–30.

Lin, Nan. 1999. "Social Networks and Status Attainment." *Annual Review of Sociology,* 25, 467–87.

Lincoln, James R., Mitsuyo Hanada, and Kerry McBride. 1986. "Organizational Structures in Japanese and U.S. Manufacturing." *Administrative Science Quarterly,* 31, 338–64.

Lincoln, James R., and Gerald Zeitz. 1980. "Organizational Properties from Aggregate Data." *American Sociological Review,* 45, 391–405.

Lipset, Seymour Martin. 1960. *Agrarian Socialism.* Berkeley and Los Angeles: University of California Press.

Lipset, Seymour Martin, Martin A. Trow, and James S. Coleman. 1956. *Union Democracy.* New York: Free Press.

Litwak, Eugene. 1961. "Models of Organizations Which Permit Conflict." *American Journal of Sociology,* 76, 177–84.

Litwak, Eugene, and Lydia Hylton. 1962. "Interorganizational Analysis: A Hypothesis on Coordinating Agencies." *Administrative Science Quarterly,* 6, 395–420.

Long, J. Scott, Paul D. Allison, and Robert McGinnis. 1993. "Rank Advancement in Academic Careers: Sex Differences and the Effects of Productivity." *American Sociological Review,* 58, 703–22.

Long, J. Scott, and Robert McGinnis. 1981. "Organizational Context and Scientific Productivity." *American Sociological Review,* 46, 422–42.

Lord, R. G., C. L. DeVader, and G. M. Alliger. 1986. "A Meta-Analysis of the Relations Between Personality Traits and Leadership Perceptions: An Application of Validity Generalization Procedures." *Journal of Applied Psychology,* 71, 402–10.

Lounsbury, Michael. 2001. "Institutional Sources of Practice Variation: Staffing College and University Recycling Programs." *Administrative Science Quarterly,* 46, 29–56.

Lozano, Beverly. 1989. *The Invisible Work Force: Transforming American Business with Outside and Home-Based Workers.* New York: Free Press.

Maas, Meridean Leone. 1979. "A Formal Theory of Organizational Power." PhD diss., Department of Sociology, Iowa State University.

MacDuffie, John Paul. 1995. "Human Resource Bundles and Manufacturing Performance: Organizational Logic and Flexible Production Systems in the World Auto Industry." *Industrial and Labor Relations Review,* 48, no. 2, 197–221.

Malan, Leon. 1994. "Organizational Responses to Turbulent Environments." PhD diss., State University of New York at Albany.

Manning, Peter K. 1992. *Organizational Communication.* New York: Aldine de Gruyter.

Manns, Curtis L., and James G. March. 1978. "Financial Adversity, Internal Competition, and Curricular Change in a University." *Administrative Science Quarterly,* 23, 541–52.

Mansfield, Roger. 1973. "Bureaucracy and Centralization: An Examination of Organizational Structure." *Administrative Science Quarterly,* 18, 77–88.

March, James G. 1991. "Exploration and Exploitation in Organizational Learning." *Organization Science,* 2, 71–87.

March, James G., and Herbert A. Simon. 1958. *Organizations.* New York: John Wiley.

March, James G., and Lee S. Sproul. 1990. "Technology, Management, and Cooptative Advantage," in *Technology and Organizations,* eds. Paul S. Goodman, Lee Sproul, and Edwin Amenta, 144–73. San Francisco: Jossey-Bass.

Marcus, Alfred A., and Robert S. Goodman. 1991. "Victims and Shareholders: The Dilemmas of Presenting Corporate Policy During a Crisis." *Academy of Management Journal,* 34, 281–305.

Markham, William T., Charles M. Bonjean, and Judy Corder. 1984. "Measuring Organizational Control: The Reliability and Validity of the Control Graph Approach." *Human Relations,* 37, no. 4, 263–95.

Marquis, Christopher, Mary Ann Glynn, and Gerald F. Davis. 2007. "Community Isomorphism and Corporate Social Action." *Academy of Management Review,* 32, no. 3, 925–45.

Marsden, Peter V., Cynthia R. Cook, and David Knoke. 1996. "American Organizations and Their Environments: A Descriptive Overview," in *Organizations in America: Analyzing their Structures and Human Resource Practices,* eds. Arne L. Kalleberg, David Knoke, Peter Marsden, and Joe L. Spaeth, 69–86. Thousand Oaks, CA: Sage.

Marsh, Robert M., and Hiroshi Mannari. 1980. "Technological Implications Theory: A Japanese Test." *Organization Studies,* 1, 161–83.

Massie, Joseph L. 1964. *Essentials of Management.* Englewood Cliffs, NJ: Prentice Hall.

Maurice, Marc, Arndt Sorge, and Malcolm Warner. 1980. "Societal Differences in Organizing Manufacturing Units: A Comparison of France, West Germany and Great Britain." *Organization Studies,* 1, 59–86.

McCarthy, John D., and Mayer N. Zald. 1973. *The Trend of Social Movements in America: Professionalization and Resource Mobilization.* Morristown, NJ: General Learning Press.

McEvily, Bill, and Alfred Marcus. 2005. "Embedded Ties and the Acquisition of Competitive Capabilities." *Strategic Management Journal,* 26, no. 11, 1033–55.

McEvily, Susan K., Kathleen M. Eisenhardt, and Jill E. Prescott. 2004. "The Global Acquisition, Leverage and Protection of Technological Competencies." *Strategic Management Journal,* 24, no. 8, 713–22.

McKelvey, Bill. 1982. *Organizational Systematics: Taxonomy, Evolution, Classification.* Berkeley and Los Angeles: University of California Press.

McKinley, William. 1987. "Complexity and Administrative Intensity: The Case of Declining Organizations." *Administrative Science Quarterly,* 32, 81–105.

McLean, Bethany, and Peter Elkind. 2004. *Smartest Guys in the Room: The Amazing Rise and Scandalous Fall of Enron.* New York: Portfolio.

McMillan, Charles J. 1973. "Corporations Without Citizenship: The Emergence of Multinational Enterprise," in *People and Organizations,* eds. Graeme Soloman and Kenneth Thompsons, 128–37. London: Longman Group Limited.

Mechanic, David. 1962. "Sources of Power of Lower Participants in Complex Organizations." *Administrative Science Quarterly,* 7, 349–64.

Meindl, James R., Sanford B. Ehrlich, and Janet M. Dukerich. 1985. "The Romance of Leadership." *Administrative Science Quarterly,* 30, 78–102.

Merriam-Webster. 2002. *Merriam-Webster's Collegiate Dictionary, Tenth Edition.* Springfield, MA: Merriam-Webster.

Merton, Robert K. 1949. "Manifest and Latent Functions," in *Social Theory and Social Structure,* 21–82. Glencoe, IL: Free Press.

———. 1957. *Social Theory and Social Structure,* rev. ed. Glencoe, IL: Free Press.

Meyer, Alan D. 1982. "Adapting to Environmental Jolts." *Administrative Science Quarterly,* 27, 515–37.

Meyer, John W., and Brian Rowan. 1977. "Institutionalized Organizations: Formal Structure as Myth and Ceremony." *American Journal of Sociology,* 83, 340–63.

Meyer, John W., and W. Richard Scott. 1983. *Organizational Environments: Ritual and Rationality.* Beverly Hills, CA: Sage.

Meyer, Marshall W. 1968a. "Automation and Bureaucratic Structure." *American Journal of Sociology,* 74, 256–64.

———. 1968b. "Two Authority Structures of Bureaucratic Organization." *Administrative Science Quarterly,* 13, 211–18.

———. 1971. "Some Constraints in Analyzing Data on Organizational Structures." *American Sociological Review,* 36, 294–97.

———. 1975. "Leadership and Organizational Structure." *American Journal of Sociology,* 81, no. 3, 514–42.

Meyer, Marshall W., and M. Craig Brown. 1977. "The Process of Bureaucratization." *American Journal of Sociology,* 83, 364–85.

Meyer, Marshall W., and Lynn G. Zucker. 1989. *Permanently Failing Organizations.* Newbury Park, CA: Sage.

Mezias, Stephen J. 1990. "An Institutional Model of Organizational Practice: Financial Reporting at the Fortune 200." *Administrative Science Quarterly,* 35, 431–57.

Michels, Robert. 1949. *Political Parties.* New York: Free Press.

Miller, C. Chet, William H. Glick, Yau-de Wang, and George P. Huber. 1991. "Understanding Technology-Structure Relationships: Theory Developing and Meta-Analytic Theory Testing." *Academy of Management Journal,* 34, 370–99.

Miller, George A. 1967. "Professionals in Bureaucracy, Alienation Among Industrial Scientists and Engineers." *American Sociological Review,* 32, 755–68.

Milliken, Frances J. 1990. "Perceiving and Interpreting Environmental Change: An Examination of College Administrators' Interpretation of Changing Demographics." *Academy of Management Journal,* 33, 42–63.

Milliken, Frances J., and Theresa K. Lant. 1991. "The Effects of an Organization's Recent Performance History on Strategic Persistence and Change." *Advances in Strategic Management,* 7, 125–52.

Mills, C. Wright. 1956. *The Power Elite.* New York: Oxford University Press.

Miner, Anne S. 1987. "Idiosyncratic Jobs in Formalized Organizations." *Administrative Science Quarterly,* 32, 327–51.

Miner, Anne S., Paula Bassoff, and Christine Moorman. 2001. "Organizational Improvisation and Learning: A Field Study." *Administrative Science Quarterly,* 46, 304–37.

Miner, Anne S., and Pamela R. Haunschild. 1995. "Population-Level learning," in *Research in Organizational Behavior,* Vol. 17, 115–66. Greenwich, CT: JAI Press.

Mintz, Beth, and Michael Schwartz. 1981. "Interlocking Directorates and Interest Group Formation." *American Sociological Review,* 46, 951–69.

Mintzberg, Henry. 1983. *Power In and Around Organizations.* Upper Saddle River, NJ: Prentice Hall.

Mizruchi, Mark S. 1989. "Similarity of Political Behavior Among Large American Corporations." *American Journal of Sociology,* 95, 401–24.

———. 1992. *The Structure of Corporate Political Action: Interfirm Relations and Their Consequences.* Cambridge: Harvard University Press.

———. 1996. "What Do Interlocks Do?" *Annual Review of Sociology,* 22, 271–98.

———. 2004. "Berle and Means Revisited: The Governance and Power of Large U.S. Corporations." *Theory and Society,* 33, no. 3, 579–617.

Mizruchi, Mark S., and David Bunting. 1981. "Influence in Corporate Networks: An Examination of Four Measures." *Administrative Science Quarterly,* 26, 475–89.

Mizruchi, Mark S., and Lisa C. Fein. 1999. "The Social Construction of Organizational Knowledge: A Study of the Uses of Coercive, Mimetic, and Normative Isomorphism." *Administrative Science Quarterly,* 44, 653–83.

Mizruchi, Mark S., and Linda Brewster Stearns. 1988. "A Longitudinal Study of the Formation of Interlocking Directorates." *Administrative Science Quarterly,* 33, 194–210.

Moch, Michael K. 1976. "Structure and Organizational Resource Allocation." *Administrative Science Quarterly,* 21, 661–74.

Moch, Michael K., and Edward V. Morse. 1977. "Size, Centralization, and Organizational Adoption of Innovation." *American Sociological Review,* 43, 716–25.

Mohan, Mary Leslie. 1993. *Organizational Communication and Cultural Vision: Approaches for Analysis.* Albany: State University of New York Press.

Molnar, Joseph J. 1978. "Comparative Organizational Properties and Interorganizational Interdependence." *Sociology and Social Research,* 63, 24–48.

Molotch, Harvey, and Marilyn Lester. 1975. "Accidental News: The Great Oil Spill as Local Occurrence and National Event." *American Journal of Sociology,* 81, 235–60.

Morgan, Gareth. 1986. *Images of Organizations.* Beverly Hills, CA: Sage.

Morgan, Glenn. 2004. "Understanding Multinational Corporations," in *The Oxford Handbook of Work and Organizations,* eds. S. Ackroyd, R. Batt, P. Thompson, and P. Tolbert, 554–76. London: Oxford University Press.

Morrill, Calvin. 1991. "Conflict Management, Honor, and Organizational Change." *American Journal of Sociology,* 97, 585–621.

Mulford, Charles L. 1980. "Dyadic Properties as Correlates of Exchange and Conflict Between Organizations." Unpublished paper, Department of Sociology, Iowa State University.

Nee, Victor. 1992. "Organizational Dynamics of Market Transition: Hybrid Forms, Property Rights, and Mixed Economy in China." *Administrative Science Quarterly,* 37, 1–27.

Needleman, Martin L., and Carolyn Needleman. 1979. "Organizational Crime: Two Models of Criminogenesis." *Sociological Quarterly,* 20, 517–28.

Ocasio, William. 1994. "Political Dynamics and the Circulation of Power: CEO Succession in U.S. Industrial Corporations, 1960–1990." *Administrative Science Quarterly,* 39, no. 6, 285–312.

O'Connor, Joseph P., Richard L. Priem, Joseph E. Coombs, and K. Matthew Gilley. 2006. "Do CEO Stock Options Prevent or Promote Fraudulent Financial Reporting?" *Academy of Management Journal,* 49, no. 6, 483–500.

Oliver, Christine. 1991. "Strategic Responses to Institutional Processes." *Academy of Management Review,* 16, 145–79.

Ornstein, Michael. 1984. "Interlocking Directorates in Canada: Intercorporate or Class Alliance?" *Administrative Science Quarterly,* 29, 210–37.

Osterman, Paul. 2006. "Overcoming Oligarchy: Culture and Agency in Social Movement Organizations." *Administrative Science Quarterly,* 51, 622–49.

Ott, J. Steven. 1989. *The Organizational Culture Perspective.* Chicago: Dorsey Press.

Ouchi, William G. 1977. "The Relationship Between Organizational Structure and Organizational Control." *Administrative Science Quarterly,* 22, 95–113.

———. 1980. "Markets, Bureaucracies and Clans." *Administrative Science Quarterly,* 25, 129–41.

Ouchi, William G., and Alfred M. Jaeger. 1978. "Social Structure and Organizational Type," in *Environments and Organizations,* eds. Marshall W. Meyer and Associates, 110–30. San Francisco: Jossey-Bass.

Ouchi, William G., and Jerry B. Johnson. 1978. "Types of Organizational Control and Their Relation to Emotional Well-Being." *Administrative Science Quarterly,* 23, 293–317.

Padgett, John F. 1980. "Managing Garbage Can Hierarchies." *Administrative Science Quarterly,* 25, 583–604.

Palmer, Donald A., Roger Friedland, and Jitendra V. Singh. 1986. "The Ties That Bind: Organizational and Class Bases of Stability in a Corporate Interlock Network." *American Sociological Review,* 51, 781–96.

Palmer, Donald A., P. Devereaux Jennings, and Xueguang Zhou. 1993. "Late Adoption of the Multidivision Form by Large U.S. Corporations: Institutional, Political, and Economic Accounts." *Administrative Science Quarterly,* 38, 100–131.

Parsons, Talcott. 1960. *Structure and Process in Modern Society.* New York: Free Press.

Pascale, Richard. 1985. "The Paradox of 'Corporate Culture': Reconciling Ourselves to Socialization." *California Management Review,* 27, 26–41.

Pazy, Asya, and Israela Oron. 2001. "Sex Proportion and Performance Evaluation Among High-Ranking Military Officers." *Journal of Organizational Behavior,* 22, 689–702.

Pennings, Johannes M. 1973. "Measures of Organizational Structure: A Methodological Note." *American Journal of Sociology,* 79, 686–704.

———. 1980a. "Environmental Influences on the Creation Process," in *The Organizational Life Cycle,* eds. John R. Kimberly, Robert H. Miles, and Associates, 134–60. San Francisco: Jossey-Bass.

———. 1980b. *Interlocking Directorates.* San Francisco: Jossey-Bass.

———. 1987. "On the Nature of New Technology as Organizational Innovation," in *New Technology in Organizational Innovation: The Development and Diffusion of Microelectronics,* eds. Johannes M. Pennings and Arend Buitendam, 3–12. Cambridge, MA: Ballinger.

Pennings, Johannes M., and Paul S. Goodman. 1977. "Toward a Workable Framework," in *New Perspectives on Organizational Effectiveness,* eds. S. Goodman and Johannes M. Pennings, 146–84. San Francisco: Jossey-Bass.

Perlow, Leslie A. 1998. "Boundary Control: The Social Ordering of Work and Family Time in a High-Tech Corporation." *Administrative Science Quarterly,* 43, 328–56.

Perratta, Heather G. 2007. "Better Dead than Coed? The Survival and Decline of Single-Sex Colleges in the United States." PhD diss., Cornell University.

Perrow, Charles. 1961. "The Analysis of Goals in Complex Organizations." *American Sociological Review,* 26, 688–99.

———. 1967. "A Framework for the Comparative Analysis of Organizations." *American Sociological Review,* 32, 194–208.

———. 1970. "Departmental Power and Perspective in Industrial Firms," in *Power in Organizations,* ed. Mayer N. Zald, 59–89. Nashville, TN: Vanderbilt University Press.

———. 1977. "Three Types of Effectiveness Studies," in *New Perspectives on Organizational Effectiveness,* eds. Paul S. Goodman and Johannes M. Pennings, 96–105. San Francisco: Jossey-Bass.

———. 1984. *Normal Accidents: Living with High-Risk Technologies.* New York: Basic Books.

———. 1986. *Complex Organizations: A Critical Essay,* 3rd ed. New York: Random House.

———. 1991. "A Society of Organizations." *Theory and Society,* 20, 725–62.

Perrucci, Robert, and Marc Pilisuk. 1970. "Leaders and Ruling Elites: The Interorganizational Bases of Community Power." *American Sociological Review,* 35, 1040–57.

Peter, Laurence J., and Raymond Hull. 1969. *The Peter Principle.* New York: William Brown.

Peters, Thomas J., and Robert H. Waterman Jr. 1982. *In Search of Excellence: Lessons from America's Best-Run Companies.* New York: Harper and Row.

Peterson, Richard A. 1970. "Some Consequences of Differentiation," in *Power in Organizations,* ed. Mayer N. Zald, 144–49. Nashville: Vanderbilt University Press.

Pfeffer, Jeffrey. 1972. "Size and Composition of Corporate Boards of Directors." *Administrative Science Quarterly,* 17, 218–28.

———. 1981. *Power in Organizations.* Marshfield, MA: Pitman.

———. 1982. *Organizations and Organization Theory.* Boston: Pitman.

———. 1983. "Organizational Demography," in *Research in Organizational Behavior,* Vol. 5, eds. L. L. Cummings and Barry M. Staw, 299–357. Greenwich, CT: JAI Press.

———. 1993. "Barriers to the Advance of Organizational Science: Paradigm Development as a Dependent Variable." *Academy of Management Review,* 18, 599–620.

Pfeffer, Jeffrey, and James N. Baron. 1988. "Taking the Workers Back Out: Recent Trends in the Structuring of Employment," in *Research in Organizational Behavior,* Vol. 10, 257–323. Greenwich, CT: JAI Press.

Pfeffer, Jeffrey, and Anthony Long. 1977. "Resource Allocation in United Funds: Examination of Power and Dependence." *Social Forces,* 55, 776–90.

Pfeffer, Jeffrey, and William L. Moore. 1980. "Average Tenure of Academic Department Heads: The Effects of Paradigm, Size, and Departmental Demography." *Administrative Science Quarterly,* 25, 387–406.

Pfeffer, Jeffrey, and Gerald R. Salancik. 1974. "Organizational Decision Making as a Political Process: The Case of a University Budget." *Administrative Science Quarterly,* 19, 135–51.

———. 1978. *The External Control of Organizations: A Resource Dependence Perspective.* New York: Harper and Row.

Podolny, Joel M., and Karen L. Page. 1998. "Network Forms of Organizations." *Annual Review of Sociology,* 24, 57–76.

Polzer, Jeffrey T., C. Brad Crisp, Sirkka L. Jarvenpaa, and Jerry W. Kim. 2006. "Extending the Faultline Model to Geographically Dispersed Teams: How Co-Located Subgroups Can Impair Group Functioning." *Academy of Management Journal,* 49, no. 4, 679–92.

Pondy, Louis R. 1967. "Organizational Conflict: Concepts and Models." *Administrative Science Quarterly,* 12, 296–320.

———. 1969. "Varieties of Organizational Conflict." *Administrative Science Quarterly,* 14, 499–505.

———. 1970. "Toward a Theory of Internal Resource Allocation," in *Power in Organizations,* ed. Mayer N. Zald, 270–311. Nashville, TN: Vanderbilt University Press.

Porter, Michael E. 1980. *Competitive Strategy.* New York: Free Press.

———. 1998. *Competitive Advantage: Creating and Sustaining Superior Performance.* New York: Free Press.

Powell, Walter W., Kenneth W. Koput, and Laurel Smith-Doerr. 1996. "Interorganizational Collaboration and the Locus of Innovation: Networks of Learning in Biotechnology." *Administrative Science Quarterly,* 41, 116–45.

Price, James L., and Charles W. Mueller. 1986. *Handbook of Organizational Measurement.* Marshfield, MA: Pitman.

Priest, T. B., and Robert A. Rothman. 1985. "Lawyers in Corporate Chief Executive Positions: A Historical Analysis of Careers." *Work and Occupations,* 12, 131–46.

Prokesch, Steven E. 1985. "Keeping Tabs on Competitors." *New York Times,* October 28, sec. D.

Provan, Keith G., Janice M. Beyer, and Carlos Kruytbosch. 1980. "Environmental Linkages and Power in Resource-Dependence Relations Between Organizations." *Administrative Science Quarterly,* 25, 200–225.

Provan, Keith G., and H. Brinton Milward. 1995. "A Preliminary Theory of Interorganizational Network Effectiveness: A Comparative Study of Four Community Mental Health Systems." *Administrative Science Quarterly,* 40, 1–33.

Pugh, Derek S., David J. Hickson, C. R. Hinings, K. M. Lupton, K. M. McDonald, C. Turner, and T. Lupton. 1963. "A Conceptual Scheme for Organizational Analysis." *Administrative Science Quarterly,* 8, 289–315.

Pugh, Derek S., D. J. Hickson, C. R. Hinings, and C. Turner. 1968. "Dimensions of Organizational Structure." *Administrative Science Quarterly,* 13, 65–105.

Ragins, Belle R., Bickley Townsend, and Mary Mattis. 1998. "Gender Gap in the Executive Suite: CEPs and Female Executives Report on Breaking the Glass Ceiling." *Academy of Management Executive,* 12, 28–42.

Rahim, M. Afzahur. 1986. *Managing Conflict in Organizations.* New York: Praeger.

———. 1989. *Managing Conflict: An Interdisciplinary Approach.* New York: Praeger.

Raphael, Edna. 1967. "The Andersen-Warton Hypothesis in Local Unions: A Comparative Study." *American Sociological Review,* 32, 768–76.

Reagans, Ray, and Bill McEvily. 2003. "Network Structure and Knowledge Transfer: The Effects of Cohesion and Range." *Administrative Science Quarterly,* 48, 240–67.

Reich, Robert, and James D. Donahue. 1985. "Lessons from the Chrysler Bailout." *California Management Review,* 27, 157–83.

Reinganum, Marc R. 1985. "The Effect of Executive Succession on Stockholder Wealth." *Administrative Science Quarterly,* 30, 46–60.

Reskin, Barbara F. 1998. *The Realities of Affirmative Action in Employment.* Washington, DC: American Sociological Association.

———. 2003. "Including Mechanisms in Our Models of Ascriptive Inequality." *American Sociological Review,* 68, 1–21.

Reskin, Barbara F., and Denise D. Bielby. 2005. "A Sociological Perspective on Gender and Career Outcomes." *Journal of Economic Perspectives,* 19, 71–86.

Reskin, Barbara F., and Patricia A. Roos. 1990. *Job Queues, Gender Queues: Explaining Women's Inroads into Male Occupations.* Philadelphia, PA: Temple University Press.

Revkin, Andrew C. 1997. "Babbitt Assails GE over Ridding Hudson of Chemicals." *New York Times,* September 26, sec. B.

Ridgeway, Cecilia L., and Shelley J. Correll. 2006. "Consensus and the Creation of Status Beliefs." *Social Forces,* 85, 431–53.

Rifkin, Jeremy. 1995. *The End of Work: The Decline of the Global Labor Force and the Dawn of the Post-Market Era.* New York: Putnam.

Ritzer, George. 2000. *The McDonaldization of Society.* Thousand Oaks, CA: Pine Forge Press.

Roethlisberger, Fritz, and W. J. Dickson. 1934. *Management and the Worker: Technical vs. Social Organization in an Industrial Plant.* Boston, MA: Graduate School of Business Administration, Harvard University Press.

Rogelberg, Steven G., Desmond J. Leach, Peter Warr, and Jennifer L. Burnfield. 2006. " 'Not Another Meeting!' Are Meeting Time Demands Related to Employee Well-Being?" *Journal of Applied Psychology,* 91, 83–96.

Romo, Frank P., and Michael Schwartz. 1995. "The Structural Embeddedness of Business Decisions: The Migration of Manufacturing Plants in New York State, 1960 to 1985." *American Sociological Review,* 60, 874–907.

Rosenbaum, James E. 1979. "Organizational Career Mobility: Promotion Chances in a Corporation During Periods of Growth and Contraction." *American Journal of Sociology,* 85, 21–48.

Rosenweig, Philip M., and Jitendra V. Singh. 1991. "Organizational Environments and the Multinational Enterprise." *Academy of Management Review,* 16, no. 2, 340–61.

Rosow, Jerome M., ed. 1974. *The Worker and the Job: Coping with Change.* Upper Saddle River, NJ: Prentice Hall.

Ross, Jerry, and Barry M. Staw. 1993. "Organizational Escalation and Exit: Lessons from the Shoreham Nuclear Power Plant." *Academy of Management Journal,* 36, 701–32.

Rothschild, Joyce, and J. Allen Whitt. 1986. *The Cooperative Workplace: Potentials and Dilemmas of Organizational Democracy and Participation.* New York: Cambridge University Press.

Rothschild-Witt, Joyce. 1979. "The Collectivist Organization: An Alternative to Rational Bureaucratic Models." *American Sociological Review,* 44, 509–27.

Rowan, Brian. 1982. "Organizational Structure and the Institutional Environment: The Case of Public Schools." *Administrative Science Quarterly,* 27, 259–79.

Roy, William G. 1981. "The Process of Bureaucratization of the U.S. State Department and the Vesting of Economic Interests, 1886–1905." *Administrative Science Quarterly,* 26, 419–33.

———. 1983a. "Toward Clearer Thinking: A Reply." *Administrative Science Quarterly,* 28, 61–64.

———. 1983b. "The Unfolding of the Interlocking Directorate Structure of the United States." *American Sociological Review,* 48, 248–57.

Rushing, William. 1967. "The Effects of Industrial Size and Division of Labor on Administration." *Administrative Science Quarterly,* 12, 267–95.

Sabel, Charles F. 1982. *Work and Politics.* New York: Cambridge University Press.

Salancik, Gerald R., and James R. Mindl. 1984. "Corporate Attributions as Strategic Illusions of Management Control." *Administrative Science Quarterly,* 29, 238–54.

Salancik, Gerald R., and Jeffrey Pfeffer. 1974. "The Bases and Use of Power in Organizational Decision Making: The Case of a University." *Administrative Science Quarterly,* 19, 453–73.

———. 1977. "Constraints on Administrator Discretion: The Limited Influence of Mayors on City Budgets." *Urban Affairs Quarterly,* 12, 475–98.

Sanford, R. Nevitt. 1964. "Individual Conflict and Organizational Interaction," in *Power and Conflict in Organizations,* eds. Robert L. Kahn and Elise Boulding, 95–104. New York: Basic Books.

Satow, Roberta. 1975. "Value-Rational Authority and Professional Organizations: Weber's Missing Type." *Administrative Science Quarterly,* 20, 526–31.

Schein, Virginia E. 1973. "The Relationship Between Sex-Role Stereotypes and Requisite Management Characteristics." *Journal of Applied Psychology,* 57, 95–100.

Schmidt, Stuart M., and Thomas A. Kochan. 1972. "Conflict: Toward Conceptual Clarity." *Administrative Science Quarterly,* 17, 371–81.

Schneiberg, Marc, Marissa King, and Thomas King. 2008. "Social Movements and Organizational Form: Cooperative Alternatives to Corporations in the American Insurance, Dairy and Grain Industries." *American Sociological Review,* 73, 635–67.

Schooler, Carmi, M. S. Mulatu, and G. Oates. 2004. "Occupational Self-Direction, Intellectual Functioning, and Self-Directed Orientation in Older Workers: Findings and Implications for Individuals and Societies." *American Journal of Sociology,* 110, no. 1, 161–97.

Schoonhoven, Claudia Bird. 1981. "Problems with Contingency Theory: Testing Assumptions Hidden Within the Language of Contingency 'Theory." *Administrative Science Quarterly,* 26, 349–77.

Schumpeter, Joseph A. 1934. *The Theory of Economic Development.* Cambridge, MA: Harvard University Press.

Scott, W. Richard. 1981. *Organizations: Rational, Natural and Open Systems.* Upper Saddle River, NJ: Prentice Hall.

————. 2004. "Reflections on a Half Century of Organizational Sociology." *Annual Review of Sociology,* 30, 1–21.

————. 2007. *Institutions and Organizations: Ideas and Interests.* Thousand Oaks, CA: Sage.

————. 2008. "Lords of the Dance: Professionals as Institutional Agents," *Organization Studies,* 29, 219–38.

Scott, W. Richard, and Gerald F. Davis. 2007. *Organizations and Organizing: Natural, Rational and Open System Perspectives.* Upper Saddle River, NJ: Prentice Hall.

Scott, W. Richard, Martin Ruef, Peter J. Mendel, and Carol A. Caronna. 2000. *Institutional Change and Healthcare Organizations: From Professional Dominance to Managed Care.* Chicago: University of Chicago Press.

Seabright, Mark A., Daniel A. Levinthal, and Mark Fichman. 1992. "Role of Individual Attachments in the Dissolution of Interorganizational Relationships." *Academy of Management Journal,* 35, 122–60.

Seashore, Stanley E. 1977. "An Elastic and Expandable Viewpoint," in *New Perspectives on Organizational Effectiveness,* eds. Paul S. Goodman and J. M. Pennings, 185–92. San Francisco: Jossey-Bass.

Seashore, Stanley E., and Ephraim Yuchtman. 1967. "Factorial Analysis of Organizational Performance." *Administrative Science Quarterly,* 12, 377–95.

Seiler, Lauren H., and Gene F. Summers. 1979. "Corporate Involvement in Community Affairs." *Sociological Quarterly,* 20, 375–86.

Selznick, Philip. 1957. *Leadership in Administration.* New York: Harper and Row.

————. 1966. *TVA and the Grass Roots,* ed. Harper Torchbook. New York: Harper and Row.

Sewell, William H. 1992. "A Theory of Structure: Duality, Agency, and Transformation." *American Journal of Sociology,* 98, 1–29.

Sills, David L. 1957. *The Volunteers.* New York: Free Press.

Simon, Herbert A. 1957. *Administrative Behavior.* New York: Free Press.

————. 1964. "On the Concept of Organizational Goal." *Administrative Science Quarterly,* 9, 1–22.

Simpson, Richard L. 1969. "Vertical and Horizontal Communication in Formal Organizations." *Administrative Science Quarterly,* 14, 188–96.

Sine, Wesley D., Heather A. Haveman, and Pamela S. Tolbert. 2005. "Risky Business? Entrepreneurship in the New Independent-Power Sector." *Administrative Science Quarterly,* 50, 200–232.

Sine, Wesley D., Hitoshi Mitsuhashi, and David A. Kirsch. 2006. "Revisiting Burns and Stalker: Formal Structure and New Venture Performance in Emerging Economic Sectors." *Academy of Management Journal,* 49, no. 1, 121–32.

Smircich, Linda. 1985. "Is the Concept of Culture a Paradigm for Understanding Organizations and Ourselves?" in *Organizational Culture,* eds. Peter J. Frost, Larry F. Moore, Meryl Reis Louis, Craig C. Lundberg, and Joanne Martin, 55–72. Beverly Hills, CA: Sage.

Smith, Kenwyn. 1989. "The Movement of Conflict in Organizations: The Joint Dynamics of Splitting and Triangulation." *Administrative Science Quarterly,* 34, 1–20.

Somaya, Deepak, Ian O. Williamson, and Xiaomeng Zhang. 2007. "Combining Patent Law Expertise with R&D for Patenting Performance." *Organization Science,* 18, 922–37.

Spangler, Eve. 1986. *Lawyers for Hire: Salaried Professionals at Work*. New Haven, CT: Yale University Press.

Staggenborg, Suzanne. 1986. "Coalition Work in the Pro-Choice Movement: Organizational and Environmental Opportunities and Obstacles." *Social Problems, 33,* 375–90.

Starbuck, William H. 1976. "Organizations and Their Environments," in *Handbook of Industrial and Organizational Psychology*, ed. Marvin D. Dunnette, 1069–1123. Chicago: Rand McNally.

Starbuck, William H., and Paul C. Nystrom. 1981. "Designing and Understanding Organizations," in *Handbook of Organizational Design*, Vol. 1, eds. Paul C. Nystrom and William H. Starbuck, ix–xxii. New York: Oxford University Press.

Staw, Barry M., and Jerry Ross. 1989. "Understanding Behavior in Escalation Situations." *Science, 246,* 216–20.

Steckmest, Francis W. 1982. *Corporate Performance: The Key to Public Trust*. New York: McGraw-Hill.

Steers, R. M. 1977. *Organizational Effectiveness: A Behavioral View*. Pacific Palisades, CA: Goodyear.

Stevenson, William B. 1990. "Formal Structure and Networks of Interaction Within Organizations." *Social Science Research, 19,* 112–31.

Stevenson, William B., and Danna Greenberg. 2000. "Agency and Social Networks: Strategies of Action in a Social Structure of Position, Opposition and Opportunity." *Administrative Science Quarterly, 45,* 651–78.

Stimson, Gerry. 2007. *Drinking in Context: Patterns, Interventions and Partnerships*. New York: Routledge.

Stinchcombe, Arthur L. 1965. "Organizations and Social Structure," in *Handbook of Organizations*, ed. James G. March, 142–93. Chicago: Rand McNally.

———. 1990. *Information and Organizations*. Berkeley and Los Angeles: University of California Press.

Stogdill, R. M. 1974. *Handbook of Leadership*. New York: Free Press.

Storing, Herbert J. 1962. "The Science of Administration: Herbert A. Simon," in *Essays on the Scientific Study of Politics*, ed. H. J. Storing, 63–105. New York: Holt, Rinehart and Winston.

Strang, David, and James N. Baron. 1990. "Categorical Imperative: The Structure of Job Titles in California State Agencies." *American Sociological Review, 55,* 479–95.

Sutherland, Edwin H. 1949. *White Collar Crime*. New York: Dryden Press.

Sutton, John R., and Frank Dobbin. 1996. "The Two Faces of Governance: Responses to Legal Uncertainty in U.S. Firms 1955–1985." *American Sociological Review, 61,* 794–811.

Sutton, John R., Frank Dobbin, John Meyer, and W. Richard Scott. 1994. "The Legalization of the Workplace." *American Journal of Sociology, 99,* 944–71.

Tannenbaum, Arnold S. 1968. *Control in Organizations*. New York: McGraw-Hill.

Tannenbaum, Arnold S., Bogdan Kovacic, Menochen Rosner, Mino Vianello, and George Wieser. 1974. *Hierarchy in Organizations*. San Francisco: Jossey-Bass.

Tannenbaum, Arnold S., and Tamas Rozgonyi. 1986. *Authority and Reward in Organizations: An International Research*. Ann Arbor, MI: Survey Research Center.

Taylor, Fredrick W. 1911. *The Principles of Scientific Management*. New York and London: Harper & brothers.

Terkel, Studs. 1974. *Working*. New York: Pantheon Books.

Terlaak, Anne. 2007. "Order Without Law? The Role of Certified Management Standards in Shaping Socially Desired Firm Behaviors." *Academy of Management Review*, 32, no. 3, 968–85.

Terreberry, Shirley. 1968. "The Evolution of Organizational Environments." *Administrative Science Quarterly*, 12, 590–613.

Thatcher, Sherry M. B., and Xiumei Zhu. 2006. "Changing Identities in a Changing Workplace: Identification, Identity Enactment, Self-Verification and Telecommuting." *Academy of Management Review*, 31, 1091–93.

Thomas, Alan Berkeley. 1988. "Does Leadership Make a Difference to Organizational Performance?" *Administrative Science Quarterly*, 33, 388–400.

Thompson, James D. 1967. *Organizations in Action*. New York: McGraw-Hill.

Thompson, James D., and William McEwen. 1958. "Organizational Goals and Environment: Goalsetting as an Interaction Process." *American Sociological Review*, 23, 23–31.

Thompson, Victor. 1961. *Modern Organizations*. New York: Knopf.

Tickner, Joseph A. 2002. "The Precautionary Principle and Public Health Trade-Offs: Case Study of West Nile Virus." *Annals of the American Academy of Political and Social Science*, 584, 69–79.

Tilly, Charles. 1978. *From Mobilization to Revolution*. Reading, MA: Addison-Wesley.

Tilly, Chris, and Charles Tilly. 1998. *Work under Capitalism*. Boulder, CO: Westview Press.

Tolbert, Pamela S. 1985. "Institutional Environments and Resource Dependence: Sources of Administrative Structure in Institutions of Higher Education." *Administrative Science Quarterly*, 30, 1–13.

———. 1986. "Organizations and Inequality: Sources of Earnings Differences Between Male and Female faculty." *Sociology of Education*, 59, 227–45.

———. 1988. "Institutionalization and Organizational Culture in Major Law Firms," in *Institutional Patterns and Organizations: Culture and Environment*, ed. L. Zucker, 101–13. Boston, MA: Ballinger Press.

———. 2004. "Introduction," in *Handbook of Work and Organizations*, eds. Stephen Ackroyd, Rose Batt, Paul Thompson, and Pamela Tolbert, 329–37. Oxford: Oxford University Press.

Tolbert, Pamela S., and Shon Hiatt. (Forthcoming). "On Organizations and Oligarchy: Michels in the 21st Century," in *The Oxford Handbook of Sociology and Organization Studies: Classical Resources*, ed. P. Adler. New York: Oxford University.

Tolbert, Pamela S., Tal Simons, Alice O. Andrews, and Jaehoon Rhee. 1995. "The Effects of Gender Composition in Academic Departments on Faculty Turnover." *Industrial and Labor Relations Review*, 48, 562–79.

Tolbert, Pamela S., and Lynne G. Zucker. 1983. "Institutional Sources of Change in the Formal Structure of Organizations: The Diffusion of Civil Service Reforms, 1880–1935." *Administrative Science Quarterly*, 28, 22–39.

———. 1996. "The Institutionalization of Institutional Theory," in *Handbook of Organization Studies*, eds. Stewart R. Clegg, Cynthia Hardy, and Walter R. Nord, 175–90. Thousand Oaks, CA: Sage.

Toynbee, Arnold. 1974. "As I See It." *Forbes*, 113, 68.

Trice, Harrison M., and Janice M. Beyer. 1993. *The Cultures of Work Organizations.* Upper Saddle River, NJ: Prentice Hall.

Tsui, Anne S. 1990. "A Multiple-Constituency Model of Effectiveness: An Empirical Examination at the Human Resources Subunit Level." *Administrative Science Quarterly,* 35, 458–83.

Turk, Herman. 1973. "Comparative Urban Structure from an Interorganizational Perspective." *Administrative Science Quarterly,* 18, 37–55.

———. 1975. "Policy Outputs and Conflicts of Large Communities from an Interorganizational Viewpoint." *Sociological Focus,* 8, no. 2, 111–23.

Turner, Jonathan H., and Leonard Beeghley. 1981. *The Emergence of Sociological Theory.* Homewood, IL: Dorsey Press.

Useem, Michael. 1979. "The Social Organization of the American Business Elite and Participation of Corporate Directors in the Governance of American Institutions." *American Sociological Review,* 44, 553–72.

———. 1982. "Classwide Rationality in the Politics of Managers and Directors of Large Corporations in the United States and Great Britain." *Administrative Science Quarterly,* 27, 199–226.

———. 1984. *The Inner Circle.* New York: Oxford University Press.

Uzzi, Brian. 1996. "The Sources and Consequences of Embeddedness for the Economic Performance of Organizations: The Network Effect." *American Sociological Review,* 60, 674–98.

———. 1997. "Social Structure and Competition in Interfirm Networks: The Paradox of Embeddedness." *Administrative Science Quarterly,* 42, 35–67.

Uzzi, Brian, and Zoe I. Barsness. 1998. "Contingent Employment in British Establishments: Organizational Determinants of Fixed-Term Hires and Part-Time Workers." *Social Forces,* 76, 976–1005.

Uzzi, Brian, and Ryon Lancaster. 2004. "Embeddedness and Price Formation in the Corporate Law Market." *American Sociological Review,* 69, 319–44.

Valcour, P. Monique. 2002. "Managerial Behavior in a Multiplex Role System." *Human Relations,* 55, 1163–88.

Van de Ven, Andrew H. 1979. "Howard E. Aldrich: Organizations and Environments." *Administrative Science Quarterly,* 24, 320–26.

Van de Ven, Andrew H., Andre L. Delbecq, and Richard Koenig Jr. 1976. "Determinants of Coordination Modes Within Organizations." *American Sociological Review,* 41, 322–38.

Van de Ven, Andrew H., and Diane L. Ferry. 1980. *Measuring and Assessing Organizations.* New York: Wiley.

Van Houton, Donald R. 1987. "The Political Economy and Technical Control of Work Humanization in Sweden During the 1970s and 1980s." *Work and Occupations,* 14, 483–513.

Vaughan, Diane. 1983. *Controlling Unlawful Organizational Behavior: Social Structure and Corporate Misconduct.* Chicago: University of Chicago Press.

———. 1996. *The Challenger Launch Decision: Risky Technology, Culture, and Deviance at NASA.* Chicago: University of Chicago Press.

———. 1999. "The Dark Side of Organizations: Mistake, Misconduct, and Disaster." *Annual Review of Sociology,* 25, 271–305.

Vroom, Victor H., and Philip W. Yetton. 1973. *Leadership and Decision Making*. Pittsburgh, PA: University of Pittsburgh Press.

Wade, James B., Anand Swaminathan, and Michael S. Saxon. 1998. "Normative and Resource Flow Consequences of Local Regulations in the American Brewing Industry, 1845–1918." *Administrative Science Quarterly*, 43, no. 4, 905–35.

Walker, Henry A., Barbara C. Ilardi, Anne M. McMahon, and Mary L. Fennell. 1996. "Gender, Interaction and Leadership." *Social Psychology Quarterly*, 59, 255–72.

Warren, Roland. 1967. "The Interorganizational Field as a Focus for Investigation." *Administrative Science Quarterly*, 12, 396–419.

Weber, Klaus, Kathryn Heinze, and Michaela DeSoucey. (Forthcoming). "Forage for Thought: Mobilizing Codes in the Movement for Grass-Fed Meat and Dairy Products." *Administrative Science Quarterly*.

Weber, Max. 1946. *From Max Weber: Essays in Sociology*, trans. and ed. H. Gerth and C. W. Mills. New York: Oxford University Press.

———. 1947. *The Theory of Social and Economic Organization*, trans. A. M. Parsons and T. Parsons. New York: Free Press.

Weick, Karl E., and Karlene H. Roberts. 1993. "Collective Mind in Organizations: Heedful Interrelations on Flight Decks." *Administrative Science Quarterly*, 38, 357–81.

Weiner, Nan. 1977. "Situational and Leadership Influence on Organizational Performance." Unpublished paper, College of Administrative Science, Ohio State University, Columbus.

Westphal, James D., Ranjay Gulati, and Steven M. Shortell. 1997. "Customization and Conformity: An Institutional and Network Perspective on the Content and Consequences of TQM Adoption." *Administrative Science Quarterly*, 42, 366–94.

Westphal, James D., Marc D. Seidel, and Katherine J. Stewart. 2001. "Second-Order Imitation: Uncovering Latent Effects of Board Network Ties." *Administrative Science Quarterly*, 46, 717–47.

Wharton, Amy S., and James N. Baron. 1987. "So Happy Together? The Impact of Gender Segregation on Men at Work." *American Sociological Review*, 52, 574–87.

Whitley, Richard. 1999. *Divergent Capitalisms*. London: Oxford University Press.

Wilensky, Harold. 1967. *Organizational Intelligence: Knowledge and Policy in Government and Industry*. New York: Basic Books.

Williams, Katherine Y., and Charles A. O'Reilly. 1998. "Demography and Diversity in Organizations: A Review of 40 Years of Research." *Research in Organizational Behavior*, 20, 77–140.

Williamson, Oliver E. 1981. "The Economics of Organization: The Transaction Cost Approach." *American Journal of Sociology*, 87, 548–77.

———. 1983. *Markets and Hierarchies: Analysis and Anti-Trust Implications*. New York: Free Press.

———. 1991. "Comparative Economic Organization: The Analysis of Discrete Structural Alternatives." *Administrative Science Quarterly*, 39, no. 2, 269–96.

Wood, James R. 1975. "Legitimate Control and Organizational Transcendence." *Social Forces*, 54, 199–211.

Woodward, Joan. 1958. *Management and Technology*. London: Her Majesty's Stationery Office.

———. 1965. *Industrial Organizations: Theory and Practice*. London: Oxford University Press.

Work in America. 1973. Prepared under Auspices of W. E. Upjohn Institute. Cambridge, MA: MIT Press.

Wrong, Dennis H. 1961. "The Oversocialized Conception of Man in Modern Sociology." *American Sociological Review,* 26, no. 2, 183–93.

Yeager, Peter C. 1982. "Review of Francis W. Steckmest, Corporate Performance: The Key to Public Trust (New York: McGraw-Hill)." *Contemporary Sociology,* 11, 747–48.

Young, Ruth C. 1988. "Is Population Ecology a Useful Paradigm for the Study of Organizations?" *American Journal of Sociology,* 94, 1–24.

———. 1989. "Reply to Freeman and Hannan and Brittain and Wholey." *American Journal of Sociology,* 95, 445–46.

Yuchtman, Ephraim, and Stanley Seashore. 1967. "A System Resource Approach to Organizational Effectiveness." *American Sociological Review,* 32, 891–903.

Yukl, Gary A. 2002. *Leadership in Organizations,* 2nd ed. Upper Saddle River, NJ: Prentice Hall.

Yukl, G. A., S. Wall, and R. Lepsinger, 1990. "Preliminary Report on the Validation of the Management Practices Survey," in *Measures of Leadership,* eds, K. E. Clark and M. B. Clark. West Orange, NJ: Leadership Library of America.

Zajac, Edward J., and James D. Westphal. 1996. "Director Reputation, CEO-Board Power, and the Dynamics of Board Interlocks." *Administrative Science Quarterly,* 41, 507–29.

———. 2004. "The Social Construction of Market Value: Institutionalization and Learning Perspectives on Stock Market Reactions." *American Sociological Review,* 69, 433–57.

Zald, Mayer, ed. 1970. *Organizational Change: The Political Economy of the YMCA.* Chicago: University of Chicago Press.

Zald, Mayer N., and Patricia Denton. 1963. "From Evangelism to General Service: The Transformation of the YMCA." *Administrative Science Quarterly,* 8, no. 2, 214–34.

Zalkind, Sheldon, and Timothy W. Costello. 1962. "Perceptions: Some Recent Research and Implications for Administration." *Administrative Science Quarterly,* 7, 218–35.

Zaltman, Gerald, Robert Duncan, and Jonny Holbek. 1973. *Innovations and Organizations.* New York: Wiley Interscience.

Zammuto, Raymond F. 1982. *Assessing Organizational Effectiveness.* Albany: State University of New York Press.

———. 1984. "A Comparison of Multiple Constituency Models of Organizational Effectiveness." *Academy of Management Review,* 9, 606–16.

Zammuto, Raymond F., Terri L. Griffith, Ann Majchrak, Deborah J. Dougherty, and Smaer Faraj. 2007. "Information Technology and the Changing Fabric of Organizations." *Organization Science,* 18, 749–62.

Zeitlin, Maurice. 1974. "Corporate Ownership and Control: The Large Corporation and the Capitalist Class." *American Journal of Sociology,* 79, 1073–1119.

———. 1976. "In Class Theory of the Large Corporation: Response to Others." *American Journal of Sociology,* 81, 894–903.

Zenger, Todd R., and Barbara S. Lawrence. 1989. "Organizational Demography: The Differential Effects of Age and Tenure Distributions on Technical Communication." *Academy of Management Journal,* 32, 353–76.

Zey, Mary. 1992. "Criticisms of Rational Choice Models," in *Decision Making: Alternatives to Rational Choice Models,* ed. Mary Zey, 9–31. Newbury Park, CA: Sage.

Zilber, Tammar B. 2002. "Institutionalization as an Interplay Between Actions, Meanings, and Actors: The Case of a Rape Crisis Center in Israel." *Academy of Management Journal,* 45, no. 1, 234–54.

Zimmerman, Monica A., and Gerald J. Zeitz. 2002. "Beyond Survival: Achieving New Venture Growth by Building Legitimacy." *The Academy of Management Review,* 27, 414–31.

Zucker, Lynne G. 1977. "The Role of Institutionalization in Cultural Persistence." *American Sociological Review,* 42, 726–43.

———. 1986. "Production of Trust: Institutional Sources of Economic Structure 1840–1920." *Research in Organizational Behavior,* 8, 53–111.

Zucker, Lynne G., Michael R. Darby, and Marilynn B. Brewer. 1998. "Intellectual Human Capital and the Birth of US Biotechnology Enterprises." *American Economic Review,* 88, no. 1, 290–306.

Zucker, Lynne G., Michael R. Darby, and M. Torero. 2002. "Labor Mobility from Academe to Commerce." *Journal of Labor Economics,* 20, no. 3, 629–60.

Name Index

A

Abbott, Andrew, 16, 66, 81, 143
Adler, Nancy J., 96
Aharonson, Barak S., 143
Ahuja, Gautam, 146
Alba, Richard D., 136
Albert, Stuart, 204
Aldrich, Howard E., 37, 38, 49, 53, 85, 122, 142, 144, 145, 177, 179, 180, 182
Allen, Michael Patrick, 73, 103, 104, 107
Alliger, G. M., 96
Allison, Paul D., 10
Allmendinger, Jutta, 156
Alter, Catherine, 144
Alutto, Joseph, 120
Alvesson, Mats, 76
Amburgey, Terry L., 182, 206
Anderson, Theodore R., 46
Andrews, Alice O., 158
Angle, Harold L., 193
Ansell, C. K., 73
Appelbaum, Eileen, 43
Appold, Stephen J., 63
Argote, Linda, 35, 199, 202, 203, 206
Argyris, Chris, 49
Aronowitz, Stanley, 3
Arum, Richard, 2
Ash, Michael, 156
Astley, W. Graham, 162
Athanassaides, John C., 125
At-Twarjri, Mohammad I., 63

B

Bacharach, Samuel B., 72, 73, 120, 179
Bachrach, Peter, 118
Badgett, M. V. L., 156
Baldridge, J. Victor, 29
Bales, Robert F., 93
Balser, Deborah B., 9
Bamberger, Peter, 179
Banerjee, Abhijit, 66, 177
Baratz, Morton S., 118
Barley, Stephen R., 4, 5, 16, 21, 28, 36, 82, 83, 154
Barnard, Chester I., 71
Barnett, William P., 142, 182
Baron, James N., 10, 27, 32, 81, 155, 158
Barsness, Zoe I., 5
Bartley, Timothy, 156
Bass, Bernard M., 122, 206
Bassoff, Paula, 200
Batt, Rosemary, 43
Baum, Joel A. C., 143, 184, 206, 207
Baumol, William J., 32
Bavelas, Alex, 133
Beamish, Thomas D., 115
Becker, Gary S., 173
Beckman, Christine M., 57, 116, 146, 149, 154, 180
Beeghley, Leonard, 140
Belasco, James A., 120
Belliveau, Maura A., 151
Benson, J. Kenneth, 145

Berger, Joseph, 5, 96
Bergesen, Albert J., 9
Berle, Adolph A., 65, 107, 151
Beyer, Janice M., 58, 117, 151
Bianco, Anthony, 9
Bidwell, Charles E., 177
Bielby, Denise D., 158
Bielby, William T., 10
Bielefeld, Wolfgang, 151
Bierstedt, Robert, 69
Biggart, Nicole Woolsey, 64
Bikchandani, Sushil, 177
Birnbaum, Phillip H., 63
Blake, R. R., 94
Blalock, Hubert M., 158
Blau, Francine D., 6, 10, 158
Blau, Judith R., 54, 136
Blau, Peter M., 15, 20, 28, 31, 32, 36,
    37, 38, 41, 42, 46, 47, 53, 69, 73,
    78, 129, 141, 186, 188
Blinder, Alan S., 32
Blum, Terry C., 61, 183
Boeker, Warren, 77, 104, 151, 202
Boje, David M., 34, 37, 145
Bonjean, Charles M., 38
Boraas, Stephanie, 81
Borman, W. C., 91
Boulding, Kenneth E., 83
Boychuk, Terry, 62
Brantley, Peter, 72, 151
Brass, Daniel J., 72
Brewer, John, 129
Brewer, Marilynn B., 152
Broschak, Jospeh P., 10, 149
Brown, M. Craig, 59, 60, 62, 103,
    168, 176
Brown, Richard Harvey, 18
Brown, Warren B., 104
Browning, Larry D., 117
Brunsson, Nils, 123
Brush, D. H., 91
Bucher, Rue, 76
Budros, Art, 32, 116
Bugùra, Ayse, 67
Bunting, David, 150

Burke, John P., 18
Burkhardt, Marlene E., 72
Burnham, Robert A., 201
Burns, James M., 206
Burns, Tom, 27, 31, 42, 163
Burrell, Gibson, 162
Burt, Ronald S., 73, 149, 151
Burton, M. Diane, 57, 154, 180

C

Cameron, Kim, 194
Campbell, John P., 190, 194
Caplow, Theodore, 144
Caragonne, P., 146
Carley, Kathleen, 199
Carli, Linda, 96
Carroll, Glenn R., 64, 65, 105, 155,
    177, 178, 179, 182
Carruthers, Bruce G., 143
Carstensen, Fred V., 11
Casciaro, Tiziana, 170
Champagne, Anthony, 11
Chandler, A. D., Jr., 65, 115, 170
Chemers, M. M., 99
Chen, Ming-Jer, 48
Child, John, 36, 37, 38, 46, 65,
    169, 198
Christenson, James A., 8
Christman, Kenneth P., 149
Clark, Burton, 205
Clarke, Lee B., 87, 115
Clawson, Dan, 150
Clegg, Stewart R., 13, 33, 67,
    69, 122
Clinard, Marshall B., 12
Coase, R. H., 172
Cohen, Lisa E., 10
Cohen, Michael D., 112, 115, 208
Cohen, Wesley M., 199
Coleman, James S., 7, 108, 154, 169
Collins, Randall, 140
Conaty, Joseph, 63
Conlon, Edward J., 194

Connolly, Terry, 194
Cook, Cynthia R., 15
Cook, Karen S., 143
Cooper, David J., 83
Corder, Judy, 38
Correll, Shelley J., 5
Coser, Lewis, 85
Costello, Timothy W., 124, 125
Craig, John G., 78
Crittenden, Ann, 9
Crozier, Michael, 74
Cummings, Larry C., 81
Cummings, Larry L., 193
Curphy, Gordon J., 93
Cyert, Richard M., 112, 115, 116, 171,
    189, 199, 201

D

Dahl, Robert, 69
Dalin, M. Tina, 64
Dalton, Melville, 80
Damanpour, Fariborz, 200, 201
Darby, Michael R., 152, 154
Darr, Eric, 202
D'Aunno, Thomas D., 62
David G. McKendrick, 142, 182
David, Robert J., 59, 61, 172, 174
Davis, Gerald F., 59, 116, 147, 150,
    151, 156, 168, 170, 188
Davis, Kingsley, 140
Davis, Stanley M., 54
Davis-Blake, Allison, 4
Day, D. V., 106
Delacroix, Jacques, 155, 179
Delbecq, Andre L., 38, 54
Della Fave, L. Richard, 150
Denton, Patricia, 205
DeSoucey, Michaela, 157
Deutsch, Stuart J., 194
DeVader, C. L., 96
Dewar, Robert D., 34, 37, 201
Dickson, W. J., 21
Diekmann, Kristina A., 170

Digman, J. M., 93
DiMaggio, Paul J., 59, 60, 61,
    176, 177
Dirsmith, Mark W., 67
DiTomaso, Nancy, 158
Dobbin, Frank R., 61, 62, 67, 155
Domhoff, G. William, 11, 150
Donahue, James D., 11
Donaldson, Lex, 25, 37, 38, 46,
    65, 162
Donaldson, Thomas, 194
Dornbusch, Sanford M., 39, 52, 71
Dowell, Glenn, 142, 151, 184
Dowell, Myron, 151
Downs, Anthony, 136
Dukerich, Janet M., 91, 204
Dun and Bradstreet, 15
Duncan, Robert B., 159, 200, 201
Dunkerley, David, 13, 33, 122
Durkheim, Emile, 59
Dutton, Jane E., 204

E

Eagly, Alice H., 96
Easterlin, Richard A., 157
Edelman, Lauren B., 61, 154, 155
Edmondson, Amy C., 202
Egelhoff, William G., 13
Ehrlich, Sanford B., 91
Eisenhardt, Kathleen M., 152,
    163, 170
Eitzen, D. Stanley, 103
Elkind, Peter, 195, 208
Emerson, Richard M., 71, 164
Emery, Fredrick E., 43, 142
England, Paula, 10, 81
Enz, Cathy A., 76
Etzioni, Amitai, 18, 72, 73, 78, 91,
    94, 187, 193
Evan, William M., 144, 147,
    164, 200
Evanisko, Martin J., 200
Evans, James, 83

F

Faulkner, Robert R., 28
Fayol, Henri, 23
Fein, Lisa C., 61
Feldman, Martha S., 123
Feldman, Maryann P., 143
Fennell, Mary C., 28, 147
Ferber, Marianne A., 6, 10, 158
Fernandez, Roberto M., 10, 73, 157
Ferry, Diane L., 37, 145
Fichman, Mark, 145, 151
Fiedler, Fred E., 95, 199
Fields, David, 61, 183
Filardo, E. K., 96
Filley, Alan C., 98
Finkelstein, Sydney, 72
Fligstein, Neil, 61, 67, 72, 74, 104,
    151, 171, 177
Fogarty, Timothy J., 67
Follet, Mary P., 23
Freeland, Robert F., 104, 115
Freeman, John H., 65, 177, 178, 179,
    180, 196
Freeman, R. Edward, 197
Freidson, Eliot, 40, 82, 83
French, John R. P., 73
Friedland, Roger, 150
Fu, P. P., 96
Fuller, Sally Riggs, 155

G

Galaskiewicz, Joseph, 9, 146, 150, 151
Galbraith, Jay R., 54, 57
Gamson, William, 102
Garcia, J. E., 99
Gargiulo, Martin, 149, 169
Geeraerts, Guy, 47, 48
Georgiou, Petro, 190, 192
Gersick, Connie J. G., 142
Giddens, Anthony, 21
Giordano, Peggy C., 14, 194

Glaser, Jurgen, 5
Glass, Jennifer, 5
Glisson, Charles A., 53
Glynn, Mary Ann, 59, 199
Goes, James B., 144
Gooderham, Paul N., 62, 184
Goodman, Jodi, 61, 183
Goodman, Robert S., 197
Goodstein, Jerry D., 61, 183
Gould, Roger V., 73
Gouldner, Alvin, 93, 141
Govindarajan, Vijay, 63
Graebner, Melissa A., 170
Granovetter, Mark, 116, 149
Grant, Donald Sherman, II, 9
Greenberg, Danna, 73
Greenwood, Royston, 38
Gresov, Christopher, 197
Greve, Henrich R., 199
Gross, Edward, 78, 190
Grusky, Oscar, 102, 103
Guest, Robert, 100
Guetzkow, Harold, 133, 134
Guillen, Mauro F., 64, 116
Gulati, Ranjay, 59, 117, 146,
    149, 169
Guler, Isen, 64, 116
Gulick, Luther, 23
Gupta, Anil, 63
Gupta, Parveen P., 67

H

Haas, Martine R., 119
Hackman, J. Richard, 40, 156
Hage, Jerald, 25, 28, 29, 33, 34, 35, 37,
    38, 42, 52, 83, 129, 130, 132, 144,
    147, 169, 200, 201
Halberstam, David, 128
Hall, Richard H., 3, 22, 26, 36, 41, 64,
    81, 83, 97, 177
Halliday, Terence C., 143
Hambrick, Donald C., 48, 74

Hamilton, Gary L., 64
Hamner, W. Clay, 98
Han, Shin-Kap, 172, 174
Hanada, Mitsuyo, 64
Hannan, Michael T., 65, 177, 178, 179,
    180, 182, 196
Hansen, Morten T., 119
Hardy, Cynthia, 69
Harquail, Cecilia V., 204
Harrison, Jeffrey S., 197
Haunschild, Pamela R., 116, 143, 146,
    149, 182, 199
Haveman, Heather A., 10, 67, 156,
    177, 182, 184, 207
Hawley, Amos H., 139
Healy, Kieran, 147
Heilbroner, Robert, 13
Heinze, Kathryn, 157
Heller, Frank A., 120
Helmich, Donald, 104
Heydebrand, Wolf V., 26, 31, 46,
    47, 129
Hiatt, Shon, 65, 107, 190
Hickson, David J., 46, 47, 53,
    73, 74
Hills, Frederick S., 77
Hinings, C. R., 38, 141
Hirsch, Paul M., 66, 177
Hirschman, Albert O., 78
Hirshleifer, David, 177
Hochschild, Arlie Russell, 14
Hoff, Timothy, 82
Hogan, Joyce, 93
Hogan, Robert, 93
Holbek, Jonny, 200, 201
Hollander, Edwin P., 95
Hornug, Severin, 5
Hougland, James G., 78
House, Robert J., 94, 95, 98
Huber, George P., 81
Huffington, Arianna, 107
Hull, Raymond, 129
Hyde, Cheryl, 58
Hylton, Lydia, 143, 145, 146

I

Ingram, Paul, 145, 179, 184, 206
Inkson, J., 46, 47
Inman, Crist, 179, 184

J

Jackall, Robert, 18, 118
Jacoby, Sanford, 78
Jaeger, Alfred M., 62, 63
James, David R., 107, 151
Jenkins, J. Craig, 190
Jennings, P. Devereaux, 61, 155, 177
Jensen, Michael C., 149, 195
John, D., 146
Johnson, George, 10
Johnson, Jerry B., 62, 63
Jones, Andrew W., 9
Judge, Timothy A., 206
Judy C. Shetler, 117
Julian, James W., 95

K

Kabanoff, Boris, 81
Kahn, Robert L., 91, 123, 126,
    127, 130
Kalev, Alexandra, 155
Kalleberg, Arne L., 10, 26
Kane, Aimee A., 202, 203
Kanter, Rosabeth Moss, 7, 73, 76,
    78, 122, 158
Kaplan, Abraham, 69
Karasek, Robert A., 40
Karau, Steven J., 96
Karichalil, Richard, 104
Kasarda, John D., 63, 177
Katz, Daniel, 79, 80, 81, 91, 123,
    126, 127, 130
Katz, Harry C., 179
Katz, Ralph, 137

Kaufman, Herbert, 204
Kaufman, Robert L., 26
Keeley, Michael, 195
Keister, Lisa A., 150
Kellogg, Katherine C., 57
Kelly, Dawn, 182, 206
Kelly, Erin L., 155
Kerbo, Harold R., 150
Kessler-Harris, Alice, 158
Khanna, Tarun, 146
Kidder, Tracy, 16
Kieser, Alfred, 198
Kilburn, Harold C., Jr., 149
Kim, Yong-Hak, 11
Kimberly, John R., 49, 200
King, Brayden G., 156
King, Marissa, 156
King, Thomas, 156
Kirsch, David A., 32
Klatzky, Sheila, 31, 46, 47
Klauss, Rudi, 122
Klonglan, Gerald E., 145
Knoke, David, 11, 15, 18
Kochan, Thomas A., 81
Koenig, Richard, Jr., 38, 54
Kogut, Bruce, 149
Kohn, Melvin L., 4, 41
Koput, Kenneth W., 148, 149, 206
Kornhauser, William, 36
Kraatz, Matthew S., 178, 207
Kralewski, John E., 47
Krohn, Karl R., 9
Kruytbosch, Carlos, 151
Kuhn, Thomas S., 162
Kunda, Gideon, 4, 5, 28, 58, 83
Kurtzberg, Terri, 202

L

Lachman, Ron, 77
Lammers, Cornelius J., 18, 40, 77
Lancaster, Ryon, 149
Lant, Theresa K., 199, 201
Laumann, Edward O., 11, 18

Lawler, Edward J., 72, 73, 120, 179
Lawrence, Barbara S., 6, 125, 157, 158
Lawrence, Paul R., 28, 29, 31, 41, 54,
    79, 87, 142, 152, 153, 162, 198
Leavitt, Harold J., 133
Lee, Brandon H., 157
Leicht, Kevin T., 26, 28
Lester, Marilyn, 197
Levine, Adeline Gordon, 12
Levine, John M., 202, 203
Levine, Sol, 142, 143, 145
Levinthal, Daniel A., 145, 151, 199
Levitt, Barbara, 116, 199
Lieberson, Stanley, 105
Lin, Nan, 73
Lincoln, James R., 53, 64
Lipset, Seymour Martin, 108, 206
Litwak, Eugene, 26, 143, 145, 146
Long, Anthony, 77,
Long, J. Scott, 10
Lord, R. G., 96, 106
Lorsch, Jay W., 28, 29, 31, 41, 54, 79,
    87, 142, 152, 153, 162, 198
Lotz, Roy E., 103
Lounsbury, Michael, 66, 156, 177
Lozano, Beverly, 5

M

Maas, Meridean Leone, 146
MacDuffie, John Paul, 43
MacPherson, J. M., 64, 116
Mahmoudi, Hoda, 63
Mahoney, Thomas A., 77
Makowsky, Michael, 140
Malan, Leon, 62
Mannari, Hiroshi, 63
Manning, Peter K., 123
Manns, Curtis L., 201
Mansfield, Roger, 38, 46, 47
Mara-Drita, Iona, 155
March, James G., 112, 113, 115, 116,
    119, 123, 128, 142, 171, 189, 199,
    201, 208

Marcus, Alfred A., 143, 197
Markham, William T., 38
Marquis, Christopher, 59
Marrett, Cora Bagley, 129
Marsden, Peter V., 15, 142, 179
Marsh, Robert M., 63
Massie, Joseph L., 25
Mattis, Mary, 96
Maurice, Marc, 63
McBride, Kerry, 64
McCaffrey, David, 82
McCarthy, John D., 156
McEvily, Bill, 143, 159
McEvily, Susan K., 152
McEwen, William, 164, 167, 168
McGinnis, Robert, 10
McKelvey, Bill, 177
McKinley, William, 32, 54
McLean, Bethany, 195, 208
McMillan, Charles J., 13
Means, Gardiner C., 65, 107, 151
Mechanic, David, 71, 73
Meindl, James R., 91
Merriam-Webster, 161
Merton, Robert K., 2, 20, 35,
    144, 147
Meyer, Alan D., 142, 207
Meyer, John W., 23
Meyer, Marshall W., 29, 38, 46, 59, 60,
    62, 159, 168, 176, 194
Mezias, Stephen J., 61
Michels, Robert, 65, 77, 107, 190
Miller, C. Chet, 53
Miller, George A., 36, 63
Milliken, Frances J., 160, 199, 201
Mills, C. Wright, 11, 150
Milward, H. Brinton, 144
Mindl, James R., 105
Miner, Anne S., 4, 143, 182, 200
Mintz, Beth, 150
Mintzberg, Henry, 69
Mitsuhashi, Hitoshi, 32
Mizruchi, Mark S., 61, 149, 150, 167
Moch, Michael K., 200
Mohan, Mary Leslie, 123

Molnar, Joseph J., 145
Molotch, Harvey, 197
Montansani, John R., 63
Moore, Wilbert, 140
Moore, William L., 105
Moorman, Christine, 200
Morgan, Gareth, 79, 151, 162
Morgan, Glenn, 62
Morrill, Calvin, 88
Morse, Edward V., 200
Mouton, J. S., 94
Mueller, Charles W., 26
Mulatu, M. S., 41
Mulford, Charles L., 145

N

Nagel, Stuart, 11
Nee, Victor, 64
Needleman, Carolyn, 12
Needleman, Martin L., 12
Neef, Marian, 11
Neustadt, Alan, 150
Nohria, Nitin, 146
Nordhaug, Odd, 62, 184
Nuss, Clifford, 116
Nystrom, Paul C., 48

O

Oates, G., 41
Ocasio, William, 151
O'Connor, James F., 105
O'Connor, Joseph P., 151
Oldham, Greg R., 40
Oliver, Christine, 177, 183
Olsen, Johan P., 112, 115, 208
O'Reilly, Charles A., 151, 158, 159
Organ, Dennis, 98
Orlikowski, Wanda J., 57
Ornstein, Michael, 150
Oron, Israela, 158
Osterman, Paul, 107

Ott, J. Steven, 58
Ouchi, William G., 54, 58, 62, 63

P

Padgett, John F., 73, 119
Page, Karen L., 146
Palmer, Donald A., 61, 150, 177
Panian, Sharon K., 73, 103, 104
Parcel, Toby L., 26
Park, Seung Ho, 144
Parks-Yancy, Rochelle, 158
Parsons, Talcott, 82
Paruchuri, Srikanth, 156, 184
Pascale, Richard, 126
Paul, Benjamin D., 143
Paul S. Goodman, 190, 194, 195
Pazy, Asya, 158
Pennings, Johannes M., 26, 34, 149,
    150, 190, 194, 195, 200
Perlow, Leslie A., 40
Perratta, Heather G., 179
Perrow, Charles, 1, 9, 51, 74, 112,
    113, 115, 141, 167, 171, 187,
    188, 194
Perrucci, Robert, 9
Perry, James L., 193
Peter, Laurence J., 129
Peters, Thomas J., 58, 189
Peterson, Richard A., 78
Pfeffer, Jeffrey, 10, 32, 73, 74, 77, 105,
    106, 118, 120, 158, 162, 163, 164,
    167, 170, 175, 171, 177, 182
Pheysey, Diana C., 46, 53, 74
Phillips, Damon J., 146
Piccolo, Ronald F., 206
Pilisuk, Marc, 9
Piskorski, Mikotaj J., 170
Pitt, Laura, 47
Podolny, Joel M., 146
Polzer, Jeffrey T., 57
Pondy, Louis R., 77, 85
Porter, Michael E., 65, 163
Post, Corinne, 158

Powell, Walter W., 59, 60, 61, 148,
    149, 176, 206
Prescott, Jill E., 152
Preston, Lee E., 194
Price, James L., 26
Price, Richard H., 62
Priest, T. B., 74, 154
Prokesch, Steven E., 177
Provan, Keith G., 144, 151
Pugh, Derek S., 28, 29, 34, 38, 41,
    46, 47, 52, 53, 74

R

Ragins, Belle R., 96
Rahim, M. Afzahur, 86, 87
Rao, Hayagreeva, 67, 156, 184
Raphael, Edna, 30
Raven, Bertram, 73
Reagans, Ray, 159
Reich, Robert, 11
Reinganum, Marc R., 105
Reskin, Barbara F., 5, 7, 10, 81, 158
Revkin, Andrew C., 9
Rhee, Jaehoon, 158
Ridgeway, Cecilia L., 5
Rifkin, Jeremy, 3
Ringdal, Kristen, 62, 184
Ritzer, George, 27
Roberts, Karlene H., 132
Roberts, Peter W., 145
Rodgers, William M., 81
Roethlisberger, Fritz, 21
Rogelberg, Steven G., 136
Romo, Frank P., 117
Roos, Patricia A., 7
Rosenbaum, James E., 7
Rosenweig, Philip M., 63
Rosow, Jerome M., 3
Ross, Jerry, 116
Rosseau, Denise M., 5
Rothman, Robert A., 74, 154
Rothschild, Joyce, 38
Rothschild-Witt, Joyce, 16

Rowan, Brian, 23, 61
Roy, William G., 11, 150
Rozgonyi, Tamas, 39
Rushing, William, 46

S

Sabel, Charles F., 79
Salancik, Gerald R., 73, 74, 77,
    105, 106, 163, 164, 167, 170,
    171, 175
Sanford, R. Nevitt, 79
Satow, Roberta, 82
Saxon, Michael S., 156
Schein, Virginia E., 96
Schmidt, Stuart M., 81
Schneiberg, Marc, 156
Schoenherr, Richard A., 28, 31, 32,
    41, 42, 46, 47, 53
Schooler, Carmi, 4, 41
Schoonhoven, Claudia Bird, 162
Schumpeter, Joseph A., 152
Schwartz, Michael, 117, 150
Scotch, Norman, 102
Scott, W. Richard, 15, 21, 25, 32, 36,
    39, 52, 59, 62, 71, 76, 129, 186,
    147, 157, 163, 176
Seabright, Mark A., 145
Seashore, Stanley E., 191, 197
Seidel, Marc D., 116
Seiler, Lauren H., 8
Selznick, Philip, 92, 141, 168, 205
Sewell, William H., 21
Shatin, Deborah, 47, 144, 145
Shepard, Jon M., 78
Shortell, Steven M., 59
Siengthai, Sununta, 63
Sills, David L., 190, 205
Simon, Herbert A., 66, 111, 112, 113,
    119, 142, 187, 199
Simons, Tal, 158
Simpson, Richard L., 130
Sine, Wesley D., 32, 184
Singh, Jitendra V., 63, 150

Slater, Philip E., 93
Smircich, Linda, 58
Smith, Kenwyn, 84
Smith-Doerr, Laurel, 148, 149, 206
Somaya, Deepak, 197
Sonnenstuhl, Walter, 179
Soref, Michael, 107, 151
Sorge, Arndt, 63
Soule, Sarah A., 156
Spangler, Eve, 34
Sproul, Lee S., 128
Stafford, Frank, 10
Staggenborg, Suzanne, 156
Stalker, G. M., 27, 31, 42, 163
Starbuck, William H., 48, 159, 160
Stauffer, Robert E., 46, 47, 129
Staw, Barry M., 116
Stearns, Linda Brewster, 150
Steckmest, Francis W., 18
Steers, R. M., 191, 193
Stevenson, William B., 29, 40, 73
Stewart, Katherine J., 116
Stimson, Gerry, 157
Stinchcombe, Arthur L., 22, 26,
    48, 122
Stogdill, R. M., 93
Storing, Herbert J., 112
Strang, David, 27, 59, 61
Suarez, Sandra L., 64
Suchman, Mark C., 154, 155
Sullivan, Bilian N., 199
Summers, Gene F., 8
Sutherland, Edwin H., 12
Sutton, John R., 61, 67
Sutton, Robert I., 62
Swaminathan, Anand, 156, 177

T

Tannenbaum, Arnold S., 38, 39
Taylor, Fredrick W., 23
Terkel, Studs, 3
Terlaak, Anne, 61
Terreberry, Shirley, 142

Thatcher, Sherry M. B., 5
Thomas, Alan Berkeley, 106
Thompson, James D., 50, 114, 163,
    164, 165, 166, 167, 168
Thompson, Victor, 35
Thye, Shane, 179
Tickner, Joseph A., 115
Tilly, Charles, 4, 156
Tilly, Chris, 4
Tinsley, Catherine H., 170
Tittle, Charles R., 48
Tolbert, Pamela S., 6, 10, 16, 25, 36,
    58, 61, 62, 65, 66, 67, 82, 107,
    141, 154, 157, 158, 175, 176,
    177, 179, 184, 190
Torero, M., 154
Townsend, Bickley, 96
Toynbee, Arnold, 13
Trice, Harrison M., 58
Trist, Eric L., 43, 142
Trow, Martin A., 108
Tsui, Anne S., 194, 197
Turk, Herman, 143, 146
Turner, Jonathan H., 140

U

Urwick L., 23
Üsdiken, Behlül, 67
Useem, Michael, 9, 11, 150
Uzzi, Brian, 4, 5, 117, 149

V

Valcour, P. Monique, 78, 108
Van Buren, Mark E., 10
Van de Ven, Andrew H., 37, 38, 54,
    145, 162, 183
Van Houton, Donald R., 67
Vaughan, Diane, 29, 110
Vroom, Victor H., 94, 95

W

Wade, James B., 151, 156
Walker, Gordon, 149
Walker, Henry A., 96
Warkov, Seymour, 46
Warner, Malcolm, 46, 63
Warren, Roland, 143
Waterman, Robert H., Jr., 58, 189
Weber, Klaus, 157
Weber, Max, 22, 69, 70
Weick, Karl E., 132
Weinberg, Nancy, 10
Weiner, Nan, 106
Welch, Ivo, 177
Werking, Richard Hume, 11
Westphal, James D., 59, 116, 151,
    178, 195
Wharton, Amy S., 158
Whetten, David A., 34, 37, 145,
    194, 204
White, Paul E., 142, 143, 145
Whitley, Richard, 64
Whitt, J. Allen, 38
Wilensky, Harold, 128
Williams, Katherine Y., 158,
    159
Williamson, Ian O., 197
Williamson, Oliver E., 65, 172,
    173, 175
Willmott, Hugh, 76
Winkler, Anne E., 6, 10, 158
Wolff, Edward N., 32
Wong, Gilbert Y. Y., 63
Wood, James R., 78
Woodward, Joan, 24, 25, 50
Work in America, 3
Wrong, Dennis H., 66, 177

X

Xu, Weiman, 64

Y

Yates, JoAnne, 57
Yeager, Peter C., 12, 18
Yetman, Norman R., 103
Yetton, Philip W., 94, 95
Yoon, Yeongkoo, 179
Young, Ruth C., 183
Yuchtman, Ephraim, 191
Yukl, Gary A., 90, 92, 96

Z

Zajac, Edward J., 151, 178, 195, 207
Zald, Mayer, 75, 77, 151, 156, 205
Zalkind, Sheldon, 124, 125

Zaltman, Gerald, 200, 201
Zammuto, Raymond F., 57, 194, 196
Zeitlin, Maurice, 107
Zeitz, Gerald J., 53, 180
Zelditch, Morris, 5
Zenger, Todd R., 125
Zey, Mary, 111
Zhang, Xiaomeng, 197
Zhou, Xueguang, 61, 177
Zhu, Xiumei, 5
Zilber, Tammar B., 58, 62, 145
Zimmerman, Monica A., 180
Zucker, Lynne G., 25, 61, 62, 66, 70,
    141, 152, 154, 168, 175, 176, 177,
    184, 194

Subject Index

A

Absorption of uncertainty, 119
Adaptive learning approach, 199–201
Administrative intensity, 32
Affirmative action, 81
Agenda setting, 118–19
Airline industry, 206–7
American companies, characteristics
    of, 63
Ascriptive characteristics, 5–6
Asset specificity, 173, 174
Aston group, 34, 52, 53
Authority, 69–71, 118. *See also*
    Power
Authorized power, 71
Autokinetic effect, 60
Awareness, interorganizational
    relationship analysis, 145

B

Bargaining, 167
Baseball organizations, 102–3
Beatrice Foods, 170
"Beliefs about cause/effect relations,"
    114
Bounded rationality, 66, 111–12
Buffering, 165
Bureaucracy, ideal type of, 21–22, 23
Bureaucratic personality, 35
Bureaucratization, 36

C

Capacity
    environmental, 142
    physical, 49
Catholic Church. *See* Roman Catholic
    Church
Centralization, 37–41
    consequences of, 40–41
    definition, 37
    measuring, 38–39
    power, 68
    relation with other
        dimensions, 41–42
    routineness relationship, 53
    size and, 47
Challenger shuttle, 110
Change. *See* Organizational change
Charismatic authority, 70
Chernobyl accident, 9
Chrysler, 11, 146, 169
Coalitions
    dominant coalition, 189, 195
    formation in decision-making,
        119–20
    organization combining, 169–70
Coding, 134
Coercion, 72
Columbia shuttle, 110
Communication
    external communication, 135–36
    hierarchy dysfunctions, 128–30
    horizontal communication, 130–33

Communication   (*Cont.*)
  importance of, 122–24
  individual factors, 124–26
  networks, 133
  organizational factors, 126
  overview, 121–22
  problems, 133–35
  vertical communication, 126–28
Communities, organizations and, 7–9
Competition
  intraorganizational conflict, 80
  professional–organizational
    relationships, 81–83
Competitive merger, 170
Complexity
  covariation in forms of, 31–33
  horizontal, 27–29
  relation with other dimensions,
    41–42
  size and, 46–47
  spatial, 30–31
  vertical, 29–30
Compliance, 78–79
Concentration, environmental, 142–43
Conflict
  bases of, 79–81
  components of situations, 83–85
  decision-making and, 113–14
  by differentiation, 79–80
  by duplication of functions, 80
  hierarchical conflict, 80–81
  outcomes, 85–86
  professional–organizational
    relationships, 81–83
  resolution, 84–85
Constraints, 196–97
Contingency paradigm, 162–63
Contingency theory, 25
Co-optation, 167–68

D

Decentralization, 47
Decision-making

  bounded rationality, 111–12
  constraints on, 116–17
  garbage can model, 115–16
  organizational structure and, 112–13
  role of politics and conflict in, 113–14
  strategic choice, 65, 163
  strategies of power and, 118–20
  styles, 94
  uncertainty and strategic decisions,
    115–16
Demographics, organizational
    environmental conditions, 157–59
Differentiation, 27
  horizontal, 31
  vertical, 31
  See also Complexity
Directorates, interlocking, 149–51
Distortion, 134
Diversified mergers, 170
Domain consensus, 143
Dominant coalition, 189, 195
Downward communication, 126–27
Drug Abuse Resistance Education
    (DARE), 157
Dual ladder, 83
Dual leadership, 94
Dyadic interorganizational
    relationships, 145–47

E

Effectiveness models
  participant-satisfaction model,
    192–94
  stakeholder approach, 194–96
  system-resource model, 191–92
Emergent leaders, 93
Employees
  productivity, 10–11
  temporary, 4
Endorsed power, 71
Environment. *See* Organizational
    environment
Equifinality, 65

Escalation situations, 116
Evolutionary approach, 196
Externalities, generation of, 12
ExxonMobil, 187

F

Family control, 104
Field of conflict, 84
Filtering, communications, 135
Ford Motor Company, 118, 146, 169
Forecasting, 166
Formalization, 33
  individual consequences of, 35
  organizational consequences of,
    34–35
  professionals and, 36–37
  relation with other dimensions,
    41–42
  size and, 47–48
Formal structure, 20

G

Garbage can model of decision-
    making, 115–16
Gender equality
  conflict, 81
  leadership, 96
General Electric Corporation, 8
General Mills, 31
General Motors (GM), 115, 146, 169
Geographical dispersion. *See* Spatial
    complexity
Geographical proximity, 145
Gossip, 126

H

Halo effect, 125
Health maintenance organization
    (HMO), 82

Heterogeneity, environmental, 142
Hierarchical conflict, 80–81
Hierarchy, communication and, 128–30
High-performance work systems
    (HPWS), 43
Horizontal communication, 130–33
Horizontal complexity
  consequences of, 28–29
  measuring, 27–28
Human organ transplantation network,
    147–49
Hybrid electric vehicle (HEV) project,
    146, 169

I

Individuals
  communication factors, 124–26
  leadership characteristics, 92–93
  organizational impacts on, 3–7
  professional–organizational
    relationships and conflict, 81–83
Informal structure, 20
Information control, 119
Information technology
  effects on organizational
    structure, 57
  use by management, 128
Innovation, 29, 35
  adaptive learning approach and,
    200–201
  definition, 200
  interorganizational networks and,
    148–49
In Search of Excellence (Peters and
    Waterman), 189, 196
Institutional paradigm, 176–77
Institutional theory, 59–62
Intensive technology, 51
Interlocks, 149–51
Internal culture, 57–58
Interorganizational relations (IORs), 9,
    143–51
  forms of, 144–45

Interorganizational relations
(IORs)　(*Cont.*)
interorganizational networks, 147–51
interorganizational set, 147
pairwise interorganizational
relationships, 145–47
Inter-University Consortium for
Political and Social Research
(ICPSR), 169
"Iron Law of Oligarchy," 108

J

Japanese companies, characteristics
of, 63
Joint ventures, 146–47
Jones and Laughlin steel company, 8

K

Knowledge development approach,
202–3

L

Labor unions, 78
Leadership
components of, 92–98
definition, 90–91
follower/situational characteristics,
95–98
functions of, 91–92
gender equality, 96
importance of, 106–7
individual characteristics, 92–93
leader behavior and styles, 93–95
motivation of leaders, 107
outcome productivity, 98–99
outcome satisfaction, 98–99
overview, 89–90
succession, 100–107
in voluntary organizations, 107–8

Legal conditions, organizational
environment, 154–55
Legitimation, 176, 182
Liability of newness, 48, 179
Localized dependence,
interorganizational relations, 146
Love Canal case, 12

M

Make-or-buy decisions, 174
Management by participation, 40
Managerial Theorists, 23, 24
March of Dimes Foundation, 190, 205
Mergers, 169–71
Multidisciplinary partnership
(MDP), 83
Multinational corporations, 13
Mutual dependence, 71

N

National Council of Churches, 190
National culture, as organizational
structure determinant, 62–64
National Football League (NFL), 103
National Labor Relations Board, 78
National Renewable Energy
Laboratory, 169
Networks
communication, 133
human organ transplantation, 147–49
interindustry ties, 116–17
interorganizational, 147–51
"No Irish Need Apply," 6
Normative rewards, 72

O

Official goals, 187–88
Omission, 133–34
Operative goals, 188

Organization
  authority system in, 16
  communication factors, 126
  definition, 14
  functional form of, 54–55
  influence on individual career
    choice, 6–7
  innovation in, 200–201
  matrix form of, 56–57
  nature of, 14–17
  product form of, 55, 56
  reasons to study, 1–3
  as systems of decisions, 111–14
  transformational change in, 204
Organizational change, 198
  adaptive learning approach,
    199–201
  knowledge development approach,
    202–3
Organizational culture, 58
Organizational demography, 157–58
Organizational effectiveness,
    approaches, 190
  participant-satisfaction, 192–94
  stakeholder, 194–96
  system-resource, 191–92
Organizational environment
  demographic conditions, 157–59
  dimensions of environment, 142–43
  interorganizational relations, 143–51
  legal conditions, 154–55
  overview, 139–40
  perception, 159–60
  political conditions, 155–57
  technological conditions, 152–54
Organizational goals, problems
    in defining, 187–90
Organizational impacts
  on communities, 7–9
  on individuals, 3–7
  on international communities, 12–13
  on societies, 9–12
Organizational inertia, 116, 178–79
Organizational performance,
    evaluation of, 196–98

Organizational set, 147
Organizational structure
  building analogy, 19–20, 44–45
  bureaucracy form and, 21–25
  categories of, 45
  centralization, 37–41
  complexity, 27–33
  cross-cultural variations in, 62–64
  debate in creating formal, 64–66
  decision-making and, 112–13
  definition, 20–21
  effects of internal culture on, 57–58
  effects of size on, 46–49, 53–54
  formalization, 33–37
  forms of, 42–43
  institutional theory and, 59–62
  national culture and, 62–63
  research on size and, 48–49
  sociological studies of, 25–27
  technology effects on, 50–54
Organizational transformation
  case studies of, 204–6
  comparative studies of, 206–8
Overload, 134–35

P

Pairwise interorganizational
    relationships, 145–47
Paradigm, defined, 161–62
Paradigm development, 105
Participant-satisfaction model, 192–94
Participative management, 40
Patterns of Industrial Bureaucracy
    (Gouldner), 100
Peaceableness, 84–85
Performance programs, 113
Personality characteristics, 93
Politics
  decision-making and, 113–14
  influence of organization in, 11–12
  leadership succession, 104–5
  organizational environment
    conditions, 155–57

Pooled interdependence, 50
Population ecology paradigm,
    177–83
Power
    centralization, 68
    definition, 69
    outcomes, 78–86
    shifts in power, 77–78
    in stakeholder approach, 195
    types of, 69–76
"Preferences regarding possible
    outcomes," 114
Productivity, leadership impact,
    98–99
Professionalization, 36–37
Professional–organizational
    conflict, 81–83
Project groups, communications, 137
Projection, 125

Q

Queuing, communications, 134–35

R

Rational–legal authority, 23, 70
Rationing, 166
Reciprocal interdependence, 50–51
Relativist approach, 194–95
Remunerative rewards, 72
Resource dependence paradigm,
    163–71
    autonomous strategies, 165–66
    comparison with transaction costs
        paradigm, 174–76
    internal power relations, 171
    interorganizational strategies,
        166–71
Resources
    access to power, 72–73
    strategic contingencies and, 73–76

Ritual scapegoating no-way casualty
    theory, 102–3
Roman Catholic Church, 31, 71
Routineness, centralization
    relationship, 53

S

Scientific Management, 23–24
Sequential interdependence, 50
Size
    centralization and, 47
    complexity and, 46–47
    formalization and, 47–48
    paradigm development relationship
        and, 105
    research on organizational structure
        and, 48–49
Smoothing, 165–66
Social embeddedness, 116
Social justice approach, 195–96
Social stratification, 10–11
Societies, organizational impacts
    on, 9
    externalities, generation of, 12
    politics and national policies,
        11–12
    social stratification, 10–11
Spatial complexity, 30–31
Stability, environmental, 142
Stakeholder approaches
    evolutionary approach, 196
    power approach, 195
    relativist approach, 194–95
    social justice approach, 195–96
State University of New York
    (SUNY), 31
Stereotyping, communication
    impact, 125
Strategic alliances, 146–47
Strategic choice, 65, 163
Strategic contingency, 73–76
Structural duality, 21

Structure. *See* Organizational
    structure
Succession, leadership, 100–107
Symbiotic mergers, 169–70
System-resource model, 191–92

T

Technological uncertainty, 51
Technology
    effects on organizational structure,
        50–53
    organizational environment
        conditions, 152–54
    size relationships and, 53–54
    See also Information technology
Telecommuting, 5
Tennessee Valley Authority
    (TVA), 205
Traditional authority, 71
Transaction cost paradigm,
    171–76
    comparison with resource
        dependence paradigm, 174–76
Transformational change
    case studies of, 204–6
    comparative studies of, 206–8
Turbulence, environmental, 143

U

United Fund, 77
University at Albany, 197
Upward communication, 127–28

V

Vertical communication
    downward communication, 126–27
    upward communication, 127–28
Vertical complexity, 29–30
Voluntary organizations
    leadership, 107–8
    moral involvement, 78

W

Whistle-blowers, 128
Workers. *See* Employees
Written communication, 137

Y

Young Men's Christian Association
    (YMCA), 205